selected
* letters
* * of * * * *
marjorie
kinnan * *
rawlings

edited by
Gordon E. Bigelow
and Laura V. Monti

A University of Florida Book
University Presses of Florida / Gainesville

Frontispiece, Marjorie Kinnan Rawlings at her orange grove in Cross Creek, Florida, ca. 1933-34.

Most of the photographs in this book belong to the Rawlings Collection at the University of Florida Library, Gainesville, and are published through the courtesy of the library's Department of Rare Books and Manuscripts.

Library of Congress Cataloging in Publication Data
Rawlings, Marjorie Kinnan, 1896–1953.
    Selected letters of Marjorie Kinnan Rawlings.

"A University of Florida book."
    1. Rawlings, Marjorie Kinnan, 1896–1953—Correspondence. 2. Authors, American—20th century—Correspondence. I. Bigelow, Gordon E. II. Monti, Laura Virginia. III. Title.
PS3535.A845Z48   1982   813'.52 [b]   82-2674
ISBN 0-8130-0728-3   AACR2

University Presses of Florida, the agency of the State of Florida's university system for the publication of scholarly and creative works, operates under the policies adopted by the Board of Regents. Its offices are located at 15 Northwest 15th Street, Gainesville, Florida 32603.

contents * * * * *

preface * * * * * *

The letters published here are all drawn from the Rawlings Collection at the University of Florida library in Gainesville, Florida. This collection, which contains more than a thousand letters, was established by Mrs. Rawlings' own gift of manuscripts and personal papers in 1950 and was augmented by a systematic canvass of her correspondents in 1959–62 and by generous gifts from a number of individuals including Norton S. Baskin, Carl Van Vechten, Bernice Gilkyson, Beatrice Humiston McNeill, Philip May, and many others. The invaluable correspondence of MKR with Maxwell Perkins was microfilmed from the files of Charles Scribner's Sons and deposited in the collection by her literary executrix, Julia Scribner Bigham. Photocopies of her extensive correspondence with Norman Berg, the originals of which are at the University of Georgia library in Athens, were deposited in the Rawlings Collection by Mr. Berg.

Since MKR wrote vividly in virtually all of her letters, even those devoted to mundane business, it has not always been easy to select those which were "best" for the present volume. But we have tried to choose those which best represent the many facets of her character, which convey a good idea of her theory and practice of the literary art, and which give glimpses into her world, her acquaintance with celebrated people of her time, and, equally important, her acquaintance with the people of rural Florida. Within these rubrics we have also tried to represent with as much continuity as possible the main shape of events in her life and to include a variety of correspondents.

Some readers may be struck by an apparent disproportion in the large number of letters to Maxwell Perkins. It has seemed desirable to include these letters in such number for two reasons: first, sheer necessity, since the letters to Perkins are virtually the *only* surviving letters from 1931 to 1937; second (making a great boon of necessity), these letters are clearly among the most interesting and significant in the entire correspondence. They provide fascinating glimpses of the Florida frontier, a running account of her struggle and growth as a writer, and serious discussion of ideas of many kinds.

Our general rule has been to leave a letter intact whenever possible and to take out only repetitive material, nonessential business matters, or other trivia that lack either substantive or structural importance; such deletions are indicated by ellipsis marks. Since MKR was an excellent speller and was grammatically scrupulous even when writing informally, there has been little need to make emendations. Occasional typographical slips we have altered silently, but most of MKR's idiosyncrasies and inconsistencies in punctuation, spelling, and capitalization we have let stand. Dates and places in letter headings have been supplied in brackets, where necessary, from evidence derived from context or from postmarks. For the sake of economy, we have consistently referred to the author in textual commentary and footnotes by the initials MKR. We have tried to keep such commentary as brief and unobtrusive as possible while still supplying necessary factual and background information. For the early years (1918–31), because of the small number of letters available and thus the large gaps in time, it has been necessary to supply considerably more biographical background than was required for later years, for which such material was more adequately supplied by the letters themselves. Occasionally, for the reader's convenience, we have interpolated names or places in brackets in the text rather than in a footnote. In all these matters our intention has been to stay out of the way so that the voice one chiefly hears in this book is that of Marjorie Kinnan Rawlings herself.

It is a pleasure to record a considerable debt to Norton S. Baskin, MKR's second husband, who made the present edition much richer by his donation of many valuable letters, and by his patient and cordial response to innumerable questions over a number of years. Bouquets of thanks should go also to Kate Kent and Kathy Eldridge, who made typescript copies of many of the letters, and to Deidre Bryan, who added a generous measure of personal warmth and charm to a sharp-eyed editing of the manuscript.

introduction *

Marjorie Kinnan Rawlings first came to public attention in the 1930s with a series of novels and stories about southern poor whites in a little-known semitropical part of north central Florida. Her stories carried the reader into an unfamiliar but exotically beautiful countryside and into a way of life that was hauntingly reminiscent of an earlier frontier period in American life. They were rich in details of animal lore and bird lore, of bear hunts in a primitive wilderness, of rafting on moss-hung rivers, of moonshining on a hidden creek, and they had so wide an appeal (four of her five longer works were adopted by major book clubs) that by the late thirties she had become something of a national celebrity and something of a legend. She began to be represented in magazine feature articles as an outdoorswoman extraordinary, a kind of great white huntress in boots, breeches, and slouch hat, whose passion when she was not hunting quail or gigging frogs was cooking up swamp cabbage or alligator tail or other forest delicacy in her kitchen.

This image and the legend behind it, while true in a way, were only part of the truth about this remarkable woman. Underneath the slouch hat was a northern city woman, born (August 8, 1896) and brought up in Washington, D.C., a brilliant college graduate with a Phi Beta Kappa key from the University of Wisconsin, a successful reporter and syndicated columnist for newspapers in Louisville, Ky., and Rochester, N.Y., who until she came to Florida in 1928 at the age of thirty-two had had little to do with the outdoors except for summers spent on a farm, little to do with sports of any kind—who had seldom held a fishing pole or hunted so much as a rabbit. "All this strenuous out-door stuff," she wrote in 1933, "is new to me since coming to Florida. I've taken to it naturally, but my chief claim to capability in such matters lies only in being game for anything."

From girlhood she had taken herself seriously as a writer, was strongly success-oriented, and grew up with the confident expectation that as a matter of course she would achieve fame in the literary world. This fame was so long coming that at one time she despaired of its coming at all. She won a two-dollar prize for a story on the children's page of the *Washington Post* when she was eleven, and she wrote energetically for her high school paper and for the University of Wisconsin *Lit* magazine when she was an undergraduate. In the decade after college graduation when she worked as a journalist she wrote stories and poems continuously, puzzled at first and then increasingly dismayed when she was unable to place a single one. Part of the idea of the move to Florida was to give the writing one more try in radically new surroundings and then, if it didn't work out, to abandon it entirely.

But her frustrated ambition as a writer was only one reason for the dramatic move. In 1919 she married a college classmate, Charles A. Rawlings, who had also been on the staff of the Wisconsin *Lit,* and who also made his living as a reporter and feature writer, specializing in Great Lakes yachting events. But the marriage did not go well and by the late twenties was involving both partners in daily and growing tension. She became progressively dissatisfied with the whole pattern of her life, with the routine of her work, and with the irritations of life in the city. Suddenly and impetuously, using money from a modest inheritance, she and her husband abruptly left city and jobs in 1928 to try a new life in rural Florida.

Thousands of people try some kind of escape from the frustrations of the city to a life seen as simpler and closer to nature—but few make so complete a break with the past as this woman did, and few find such rich and lasting reward in a new life. Although the marriage continued to falter and ended in divorce in 1933, the writing suddenly began to flourish.

She had a theory, expressed in many of her writings, that human happiness is radically related to place. She felt that places quite as much as people have a definite character, and that just as a person has natural affinity for some people and not for others, in the same way he has affinity for some places and not for others. She believed that for a person to find lasting happiness or fulfillment, it is essential for him to find a place with which his spirit can live in harmony, and that for a person to live in a place where he is out of harmony with his surroundings would lead to a frustration amounting to a kind of death. She had the conviction, immediately upon her move to the orange grove in the tiny hamlet of Cross Creek, Florida, that she had found a place where her soul could be at ease.

The half-wild country fascinated her from the very beginning with its profuse natural beauty, the alien but exciting flavor of the subtropics, but she also discovered, more gradually and quite unexpectedly, a fascination for the cracker natives. To her city eyes they seemed at first to be merely quaint and backward, with picturesque customs and archaic speech, but as she came to know them better she recognized a grace and beauty in their way of life which seemed to come from the way they lived in great harmony with the exotic place. Physically their life was hard, bringing them daily close to danger and often to actual hunger. They did some farming, they sometimes grazed scrub cattle, but much of their living depended upon axe and gun, upon what they could take from the forest and the rivers, or in some cases from secluded moonshine stills. They were, she came to understand, an authentic, living remnant of the American frontier, surviving into the twentieth century. Once she recognized this fact, she was so stirred that she could hardly write fast enough to record what she saw before it was destroyed by advancing civilization or before her eyes and ears became blunted by familiarity. These people were far different from the grotesque stereotypes of the southern poor whites in the comics, or the moral degenerates of *Tobacco Road;* they had an intelligence and pride, a sense of humor and an awareness of natural beauty, which she found wholly attractive. To experience their way of life in its purest form, she left the comparatively civilized area at Cross Creek and for more than two months in the late summer of 1931 lived with the Fiddia family in a cabin located on a high bluff over the Oklawaha River in a wilderness area known as the Big Scrub. While she was there, as she wrote in one of her letters, she found the way of life "peculiarly right" and she did all the illegal things the Fiddias did to make a living—shot deer at night out of season, dynamited fish in the river, shot the forbidden limpkin for food. She came back from the scrub with deepened admiration for the cracker people, with bulging notebooks and a strong urge to commit what she had learned to print.

Within two years of her coming to Florida she had sketched out in her notes the main substance of all her later Florida writing and in the fall of 1930 *Scribner's Magazine* bought the first piece she sent out, a group of sketches called "Cracker Chidlings." In this way she came under the eye of Maxwell Perkins, the great editor in Scribner's publishing department, who urged her to try a longer fiction based on this material, and for the next twelve years the Florida stories poured out, with a major title coming every two or three years: *South Moon Under* (1933), *Golden Apples* (1935), *The Yearling* (1938), *When the Whippoorwill* (1940), *Cross Creek* (1942). Beginning with *South Moon Under* she had not only a substantial popular success but a critical success as well, with reviewers praising the lyric beauty of her nature writing and the lucid realism of her depiction of cracker life. But in the first five years at the grove, before royalties began to come in, there was close living and considerable worry about money, and the physical labor of running house and grove sometimes seemed almost more than she could bear. By 1938 and the great success of *The Yearling,* the money worries were over. This book received the Pulitzer Prize, was sold to a major film studio, and was translated into thirteen languages to spread her name almost literally around the world. She received honorary degrees from the University of Florida and Rollins College; she had more invitations to lecture than she cared to fill; she was invited to speak at the Women's Press Club in Washington and to have lunch with Eleanor Roosevelt at the White House; she came to know many of the literary great of her time, including Hemingway, Fitzgerald, Wolfe, Stevens, Frost, and Ellen Glasgow, and many celebrated persons from other walks of life. Though it came years later than she had hoped, here was literary success and public recognition as large as her girlhood ambition had projected.

In 1941 she was married for the second time, to Norton S. Baskin, a hotel manager and friend of some years, whose work required that he be in St. Augustine. To be with her husband she moved away from the shabby, beloved farmhouse in Cross Creek to spend more and more time in St. Augustine or at their beach home a few miles south of that city. Then, to show that her talent could encompass an entirely different subject matter, she deliberately turned away from the Florida material and began a novel based on the life of her maternal grandfather, who had been a farmer in Michigan in the years following the Civil War. But the work went slowly, interrupted by World War II and by the five-year harassment of the famous "Cross Creek Trial," in which she was sued by one of her neighbors for "invasion of privacy" for remarks made about her in the book *Cross Creek*. After long, dragged-out legal proceedings, MKR won the trial in the circuit court, but upon appeal the decision was reversed by the Florida Supreme Court, and she was forced to pay one dollar and costs. This decision rankled, but she took comfort in the fact that virtually all of her Cross Creek neighbors had come to her support in the course of the trial.

To get the feeling for the northern rural setting that she needed for her next book, in 1947 she bought and renovated a farmhouse in upper New York state near the little town of Van Hornesville and began to spend her summers there, driving herself relentlessly to complete the book. It was published as *The Sojourner* in 1953, after ten years of false starts and repeated rewriting that left her mentally and physically exhausted and resulted in a book with which she was never really satisfied. Without pause for rest, she plunged into a biography of Ellen Glasgow and in the spring of 1953 rented a house in Richmond, Virginia, in order to conduct interviews as part of her research. But in December of that year, before she could begin writing, she was struck down by a massive cerebral hemorrhage while at her home in Crescent Beach, Florida. She was buried in Antioch Cemetery near Island Grove, Florida, in the midst of the Cross Creek country which had been her truest home.

Seen in overview, her life as a writer assumes a kind of wave form, with the thirty-two years in northern cities taking the aspect of a long preparation for a career which began only after she left the North and settled in the orange grove at Cross Creek. Once begun, the upward curve of literary achievement and success rose swiftly, cresting in the late thirties with *The Yearling* and continuing on a high plateau with *Cross Creek* in the early forties. Then, with her leaving the grove and turning away from Florida to a northern setting for her last novel, the curve began to slope down and the power in the wave to recede. Her encounter with the Florida countryside had many resemblances to a love affair, and though she never ceased to feel the pull of Florida, the pitch of early ecstasy was not sustainable and of necessity became tempered with other attachments and demands. In perspective it appears almost as if, without being aware of it, she illustrated in her own experience her theory of the radical relation between place and personal happiness and fulfillment. As long as she breathed the magic air of Cross Creek her writing and her life had a glow which they began to lose when she left the grove for other places.

One recognizes at once in the person an extraordinary human being, warm and vital as well as gifted, generous almost to a fault, whose career reminds one that there were liberated women in America long before the movement of the 1960s and '70s. Her significant achievement as a literary artist was all the result of her own doing, of her own talent and intelligence, her own ambition and independence of spirit, her courage and persistence in the face of reverses. She was a self-reliant professional who taught herself to milk a cow and manage a grove and truck-farming operation as well as write best-selling fiction. She was socially adept and a brilliant cook and hostess, but also a lover of solitude with a romantic, half-mystic love of the wild countryside and all natural processes. She made friends easily, with blacks as well as whites, with cracker backwoodsmen and moonshiners as easily as with governors, college presidents, or other artists and writers. This largeness of heart shows in all her published writings, and it shows in the letters that make up the present volume.

chronology * * *

1896   Born August 8, Washington, D.C. Her father, Arthur Frank Kinnan, an examiner in the U.S. Patent Office; her mother, Ida May Traphagen Kinnan.

1907   Wins a $2.00 prize for a story published in the *Washington Post*.

1913   Father dies.

1914   June, graduates from Western High School in Washington. Mother moves with Marjorie and younger brother Arthur to Madison, Wisconsin. September, Marjorie enters University of Wisconsin as an English major.

1918   Graduates from University of Wisconsin (Phi Beta Kappa in junior year). Moves to New York City; works as an editor for the National Board of the YWCA.

1919   May, marries Charles A. Rawlings; they take up residence in his home city of Rochester, N.Y.

1920–
1928   MKR a feature writer for the Louisville *Courier-Journal* and the Rochester *Journal-American*. Writes daily syndicated feature, "Songs of the Housewife," May 1926 to February 1928. Works continually on short fiction but cannot find a publisher.

1928   March, takes first trip to Florida. Buys Cross Creek grove property in late summer and moves to Florida in early November.

1929   Immediately begins to record impressions of countryside and Florida people.

1930   March, sells first story, "Cracker Chidlings," to *Scribner's* magazine for $150. December, sells second story, "Jacob's Ladder," to *Scribner's* for $700. Becomes protégée of Maxwell Perkins.

1931   "Cracker Chidlings" published in February issue of

Scribner's; "Jacob's Ladder" published in April issue. August to October, lives in the Big Scrub with the Fiddia family.

1932   Continues to publish short fiction on Florida subjects. Now working on first novel of the Big Scrub.

1933   March, *South Moon Under* published, an immediate critical and popular success. June, first mention of *The Yearling* in an exchange of letters with Maxwell Perkins. July, lives with family of Cal Long in the Big Scrub, gathering material for *The Yearling.* August to September, voyage to England. November, divorce from Charles Rawlings made final. Receives $500 O. Henry Award for "Gal Young 'Un."

1934   December, completes draft of *Golden Apples* after severe struggle. Cut version of book sold to *Cosmopolitan.*

1935   February, breaks neck in fall from horse; wearing neck brace, completes revisions of *Golden Apples.* August, visits brother Arthur in Seattle. They take boat trip on Inland Waterway to Alaska.

1936   May, meets Hemingway in Bimini. June–July, hunts bear in Big Scrub with Barney Dillard. September, begins writing *The Yearling* in mountain cabin at Banner Elk, North Carolina. October, meets Fitzgerald at Grove Park Inn, Asheville.

1937   June, drives to New York City with partial version of novel. Perkins introduces her to Thomas Wolfe.

1938   February, *The Yearling* published; April, film rights sold to MGM for $30,000. Book becomes a major best-seller and MKR becomes a national celebrity.

1939   January, elected to National Institute of Arts and Letters. May, *The Yearling* receives the Pulitzer Prize for fiction. Begins research for book on Zephaniah Kingsley, an eccentric early-19th-century Florida planter. Buys cottage at Crescent Beach, Florida, near St. Augustine.

1940   March, publishes *When the Whippoorwill,* a collection of short stories. Abandons Kingsley novel and begins work on *Cross Creek.*

1941   May, MGM begins production of movie version of *The Yearling* on location in the Big Scrub. October, completes writing of *Cross Creek*. Marries Norton Sanford Baskin, owner of Castle Warden Hotel, St. Augustine. Divides time between living in Cross Creek and in St. Augustine.

1942   February, *Cross Creek* published, another major best-seller. May, awarded Doctor of Humane Letters by the University of Florida. August, *Cross Creek Cookery* published.

1943   January, Zelma Cason enters $100,000 suit against MKR for libel. June, MKR begins work on a novel based on her grandfather Traphagen (*The Sojourner*).

1944   Begins massive correspondence with American service-men. In spite of repeated starts, novel goes badly. June, Florida Supreme Court rules that grounds for suit exist if charge is changed from libel to "invasion of privacy."

1945   Continues to labor over *The Sojourner*. Continues to publish short fiction, but stories are based less and less on Florida material.

1946   May, "Cross Creek Trial" held in Gainesville, Florida. MKR wins decision, but Zelma Cason appeals and case goes a second time to the state supreme court.

1947   May, Florida Supreme Court reverses decision of circuit court in a 3–4 decision, directing that MKR pay nominal damages of one dollar and court costs. June, MKR spends summer in Van Hornesville, New York, in cottage lent by Owen D. Young. Maxwell Perkins dies. MKR buys and renovates old farmhouse in Van Hornesville. Novel *Mountain Prelude* serialized in *Saturday Evening Post*. Begins to spend winters in Florida, the rest of the year in Van Hornesville.

1952   February, suffers heart attack while alone in house at Cross Creek. Recovers and continues laboring on *The Sojourner*, which is finally completed in August.

1953   January, *The Sojourner* published; adopted by Literary Guild, but receives lukewarm critical response. February, begins research for biography of Ellen Glasgow. In Richmond for several months to gather data. December 14, dies of a cerebral hemorrhage at Crescent Beach, Florida. Buried in Antioch Cemetery near Island Grove, Florida.

Marjorie Kinnan at age 22, about 1918.

the letters * *

Marjorie Kinnan and Charles A. Rawlings, Jr., became acquainted while both were working on the *Lit,* the campus literary magazine at the University of Wisconsin, and by the end of their senior year they were talking seriously of marriage. They graduated together in June of 1918 when the excitement of World War I was running high, and Charles, following the impulse of many graduates of that year, "joined the colors" and in late August was sent to Camp Upton on Long Island for training. In spite of the war fever, or perhaps because of it, Marjorie and Charles were engaged to be married before he climbed on the troop train that was to carry him east. In a few weeks she followed, stopping off in Rochester to visit the Rawlings family on the way to New York City, where she hoped to accomplish the double purpose of locating near Charles and starting a career in the publishing world.

Accompanied by her mother, who wanted to be sure her daughter was safely established in the big city, she began looking for permanent quarters and made application to the various magazines and publishing houses for work. She soon found a job doing editorial work for the national headquarters of the YWCA and began to send out to the slick magazines some of the poems and stories she had brought with her from Wisconsin. Then she and Charles began to suffer the poignant frustration of being separated by only a few miles but being unable to see one another except for brief occasions when Charles had liberty from camp. They filled the separation as best they could with an almost daily exchange of letters, which are like such letters the world over— garrulous, full of intense trivia, lovesick yearning, and private allusions. MKR's letters also show a young woman with strong will and independence of spirit, a touching mixture of innocence and romantic idealism, and some inclination toward the occult.

1. To Charles A. Rawlings, Jr.

Carolyn Court
414 W. 121st.
N.Y. City
Saturday Night
[September 14, 1918]

My sweetheart:—

Oh, such a strenuous day! And, I suppose, your days are
crowded so full of hard work you hardly know where you're
going. I haven't been able to hear from you since Wednesday
night—and I'm so anxious to know how things are going. Honey,
Camp Upton is only several hours' ride—don't lots of the boys
come in on Saturday afternoon? I can feel it in my bones that it
won't be very long after mother goes before I have to send for
you post-haste. How are your finances? This place certainly costs
to move around in—mother's afraid she's going broke before I
get a position & get settled.

Agnes Durrie[1] was terribly discouraging. $18 per week is all
she gets, & all Mary Worsell gets & they didn't seem to think
I could do any better—they say you can only exist on that.
Agnes expects to get her clothes out of her mother, & Mary
simply doesn't have any. But after dinner we went over & saw
Imo Burch & Lois Clark, & they were much more encouraging—
said after Agnes & Mary left, that there was no reason for a
girl's holding such inferior positions—that there were lots of $25
positions open. Proof-reading only pays $18. Imogene knew of
two assistant editorships open, one on McCall's & one on the
Designer. They pay $25 a week, & she thought possibly I could
get one. I went to the Designer today, but the man had gone.
The approach to the building is *terrible*—through blocks of horrible slums, after you leave the car. Imo said the McCall
building was an awful old rat-trap. My enthusiasm is waning,
but I will *not* go back to Madison & be a piker. I expect to hear
from P.J. Campbell Monday or Tuesday.

Mother & I went to the matinee today—saw Lenore Ulric
in *Tiger Rose*. She was great.

Say listen, The Follies are only going to be here 2 weeks
longer. Jimmy[2] said if he came to N.Y. in the car, to see you,
with Mrs. Boucher & the folks, he'd take me, & then to the

Amsterdam Roof Garden & Frolic, & I said no, I had to save that for you—you asked me to. Do you suppose you'll be in, & have enough money, before they go—or shall I go with Jimmy? I'd rather take every chance of going with you if there's the least possibility.

I'm so tired tonight I ache all over. We've torn all over kingdom come. Mother is really satisfied I can take care of myself. She's left everything to me, on purpose, & I haven't had a bit of trouble. She pulled a boner last night coming home from down town. It was about 10:30, & when we got off the Subway, she sang out, as she stopped & looked all around, "Now I'm all turned around. Where do we go?" There were two men standing on the corner who heard, and I grabbed mother's arm & started off towards home at a quick pace. One of the men followed us for several blocks, until he realized from my manner that I, at least, knew where I was going and why. I tell mother she needs protection worse than I do.

Dearest boy, it's going to be a lonesome city. I've had a wonderful time so far—N.Y. is great—but I know how forlorn it can be. And I love you so, it buoys me up thru it all. I'll be good & ready to come, when you are ready for me, & I've had my fight here. Goodnight, sweetheart. Come & kiss me tonight—every night.   Marjorie

Did you know Camp Grant was sailing about now? And Agnes told me she & Skip Clark had broken their engagement. I know he did it. She's better-looking than ever.

1. Most of the persons mentioned in these early letters to Charles Rawlings were acquaintances from college.

2. Charles Rawlings' brother, James.

2. *To Charles A. Rawlings, Jr.*

414 W. 121st.
N.Y. City
Sunday night
[September 15, 1918]

My dearest—

I've had a very stormy sort of day. We got up late, & went to a couple of places to see about rooms. I don't think I want to

be with Agnes Durrie & Mary Worsell—they are bad man-
agers, and unambitious, and seem to enjoy living down in the
business section, in order to be "near things" and their work. I'd
rather take a little longer to get to and from my work, and
have a better, healthier, quieter, residence district to go to. I
found almost an ideal place—except the price—to live, this
morning. It's just around the corner from here, in a most attractive apartment house on Morningside Drive. A Miss Matthews, a very nice, middle-aged spinster, rents two apartments
there & furnishes the individual rooms—sub-lets them. I can
get a very cozy little single room in the apartment she lives in,
at $6 per week. That takes a big piece out of a fellow's salary,—
I don't think I could eat for less than $10 per week. Then there
are incidentals, carfare & clothes—and I do want to save
something. The room is very attractively furnished, & Miss
Matthews would make me very comfortable. She has a kitchen,
& lets the girls in the apartment fix tea & things for their
callers. She settled one thing for me. Mother asked where the
girls received men callers, & she said, "Oh, right in their rooms.
It's considered perfectly proper. All of us are going back and
forth along the hall constantly, & if anything seems wrong I
would be where I would know about it. I've never had the least
bit of trouble, because I don't take young women that seem
questionable—I've had enough experience in the world to know.
The girls usually leave their doors part-way open when they
have callers, though not necessarily. There's no other way to
manage. And of course, tho' I try to look out for my girls, I
expect them to be able to take care of themselves."

So *that* question is settled, & even mother is satisfied.

My dearest lover—it was *so* thoughtful of you to send the
telegram—bless your sweet heart for it. Don't you worry—I'm
having a *good time,* & also being wary. Of course, I'm smack up
against a big proposition—but I won't go back with mother,
tho' she says, "Better come back to Madison" every time I remark on the High Cost of Living.

Chuck sweetheart—you've got to make most whopping good,
if only to give me a little peace and comfort, from her. She
acts worse every day. She makes some horrid comment now,
EVERY TIME I mention your name. She said this morning, "Oh,

this Chuck business makes me tired." And when I told her who my telegram was from, she said, "Oh, what a fool! I was hoping it was from Campbell." She said tonight, "If you could explain to me just what you love about him, perhaps I could understand the interest a little better." Don't you see why Madison would be impossible? She keeps me sick at heart all the time, although she worships me—or rather the part of me that can do *creditable* things—and if you could hear her, & feel her attitude, YOU WOULDN'T WANT ME TO HAVE TO SEE YOU DAY AFTER DAY THROUGH HER EYES—you wouldn't dare ask it. So let's consider the Madison possibility closed, honey. It's N.Y. for me until you can take me away from it.

We had the wildest time with my aunt in Pelham today. I guess I told you—well I'll tell you all about it when I see you. At any rate, that avenue is closed now.

Goodness, this sounds discouraged as I read it over—I'm *not*. I've got as much nerve as ever. If I can get a $25 per week job, I'll be O.K., tho' I can't run around in a taxicab. Oh sweetheart, I want to hear from you soon badly—if I could only see you a few minutes tonight—just a few! I'm crazy to know how you're getting on.

M.

Ran into Lora Ziesel on the street this morning. She's Bob Jackson's wife. They live just around the corner. They'll be near me if I take Miss Matthews' room.

3. To Charles A. Rawlings, Jr.

100 Morningside Drive
New York City
Thursday Night
[October 1918]

Dearest—

I'm unconscionably mixed-up tonight—in fact, dear, I feel so confused I don't believe I can write much. I don't believe I could follow out a logical sequence of thought. I'll see what I can do, though. Oh, but I feel as if I were groping in a mist—I'm at such an obvious cross-roads—obvious to me—and the fog on either side is so thick—all I can see is the two roads—not

even the sign-posts—and I don't know which way to go. I seem
to be in sort of a trance, incapable of decisive thought or action—it's one of those nightmares, where you can't move or
think, but know you have to do *something*—with invisible forces
all around, pressing in against you.

Oh——

I can't write, somehow——

Nothing's clear in my mind——

Oh—darn it——*darn* it!

Chuck, I can't get it out—I think I'm tangled up in that
Hinkel woman's[1] psychic radiations or something—I felt her
concentrating on me last night about 11 o'clock.

I talked to Mrs. Wilkie over the 'phone today. She has a position for me on the Delineator [Magazine], under that Miss
Blaine. It won't be ready for a week or two—they're going to
call me up about it next week. But I don't think I want it. Don't
know what it is—but I don't want it.

Called up Dr. Hinkel as per schedule. She wants to see me
Monday when I get through my work. She wants me all right.
She said she'd tell me when we could talk about it then, what
she did about that month's vacation difference in salary I
brought up. I don't know what to do. Asked Mrs. Wilkie—she
said right off (the kind of snappy judgment, as I told you too, I
don't need in this case) not to take it—she thought it would be
unwholesome.

Had a most satisfying talk with that nice Miss Avery out in
Flushing, over the phone. She saw it just as I do—it crystallizes
into words what I had *felt* about it. She felt, as I do, that it
might be the making of me as a writer—I *feel* that I might do
something really big as a result of it, Chuck, if I took it, but she
put into words my secret fear that it might spoil my happiness as a wholesome, normal human being. She said that since I
was really so young, after all, it might have a morbid effect
on me to get into that line of thought, and know the most intimate cores of people's lives and thoughts—things they couldn't
even tell to *themselves,* except under this sort of hypnotic
psycho-analysis—under it they deliver up their very souls. It
involves sex a great deal, you know—it might be fearfully unhealthy. Miss Avery really understood the situation, and is

thinking it over. She will call me up Sat. night and tell me what she thinks—meanwhile she's going to ask another doctor— who also uses psycho-analysis—a very *sane* sort of man—what Dr. Hinkel really is—he knows all about her, Miss Avery knows.

Meantime, I go ahead—taking Y.W. notes from the religious weeklies. Religion is an awfully morbid thing isn't it? A positive taint—very unhealthy—much more unnatural than sex problems!

Chuck—I've promised to marry you. For heaven's sake see if you can help me straighten out this thing. Can I go ahead with that psychoanalysis job, get my big material out of it, and yet keep rational and normal and happy? Could I be a bigger writer than I ever before thought I had a chance of being, and yet make the right go of our two lives together? Can you gather all of me—my work, my thoughts, my poor female inconsistencies—into one co-ordinated whole under your guidance? Do you have the big quiet strength to do it? Can I be as big as I want to be—and yet know you're bigger? Tell me the truth because I love you.

1. MKR has apparently been offered a job as assistant to Dr. Hinkel, a psychoanalyst.

4. To Charles A. Rawlings, Jr.

100 Morningside Drive
N.Y. City
Friday night.
[November 15, 1918]

Dearest sweetheart—

Life is interesting again! All of sudden I enjoy living. You surely have a feeble-minded imbecile on your hands.

No letter from you today. Isn't it awful not to get that letter? It spoils the whole day. Unconsciously I live the day waiting for it—and when it isn't there—bang! drops the whole world. Then I go to sleep impatiently, wanting morning to hurry up, so I can hear from you.

But I'm not such a silly tonight, and it didn't make me blue or anything like that.

Marjorie Kinnan and Charles Rawlings at the University of Wisconsin, about 1918.

Well, I didn't get the hat, but I bought the tea-pot—and the blamed thing LEAKS. I can't afford $4 on just an ornament, so I'll have to take it back tomorrow. I'm so provoked. Went in & priced one hat on 5th Ave. today, that I sort of liked the looks of. Thinks I—"If it's $10 I'll take it. If it's $15 I'll try it on & think a long time, and take it if it looks wonderful. If it's $20, I'll try it on, & then ask mother if she thinks I'd be foolish." And it was $55! ONE hat!

Saw one combination in a 5th Ave. shopwindow I yearn for passionately. A black velvet dress embroidered in orange & yellow, and an orange & yellow feather hat. I didn't even price them!

Do you know what I want to do? Marry you & go to Russia

or France or Italy, & bum around at something interesting.
Don't you honestly think, after the war is over, that the Red
Cross would have use for a man & wife in reconstruction work?
Prof. & Mrs. Slaughter from Wisconsin, for instance, were
sent by the Red Cross to Italy—& I know the gov't. needs
women desperately for work abroad. Some branches of course
don't take a married woman—but still, I guess that applies to
war-time, with her husband in service. Doesn't that appeal to
you like everything? If we could only make enough to pay our
expenses, it would be worth it by a long shot—don't you think
so? We could write a couple of books, and lots of articles, & when
we come home the papers & magazines would gobble us up—
if we'd written anything worth while. Golly, wouldn't that be
slick? And we'd have goats' milk, and peasants, and fur coats if
we went to Russia—and oh jiminy, it would be great. And
think how fond we'd be of each other, among foreigners. We'd
never fuss at all. (Not that we're going to, anyhow. Once we're
married, we mustn't do it.) And we'd run around in ox-carts, and
maybe go to England during the summer, & tramp along the
English lanes like gypsies—Oh Chuck! I HONESTLY would start
TOMORROW if it were possible. I mean it—I'm CRAZY to do it.
Why not do something fascinating while we're young and peppy.
If we don't do it then, we never will. And if you go into the
newspaper game, we won't have money enough to go interesting
places until we're old and decrepit and have scrimped & saved
all our lives. Let's go out—*now*—the minute you're released
from service—for something adventuresome and marvelous! Just
imagine starting off together—for "parts unknown," with life
preservers and boxes of sterno canned heat! Oh Chuck—don't
you think there would be more comfort in that than in an
Avenue bungalow—for a few years, anyway? And we could have
our candlelight and big chair *wherever* we were! And think
how nice and interesting we'd be when we came back! And there
would be plenty of time for the bungalow, & the newspapers
& magazines—and babies and comfort and quiet. LET'S do it—
PLEASE! I MEAN it! We might even want to live in England for
good! With so many men gone from there, there ought to be
wonderful opportunities there for wide-awake Americans.
Wouldn't it be GORGEOUS? It's not just a mood—I *want* it. It

seems as if the combination of you & that would satisfy the last fibre of my being.

And we'd be away from relatives that think they own us body & soul!

Now I'll tell you something along that line that startled me. It was quite a while ago, when you asked me—over the 'phone, I guess,—if your Dad's letters got on my nerves. And I said there was just one thing—but didn't tell you what it was. When your Dad urged me to come & stay with them, he added, "Now, little Marjorie, Mother and I aren't doing this without a selfish motive. We're looking forward to the day, not so very far away, when we want to take life easy, and would like to live with Charles and Marjorie."

Don't EVER let on I mentioned that to you, dear. You feel just as I do, I know—it isn't that we want to be selfish, or ungrateful, or don't care for the older generation. But you know as well as I do what a mess that situation ALWAYS makes. My mother knows it, poor dear. And for that very reason she is being careful of her principal, so that in her old age she won't HAVE to break her principles for financial reasons, & live with her children, if they're married.

I struck a REALLY Bohemian place for lunch today. It's Italian—with real spaghetti, & a tragic-hero sort of Pagliacci who stands in a box at the back with his head thrown back, and seals letters with a vicious, sweeping lick of the tongue as if he were sending Black-Hand warnings. The food is GREAT—& it's clean, & a perfect joy—really Bohemian as I said—first time I've felt a place was that—they usually just try to be.

Well, the city is pretty sober & sheepish today. Only stray corners still hide confetti—but the consensus of opinion is, "It was worth-while anyhow, just to let loose. And peace is almost here anyhow." How long do you suppose they'll keep you in camp after the war is over? If they send you off to Russia to guard the Siberian steppes—darn it, I'm going too.

But now honest to goodness—no lunacy, no moodiness—I want to go abroad with you, as soon as we can get passports & an expense-paying job. What do you think? If I could look forward to that, I could clean the incense-pot in the Catholic Church for a living, & not have a bored moment.

What do you honestly think? Isn't it worth breaking our necks for? I'm so thrilled at the thought. I love you—oh you khaki-clad lecturer—I do, I do, I do, I REALLY do!!

5. To Mrs. Charles A. Rawlings, Sr.

> [New York City]
> Wednesday morning—
> at the office
> [December 11, 1918]

Dear Mother Rawlings [in Rochester, N.Y.]—

Please don't think I'm absolutely "off"—but I'm worried to death about Chuck. I haven't heard from him since Monday morning—and in the letter I got then (written Sunday morning) he said he was going to write that night. Now the real reason I'm acting so about it, is one of those "feelings" that we super-sensitive people like you and I get. Sunday night, from about ten o'clock or so, on until morning, I was absolutely in the grip of the most terrible consciousness that either Chuck or Art[1] was going through some *terrible* danger. I could hardly get to sleep, I was trembling so. Then several times in the night I woke up, and that perfect *panic* of *fear* seized me. I couldn't tell whether it was Chuck or Art. Really, Mother Rawlings, it was absolutely REAL—I've had things like that before, and they've always proved to be true. Monday I didn't get a telegram, so knew nothing had actually happened, and Chuck's letter made me feel better—so I put it all out of my mind. But now, not having heard from Chuck for so long, I'm just almost crazy. If it hadn't been for that awful feeling Sunday night, I wouldn't be so worried. Now please—please—please—if he's very ill, let me know RIGHT AWAY and I'll come—I'd have to. It may be—Heaven knows I pray it—that he's going on his fat, contented way just as usual—but oh, I'm so frightened. You don't think I'm a perfect idiot, do you? You've had those uncannily true feelings yourself. So PLEASE let me know if everything isn't all right—and let me come—please—please. And don't laugh at me, if everything IS all right. Chuck is the only thing in the world that matters to me.

> Love—
>
> Marjorie

1. MKR's brother, Arthur Kinnan.

6. To Charles A. Rawlings, Jr.

[New York City]
Sunday afternoon
[December 15, 1918]

My very dearest one—

Bless your old heart—I had a feeling I'd get a special from
you this morning. And sure enough, in the midst of my dreams
of you, early this morning, came a loud ring. Nobody else in
the house ever answers an early or a late ring—they assume it's
for me, from you. It's a good thing I don't look the way some
women do in a kimono, with hair down, or that poor postman
would be ill by now. You know, I really look best in the costumes
nobody ever sees! A desert rose born to blush unseen—only
when you take me out of the desert, my fragrance *won't* be
wasted. N'est-ce pas?

Sweetheart, I can see just what's happened. Your folks are
counting on our living in Rochester, and pitching our tent in
their back-yard, and just being nothing but the dutiful son and
daughter. As they see it, it would be an ideal arrangement.
Daddy R. would "advise" you in business matters, and Mother R.
would tell me how to bring up the baby—and would ask muchly
questions if we didn't have one when she thought it was time.
They're just dear and fine and kind—but it really is a sort of
selfishness on their part. Don't you think so? I wouldn't talk this
way, dear, if I thought you *wanted* to be there—but I know
you yearn as much as I do, to go packing down the open road
without anyone to say yes or no. We're so intensely *individualistic,* both of us—it just happens that our individualities cuddle
down in the same box together, like the two halves of a pecan
(*very* good simile, don't you think?); and we can't stand it to be
unduly interfered with. What's right for us is perfectly wild to
the average, normal human being. Going to Rochester to *settle down* in our middle-age would be *quite* a different matter.
But dear God, the last thing in the world we want now is to *settle down*! We've got to be *out,* where things are moving, and
we can catch some of the enchantment and swing of life—and
feel free to tear off and do perfectly absurd, glorious, romantic
things. We aren't starting out as most young couples start out—
making a *permanent* home, and counting on never budging

from the life we take up on our return from the honeymoon. (I
came across a very interesting statement of Arnold Bennett's
about honeymoons. It's in a recent volume of his, a compilation
of critical articles. In one of them he discusses H. G. Wells,
and especially *Tono Bungay.* You never finished that, did you?
Well, Bennett was objecting violently to some statements of
some critics on *Tono Bungay,* who called the next to the last
chapter, where the man and the Lady Beatrice (the one he
kissed as a boy, at that old manor, you know) go off together for
two weeks, "an orgy of lust." It was really a wonderful thing—
their insisting on coming together because they loved each other,
even tho' they could not marry, as she saw it. Well, Bennett
defended it magnificently, and then said, "The most correct honeymoon is an orgy of lust." Then he backed up, and said, no,
it wasn't. Then he said, "But if it isn't, it *ought* to be." Isn't that
a daring statement? Bennett is such a queer mixture. Have
you read his *Old Wives' Tale?* It's Dickinsonian [Dickensian?]—
and tremendous. Every sentence *thrills* you with its style and
thought.

How on earth did I get off on Bennett?

I was talking about Rochester! Oh yes—I see. Well, to return
to the original subject under discussion—

As I said, the idea in our marrying, and even in our working, is not settling down—but making life one glorious adventure together. Chuck dearest, will you promise me never to lose
sight of that? I'm lazy, and get into a rut every now and then
(I'm not stale any more, though, dear!) and you've got to "keep
the vision" constantly. I don't mean that we must live a nervous, hectic life—far from it—we've got to learn to let down
more—but we must always keep that sense of something interesting and strange and ecstatic just around the corner. We
must always be *lovers*—never staid old placid "married folks."
We don't want to *feel married*—just feel *together.*

In Rochester, we'd be settled. We'd be Mr. and Mrs. C. A. Rawlings, Jr.—not Marjorie Kinnan and Chuck Rawlings. And
what would *I* do there? However good the opportunities for you,
there certainly wouldn't be as good ones for me. *If I ever became willing to go to Rochester,* (because you were there) *it
would mean that we would settle into a hum-drum domesticity,*

and actually even come to bore each other sometimes—and I'd be willing to have 3 or 4 babies right away (because there wouldn't be much else for me to do!)—and then our chance at an interesting life would be gummed for good!!! Can't you see what it would mean? I love you so much that, if you *insisted* on staying away from me for a year or so, I'd probably say I'd come, just because *anything* would be better than being away from you. But why spoil every thing? What is "a good proposition" compared to an interesting life? Can't you just tell your folks that you want to try New York now, while they need men badly here, and you'd have a fine chance? And couldn't you appease them by saying that it would be better to make good in a big place like New York, and *then* come back to Rochester, and have *everything* offered you, as a successful New York man? Can't you get away now by making them feel you fully expect to go back there? I shouldn't think you'd need to hurt their feelings at all. And oh—that importing game—if you get with a whopping big concern—sounds so *blamed* good!

And there's this, too: *every day* you delay, means that some good position in N.Y. is being filled by a returning soldier! ! Now is the time to strike. If you dare wait until Dec. 30 (the Monday after Christmas) to start your "visiting"—why I'll come to Rochester for Christmas. If I stayed that long, it would mean I couldn't reach there, probably, until Christmas morning. You see it's this way (*get this,* and decide right away what you want me to do):

Mon.	Tues.	Wed.	Thurs.	Fri.	Sat.	Sun.
23	24	25	26	27	28	29

? ?

We get the 25th and the 26th off, anyhow. Then we secretaries have our choice of *either* the 24th or the 27th in addition. And we have to let the office know pretty soon which we're going to take. Now if I take Friday the 27th, why I'd ask to have Saturday morning too. It would be foolish to come clear back from Rochester just to work Saturday morning. But that would mean taking a night train, (probably), the 24th—even if I

Marjorie in 1918 at the University of Wisconsin.

asked to go at about 3 o'clock, I wouldn't get in to Rochester until midnight—and I wouldn't have Christmas Eve with you. But if I took the 24th off, I wouldn't have the nerve to ask for Friday and Saturday too. But if you want your Skinney[1] to arrive like a thin, soft Christmas package—all wrapping and tissue-paper, and nothing inside!—Christmas morning at 8:15— and then have *me* take the night train back to N.Y., Sunday—why, I'd love to come. You'd have to tell your folks I'd have to use the mileage book as a gift—do they want me $15 worth? And if I didn't get paid before I came, you'd have to lend me carfare to come back on! Unless you want to give me my ticket back for my Xmas present. It's all up to you—I've told you how I can manage. If you dare wait that long, and are going to be there for sure—I *really* would love to come. I think it would be most awfully jolly. If you want me to come, let me know how much "gadding" I'd have to do. I'd rather not do much, because then I'd have to bring a rickety old steamer trunk—I have nothing in-between—Mother took my portmanteau back to Madison, as I didn't expect to need it. I'd rather come with just my little band-bag and an extra shirt-waist. But tell me what places I'd have to go.

Our being here at the apartment Christmas is out of the question. Miss Mary is going to be here *surely,* and possibly Miss Clara, and Miss Haverhill will be here for sure. We lost our chance Thanksgiving, when I had the apartment absolutely to myself—all day and until 9:30.

I'm so lonesome for you. Whenever I have on this dress (the old fashioned blue one, with the bodice, that you always thought so quaint) it comes over me so vividly and acutely, how many times I wore it for you.

You know, my little room is as cozy as can be, and really sufficient for my needs, when you're not here. You fill it so full, and the furniture isn't right for you, and it isn't big and comfy enough for you. I don't miss the solid comfort so much, because when I'm not actually in bed, I'm sitting at my desk writing. I never just sit and think, or read—don't have time. What are we going to do when you come to N.Y.? If you get a room in Greenwich Village, as you spoke of doing, it will take an awfully long time to get up here, on the El or the Subway. Greenwich

Village is cozy and dandy in the winter-time—but after all, this part of the city is *much* preferable in warm weather—high up, with fresh air, all the breezes—and green trees in Morningside Park.

Ran into my friend Mr. Huang this afternoon. I was supposed to be working very hard last week, you know—and he said he saw me with a very fine-looking soldier Wed. or Thursday. I told him it was my fiancé—which ought to finish him for good. In China, I suppose I'd be under lock and key if I had such a thing as a fiancé—to keep me for him like a hot-house fern.

I'm going to have such a nice little supper here. You'd enjoy my room too, and my suppers, if you didn't have that tense, nervous feeling about someone's bursting in. I'm going to have grape-fruit, Snappy Cheese sandwiches, hot chocolate and a cinnamon bun. Good enough for anybody.

Well—you decide what you want me to do, and let me know right away.

And I'm sure you can reconcile your people to your starting out in N.Y., without hurting them.

Tell your folks I'm going to write them as soon as I can, and give them my best. I suppose Jimmy will be home for the holidays, won't he? Oh boy—remember the two-weeks' vacation at school—golly! The Delta Gammas are on Art's trail—good-looking devil.

Well, good night, old darling—I just love you and love you until it seems I'll have to grow a bigger body to keep it in—Come to me again tonight, dear, as you did last night.

1. Charles Rawlings' nickname for MKR during their courting days.

Charles Rawlings was mustered out of the army in February of 1919 and took a job in New York City as publicity representative for an import-export firm; but the company folded soon afterward, and he and Marjorie Kinnan found it expedient to move to Rochester, where his family lived. They were married in May, and Charles went to work as a traveling salesman for the shoe company of which his father was part owner. MKR stayed at home writing more stories and poems and sending them out to the magazines, still without success. In the winter of 1922, to relieve her loneliness during one of Charles' long road trips, she went out to visit her Aunt Ethel Riggs at a farm in Linden, Michigan, which had been settled and worked by her maternal grandfather. This farm and this grandfather were to come back into her life twenty-five years later as the central substance of her last novel, *The Sojourner.*

7. To Charles A. Rawlings, Jr.

Linden, Mich.
Friday afternoon
[January 1922]

Sweetheart:

—I am just sick lonesome for you today—so much that I had to get up from the bed, where I was stealing an afternoon siesta, and write to you. I'm in the sort of place where I could be blissfully happy if you were here, but without you am miserable.

Aunt Ethel [Riggs] came for me yesterday, and I'm still here, after spending the night.

Her farmhouse has the most glorious view. It's on a knoll, and overlooks little hills and valleys, woods and a tiny lake. The whole front of her house, almost, is one big living room— 15 x 22, with an alcove that widens it still further at one end. It has six big cheery windows, facing East and South, and the bright winter sun has been streaming in all morning through the snowy white dotted Swiss curtains. The room has paneling a third of the way up the walls from the floor, and it, and the woodwork, is painted a warm, old-fashioned cream color.

It's a room I'd like a whack at with some real old fashioned furniture and good pictures.

I slept in a downstairs bedroom that completes the front of the house, and the soft pink sun looked in across the road at me this morning, so invitingly that I didn't mind getting up. For breakfast we had buckwheat pancakes, sausage and fried cakes.

Lauren let me turn the separator, and a whole pail of golden, thick cream was my reward. I was also given the privilege— at my request—of washing the separator—which has some 50 different be-creamed parts to be laundered!

This afternoon a fine snow is sifting across the Christmas post

card view from the windows. Aunt Ethel is taking a nap, and
I am all alone with the ticking of the clock, the snow, and you.

"Emily's Mistake" last night at the Opera House was worth
going far to hear excused. The wooden hall, with two big stoves,
smelled of hay and milk and cows. The orchestry sounded like
a deliberate take-off and attempt to be funny—the worst collection of discords you can imagine. No two instruments hit the
same note or the same key at the same time.

There was a "fairy"—a country lass with a voice like On-
tario's fog horn.

"I am a fairy" she announced in train caller's tones.

A village youth, passing for an Eskimo, had his big hound
drawing a sled, as a sledge dog—and in the midst of his speech,
the dog stretched, yawned prodigiously—and lay down on the
stage for a nap.

Eight little boys, about 10 years old, some fat, some lean,
freckled and all Penrodian, were "Scottish chiefs," with turned-
down stockings, plaid kilts, and Scotch tams, be-quilled, that
either sat on the backs of their heads like halos, or dangled
perilously over one eye. In a timid sing-song their leader announced that they would sing "the fierce battle song of the
Campbell's"—whereupon, with some giggles, much arm-swing-
ing and a great scuffling, they galloped round the stage, singing, "The Campbell's are coming, oh ho, oh ho!" About two of the
eight were doing the singing, and in so feeble a voice, so frag-
mentary a manner, that the "fierce battle song" would never
have alarmed a rabbit.

The school superintendent made a speech thanking "the folks"
for coming out on so cold a night.

It was delicious.

Well angel, you are a most unlucky man. I tried my very
best to kill myself this morning, but, you will regret to hear,
made a total failure of it.

I sprawled headlong through a trap door into the cellar. I
started into the dining room to look out of the window at a
damn yellow cat. The trap door was open, as Lauren was in the
cellar. I never gave a thought to hidden precipices in a civilized house—and bingo!—there I was in space, with the heavy
cellar steps banging past me. Aunt Ethel saw me go, and said I

turned a complete somersault in the air, landed on my behind, and fell with my head crashing against the stone wall at the bottom. I don't remember the somersault, but believe me, I remember the crash! By every right I should have broken, first, my neck, and then every other bone in my body.

But aside from a hunk clipped out of one leg, my knees and elbows skinned, a couple of small bruises and a very creditable lump on my head, it did no more harm than a walk across the room.

With all the catastrophes that have been on my trail lately, I wondered if my days were numbered. This spill this morning certainly answers me—my days are numberless, and as the grains of sand of the sea.

Poor Chuck, they cannot kill me! You are doomed to have me on your hearth for many moons.

Tomorrow morning I go to Clarkston. From there to Bay City. Since I only have your route through Lexington, you may have to skip several days of letters from me after that. It is hard for me to get you a daily letter, for the mails go out of here so infrequently, the postman comes once a day, quite early in the morning, and I get downtown so seldom. I know you'll forgive any lapses—it's not that I don't love you or think of you just as much!

I love you most mightily—and wish that you were here, or I there. I feel in no hurry to get back to Rochester without you. I am abominably lazy and passive and hungry.

Be sure and let me know in time when you complete your quota of selling, so that you won't get home ahead of me.

I love you
Marjorie

For nearly four years Charles traveled a round of midwestern cities selling shoes, but he detested the life and left it as soon as he could for more congenial work as a reporter, first for the Louisville *Courier-Journal,* then for the Rochester *Times-Union.* MKR also turned to journalism and worked as a reporter and feature-writer for these same papers. She achieved considerable success with a syndicated feature called "Songs of a Housewife," in which she wrote a daily poem about the cheery, pleasant side of running a household—"the romance of the dishpan and kettle," as an editorial note put it.

But her whole work and way of life in the city left her with a growing hunger for something simpler and more elemental, something closer to the land. In March of 1928, she and Charles took a spring vacation to Florida, sailing from New York City on a Clyde-Mallory steamship to Jacksonville. Then they went inland to meet Charles' brothers, Wray and James, who were staying in the little town of Island Grove, about seventy-five miles southwest of Jacksonville. With the brothers as guides, they had a fascinating tour of the half-wild countryside, including boating trips on the Oklawaha and Withlacoochee rivers, a tramp through the wilderness area known as the Ocala scrub, fishing trips on the Gulf of Mexico, and oyster roasts around a campfire on the beach of an uninhabited key. They were completely seduced by the place and the way of life, and before the two-week vacation was up had decided to move down for good. MKR had recently inherited $18,000 as her share of the sale of a farm her father had owned on the outskirts of Washington, D.C., and before they returned to Rochester, she left instructions with the brothers to find her and Charles a farm that could support them while they tried to write. In July, Wray wired that he had found what she wanted: seventy-four acres of rich hammock land, about half of it orange grove, with an eight-room house, barn, tenant house, and farm implements, on the shore of Orange Lake in a tiny place called Cross Creek. She sent a check for $7,400 as down payment and signed a mortgage for $7,000 more; she and Charles resigned their jobs, sold their house in Rochester, and in early November moved to Florida.

From the first, MKR felt that she had "come home." She loved the whole exciting new experience, the beauty of the semitropical countryside, the quaint ways and speech of her cracker neighbors, the hunting and fishing and boating, even the hard physical labor of working the place. Most important, the new life did stimulate the writing, so that her notebooks quickly began to fill with her accounts of the place and people. In early spring of 1930, only a little over a year from her first coming, she polished up a number of sketches from her notes, gave them the name "Cracker Chidlings," and sent them off to *Scribner's Magazine,* which promptly accepted them for publication.

After more than ten years of discouragement from sending out story after story with nothing but rejections slips to show, she was understandably thrilled to have her first Florida piece accepted by one of the country's most prestigious literary magazines. Alfred S. Dashiell, the editor, asked her to give him information on her background and on how she had gathered material for the sketches. A fragment of her response survives.

8. To Alfred S. Dashiell (fragment)

[Cross Creek
March 1930]

My dear Mr. Dashiell:

I am so glad that you share my interest in "Cracker Chidlings," and that you think Scribner's will accord them its prestige in publication. There seems to me something so moving in these lives in the Florida interior, that I felt the fault surely would lie with me, if I could not make them alive in print.

The price you mention for the sketches [$150.00] would be acceptable to me.

My past years have become somehow unimportant. They are a shadow, against the satisfying substance that is our life in the heart of the Florida hammock.

I was born in Washington, D.C. and took my B.A. from the University of Wisconsin in 1918. I have done journalistic writing of various sorts in Louisville, Ky., New York City, and Rochester, N.Y. Two years ago my husband, a newspaperman, and I deliberately cut our civilized ties in Rochester and migrated to this firmly entrenched outpost of the vanishing frontier. We do not expect ever to regret the move. We have a profitable orange grove on the jungle edge of Cross Creek, between two lakes, where life has as many elements of the idyllic as is quite reasonable.

You ask how I happened to become interested in this material and how I gathered my facts. This wild, beautiful country, tucked off the tourists' highways by no large number of actual miles, is in itself a challenge to the imagination. I had met only two or three of the neighboring Crackers when I realized that isolation had done something to these people. Rather, perhaps, civilization had remained too remote, physically and spiritually, to take something from them, something vital. They have a primal quality against their background of jungle hammock, moss-hung, against the tremendous silence of the scrub country. The only ingredients of their lives are the elemental things. They are a people of dignity, speaking often in Chaucerian phrases, aloof; but friendly and neighborly once even a Yankee has proved himself not too hopelessly alien.

I have gathered my facts first-hand. Most of the material is to my personal knowledge. The rest has been told me here and there in the locality, and is equally authentic. Bits about this woman or that man, mentioned casually in the course of my ordinary conversations with Cracker friends and neighbors, make up, with perhaps some salient last fact, the outline of life. A mere chance visit, as my literally recorded chat with a 'shiner's wife, suggests the drama of a personality. . . .

Scribner's Magazine held "Cracker Chidlings" for nearly a year before bringing it out in the February 1931 issue, which appeared on the newsstands in early January. As might be expected, the piece was read widely by people in north central Florida, including the editor of the Ocala *Evening Star*, who wrote a fatuous editorial, full of chamber-of-commerce indignation, accusing her of distorting the truth about the Florida backwoods. He objected to her mention of freezing weather and of "red bugs" (chiggers), and in particular he complained about her description of the cracker natives, asserting that they were nothing like what she pictured and that she must have learned what she knew about southern poor whites from visiting the Cumberland Mountains.

MKR was in the hospital in Jacksonville having an appendectomy when the editorial was published, but she saw it after she was discharged from the hospital and was furious, because she took particular pride in the truth and authenticity of her local-color material. What graveled her most was that even though she was a recent immigrant from the North, she *did* know more about the Florida crackers than he did, and she felt that he had no business finding fault with her account. Her response to the editorial

MKR's house by the orange grove at Cross Creek.

not only records her indignation but also reveals that by early 1931 she knew she had found in the Florida frontier a fascinating subject for literature and was already involved in a careful and systematic attempt to extend and deepen her knowledge of it so she could bring it to print.

9. To the editor, Ocala Evening Star

Cross Creek
January 31, 1931

Dear Sir:

Your comment on my sketches in the February SCRIBNER'S, "Cracker Chidlings," was brought to my attention yesterday as I was leaving the hospital in Jacksonville after a recent operation.[1] The paper had been kept from me until that time. Late as I am in taking up the discussion, journalistic ethics of course require that, having attacked my good faith and sincerity, you give space to my communication exactly as I submit it.

Allow me to point out that one thing that simply is not done by a trained journalist or by any writer careful of her integrity and reputation, is "palming off material collected in the Cumberlands, where she must have visited, as Florida life." I have not visited the Cumberland mountains or any other remote regions. The Florida frontier—unfortunately fast-vanishing— has been my first experience of the kind, and my Cracker friends and acquaintances have come into my life with all the freshness of new material.

Reading your editorial, I thought ruefully, "Ah, I must know more than he does about red bugs and mosquitoes." Or perhaps—come now, take a firm stand—perhaps you deny the red bug and mosquito! My dear sir, either you simply do not know the back woods and back waters of our State, or you are one of those persons Mencken had in mind when he wrote in the September *Forum:*

"There are men in the world, and some of them not unintelligent men, who have a natural appetite for the untrue, just as there are others who have a natural appetite for the ugly. A bald fact somehow affrights them; they long to swathe it in comforting illusions. Thus one hears from them that it is somehow immoral for an artist to depict human life as it actually is: the spectacle of the real must be ameliorated by an evocation of the ideal, which is to say, of the *un*-real. So Thomas Hardy becomes a bad artist, and the author of *Pollyanna* a good one."

My artistry I cannot myself becomingly defend. Of my accuracy I am so positive that I feel, in good time, as your knowledge increases, you will offer me the courtesy of an apology. My dear sir, my sketches are so true, that I have softened, not colored them, for fear that if they came to the chance attention of the subjects—all within a forty-mile radius of my home— offense would be taken at my frankness, where none was intended.

I can verify all my material with dialect which to you "sounds as if it must be spoken somewhere," but which is made up studiously only of idioms, of phrases, of turns of speech, that I have myself heard here again and again. Perhaps my newness in this country gives a pristine quality to the oddities of speech that come to my ears. Perhaps my interest as a student of etymology has made me alert to quaintnesses and to archaisms deep-rooted in the English language. One of my Cracker acquaintances in the cattle section of recent turmoil, said to me of 'coon-meat, of which he is exceedingly fond, "It has a kind of foolish taste." Do you know that one must go far back into Anglo-Saxon speech to find the word "foolish" used currently in the sense in which he used it. And have you noticed that the Georgia "hit" for "it," which persists hereabouts, is likely to be used at the beginning of a sentence, but not necessarily afterward?

Of course, it would be preposterous to credit me with implying that all Crackers or that all Florida natives use the dialectual [sic] turns I have suggested. They exist only in sections uncontaminated by the tourist or the Rotary Club. Just as it would be preposterous to insist that I was describing the average Floridian, and therefore insulting him. Heaven forbid that a storied character out of any one locality be forced, by such logic as yours, to represent his whole community. Sir, you would eliminate individuality. You would annihilate personality.

And how we disagree, you and I, in summarizing my characters. You shock me with your classifications. The lack of sympathy is yours, not mine. These people are to me all that is delightful. Yet they offend you. I am so sorry. And I am so sorry that you must have hurt the feelings of a very good man in your failure to read carefully "The Preacher Has His Fun."[2] The Rev. Mr. Plummer, well-loved chaplain of Raiford, an inspiration to its inmates, who preached what I thought a locally famous farewell sermon in a certain nearby small town, must be cut to the quick at your careless labeling of him in the public print—most of two counties know the story of his prank—as "a renegade preacher."

And how astonishing to call a Florida moonshiner a weakling! This burly breed made Florida famous long before the day of hard roads and modern hotels, and will, I do not question, in fame outlive them. No, my dear sir, do not let us hustle and deny out of existence the last of Florida's frontier. The State will so soon be just like any other. Before they have been quite swallowed up, let us know and enjoy these picturesque people, pioneer remains. They are much more vital than you and I.

Let me quarrel a moment longer, and I am through. How, in

your glass house, dare you stone my "unsympathetic manner"
after the farce your paper made of journalism and of justice,
in its handling of the recent flogging in the cattle country? I
have met, and been entertained at one of the hospitable tables
of, most of the cattle men in the Burbank section. I admire
them. They are honest, sturdy pioneers, puzzled at the superim-
position of involved modern law on the simple frontier law.
You called them "hoodlums." You implied, just short of laying
yourself open to libel charges, that the particular men under
indictment were without doubt the "hoodlums" you meant. Their
acquittal did little to temper the injustice that has been done
them.

May I ask you to reserve your charge of my lack of sympathy
until you have read my short novel, "Jacob's Ladder," a story
of a young Cracker man and woman, to be published in SCRIB-
NER'S within a few months?[3] With the encouragement of SCRIB-
NER'S acceptances, I have only begun my re-creation of this
section and these people. I am going leisurely, for I wish only to
write of what I know. Added to past days and nights in the
scrub, there must be weeks; there must be longer and further
prowlings through the piney-woods and the shadowy ham-
mocks—where, alas, my dear sir, I am never likely to meet you.
The remote, lovely core of Florida is as yet unexpressed. Having introduced you to some of her unfamiliar people, I think
hopefully: perhaps I can also introduce you to some of her unfamiliar beauty.

Sincerely,

[MKR]

1. It turned out in the course of this operation that her appendix was perfectly
healthy. The symptoms that sent her to the hospital were apparently caused by
diverticulosis, a disorder of the colon from which she was to suffer recurrently in
later years, particularly during periods of emotional stress.

2. One of the sketches in "Cracker Chidlings."

3. This novelette was published in *Scribner's Magazine,* April 1931.

Maxwell E. Perkins, chief editor in Scribner's publishing department, is now generally recognized to have been one of the
important shaping forces in American literature from the early

1920s until his death in 1947. He acted as editor and confidant to Hemingway, Fitzgerald, Wolfe, Lardner, Glasgow, and Aiken, among many others, and MKR was in a real sense his discovery and his protégée. He had noticed "Cracker Chidlings" and her novelette "Jacob's Ladder" in *Scribner's Magazine,* and, feeling that there might be the possibility for something much finer in these materials, wrote to MKR asking if she had considered writing a novel based on them. As her ebullient response indicates, this was precisely the encouragement she needed. The correspondence that began here became one of the most important factors in her professional life, and though she saw him infrequently in person, Maxwell Perkins became one of her most cherished friends. He had the special gift of providing critical advice and stimulus (without intruding upon the creative function) that helped authors to realize their best potential. Her correspondence with him provided, in her self-imposed rural isolation, a much-needed opening to the literary world, a sympathetic listener to her struggles and problems with the writing, and a quiet voice offering the sharpest kind of critical advice as well as personal encouragement and support.

These letters to Perkins are almost the only surviving letters by MKR for the years 1931–37, and they are among the most vivid in the entire Rawlings correspondence, quite as if he elicited from her the best in her writing of letters as he did in her writing of fiction. They provide a running account of her discovery of the Florida frontier and her attempt to record it in literature, and they give intimate glimpses into the process of growth through which she changed from an ambitious, unknown reporter into a professional writer of significant accomplishment. They also record the faltering of her marriage and her divorce from Charles Rawlings, the years of lonely struggle to carry on with both orange grove and career in spite of serious obstacles, and the heady satisfactions of big literary success.

10. To Maxwell E. Perkins

Cross Creek
Hawthorne, Route 1, Fla.[1]
March 31, 1931

Mr. Maxwell E. Perkins
CHARLES SCRIBNER AND SONS
New York City
My dear Mr. Perkins:

Your recent question as to the possibility of my doing a
novel makes me wish I might talk with you, for I am vibrat-
ing with material like a hive of bees in swarm. It would take
pages of necessarily vague ramblings to discuss it. At present I
see four books very definitely. Two of them need several more
years of note-taking. Of the two I am about ready to begin on,
one would be a novel of the scrub country.[2] I managed to get lost
in the scrub, the first day of the hunting season—and I encountered for the first time the palpability of silence.

So isolated a section gives a value to the scattered inhabitants. There is a handful of fascinating characters ready to be
woven into the fabric of the story. So far, I have not come on the
necessary thread of continuity. When it occurs to me, I think
it will force me to drop whatever else I may be doing. Once I
know where I am going, the book will almost write itself.

The novel that I should like to postpone a little, but that I
shall probably begin on, will be called "Hammock."[3] A few miles
away on the road to Micanopy, we cross a strange, unearthly
stream that has overflowed into the hammock itself. It is called,
inexplicably, the River Styx. It seemed to me that it might
well have been so named by one of the young Englishmen, remittance men, who colonized a section around Orange Lake in
the middle and late '80's—younger sons in disgrace, subsidized
to stay away. Some of them planted orange groves; others, I
am told, pretended to, sending home mythical accounts of their
development.

There took shape in my mind one of these young men, to
whom, coming into this jungle hammock, an embittered exile,
the strange small river would indeed seem another Styx, trans-
porting him from life into death. To his nature as I conceived
it, this country would be intolerable. This region is beautiful,

but it is not pretty. It is like a beautiful woman capable of a deep evil and a great treachery. Back of the lushness is something stark and sinister.

This man, in a desperate moment, would take a Cracker girl for wife; father a Cracker son. Both wife and son would be relegated to the kitchen almost at once, offensive to him in speech and habits. Against the one background, then, would run the two threads: the man in spiritual and physical torment, immersing himself fitfully and cynically in the social life that flourished here for a few brief years just before and after the Big Freeze of '95: fitfully in this, habitually in his liquor and his books; and the growing boy, finding exultation and beauty in all the elements that, to the other, are the essence of horror. The major characters and some of the minor ones are as sharply etched before me as though I could call them by name—and have them answer. The outline of the story is also comparatively clear to me. The book could become, incidentally, one of several things; possibly something of a study in the relativity of beauty.

I am hesitant about it, because it will be such an impossible mess if I bungle it. The characters are sufficiently complicated psychologically—the young Englishman, at least—to make me feel as a surgeon must feel the first time he tackles a major operation. The scrub story contains no more than the ordinary pitfalls, and for that reason I should feel a little more sure of myself in doing it first.

Out of the welter of equally indiscriminate praise and abuse that I have received, I am sending on three letters of favorable comment that may interest you as they did me, for they are from three of the comparatively rare souls who have seen the Florida I see. The comments of the elderly man from Massachusetts, who saw this Florida in his youth, I found quite touching. May I have the letters back, if you don't mind, for out of my gratitude for their genuine understanding, I want to answer them.

"Jacob's Ladder" was, of course, over-written. If you will be patient with me, I can do better work.

I wish you would thank for me the proof-reader who worked on the story. He has an eye like a sharp-shooter, and did an

amazing piece of work. With anything short of such perfection
of accuracy, he could have ruined the whole story.

Sincerely

Marjorie Kinnan Rawlings

1. Cross Creek had no post office. MKR's mailing address was the nearby town
of Hawthorne.

2. *South Moon Under* (1933).

3. *Golden Apples* (1935), to which she at first gave the working title of *Hammock*, or the Spanish *Hamaca*, after the central setting of rich, heavily wooded
Florida land.

Excited by her discovery that a living part of the American
frontier had survived into the twentieth century in her little-
known part of Florida, MKR set about with typical energy to
learn as much as she could about this frontier existence from personal experience. With the help of cracker neighbors at Cross
Creek she made arrangements to live with the Fiddia family in
the Big Scrub, where she could observe the old ways in their most
authentic form. In late August of 1931 she crossed the Oklawaha
River at Eureka, turned north up a narrow, sandy road running
along the river to the Fiddia house, which was located on a high
bluff above the river, and thus entered upon one of the great shaping episodes of her life. She stayed for two-and-a-half months, en-
tering fully into the life, including certain illegal things such as
poaching deer out of season and helping to run a moonshine still.
While she was there she made no attempt to disguise her note-
taking or the fact that she was gathering material for a book, but
it was part of her gift that she did so in such a way as to inspire
the friendliest kind of acceptance and approval from people who
might have had good reason to view her with hostility and
suspicion.

In her earliest published sketches about backwoods Florida one
can detect a certain condescension, something of the big-city reporter working a good story, exploiting the quaint customs of the
natives for the amusement of big-city readers. But by the time
she went to live in the scrub, she had already undergone a kind of
conversion, so that she was no longer viewing these people as an
exploiter, but as a sympathetic insider, a believer already com-

mitted to seeing the old ways as beautiful rather than as merely quaint. She came back from the Big Scrub with full notebooks, the major substance of two novels and half-a-dozen stories, and a lasting affection and admiration for the friends she had made there. The two letters that follow bracket the experience, one to Perkins before she went, one shortly after her return.

11. To Maxwell E. Perkins

> Cross Creek
> Hawthorne, Route 1, Fla.
> June 30, 1931

My dear Mr. Perkins:

My plans for a novel have advanced, since I wrote you, to this extent: that there is no question now in my mind, but that the story of the scrub country must come next. As soon as I have finished the several shorter things I am working on now, and stolen a very brief vacation on the coast, I have arranged to go over into the scrub and live, for as long as I need to gather up the intimate, accurate details that make up the background. Three of the handful of Cracker families in that section, are my good friends. The family with which I will spend most of my time, a boy as indigenous to the scrub as the deer, and his ninety-pound wisp of a white-haired mother, who ploughs, and last week with an axe cut a sapling and killed a rattlesnake in her field, is 'shining. Leonard says that when I come to board with his mother, I've got to help him run his 'shine at night. The federal agents have been very active lately, so don't be too surprised if your correspondent has the misfortune to be run in! If it should happen please don't bail me out, because the jailhouse would be a splendid place for quiet work!

I still do not know along what line of thought I mean to co-ordinate the story, I feel sure that will come to me when I am sufficiently immersed in the life. It is very possible that the simpler the narrative, the better. An absence of formal motivation may be exactly what it needs. It is a temptation, of course, to stress the 'shining. My husband, whose judgment I trust, warns me against this, saying that it is a relatively unimportant element. I suppose, if it were not handled with the most exquisite care, it could be cheapening—the Saturday Post taint. I don't know.

The actual writing of this story will only take a few months. When I return from the scrub, I am sure the story will be in such shape in my mind, that I can feel safe in naming an actual date for its completion. My stuff always goes through a long gestation period, but once I begin the actual writing, the first draft goes quite rapidly.

These are the shorter things I am working on now:

A short story, probably six to eight thousand words, "A Crop of Beans."[1] My material, basically true, is vital, and it will be my own fault if the story isn't good. I am well into it now, and I think two weeks will see it done.

A narrative about which I wrote Mr. Dashiell last week, "'Gators."[2] As it stands, it is a 3,000-word true yarn told me by one Cracker friend. I keep coming across so many more awfully funny Cracker alligator experiences, that I decided at the last minute not to enter it in the contest, but to amplify it from time to time, until I have a really comprehensive study of the Florida Cracker in humorous relation to that fast-vanishing and utterly preposterous reptile.

A short story, about 3,000 words, "Ol' Mule,"[3] half fact and half fancy, in which the most important character, and a true one, is a highly individual mule, owned jointly and quarreled over for nearly thirty years by two Cracker farmers. The first draft is done—badly done—and I have to do it all over again.

Then I have a dozen or so completed sketches about which I also questioned Mr. Dashiell. They are really "Cracker Chidlings," but if the magazine doesn't care to repeat the title, six or seven of them, perhaps more, could be grouped under some such heading as "Cracker Town," indicating the village psychology.[4]

I submitted a manuscript in the contest, "Lord Bill of the Suwannee River."[5] Modestly addressing it only to the Contest Editor. Mr Crichton informs me that it is absolutely lost in the snowstorm that has filled the offices. I should really have gone over into the scrub before the heat and the mosquitoes and the rattlesnakes began to appear, but I spent the late spring weeks on my contest narrative.

What an amazing response you have had. The office must feel like the old woman whose magic kettle kept on boiling, so that she had to eat her way through a village of soup.

I am reminded of the sad remark of a friend of mine,[6] who had novel aspirations, and who wrote tremendously well. She was a reader for Houghton Mifflin, and after nearly completing a novel, she suddenly stopped writing altogether. When I asked the reason, she said:

"I was astonished at the number of people who are writing, and writing well. I decided that the greatest contribution I could make to contemporary literature, was to get out of it."

I am not so high-minded. You have given me a fatal encouragement. I am like the old Cracker whose story I will write up some day, who fiddled his way in to jail and fiddled it out again, just because he fiddled in ecstasy as long as a single soul would listen to him.

Very sincerely,

MKR

1. Published in *Scribner's Magazine,* May 1932.

2. Published as "Alligators" in *Saturday Evening Post,* September 23, 1933.

3. Published as "Varmints" in *Scribner's Magazine,* November 1936.

4. These sketches never reached print in this form, though some were later reworked with Quincey Dover as narrator and published in MKR's collection of short stories, *When the Whippoorwill* (1940); others were reworked for *Cross Creek* (1942).

5. Published posthumously in *Southern Folklore Quarterly,* June 1961.

6. Probably Esther Forbes, whom MKR had known at the University of Wisconsin, and who did not give up writing but went on to publish a number of highly successful novels.

12. *To Maxwell E. Perkins*

Cross Creek
Hawthorne, Route 1
Florida
November 4, 1931

Dear Mr. Perkins:

About my novel of the scrub country——

I came back recently from very absorbing weeks lived with the old woman and her 'shiner son, of whom I believe I wrote you. I have voluminous notes of the intimate type, for which the most prolific imagination is no substitute. I have also, well as I thought I knew the people of this particular section, an entirely new conception of them. I knew they were gentle; honest. I knew that living was precarious, but just how hand-to-mouth it is, surprised me. I was also astonished by the *utter lack of bleakness or despair,* in a group living momentarily on the very edge of starvation and danger. Whatever else my story turns out to be, it will not be a gloomy, morose "novel of the soil." I found a zestfulness in living, a humor, an alertness to beauty, quite unexpected, and of definite value to record, if I can "get" it.

These people are "lawless" by an anomaly. They are living an entirely natural, and very hard, life, disturbing no one. Civilization has no concern with them, except to buy their excellent corn liquor and to hunt, in season, across their territory with an alarming abandon. Yet almost everything they do is illegal. And everything they do is necessary to sustain life in that place. The old clearings have been farmed out and will not "make" good crops any more. The big timber is gone. The trapping is poor. They 'shine, because 'shining is the only business they know that can be carried on in the country they know, and would be unwilling to leave.

The 'shining will have to be the main thread in my story. But I want to make it dramatic by an entire absence of melodrama. It is quite simply a part of the background; a part of the whole resistance of the scrub country to the civilizing process. The scrub, as a matter of fact, has defeated civilization. It is one of the few areas where settlements have disappeared and the scanty population is constantly thinning. Just this side of the Ocklawaha River, in the open range cattle country, the old-timers have recently heard their doom pronounced. The cattle must be fenced, which means the end of the old regime. A grand row has been raging there the past year, a Yankee family being whipped by the cattle men for not minding their own business, and I shall use the situation. Several of the old cattle men are "kin" to the 'shiner families just across the river.

There is no human habitation—there never has been and probably never will be—in the scrub itself. As far as I can determine, there is no similar section anywhere in the world. The scrub is a silent stretch enclosed by two rivers, deeply forested with Southern spruce (almost valueless), scrub oak, scrub myrtle and ti-ti, occasional gall-berry and black-jack and a few specialized shrubs and flowers, with "islands" of long-leaf yellow pine. There is an occasional small lake with its attendant marsh or "prairie." The only settlement is here and there on these bodies of water, and along the river edges, where the natural hammock growth has been bitten into by the settlers' clearings. It is a fringe of life, following the waterways. The scrub is a vast wall, keeping out the timid and the alien.

I have to go back again to stay another couple of weeks, for I need more information about the 'shining on the river of forty or fifty years ago, and the sources are of course scanty. I don't intend to dwell at any length on the past—the story will be one of the present, but I want to take the old woman of the book briefly through two or three generations of 'shining; it will indicate, as nothing else could do, the profound instincts that motivate the present generation. The 'shiner boy will be the chief protagonist.

When I facetiously urged you not to bail me out if I was caught at the still, I wasn't too far off. Just the week before I went over to stay, a cousin of my 'shiner friend betrayed him, with two others, to the federal agents, and his still was torn up and burned. I had one experience I would not have missed for a great deal—a discussion of a group of the 'shiners and their friends, of various plans for dealing with the traitor. Nothing definite has been done to him yet, for reasons too involved to go into, but in one way and another they are closing in on him, and some day he will simply disappear.

Possibly you wonder how I gain the confidence of these people without being a cold-blooded spy who intends to "use" them. It is so easy for me to live their life with them, that I am in some danger of losing all sophistication and perspective. I feel hurried sometimes, as though I must get "written out" in this country within the next few years, because so much is no longer strange or unusual to me. The life in the scrub is peculiarly right. While I was there, I did all the illegal things too; stalked deer with a light at night, out of season, kept the family in squirrels, paddled the boat while my friend dynamited mullet, shot limpkin on the river edge and had to wade waist deep in cypress swamp to get him (if you haven't eaten roast limpkin, you just haven't eaten, but you can go to county, state and federal jails for shooting them). But with food scarce, these people kill, quite correctly, I think, what they need. Incidentally, *only* what they need for food. Hunters with their licenses, on the other hand, kill a greater quantity during the legal season, and much of it is absolutely wasted—all of it entirely un-needed.

I helped the old lady do her work, helped her wash her heavy quilts that had gone two years without washing, to her despair, because she had no help with them, and can no longer lift them alone from the water and get them on the line. She cried when I left! They live cleanly and decently, and have one sheet on the bottom of the bed. For cover, they use quilts, hand-pieced, of course, summer or winter. One bed had a counterpane instead, which the occupant used over him in place of sheet or quilt, and the phrase was used, "to quilt with the counterpane. . . ."

(Innumerable phrases are fascinating. The verb "to use" is passive, not active. My friend, finding deer-tracks in the sweet potato patch, said, "Marge, let's you an' me come about moon-down tonight an' kill us the son-of-a-bitch been *usin' in* this field." The deer *use in* the hammock, as do the hammock rabbits—"them whistlin' bastards.") Many expressions are very beautiful. The fish and deer, in fact most of the game, feed "on the moon"—at moon-rise, moon-down, south-moon-over and south-moon-under. The people are conscious at all times of the position of the sun and moon and stars and wind. They *feel* the moon under the earth—south-moon-under. The simplicity of speech is most effective. Old Granny Brinson, whom we went to visit one night by way of row-boat down the river, described what you might call the state of consciousness between life and death. She answered the old lady's inquiry about her health, with the true and simple statement, "I'm sick, Piety, an' dyin'," and told us of her "spells": "I go off into the twilight; into some lonesome-looking place."

The story is clear in my mind, and I am beginning the actual writing this week. Its success will depend, I should say, almost altogether on how real, how vivid, I am able to make the individuals whose lives move along with the 'shiner boy's. The background and small details are fool-proof, but tremendously hard work in delineating each character will be necessary to make the story anything like a reality. The final effect should be one of utter absorption in the people and their lives. For that reason, the title is giving me some difficulty. I don't like to call it "Yonder in the Scrub," as the Crackers in my own section do, for the title is detached, looking at the scrub from the outside. I want a complete submersion. And I can't call it "The Scrub" or "Big Scrub," simply, for the word to any reader in the country outside of Florida suggests foot-ball! It annoys me to work without a definite heading. . . .

Shall I let you know when I am, say, half-done?

I was interested in Lewis Gannett's[1] criticism of Galsworthy's American idiom, remembering your asking me, when I discussed my other embryonic novel with you, "Hammock," whether I knew enough about young Englishmen! Gannett seems to think Galsworthy doesn't know enough about young Americans! I haven't read "Maid in Waiting,"[2] but if Galsworthy has erred, I should say it was because he made too deliberate an attempt to use an American idiom. It is my belief that there is a common academic speech, used normally by the intellectual classes, intelligible to both nations. Conspicuous idiom, particularly when used by the cultured, is a social affectation in any case—an effort at sprightliness. When I do my young Englishman, he will use a simple Anglo-Saxon that is always, to my idea, more effective than colloquialisms. The simple speech of the Scandinavian novels, for instance, creates a certain timelessness, dignifies the characters.

Of course, you were questioning more than that—my knowledge of young Englishmen psychologically. He isn't going to be entirely normal which gives me some leeway! I have recently come across a track that will help me, I think. There is still alive, in late middle-life, an Englishman who came with his two brothers to the scrub country, establishing by their own effort a prosperous orange grove on the river edge, which was killed to the ground by the big freeze. The man went to Jacksonville and was recently retired with honors as a Clyde Steamship Line agent. If he proves to be a man of ordinarily sensitive perceptions, I can ask him innumerable "lead" questions, whose answers should keep me on the right track. I have a superficial knowledge of young Englishmen, besides.

A fascinating assortment of people is being born into that book. One of our Florida friends has been strangely reticent about one of his grandmothers, but an uncle of his, with a deeper appreciation of character, told us of a hard-riding, hard-drinking woman who left her weak husband in the house and over-saw the plantation and orange groves herself. She carried mint juleps in a canteen at her saddle, and careened down sometimes on astonished strangers jogging along the sand roads in a buckboard, offering them a julep!

But that is a year or two away.

By the way, if any of your staff should come to Florida this winter, send them on to us for a few days' visit, if they're not too aesthetic. I don't mean to imply extreme aestheticism on SCRIBNER'S, for the virility of the magazine is one of its most striking features. I mean, for example, just what would I do with William Lyon Phelps.[3] We aren't entirely primitive—we set a good civilized table and have a bathroom. And we do have a powerful good time—so good that one would scarcely notice the state of our exchequer. Do you suppose the millionaires will eat oranges this winter? We begin to doubt it. But it really makes very little difference. We have a fine stand of broccoli, thick cream, home-cured hams superior to Smithfield, friends from mayors and university professors on up to sheriffs and Cracker constables, comfortable access to both seacoasts and a charge account at a gas station. As the old French valentine verse has it, "Que voulez-vous encore?"

Very sincerely,

MKR

1. Lewis S. Gannett, journalist and author (1891–1966).
2. John Galsworthy, *The End of the Chapter,* vol. 1, *Maid in Waiting* (New York, 1934).
3. William Lyon Phelps, American educator, writer, and critic (1865–1943).

With head, heart, and notebook brimming with the rich material she had gathered during her stay in the Big Scrub, MKR immediately sat down to her typewriter and for the next seven months worked with unusual absorption, completing by early summer a draft of *South Moon Under*, the promised novel of the scrub, which she sent off to Perkins in July. After several weeks he sent the manuscript back with a detailed critique, praising the work but urging her to rewrite so as to give more emphasis to the story and the development of character and less to "social chronicle," or detailed reporting of the place and way of life. She agreed with his suggestions and proceeded at once to a major revision.

13. To Maxwell E. Perkins

> Cross Creek
> Hawthorne, Route 1, Fla.
> August 31, 1932

Dear Mr. Perkins:

Your letter is tremendously helpful. Your diagnosis and prescription are so specific, that I think between us we can have the patient on his feet in no great while. You have a truly amazing genius for taking the product of another's imagination in the hollow of your hand. It is the height, I suppose, of critical sympathy and understanding.

Reading over the manuscript of *South Moon Under*, I am astonished at how far I went out of my way to be random and rambling. The direct narrative form throughout is so patently required—and through so much of the book I seem perversely to have avoided it. Looking back to my earliest conception of the book, I do not believe that I ever planned it as a true novel, but, as you express it, as "a social chronicle." But I agree heartily that the true novel form will be much more effective, and will convey the truth beyond truth, by making the characters more vital. I believe that I was afraid of two things: first, of getting into too great length in the straight narrative form, which always takes more space than a few paragraphs of generalization; and second, of not being detached enough. But I think I can lay both ghosts.

I plan to re-write altogether most of the central third to half of the book, considering what now stands as simply a collection of coherent notes. I remember I didn't answer you when you asked how long it would take me. I hate to say too defi-

nitely—it makes one nervous in spite of oneself—but if the end
of October is reasonable for your requirements; I think that
only an untoward interruption would prevent my having the
work done by that time. I could do it in a month if necessary.
I probably work better under pressure. The bad part of the book
is the part I dawdled over.

You asked me what Carl Brandt[1] said about it. I did not see
him again after I left a carbon copy for him, although I found
out later that he had wanted to talk with me about it. Miss
Baumgartner (spelling?) had read it and talked with my husband about it. She considered it "fascinating" material, made
a general comment similar to yours, saying that it lacked "a
backbone" to hold it together. Her principal suggestion toward
unifying it was to urge an emphasizing of the boy's inherited
fear. To a minor degree I shall do this, but to carry it very far I
should consider artificial, tending to make a book with too obtrusive a "theme" or "motif," which, when too much dwelled on,
I find abhorrent. Miss Baumgartner thought his fear should
be brought out in his dealings with the girl Kezzy. That would
be all tommy-rot, as I conceived of her as very much a harbor of
refuge for him, at all times. However, when I bring in the
other girl, it will automatically be his hidden fears that will
keep him from her. She will be too much a part of the civilized
world he does not know, and mistrusts; the game warden will
be an habitué of her father's house; the sheriff will be her father's friend. Everything about her, except her physical appeal
for him, will chill the very marrow in his bones, and make it
impossible for him to do anything but run from her and from his
desire; his instinct for self-preservation being more profound,
in such a situation, than the sex-instinct.

I can't tell you how deeply I appreciate your helpfulness—
your thoughtfulness and sympathy. You make it very easy for
me to go at it again. You have only asked one hard thing of
me—to give up the wolf!

Very sincerely,

MKR

1. MKR's literary agent. Bernice Baumgartner was Brandt's secretary.

14. To Maxwell E. Perkins

Cross Creek
Hawthorne, Route 1
Florida
November 12, 1932

Dear Mr. Perkins:

. . . I had no idea that you planned to move so fast on the book, *South Moon Under.* As a matter of fact, you have had more confidence in the outcome than I have had. You have been so awfully decent about everything—you really are a dear, you know—that I do want to cooperate in every way. . . .

I am anxious to know just how the revision strikes you. Now that it is done, I realize that it is not the book I wanted to write—not the picture I wanted to give. Very possibly it is a better book—probably more readable—but somehow or other the emotion I intended to convey, has escaped me. Probably it is always so with any writer except a true genius. The thing that sweeps across you, clamoring for expression, is probably always more powerful than the flabby words and phrases you begin to trot out against it. The profound reality, the essence, of an idea or a feeling, manages to slip away in the shuffle. I wonder what proportion of books gives the thing the writer wanted so much to give.

Do feel assured that you can count on me to work as fast as possible and not hold you up. I'll even promise good behavior to the extent of not raising the devil with the proofs.

Very sincerely,

Marjorie Kinnan Rawlings

15. To Maxwell E. Perkins

Cross Creek
Hawthorne, Route 1
Florida
November 18, 1932

Dear Mr. Perkins:

I was bullying my husband last night into reading some of my chapters of "South Moon Under" as I worked on them. He threw down the manuscript and said, "I'm going to make a suggestion that will infuriate you, and I'm possibly wrong about it. Take out all your profanity. If you do this, you automatically open up a wide and continuous market for the book *among boys,* entirely distinct, an accidental by-product, from your mature appeal."

Of course, I was as shocked as if he'd suggested that I sell myself into slavery. I remember, out of the red fog that enveloped me, remarking caustically that possibly the book could become the first of a series, "The Rover Boys in Florida." I remember being soothed with copious draughts of native rye. When I came to, he went on to explain that he meant nothing of the sort. He said that the book, as an accurate picture of one of the last strips of American frontier, contains so much woods and river lore that would appeal to boys in the way Huckleberry Finn, Treasure Island, and some of Kipling, appeal to them, that it was a pity to cut off the book from such a group by what he considers the casual excrudescence [*sic*] of the profanity of Lant. He didn't mean, he said, to impugn the artistic quality of the book at all; that far greater, more artistic and mature books than I will ever write, happen here and there to contain a picture or a quality that makes boys devour them ignoring the mature angle altogether. Then I remembered your speaking of Huckleberry Finn in connection with the possibilities you saw in the river chapter, and I am ready to admit there may be something in the idea.

It sounds like an affectation to say that I don't particularly care whether or not the book sells. I just happen to mean it. I should rather have it considered good by people of discernment, than popular. But I do have common sense enough to be willing to broaden its appeal if the book is not harmed in so doing. I have possibly already fallen between two stools as to its artistic unity. The mass of out-of-the-ordinary detail and native lore, may, if I am lucky, slip naturally along with the narrative. Or, it may obscure and defeat my basic conception of the cosmic conflict of man in general struggling against an obscure law and destiny. So for Heaven's sake, since this menace is already present, don't let me bring in a new one unless we're pretty sure of our ground. I mean, don't let's "purify" the book for an adolescent consumption that might never materialize, and ruin the book at the same time for the discriminating adult palate.

Now: I want you to think it over very carefully from both
the publisher's and the artist's standpoint. I don't know you well
enough to know which is dominant in you. But in spite of
your betrayal of me by handing over the manuscript to the
printer without being sure that it contained no atrocities, I trust
you implicitly as an artist and a critic, and I shall accept your
judgment in the matter without further question. I want you to
answer two questions:

Is Lant's profanity extraneous and meaningless, as my husband claims it is in 75% of the instances? (He admits the effec-
tiveness of such phrases as "the ring-tailed bastard," the "skew-
tailed bastard" and such.) Or is the profanity, as of course I
intended it to be, an amusing and vigorous part of my character? Typical changes occasioned by the deletion would be, for
instance, when Lant is trying to roll the big dead alligator in his
boat, "He sobbed, 'God damn you, you stinkin' bastard, I'll not
leave go——'." Substitutes for "son of a bitch" and "bastard"
would be "booger," "scaper," "scoundrel," "jay-bird," "buzzard"
and "jessie." There are three places that occur to me where
Lant's profanity is an integral part of the story; where his
mother accepts his son of a bitch and bastard without question,
but objects violently to his "I'll beat your butt"; where she objects to his calling her sister's son a son of a bitch or a bastard
but agrees with enthusiasm to the epithet taken up by the
whole vicinity, "the pimp"; and where Lant objects to Kezzy's
roughness of speech in front of the girl, Ardis. (About page 302)

The other question: is there so much else in the book that
would be objectionable for boys from a parent's standpoint, that
nothing is to be gained by toning down one character's language? I have already been talked into deleting one or two of
the more medical bits of folk lore. I think such bits of lore as the
doctor's comment on women in relation to child-bearing and
the moon, Zeke's remark that "a woman in the house ain't a
woman in the bed"—that type of thing would simply, I should
think, go right over an adolescent's head and not be objected to
by a Puritan parent. I may be quite wrong about that. That
leaves such things as the quarrel about the out-house and the
quarrel of the crazy man, Ramrod Simpson with "ol' Desus
Chwist." My husband thinks that since the crazy man is not

very much developed any way, in the story, that it would be as effective to replace Jesus with the devil—(always a neat and tasty change.)

Well, you figure it out. Mechanically, the changes would be quite simple. *Don't* let me emasculate either character or story to a very problematical end. *Don't* let me turn a rough woodsman into a Boy Scout! But you will see the thing absolutely clear, and I have a queer feeling there may be something in it.

This is the last time I'll be tugging at your coat-tails to have you answer questions. I hope to be quite done this week and go off hunting on the 20th with the whole thing off my mind. You will receive the last installment not later than Wednesday the 23rd. . . .

Very sincerely,

Marjorie Kinnan Rawlings

In spite of the fact that she was constantly running a low-grade fever from a malarial infection which no one diagnosed until the revision was done, MKR doggedly completed work on *South Moon Under,* which Perkins approved and sent on to the printer and scheduled for March 1933 publication. The urbane and rather proper Maxwell Perkins on several occasions had been prevailed upon to leave his editorial office to go deep-sea fishing with Hemingway in the waters off Key West, and on one occasion he had been persuaded to try duck hunting with Hemingway in a freezing blind in Arkansas. MKR, by now thoroughly ingratiated and habituated to the outdoor pleasures of her adopted Florida, tried repeatedly to persuade Perkins to make a visit to Cross Creek. But he, swamped with editorial duties, and perhaps a little leery of the rough-and-ready tone of Cross Creek life, never accepted, though she kept trying.

16. To Maxwell E. Perkins

[Cross Creek]
January 1, 1933

Dear Mr. Perkins:

I think we'd all better renounce duck-shooting for the new year——

I came in the other morning from futile hours with my husband at the sport, to find your pitiful story waiting for me. It seems to me that Hemingway drags you the most preposterous distances just to freeze you to the marrow. I remember your telling me that an icy norther had blown every time you went to Key West to fish with him. At least we were warm and comfortable on Orange Lake. Our lake is black with ducks; but they're all "in the clare," and to get a shot you need to sit in the marsh up to your neck, or have more beaters than we have ever been able to assemble. I'm no good at hitting anything on the wing, anyway.

Thank you, yes, I had a grand Christmas. We spent it at the log hunting lodge of our Tampa surgeon friend [Dr. J. C. Vinson] and were able to do full justice to his very good Burgundy and the Chauvet 1920 for whose vintage he apologized. Vintages become minor matters after more than four years on corn liquor.

What a fiendish conscience you have! You paint the most devastating picture of yourself, crouched in the Arkansas snow, worrying about as yet unborn characters in books you're publishing——. To my ignorance, Arkansas is so God-forsaken a place that of course there's no telling what one would be forced to worry about there. If you could live through Arkansas, the Rawlings needn't hesitate to try to get you to sample Cross Creek sometime.

Anyway, many thanks for your sympathy, and with the best of wishes for the year—

MKR

Nineteen thirty-three turned out to be a mixed year for MKR, with professional satisfactions of several sorts but considerable adversity in her personal life. *South Moon Under* was published in March to an almost universal acclaim, adoption by Book-of-the-Month-Club, and serious mention for the Pulitzer Prize. But just as the book appeared, her marriage, which had been suffering increasing strain for more than a decade, finally broke apart, and Charles moved away from the grove to live on the Gulf Coast, the separation becoming final with a divorce in November. With his leaving, she found herself, in spite of the success of her book, in deep depression, alone at the grove with funds exhausted, facing what seemed the possibility of actual hunger. She later wrote that it never occurred to her to ask for an advance on the royalties from the novel and that she found herself down to a box of Uneeda crackers and a can of tomato soup when, quite unexpectedly, the postman brought her notice that she had won the $500 O. Henry Memorial Award for her story "Gal Young 'Un," which had appeared in *Harper's* magazine the previous June.

Seeking a complete break from her painful associations at Cross Creek, she went on a 100-mile trip with her friend Dessie Smith Vinson in a rowboat powered with an outboard motor, down a wild, marshy section of the upper St. Johns River. Then later in the summer, with royalties from the novel coming in, but still feeling restless and depressed, she made a voyage to England, telling herself it was a research trip to learn about the home background of the young Englishman she meant to use as a central character in her next novel. During this time she was also slowly becoming aware from remarks in Perkins' letters that as one of the authors at Scribner's she was in the company of the literary great—Hemingway, Wolfe, and Fitzgerald. With the birth pangs of her first novel scarcely over, she was already gestating the second, the one she called "Hamaca" or "Hammock," which was published two years later as *Golden Apples*.

---

17. To Maxwell E. Perkins

Cross Creek
Hawthorne, Route 1, Fla.
March 3, 1933

Dear Mr. Perkins:

. . . Many thanks for the reviews [of *South Moon Under*]. They are more generous than I had expected, but they sadden me. I feel quite cheap, quite the Judas, at having apparently delivered the Cracker into the hands of the Philistines. You remember my telling you that I dreaded the thought of making the Crackers seem utterly wild and woolly, when they are not. You comforted me by saying that they didn't seem so to you;

no more queer, I believe you said, than a Maine woodsman. Well — —. The country I hoped to present as stirring and beautiful, emerges under Percy Hutchison's well manicured touch as "repellant." Good old Piety ends up "a blind and toothless hag." It's his privilege to think of her as a hag but God knows I never even mentioned her teeth! I thought I was getting in quite a nice little touch as to the sheer relativity of social viewpoints when I had Kezzy say of the Moslems, "It makes me faint-hearted to think there's sich people with sich ways," (incidentally, a remark I really heard made) but it seems to have gone by without leaving any claw marks. Anyway, the feeling that I have written a wild animal book removes any lingering doubt as to future subject matter. No more Crackers. I have two or three humorous short things in mind, but no more Cracker novels. I gave as accurate a picture as possible of a way of life and a group of people—so that's that.

What did please me in the reviews I've seen, particularly the Phila. *Public Ledger* (naturally, I suppose, as it was the most enthusiastic) was favorable comment on style, because that tends to relieve my mind somewhat of the fear that my seemingly *outré* material was carrying me along. Any good journalist, able to get the material, could have made a readable book out of the scrub stuff. The "Hamaca" will have to stand on its own feet. I'll write you about it later.

I plan to take possibly a very foolish trip, beginning this coming Wednesday or Thursday. Another woman—an amazingly capable sportswoman—and I are going down the St. Johns river by rowboat with outboard motor. We put our boat into the water at its source, which is, ominously enough, Lake Hellenblazes—about on a line with Melbourne on the east coast. I know that the first 100 miles at least lie through an utterly forsaken marsh country dotted with palm islands, and I can't help being a little afraid that false channels may get us into trouble until the river broadens and develops definite banks. But as a Cracker friend says, "No fool, no fun." All this strenuous out-door stuff is new to me since coming to Florida. I've taken to it naturally, but my chief claim to capability in such matters lies only in being game for anything. So wish me luck.

You should receive this Monday morning. If you need to get in

touch with me in a hurry about the English business, you can
reach me Monday by wire:

Care of Dr. J.C. Vinson
Embassy Apts.
Tampa, Fla.

Tuesday and Wednesday the Island Grove address will reach
me by telegram. (Or if you write me Monday, I will get the
letter Wednesday morning by the regular Hawthorne route; before I leave.) Then, leaving Thursday, I'll be gone on the river
trip for ten days if all goes well.

Do things look any brighter financially in New York? A
Tampa friend in with the politicians and such got us word on the
Q.T. today to get our fifty cents out of our Ocala bank in a
hurry—the inside word is that 26 Florida banks are folding on
Monday. It may be just one of those absurd rumors, but it's
reasonable enough so that I'm going to take out the amount of
our last orange check at least. The world infection is beginning to spread even to our peaceful backwater.

Very sincerely,

Marjorie Kinnan Rawlings

18. To Maxwell E. Perkins

Cross Creek

[March 20, 1933]

Dear Abbé:

Now what can I say to you? When you put me in such a
corner?[1] You say, in implication, "You trust me, don't you?" And
I say, "Yes, Abbé, I have publicly professed my faith." And you
say, "Very well, then, you must be entirely dutiful and think as I
tell you to think."

Ordinarily I love a good argument for its own sake—and I
think a pair of lawyers could work up a lively one over the
interpretation of that contract. But I intended you to draw it up
to suit yourself in the first place—so if you've decided to back
up Mr. Scribner (when he wouldn't back you up) in his insis-
tence that the English rights always were—or at any rate always should have been—in Scribner's hands—I sha'n't quarrel

about it ever again. At the risk of being vulgar, I tell you of
an incident that illustrates my point of view about not calling
Mr. Scribner names. One of our good friends is the Cracker
constable of a nearby village.[2] He has taken both my husband
and me in hand from the beginning, trying to make hunters and
fishermen of us. I often go off alone with him for a day's sport.
One of his minor vices is a mania for attempting to stroke a
woman's legs. A woman like myself is as safe with him as with a
ten-year-old-boy—as a matter of fact, this tendency is, I believe, more mischievous than evil—the last woman he tried it
on was a woman evangelist, sitting next to him in church,
bowed in prayer—so that it annoyed, rather than disturbed me.
I had cracked his knuckles with the butt of a revolver and
this had pleased, rather than dissuaded him. Finally I had it out
with him when fishing one day. I told him that it interfered
with our honest sport and spoiled all my pleasure in being with
him; that if he ever put his hand on me again, I should never
fish or hunt with him from that day on. He knew I meant it.

"Well," he conceded, "you can keep me from pettin' them
purty legs—but you can't keep me from wantin' to."

But really—if you knew how little the English business
means to me, or bothers me— —. I spoke my piece about it—the
Brandt people have been very decent and have made no complaint—and as far as I'm concerned, that's the end of it. It
doesn't in the least interfere with my conviction that you are my
friend and my support in time of trouble, and that the house
of Scribner is quite the noblest and most dignified with which a
(comparatively) young author could hope to be associated. I'm
an old woman of 36, you know, and after having been buffeted a
bit by life and circumstance and what-not (which accounts for
my changed character and physique from my co-ed days), I'm
deeply appreciative of kindness and goodness in any form.

Which reminds me of the river trip, from which Mrs. Vinson
and I returned yesterday. It was gorgeous. Two impressions
stay with me. One is of the just-mentioned kindness and goodness of simple people. Somehow or other, I understand such
people. I also understand lunatics. The people in between are
quite beyond me. The other impression is of the other-worldly
quality of river life. Water is, after all, an unfamiliar element,

yet our only life, our only safety, lay in continued progress down
a flowing stream. The poor fishermen we met along the way
were helpful and concerned as none of my sophisticated friends
have ever been. The first one we encountered, who gave us
channel information, begged us to send him a card when we
reached home and civilization. He said, "I don't want to keep on
worryin' about you." And when we reached Lake George, we
found that news of our passage had preceded us. The fishermen
had sent word down the river to watch for us, to see if we got
through all right. . . .

Our correspondence is frightfully one-sided. I think sometimes—usually at the end of a letter, like this, when it's too late
to do anything about it without going to a lot of trouble—that
the ramblings of writers about themselves to you must be very
wearisome. You know a great deal about me, about my way of
life, and so forth, and I know nothing at all about you, except
that you have a magnificiently lucid mind that contrives also to
be sympathetic.

Very sincerely,

MKR

P.S. On my last day up the river a great deal about "Hamaca"
suddenly straightened itself out in my mind. I am desperately
afraid of several things—one, that the first part of the book may
be too raw and disgusting—and I am so weary of the Faulkner school of filth that I should almost prefer to be a Harold Bell
Wright,[3] than to contribute to it. Yet my character and my
plot require some things that in themselves are revolting—they
are all part of the horror of an alien background, from which
my man finally emerges—rather, with which he finally identifies
himself.

Of course, I shouldn't think of anything so selfish as insisting that you come to Florida for the sole purpose of talking
about an unwritten book, when we are both perfectly literate
and able to work things out on paper. When I said that I should
like you to come, I only wanted to make very sure that you
understood the certainty of your welcome if your affairs should
bring you near us. Until you crouched in the snow with Hemingway, I had felt a little uneasily that our life here might strike

you as—I don't know what—random—messy—a little shabby. But once I realized you were entirely adaptable, I felt you would enjoy it, as widely varying persons seem to have done. So if you should plan to come south this spring any time after the next two weeks—my husband will then be home from the Gulf—please stop off with us for a week at least. I'll show you the scrub and a couple of lovely rivers.

If you're not coming, I'll take up the book in detail later. I plan several months of research, just to have my period firmly fixed. Then I feel I must get away during the worst of the summer, as another dose of malaria would be too devastating.

In all seriousness, all is forgiven and forgotten about the Brandt mix-up—I understand your viewpoint and quite harmlessly disagree with it. I'll be glad to assign "Hamaca" to you right now, if you want it.

MKR

P.S. Use your engraved stationery some time when you're not solemnly taking me to task! It's not fair to use your dressiest stuff for purposes of chastisement!

1. There had been a mix-up about whether her literary agent, Carl Brandt, or Scribner's should execute the contract for the English rights to *South Moon Under*. Perkins had urged her to trust Scribner's to act in her best interest in the matter.

2. Fred Tompkins, who was the original of Uncle Benny Mathers in her story "Benny and Bird Dogs," and from whom she had heard many tales and much cracker lore.

3. Harold Bell Wright, American novelist (1872–1944), whose books emphasized a wholesome morality.

19. To Maxwell E. Perkins

[Cross Creek
April 1933]

Dear Mr. Perkins:

I thought possibly you might like to know what sort of reader reaction I'm getting on South Moon Under—here are some letters that for obvious reasons interest me particularly. I was delighted with the one from the literary lumberman—the Wilson Cypress Co. president—for it was like having the river itself rise and approve of the book. I was only dimly aware that

the company was still in existence. I intend to make the
man's acquaintance and take him up on his offer to visit the
Dixie County logging camps. I guess it's sure-enough wild country up there.

What's the news on the book, from your end? It's a rather
queer feeling to be sitting here in the swamp and having the
merest dribbles of information come in. From personal sources I
hear, here and there, of its selling. Somebody is wild about it
and somebody else writes to the Tampa Tribune asking if they
don't consider it obscene in spots.

I had an amusing reaction from the family in the scrub where
I stay off and on. I gave them a copy, suitably and gratefully
inscribed, and the man of the family says "You done a damn
good job, for a Yankee." He is being tormented by friends and
relatives who want to borrow the book, and he's being very
choosy in the loaning. He refuses point blank to lend it to his
uncle to take home, because he's afraid his uncle's wife would
tear up the book or burn it. I asked, astonished, why she might
do such a thing. He said, "Well, she's one o' them Christian-
hearted sons o' bitches, and peculiar as Hell, to boot. You got
right smart o' cussin' in the book, and she might be scairt her
boy Lester'd learn to cuss by it. Now Lester kin out-cuss the
book right now—but his Mammy don't know it."

By the way, don't be puzzled when your sales sheets show
two or three copies disposed of in Ocala. It's not a boycott. The
whole town is standing in line to read the copy donated to the
public library, and the copy in the circulating library. Everyone
tells me with great pride, "I've got my name on the list to
read your book. I can hardly wait." I say politely, "I do hope
you'll enjoy it," and I'm bursting, like Cabell[1] with his letter
answers, to say something such as, "Do you think I'm a damn
orchid, that I can live on air?"

What is one supposed to do about answering letters anyway?
I have a whole swarm about Jacob's Ladder that I never answered because it seems so futile. I tried to keep up for a while
and found it almost impossible to hit a cordial but distant medium. I either sounded cold and heard later I was considered
high-hat—or sounded too big-hearted and had the correspondents on my neck. You just can't be bothered with old men in

Boston who send you candy. Do you think it matters in the least if you don't answer mail at all? Of course, several of those I'm sending you today I shall very much want to answer, because the contact appeals to me. So send me back this batch, please.

Very sincerely,

Marjorie K. Rawlings

1. James Branch Cabell, American novelist and essayist (1879–1958).

20. To Maxwell E. Perkins

Cross Creek
Hawthorne, Route 1, Fla.
[ca. April 15, 1933]

Dear Mr. Perkins:

I've had to stop and think just what it was I wrote you that sounded quotable for publicity. It must have been what my friend of the scrub said— —"You've done a damn good job, for a Yankee," and his statement as to why he wouldn't lend the book to his uncle, describing his aunt as "one of them Christian-hearted sons of bitches," etc. Is that what you mean?

Now— —. If what you want is to be able to quote the reaction of the scrub inhabitants, the prototypes of the characters in the book, I'm frightfully sorry, but it just can't be done. On the other hand, if you want to use the remarks as coming from Florida Crackers in some other section, that would be perfectly all right.

You have been awfully careful from the beginning in taking care of me from the local angle, and I appreciate it a lot. I scarcely need to go into detail about the present situation, because I'm sure you understand pretty well, but I'll be briefly specific. It's not a question, as it was in the "Cracker Chidlings" of hurting people's feelings by writing them up, and of bothering the Chamber of Commerce type of person as well as bringing to public notice a class of natives considered by many no special asset to the state. It would be a matter of actually getting a definite family in trouble with the law by identifying them too publicly with my book-characters. I have been nervous about that part of it from the beginning. As you know, as my friends

Publicity photograph, at the Cross Creek farmhouse, about age 36 (1932–33).

here and elsewhere know, I have spent a good deal of time with a family in the scrub whose living is made by moonshining. The young man also hunts as he pleases, very much as Lant does in the book. My character of Piety in her latter years is drawn very closely from life, from the mother of this family. Lant is a composite portrait, but many of the small details of his life are those of the life of my scrub friend. He understood all this perfectly, knew I was writing the book, that I was using all the things he told me. I checked over a great mass of detail with him, from the manuscript. He has recognized in the book the parts that are photographic—told a mutual friend "It's a good thing she didn't tell no more'n she did about my huntin'— she'd of had the game warden on my neck shore." He seems rather indifferent to danger about the illicit distilling, I think because he feels so safe about the present location of his still. So far, so good.

You keyed your publicity about the book very nicely, and there has been no public mention anywhere that I have seen of my having done any more than work from life in a general way. Now——. There are so few families in the scrub, that if any public mention is made of my connection with any one of them, people hereabouts will go even beyond the truth, and it would be quite conceivable that "one of them Christian-hearted sons of bitches" would raise a great row about moonshining in Marion County being so common and public that a Yankee writer could make a book about it. You are no doubt familiar with the depths of depravity in the reforming type of mind. Of course, the new political slant on liquor makes interference improbable, but I just couldn't run the risk of getting my friends in trouble to make a Roman holiday.

Would it answer your purpose to use the quotations as coming from Cracker friends of mine in Gulf Hammock? It would all sound alike to anyone in the north, and if the quotation were picked up here in Florida, it would be harmless, since Gulf Hammock is on the opposite side of the state. But they CAN'T be quoted as coming out of the scrub itself. If you use them, I'll have to ask you to let me see the notes before they are released, just to make sure they're all right from my point of view.

Very sincerely,

Marjorie Kinnan Rawlings

21. To Maxwell E. Perkins

Cross Creek
Hawthorne, Route 1, Fla.
May 21, 1933

Dear Mr. Perkins:

I'm glad you felt that the river article[1] had enough of value to redeem it from dullness. I couldn't judge of that, and I was very mistrustful.

I plan now to spend about all of August and the first week or two of September in England. That will put me in New York for a few days' shopping the last week in July or the first week in August. Will you be there then? I should hate to pass near your habitat and not see you.

I am limiting myself to the several English shires from which I expect, unless they are very different from my conception, to choose a locale for my young Englishman of "Hamaca." These are Lancaster (which I expect to reject), Sussex, Devon and Somerset. I should like to have you help me decide on the exact social class that fits my requirements, and that will be consistent with a particular locale. I don't want an out-and-out aristocrat. Upper middle class—rather scholarly landed people. They won't come into the story at all, but I want to be accurate.

I'm having better luck than I ever dared hope for in tracking down the remnants of the English colonists of the period I'm using—the heyday of the orange industry from 1880 to 1895, the year of the Big Freeze, and then five years more after that, bringing it to 1900. I've found some adorable old Englishmen and Englishwomen in varying stages of prosperity and poverty. They're being most cooperative. I'm unearthing all kinds of interesting stuff, including a 50-year-old scandal about the former Duke of Sutherland, whose heirs still own land on the Florida Gulf coast. One old lady (a solitary cup-bearer for the Church of England in the most desolate small Florida village you ever laid eyes on) is sending to England for some diaries of the period for me, and is making a contact for me (if her family proves as agreeable as she) with two sisters who lived in Florida at that time and went back to Lancaster after the disastrous freeze.

I'm going to Jacksonville tomorrow to keep a date with an Englishman who came to the Riverside colony on the Ocklawaha in the scrub that I mentioned in "South Moon Under." Next week I'm going to Miami and intermediate points where I've located some very promising English folk. I don't think I'll have any trouble in getting together all I need for my setting, from that angle.

Very sincerely,

MKR

1. "Hyacinth Drift," based on her long trip down the St. Johns River, which was published in *Scribner's Magazine*, September 1933, and reprinted as a chapter in *Cross Creek* (1942).

In a note to MKR on June 1, 1933, Perkins mentioned that he had a plan "in connection with writing" that he would like to discuss with her, but he did not suggest what it was. Wanting to know more, she wrote asking him what he had in mind, and Perkins replied at once, outlining his plan for her to write a book about a boy in the Florida scrub country. He was thinking of a juvenile, a book *for* boys, and this scratched MKR's pride a bit, but the idea lodged in her mind and received mention in her letters over the next several years while she was working on her second novel, *Golden Apples*. Perkins' suggestion about a "boy's book of the scrub" was to have significant consequences: it led five years later to MKR's masterpiece, *The Yearling*.

22. To Maxwell E. Perkins

Hawthorne, Route 1, Fla.
June 7, 1933

Dear Mr. Perkins:

. . . The only possible plan I can conceive of your having for me that answers the rather strange description of being "in connection with" writing, would be that you'd like to have me do a text-book for your educational department on "The Principle and Practice of Moonshine Liquor."

The difficulties you're having with Wolfe make me think I've been quite a model author. I only worried you crouched in the snow with Hemingway—certainly I never cost you a whole vacation.

Yes, I've been following the Wolfe stories.[1] It was rather startling to have the first one in the same issue of the magazine with the Hemingway story—you couldn't get a wider variance in technique if you culled over the whole field of American writers. I read the Hemingway story first and then turned immediately to the Wolfe story—and I was totally unable to read the Wolfe. Two days later I picked it up again, and read and enjoyed it. I didn't like "The Train and the City" nearly so well as "Death the Proud Brother," however, when Wolfe hits it right with his very gorgeous style, the effect is tremendously satisfying emotionally like a symphony at its best. When he beats his chest and tears his hair and pounds on the drums too lavishly, as I thought he did in the first story, you get more the effect of an awfully enthusiastic German band, and you rather long to empty pitchers of water from the third story, to shut up the tumult. I imagine he's the sort of person who has to get his effects that way or not at all, and that there's no such thing as safely toning him down.

Hemingway, damn his soul, makes everything he writes terrifically exciting (and incidentally makes all us second-raters seem positively adolescent) by the seemingly simple expedient of the iceberg principle—three-fourths of the substance under the surface. He comes closer that way to retaining the magic of the original, unexpressed idea or emotion, which is always more stirring than any words. But just try and do it!

Very sincerely,

MKR

I was amused the other day to come across a most domestic photograph of Hemingway and his progeny in "Vogue" and someone had scrawled across it, "What do you suppose is the opium of the literati?"

1. A series of stories by Thomas Wolfe published in *Scribner's Magazine*. In the May 1933 issue, Wolfe's "The Train and the City" appeared along with Hemingway's "Give Us a Prescription, Doctor."

23. To Maxwell E. Perkins

Hawthorne, Route 1, Fla.
June 12, 1933

Dear Mr. Perkins:

I really didn't intend to bait you into telling me about your plan for me "in connection with" writing—which, incidentally, is an entirely accurate phrase for what you have in mind! Such a book had never occurred to me. My first reaction was one of sheer distress, and then on second thought I was quite intrigued.

Your suggestion has brought back a whole train of memories of my Washington childhood, that I hadn't thought of in years and years. They are memories of spring and summer evenings and nights when I sat on the cool steps of a Baptist church and told stories to the other children. We'd usually play our strenuous running games in the long twilight, and then when Tony the Italian lamp-lighter had lit the red-glass gaslamps all along our street, we'd gather deliciously close together on the church steps and I'd "cut loose." I can remember very distinctly the feeling of smugness that came over me when one of the youngsters would run up the street calling to any stragglers, "Marjorie's going to tell stories!" and the hauteur with which I refused to begin until everyone was there. There was a tumultuous Irish child that shrieked and screamed if any of the details depressed him—particularly what I realize now must have been my very celebrated imitation of a wolf howl. He got to be such a nuisance that I recall saying sternly, "You'll have to take Jimmy home now—there's going to be a wolf in the next one."

It comes over me that I have always had a predilection for wolves in a story. I believe I protested so your making me take a wolf out of the scrub book because it was really quite a serious repression! I think I should almost be willing to do the book you speak of for the sole purpose of getting in that wolf again.

It really would be interesting to see if I could recapture whatever quality it is that gives glamour to stories for the young mind. We'll certainly have to talk about it. . . .

Thanks for your note,

Very sincerely,

MKR

24. To Samuel Wright

On board S.S. Minnewaska
Sept. 20, 1933

Dear Sam:

You're simply not running true to Chi Psi form—buying a book and mailing a letter! I'm tremendously flattered to have reduced you to both.

I remember very well the Chi Psi party you were angel enough to take me to—I even remember turning up the hem in the black dress. I have conveniently forgotten keeping you waiting!

I'm on my way back home after a grand summer: England. I rented an Austin in London and toured the country with a dash into Scotland, alone except for occasional days when an

English friend might go along and show me one shire. I stayed mostly at country inns—all very old and quaint and simple until you got your bill, which was usually higher than a N.Y. hotel. But I loved the country and the people—very kind and friendly once you get through the outer crust. If you sit quietly at table and don't speak and don't spill things, all of a sudden someone passes you the toast and accepts you.

Chuck is living mostly on the Gulf of Mexico. The last I heard from him he was on his way to the Bahamas with a friend on a trading schooner. He should have a yachting story out in the Sat. Eve. Post any week now. Thanks for writing, my dear, and best of luck.

Marjorie

25. To Maxwell E. Perkins

[Cross Creek]
October 4, 1933

Dear Mr. Perkins:

I'm strongly considering the desirability of doing, before the novel, the boy's book of the scrub. I found old man Long,[1] the hunter, still alive, and his wife very reproachful because I hadn't come two years ago to stay with them as I promised. I am going over next week to stay, as long as necessary to get what stories I need from the old man. I hope you can see his place some day—in the very core of the scrub, where he has lived since 1872—falling into decay under the exquisite mantle of flowering vines. They are hard put to it to make a living, principally because the deer and foxes eat their crops almost faster than they can raise them. They are in the forest preserve, and are not allowed to kill the game. When I asked Mrs. Long what to bring with me when I came, she chuckled and said, "Something to eat——."

The notes will be fresh in my mind—the book will certainly be a comparatively simple matter, and a not too long one. I happen to be in a rather distressed mental condition, and while I don't think personal happiness or unhappiness makes a scrap of difference in writing, it might be just as well to have my thinking a bit clearer for so complicated a piece of work as my Englishman's psychology. (Entirely by the way, I have come to the conclusion I shall have to begin the novel in England and move along more directly than I had planned. His whole viewpoint takes its substance from the English background and the English injustice, and it would only make for incoherence to treat it as a casual incidental, part-way through the book.)

Of course, you will tell me to do as my judgment dictates in this matter of precedence. A few months one way or the other wouldn't, I should think, make much difference in interest in the novel. If it is bad, the first book's having been a little liked will not save it. And if it's good, it wouldn't matter, would it, how soon or how late it had followed a previous novel?

I am undecided in this matter, and wish you would throw your opinion in the balance for me. Then I'll go ahead either way, without any further indecision.

Did you happen to see the review of *South Moon Under* in the London *Times Literary Supplement*? It was more benign than I had expected from an English source, but interested me particularly because the reviewer emphasized the cosmic pattern I had in mind, and which I felt I had failed to "put over," because the American reviewers weren't particularly conscious of it.

The orange grove is, more than ever, home. I doubt whether I can ever bear to leave it permanently.

Very sincerely,

M.K.R.

1. Cal Long, whose family pioneered the Big Scrub in the 1870s. He and Barney Dillard, another authentic pioneer, served as suggestive prototypes for the boy Jody in *The Yearling* and provided MKR with many details of the old way of life.

26. To Maxwell E. Perkins

Hawthorne, Route 1, Fla.
Oct. 23, 1933

Dear Mr. Perkins:

I think we must come to a much clearer understanding of what you are expecting of me as to the boys' book. By "you," in this case, I mean the house of Scribner. (I dote on infuriating you by speaking of "the house," as contraposed to you personally.) You say "The book would probably be one anyhow that men would read as well as boys," and in the same mail Mr.

Darrow writes, having talked with you, of "a book which anyone might enjoy but which would possibly ultimately become a
Juvenile."

Do you by any wild chance think that once I get into it, I
will automatically find myself doing another Cracker book for
mature consumption? Are you hoping for that? I can't say too
emphatically that that is not the case. In the first place, the
material simply is not there. And in the second place, if it were,
or if it could be induced, I have neither the taste nor the
heart for such a book. It is not impossible that in a few years I
should turn again to the backwoods field—there is an un-
touched locale I know of that might some day prove fertile—but
right now I will not, under any circumstances, consider it. I
will not consider anything but an out-and-out boy's juvenile—
written without condescension, and an attempt at a simple artistry. If that will satisfy you—if you will promise to publish
it (if good enough to publish at all) only as a juvenile, I'll go
ahead with it.

The principal reason, aside from my personal feeling in the
matter, I could not agree to an adult book, or any pretense at an
adult book, is that for the present at least I have nothing to
say for mature people along the *South-Moon-Under* line. A book
in the same general locale could only be compared with the
first book, could only be called its sequel or successor at best,
and, at worst, would be considered an attempt to capitalize on
what earlier interest there was in such characters in such a
setting. It would be ruinous. Incidentally, for the boys' book, I
should prefer to use, if not a pseudonym, at least some variation
of my name that would keep them from realizing the writer
was a woman, say, "M. Kinnan Rawlings." Boys I have found
very touchy about that. Sex antagonism is rampant in the
'teens. Don't think I'm taking myself too seriously about all this,
but it is important that we understand each other perfectly.
There will be then less likelihood of my disappointing you.

A question I'd like answered specifically, if you don't
mind——We discussed it rather vaguely before. The book being
strictly a juvenile, is it legitimate to lift three or four incidents from South Moon, particularly those of the deer playing in
the sink-hole in the moonlight, and the cat-hunt? . . .

And please make a mental note of it that I should get a

great deal of pleasure out of entertaining . . . any Scribner or personal friends who enjoy out-of-the-way and simple things. I have a roomy, if unpretentious, place, with adequate help, and I love to feed people.

Did I give you the impression that I expected to come to New York this fall or winter? I didn't intend to, at all. I considered myself "put" for a couple of years. Do you consider it necessary or desirable to talk over the boys' book when it is further along, or for me to talk with the illustrator? If the latter, it would surely, I should think, be much more to the point for him to come here.

Thank you for taking care of the money matter. Am I right in thinking of the first six months' royalty, from March 1 to Sept. 1, being due me Dec. 1? Beastly nuisance—money. I think I shall spend my royalties as soon as possible and settle down to grits and greens.

And you will make your point of view about this book clear to me, won't you?

Very sincerely,

MKR

As you love me, please don't go about inflicting S.M.U. on people like Scott Fitzgerald. You will have a huge group of sophisticates actively hating me. True, I have had some delightful correspondence with Robert W. Chambers,[1] than whom there is no one who goes in more for drawing room literature—but his secret vice is the diurnal and nocturnal lepidoptera of Florida, so you see it was his baser nature that I appealed to.

1. Robert W. Chambers, American novelist (1865–1933).

27. To Charles A. Rawlings, Jr.

[Cross Creek]
Nov. 11, 1933

Dear Chuck:

The divorce was granted yesterday——

You're free as the wind, big boy, and I hope you'll make the most of it. Take the women as they come—we're a tough breed, and can stand considerable man-handling.

Everything is going reasonably well. The roof took five weeks instead of one, but I guess it's on to stay.

Vinson said last night he had hoped to hear from you by this
time———

Had a frightfully nice letter from your mother, in answer to
mine—glad she and I can go our ways with mutual respect and
affection.

Hope you get your mail all right—proofs of Old Whee-e-e.[1]
Know you would be furious to have them go astray like the
others. Carl Brandt is really a dear. He had Talbot Mundy, the
adventure writer, and his dazzlingly beautiful young wife,
stop off to see me. We drank a quart of liquor and I made crab
newburg & peach shortcake, making two more fast friends. They
know Eustace Adams[2] & expect to spend the winter at Osprey
below Sarasota. You would like them, if you run into them. They
go to Clearwater sometimes but can't afford to live there now.
He got $17,000 for a movie once!

Glad to see 3 months ahead now.[3]

Left Moe [Sikes][4] to do odd jobs one day—he chose to line that
closet in the living room. Came home to find he had completely sealed up the 10 gals. of liquor I have up there! The
reasons I gave to induce him to cut a hatch big enough to get
it out!

Young Hawkins[5] came & got his picture this morning. Told
him he would probably hear from you.

Let me know when you want your odds & ends.

Best of luck—and hope your material is pouring out nicely.

Marjorie

Best to Wray.

1. A story by Charles Rawlings.
2. Eustace Adams, American author (1891–   ).
3. MKR had just begun to receive royalties from *South Moon Under*.
4. A Cross Creek neighbor, a carpenter sometimes employed by MKR.
5. An artist from nearby Gainesville.

28. To Maxwell E. Perkins

Hawthorne, Route 1, Florida
Nov. 11, [1933]

Dear Mr. Perkins:

I'll have to ask you to put up with my almost illegible
handwriting while my typewriter is being cleaned and oiled for
the next siege.

I imagine—fear—that I may have to come up to New York to collect the O. Henry thing,[1] although I haven't had a blessed word from anyone connected with the matter—just a copy of the book of stories from Doubleday Doran. I know that Marjory Stoneman Douglas of Miami won 2nd award one year and had to go up to get it—and naturally it cost the lion's share of the $250 to make the trip—and she had to get up, unknown and almost unannounced, no one knowing she had won a prize—and make a speech on "The Art of the Short Story"! She said she never felt quite so imbecilic in her life.

I suppose it makes a little necessary publicity for the awards and for the book, to make some fuss about the awarding, etc., and if I have to go through with it, I'll try not to be ungracious about it. But I hate to take the time—and you know how I feel about that particular story—it's like being handed a medal for committing murder—and I'd have to keep still about that!

You must be reasonably sure about the Prix Femina[2] to have mentioned it to me at all. "There is a tide in the affairs of men," etc., and it has nothing to do with merit! The moment simply arrives when material things go astonishingly right for a while—then, as astonishingly and unreasonably, they go wrong—and the trick is not to let either road fool you into thinking it will continue in the same direction forever.

I'm hoping the same favorable stars are at work in my private affairs—I was granted a divorce yesterday from my husband. The end, simply—I hope—of fourteen years of Hell—of a fourteen-year struggle to adjust myself to, and accept, a most interesting but difficult—impossible—personality. It was a question, finally, of breaking free from the feeling of a vicious hand always at my throat, or of going down in complete physical and mental collapse. That was one reason I wanted to go as far away as rural England—to be sure I had perspective on it, and to make up my mind what was best to do.

I am not riotously happy, not being interested in freedom for its own sake—I could have been a *slave* to a man who could be at least a benevolent despot—but I feel a terrific relief—I can wake up in the morning conscious of the sunshine, and thinking, "How wonderful! Nobody is going to give me Hell today!"[3]

But enough of such nonsense—I have almost definitely decided that I will have to get into the novel right away without stopping for the boys' book.

Do you realize how calmly you sat up there in your office and announced that you were expecting a boy's *classic* of me? I could toss off a 50–75,000–word simple boy's story of the scrub, without too much interfering with the novel—but I can't do a really decent boy's book quite so casually. There is more fine material to be gotten for it, that will have to come slowly, and it would be a pity to toss off a pot-boiler when by letting it go until my material has increased, and until I can give it my undivided attention, we might get something really decent out of it. A boy's mind is really too sacred a responsibility just to flip crumbs at it.

If the novel is any good, I can feel reassured as to the desirability of going on writing (that sounds hypocritical—but you know what I mean), and can draw a breath and not feel hurried—and do the boy's book leisurely.

If it is bad—the novel—I can plunge for relief into the other, thinking, "At least I can please the adolescent!" I hope you're not disappointed at my deciding this way—almost the last kindness my husband did me was to try to convince me that you were so certain that the novel would be an impossible mess, that you were doing all you could to divert my mind from it, in the hope you could steer me away from it altogether.

But I asked you that question, and I believe you would have told me honestly if you felt so. We certainly have enough mutual confidence and trust so that you would have felt free to warn me of any specific dangers you feared for me.

If you get any advance information on the necessity for my coming to New York, I'd appreciate greatly your tipping me off. I have my hands full, as you can imagine, with the grove, etc., and I'm having long-needed repairs made to my shack. My new hand-hewn-cypress shingle roof is just completed—but it took 2 men 5 weeks instead of the estimated 1.

The local carpenter lined a clothes closet the one day I was away—my only access to the attic—and I came home to find that he had completely sealed up ten gallons of liquor I had up in the attic, aging! I didn't want the local folk to know where I kept my stores—or that I had that much—and the reasons I had to think up to get him to cut a hatch big enough to get the keg down when I need it!

As ever,

Marjorie K. Rawlings

P.S. I promise NEVER to write you such a long letter in long-hand again!

1. The $500 O. Henry Memorial Award for 1933 for her short story "Gal Young 'Un," published in *Harper's*, June–July 1932.

2. MKR's *South Moon Under* was under consideration by the committee for the *Prix Femina Americain,* a subsidiary of the French *Prix Femina,* but did not win the award.

3. For a much more detailed analysis by MKR of the reasons for the collapse of her marriage, see letter 32, September 21, 1934.

From the very beginning, MKR had serious trouble with her second novel. She had outlined the basic plan for the story in the first letter she ever wrote to Perkins (March 31, 1931) and this never changed except in details. She meant the book to be a study of the contrast in the reactions of two quite different people to the same plot of Florida hammock land. The first was a young Florida cracker named Luke Brinley, a worthy but penniless orphan squatting on land he does not own, but wholly adjusted to it, loving it, and seeing its beauty and its potential for producing a fertile citrus grove. The second was an aristocratic young Englishman named Tordell, who is unjustly sent away in disgrace with a remittance to Florida land owned by the family; he is bitter because of the injustice and hates the alien place. MKR had no difficulty drawing the young cracker and describing the Florida setting, but when treating the young Englishman she tended to go off into stereotype and melodrama. Perkins was engrossed at this time with Wolfe's *Of Time and the River* and could not take time to give her more than general encouragement. She revised painfully several times but was never satisfied with the result. At one point she was tempted to turn to Chicago novelist Robert Herrick (1868–1938) for help, but was warned by Perkins not to increase confusion by seeking outside critical help. She followed Perkins' advice, though she continued to correspond with Herrick on a friendly basis until his death in 1938. She completed a draft of

Golden Apples in December 1934, and her agent sold the magazine rights to *Cosmopolitan,* which wanted a reduced version for
serial publication. In February, while she was in the midst of revision, she broke her neck in a fall from a horse and had to finish
the work in considerable physical pain, wearing a neck brace
which she said made her look like Joan of Arc listening for the
angels. Meanwhile, the idea of "the boy's book of the scrub" continued to work just below the surface, ripening very slowly.

29. *To Maxwell E. Perkins*

Hawthorne, Fla.
Feb. 11, 1934

Dear Mr. Perkins:

You do encourage me by indicating that difficulty in "getting going" is not necessarily a sign of complete incompetence.
But I had long held the theory that to allow personal turbu-
lence to interfere with one's work was a fatal weakness, and a
sure sign that the artistic impulse was not valid. Physical obstacles never bother me—I can work just as well in pain, in
fearful heat—in any place. But when I am emotionally torn up I
find myself submerged in a miasma, with clear thought seemingly impossible. It is a maddening thing to have happen, for
several reasons. When you really *want* to be working, it gives
you the nightmare sensation of trying to run and not being able
to lift your feet. You are torn between the reality of yourself
and your relations to other people, and the reality of the thing
you wish to create, and you cannot give your mind to both at the
same time. I find when I *force* myself to write, in this fog, that
I produce un-true rubbish that has to be thrown out. There is no
alternative but to put your own problems totally out of your
mind, and that proves difficult when all your most intimate
happiness is at stake. . . .

I hear much talk already of "Tender is the Night."[1] I thought,
beginning to read it after I had written you, that Fitzgerald
had filled the contract I was setting up for myself—a book disturbing, bitter and beautiful. I am totally unable to analyze
the almost over-powering effect that some of his passages create—
some of them about quite trivial people and dealing with triv-

ial situations. There is something terrifying about it when it happens, and the closest I can come to understanding it is to think that he does, successfully at such times, what I want to do—that is, visualizes people not in their immediate setting, from the human point of view—but in time and space—almost, you might say, with the divine detachment. The effect is very weird when he does it with unimportant people moving in a superficial and sophisticated setting. I shouldn't put it that way, for of course importance and un-importance are relative—if they exist at all. . . .

Thank you for writing me.

MKR

1. Novel by F. Scott Fitzgerald (New York, 1934).

30. To Maxwell E. Perkins

Hawthorne, Fla.
Wednesday
[February 17, 1934]

Dear Mr. Perkins:

Thank you for answering my wire. Our letters will probably cross and the chances are we will automatically answer each other's questions. I'll tell you what was back of the question in my wire to you, and why I was so precipitous about it.

Saturday night in Winter Park, where I went to read on a program at Rollins College, I met Robert Herrick at a supper Dr. Albert Shaw[1] gave for me. Mr. Herrick has something of your peculiarly understanding quality, and we disgraced ourselves by getting in a far corner and talking to please ourselves and ignoring the party all evening. He had an amazing enthusiasm for *South Moon Under* and had come to the party just to meet the writer of it. It appears he had told his brother-in-law, who is on the Pulitzer prize committee, before leaving the north, that "You should give the Pulitzer to S.M.U., but of course you won't." He asked me, as many people do, on what I was working—and I told him just a little of the book, in quite hazy fashion. As you know, I have a reasonably clear conception of what I want to do. He expressed some concern at the time and pointed out one or two obvious pitfalls. As a matter of fact, I doubt whether anyone could indicate to me a danger in it over which I have not already sweat blood in anticipation. He said he should like to go into it further with me—that as a teacher of many years, working with young writers, he might possibly have some concrete and practical help for me.

Meantime, Mr. Herrick and Mr. and Mrs. Winston Churchill,[2] with whom he is staying, accepted my invitation to spend a day and night with me at my place, probably this week-end. On receiving Mr. Herrick's note yesterday morning, my first impulse, in response to his sympathy and interest, was to do as he suggested in it, taking advantage in due time of any help he might give me. Then it occurred to me that on more counts than one I could get into embarrassment on it. As I said in my wire, I know nothing of his connections, really nothing of him, except that his name strikes familiarly. Personally, he is everything wise and charming. He may be a very great editor and teacher, with a great deal to give. On the other hand, as a novelist himself, he may have set ideas of his own as to how things should be done, and it would be impossible for me to profit by his experience. On the whole, it is easier for me to work with you as I did on the other book and on "Jacob's Ladder"—making my mistakes my own way, then going at it fresh and re-writing after you have showed me the trouble.

It also occurred to me that he might have definite publishing connections, and being pleasantly and satisfactorily associated with Scribner's, I would find myself embarrassed by being under some obligation to anyone who had helped me. I didn't want to cause any mix-up by accepting a seemingly desirable offer of cooperation. It was necessary to get your reaction at once, as I must write him and the Churchills today about the time of their visit, and I needed to know at once how to respond to his offer—which I feel sure is purely kindly and unselfish. Your wire confirms my second thought of avoiding this assistance, and I presume your letter will give me the reason. Unless you knew that Mr. Herrick has a special gift for such things, to be accepted gratefully, I should have preferred in any case just to bungle along as usual and count on you to straighten me out after the writing was done.

You do have your hands full. I pity you with Tom Wolfe's

gorgeous bedlam. As I see it, he *must* discipline himself. Please don't spare the blue-pencil, as far as he will stand for it without shooting you on sight. He repeats and repeats, and says in four magnificent ways, what could have been said more magnificently in any one. His own sonorousness betrays him. If you would only give him Hemingway's restraint!

I have finally satisfied myself, why, aside from my difficulty in concentrating on any work at all, I have had so much trouble in getting going. The English beginning is wrong, all wrong. It is impossible to key it to the main part of the book—it makes a totally undesirable transition in characters and locale. The English portion has no meaning, no value, *except as it exists in the man's mind in Florida*. So I have thrown out what I had done once again—and the Florida beginning, while it does not please me as to the writing, is in the mood, the key, that I want, and I am much better satisfied to go on from there. I have been forcing myself to work on something I knew inherently was off-key.

MKR

1. Member of the Rollins College faculty.
2. Winston Churchill, American novelist (1871–1947).

31. To Ida M. Tarrant

Hawthorne, Fla.
June 2, 1934

Dearest Aunt Ida [in Cincinnati]:[1]

Bless your heart, "formidable" is not the word to use about the trip to Cincinnati I had planned on all winter—and yet the obstacles in the way have proved just too much for the time being. Money and time are the trouble—the New York trip put a kink in me. It will pay me in the long run, but right now it was the last straw, for it took a hundred dollars I hadn't expected to use that way.

I bit off *almost* more than I could chew in a year's time, and yet if nothing more unexpected happens, I will come out all right and be sitting pretty, but by the skin of my teeth. Just between you and me—I wouldn't want anybody else to know my business—I got about $6,000 out of my book, to date, including the Book of the Month $4,000. Actual royalties on sales were a little disappointing. But that is a lot of money and it looked like a fortune, but here is how it went. I gave Charles $2,000 in cash, representing our *joint* savings on the Rochester house, I simply couldn't see that he had anything coming out of the grove, as the money had been entirely mine, my mother's money, and to be perfectly blunt, he had hardly earned his board, piddling around. And the packing house that he was letting run the grove was *ruining* us. I have had experts from the university out here, and the grove had been starved for fertilizer. The quality of my fruit was low this year, and another year of the same treatment would almost have ruined the trees and the crop. I was very hesitant about running the grove myself, as Charles had predicted dire disaster if I tried it—but at the last visit of my experts, they said I am absolutely O.K. Nothing to worry about. Have over 1,000 young trees in fine shape, and in 3 years they will be bearing, and 4 or 5 years from now, my grove income should be nearly double what it is now—and when that happens, I am all set, short of a bad freeze or other "act of God."

Well, back to the money. I paid $1,000 in old bills, including Charles' hospital bill in Jacksonville, some of the bills 3 and 4 years old. Bought a new car, about $500 difference to pay after trading in the old one. The English trip cost me twice what I thought, and cost about $800. There is $4300. I did put $1,000 away—bought a good bond—decided I would save that much out of so nice a hunk if it killed me. Had a new shingled roof put on, costing between 2 and 3 hundred dollars, the house painted, 150 more, nigger tenant house built, $125, so I can be sure of help—if you can house them, you are independent and can always get someone. I have a colored man so good I keep my fingers crossed for fear something will happen. Had a garage added to the side of the house, sort of a porte cochère, for the car. Bought over a hundred dollars worth of young orange trees. So there's the $6,000! Add it up. Odds and ends of money from stories, and the orange money, after I paid last year's bill with Maxy for fertilizer and young trees, have paid running expenses—taxes, interest on mortgage, etc. My mortgage notes call for payment of $750 yearly, beginning this June, which I couldn't make, but the man who holds them is very fine and reasonable and says a yearly payment of $250 will satisfy him. That is as good as a Federal farm loan, and I accepted the rates. After sending him his check, I have $400 left in the bank to last me until orange money comes in about Christmas time. I have one more application of fertilizer to buy, am still paying $22.50 a month on my car, my boy gets $5 a week and Beatrice gets $3 a week (I raised her—she earns it—all the washing and ironing, has learned to cook pretty well, milks the cow and takes care of the chickens, and is as faithful as the sun.) So you see it is going to be nip and tuck. By staying put and living quietly, if nothing queer happens, I will be all right. If I had the money, I would run out for just a couple of days. In any case I don't feel I can be away long enough to hardly be worth while. I am working hard on the book—it didn't go right, and I began six different times, my New York editor gave me fine help, but now it more or less suits me, and I don't like to interrupt it. My trip to Seattle to see my brother is out of the question. He is going to be sick, but I can't do it.

I am perfectly happy and feel good, and so far it is a fine cool summer, and I don't feel the need of any change or vacation. I don't mind not having the trip, but I do mind terribly not seeing you for so long. If I had known it was going to work out this way, think I would have begged you to come down for a good part of the winter. But I thought sure I could come out this spring, and I felt I wanted to fight my fight out here *alone*. Think you understand how I felt. This is my home, the place I love, and I wanted to get the adjustment made and over with.

I have nice men and women friends, in fact have to be careful my good times don't take up too much time and interfere with my work. I am enjoying life more than since I was a girl in college. Everyone says I look like a different person and 10 years younger.

Now don't ever let on you know—Dessie [Smith Vinson] made me promise not to tell anybody—but the Count[2] told her he had had a letter from Mother Rawlings asking him if there wasn't something he could do to bring Charles and me together again. The Count said he hadn't even answered the letter.

Charles, I am told, left for New York suddenly to finish a

story under his agent's supervision, and will go from there to Rochester, possibly to live.

If Mother R. ever says anything to you, you can say with authority that you know it is hopeless—that I am so happy to be free from a constant black cloud that I would be willing to have Charles go on the rocks (I didn't used to feel that way) before I would live with him again. I don't think he wants the old life any more than I, but if he should decide he did, I would refuse *ruthlessly*. No person is privileged to keep another in a mental black cave. I have lost all feeling for him. I hope he does well, just as I would wish luck and success and happiness for anyone.

Well my dear, something unexpected may bob up and we will get together before too long. I have the feeling it may still work out some way within a few months. Write when you can. I don't write as often as I would like to, for pure lack of time.

Lots of love,

Marjorie

P.S. It is always you I think of on Mother's Day, because you have done more for me and meant more to me and been closer than anyone but my own mother. Have always felt we understood each other.

1. Ida Tarrant was Charles Rawlings' great-aunt by marriage. In spite of the fact that there was no legal relationship between them, MKR remained devoted to "Aunt Ida," even after her divorce from Charles. She helped to move Aunt Ida from Cincinnati to Ocala, Florida, so as to have her nearer at hand, and later moved her to St. Augustine for the same reason.

2. An Englishman (name unknown) living in the Cross Creek area, who was possibly the suggestive prototype for Tordell, the English remittance man in *Golden Apples*.

32. To Beatrice H. McNeill[1]

Hawthorne, Florida
Sept. 21, 1934

Bee old darling [in Los Angeles]:

You were sweet to write me, when I've owed you for so long. Yes, the reason I didn't write, at least briefly, was because it seemed like such a hopeless job to tell you about Chuck and myself. I know you always thought it was a match made in Heaven and so on, and it really is a minor tragedy that everything turned out so wrong, because we did start out with so many of the ingredients that should have made it all right. We certainly loved each other with the real thing; common tastes and background and so on.

Bee, I just don't know where to begin. We were never happy for very long at a time. Everything I did was wrong. Nothing suited Chuck. When we came to a show-down a year ago in March, he said that he realized he had always had an inferiority complex as far as I was concerned. He had something of the sort—I still don't understand him—about the whole world. You will remember that rather ingratiating shyness and self-deprecation. He never got over it. He never, in a way, matured. He kept a high school boy's philosophy and psychology to the end. That might have been rather touching if it had taken a touching or appealing form. But with me, he was completely the bully. I took a constant abuse. And because I loved him so, and just couldn't admit, even to myself, that he was an utterly impossible person to live with, I kept on year after year kidding myself, thinking that if this was changed, or that was changed, he would be all right and we would be happy. He could never work under anyone. He quarreled with every man he ever worked for and either quit or was fired. It was always the other fellow's fault. He was the poorest of sports, the poorest of losers. And I caught the blame for everything that went wrong.

Bee, I hate to light into the poor devil like this to you of all people, because I know you saw the same charm in him that I did. I felt for years it was my fault someway that he wasn't happy, that he needed a sweeter or more patient woman, and I often wished that something had developed between you and him instead of between me and him. I made him promise me that if I died he would look you up! As I began to give up hope, I kept thinking that probably Bee was the right woman for him, and honey, when I heard from you that you were married, I had a lost and disappointed feeling. But I'll tell you now, he would have broken your heart. It almost broke me—the alternative to my divorce was, frankly, suicide. Life just wasn't worth

With Pat, in the late 1930s.

living with the black cloud of his daily disagreeableness over me. You couldn't have stood it. I'm a tougher breed of cats than you.

I thought if we had more money, he'd be happier. Well, at one time we were both making good money and were fixed nicely that way. He seemed to enjoy life a little more, but at that time I remember an incident when he and I went to Canada on his uncle's lovely yacht. One of his cousins was married to a rather stupid chap and had a little baby. We landed at the Canadian port where Chuck had covered some yacht races for his paper. He slipped away from the rest of us, and when the cousin (his own cousin) and husband and baby and I went into the local dance hall to watch, here was Chuck with his Canadian friends, and he pretended not to know us. I went off down a strange Canadian road and cried my eyes out. That's the last time he ever really hurt me. He said afterward that he just couldn't afford to introduce those people to his Canadian friends. I almost left him then in cold blood. He didn't care whom he hurt, but oh my dear, his own sensitive feelings! At the time we came to Florida, and I hoped maybe the new and exciting environment, his two brothers being with us and so on, would make things all right, but they got steadily worse.

The grove was bought with my little inheritance from mother. I did all the work, cooking three elaborate meals a day and so on. Yet one morning when I was late with breakfast Chuck roared at me, "You're the only one that's fallen down on the job." His brothers left when we all realized the place wasn't big enough to support three families, and Chuck hated it here. I felt his salvation was in his own writing, kept urging him to get to the coast and take a newspaper job or write some sea stuff. A doctor friend finally got him in with the Greeks. He wrote a story of his trip with the Greek sponge fishermen with the *Atlantic Monthly* in mind. Sent it to them without any personal letter with it and it came back. He was "through with writing" and so on. I asked if he minded if I wrote a letter to the editor for him to sign, telling the editor the material had never been handled before and so on. I knew the manuscript had never gone past the first reader. He said he didn't give a damn, so I wrote the letter and after reading it carelessly he signed it and I sent if off with the manuscript again. They accepted it, for it reached the right person, and was a fine story. When they printed a little biographical note about the author in the back of the magazine, they quoted an excerpt he would have preferred not to have been quoted, and he damned me up and down. Said I had ruined him. Said "The next time I listen to a Goddam bitch, you'll know it."

The last winter we were together, he tried to convince me I was going crazy. A little old aunt of his [Ida Tarrant] was with us, and that old dame almost tore him down. Said if she ever caught him at such a vicious thing again, she'd make his life hell. He never did it again. You can imagine how he acted when my Florida stuff began to be accepted.

I had always felt in him the potentialities of failure, but did nothing but encourage him. Many times I would have quit, but things were not going well for him and I didn't have the heart to do it when things weren't right for him. At the time I did it, the magazine world was open to him. He had had stories in the *Saturday Post, Atlantic, Adventure,* and the *Post* was clamoring for more. He had only to get to work and turn them out. I tried to be fair financially, dividing up with him what represented our life together, keeping the grove myself, since it was my own, as I say, bought with mother's money.

As I feared, he doesn't seem to be very happy. After our divorce, he had an affair with a writer that didn't seem to pan out very well. Now he is covering the America's Cup races at Newport. I had rather a sentimental note from him from Canada a while ago. All I ask of him is to leave me in peace. I have begun to find a little of the joy in living that I always had. The sun shines again, and when I wake up in the morning I feel like a normal human being, instead of being filled with dread waiting for the first ugly remark. It is a shame, because he has made himself so much more unhappy than he could make anyone else. He kept his good looks, charm, delightful personality (when he felt like it), brains and so on. But a queer kind of something to spoil it all.

Of course, I've given him a black sheet and myself a white one, and that can never be accurate. I don't question that my independence, my very love of the fight of life, all my character, were too harsh to bring out the best in him. Yet I always put his interests first. And when he was top-dog, he did things like the snobbish Canadian incident.

Bee, it is terrible to write you this. I suppose I should have just passed it off lightly, as I do to almost everyone, and let you keep your picture of the sweet college boy with the broken leg. That picture, that charm, held me periodically long after I really, in my secret heart, hated him. Yet you knew us both so well, you would never have stopped wondering what was wrong. And as I say, a gentler kind of woman might have brought out the best in him. Well, it's over, thank God, and forgive me if I've hurt you telling you all this.

I'm working like the very devil on a second novel, trying to get it done by the end of November. Can't tell yet whether it's any good or not. I had a very short story in the August *Scribner's*, "The Pardon."

What a stunning picture of Gertrude Johnson.[2] She is a peach. I surely hope we can get together, all of us, before long. I wanted so much to go to see Arthur [Kinnan] this summer, and would have gone by boat and stopped off to see you, and if money and circumstances permit, that is what I will do next summer. I just had to do the book this year. I didn't enjoy my trip last summer to England very much, because I was in such despair and torment, trying to make sure I was doing the right thing, that I might as well have been in jail. Have been in Florida all summer on my lovely grove, and it's been grand weather all the time. You would love it here. I put most of my book money (aside from four years of farm debts) in simple repairs, and while the old shack is still a shack, it's comfortable, with an atmosphere people love.

I had the nicest letter from Sidney Howard, the playwright, just before he sailed for London. I want to talk to him some day about my story "Gal Young 'Un." I was broken hearted my agents couldn't sell that to the movies for Marie Dressler. The locale wouldn't have to be Florida, and the gal young un could be kept technically pure. Aline MacMahon could do something with the middle-aged woman, too, but my agents seem stalled on it. When it won the O. Henry prize last fall I thought sure they could sell it.

I do wish you would try a full-length play. Maybe we can

collaborate on one some day! Wouldn't that be fun? If you run into Freddy March,[3] give him my best and tell him I've never forgotten his grand voice in that Union Vodvil play, or was it Edwin Booth, "The Doctor's House," was that it? Well, this isn't getting work done, darling. Loads of love,

M.

This is all between you and me, Bee. I don't yap like this to hardly anyone.

1. A close friend from college.
2. Another college friend.
3. Fredric March, well-known movie actor, whom MKR had known as Frederick Bickel at the University of Wisconsin.

33. To Maxwell E. Perkins

Hawthorne, Florida
November 9, 1934

Dear Mr. Perkins:

I'd so much rather be able to send the completed manuscript [*Golden Apples*]——. Do you mind telling me what you need "a few pages" for? I'm not crying "Wolf!" when I say that a great deal of work may have to be done over again on the latter half. I do really think, if I can make the more civilized characters real, that the book should be interesting. And there are things I do want to say in it. But whether it is of value or not, God knows. But even through my intense dissatisfaction with this manuscript, a conviction comes to me that even if it is very bad indeed, some day I shall write a good book.

It is too early to tell whether the completed manuscript will be good enough for your purposes or not, but if it should be, luckily, do you still have any idea of serialization in the Magazine? It doesn't seem likely to me that it will be suitable for the average run of popular magazines, but if you don't want to use it that way, I'd like to send Carl Brandt a copy when I send you yours, just on the off-chance of his being able to do something with it that way. It seems to me all thought of any such thing should wait until we see the quality of the book, but I suppose plans have to be made ahead, and gambled on. . . .

By the way, I have just seen Robert Herrick off after a few hours' stop with me on his way south. He has proved a delightful friend—and after reading some of his books, I have thanked my stars that I was dubious enough to query you about the advantage of letting him see my stuff, and that you were honest enough to warn me against it. His personality is infinitely beyond his literary gifts. (Entre nous.) I had a good argument with him about "Farewell to Arms." I felt he had only a superficial understanding of it, and of Hemingway. I was impudent enough to tell him so. I told him that to me the point of the thing was that there *is* no "Farewell to Arms." The man thought he could turn his back on the silly turmoil and confusion of the war. He sunk himself in what to him represented peace and ecstasy; and the casual slap in the face of circumstance, of destiny, of death, destroyed all security, all happiness, for him. There is, simply, no escape. Herrick said, astonished, "But that gives the book dignity and meaning!" I said, "Precisely." Then he questioned whether Hemingway had that in mind or whether I had read it into what to Herrick was merely a love story. I said I was sure it was in Hemingway's mind, that all his stuff had that under-current. The old gentleman grew very thoughtful and said he should like me to interpret some of the other younger writers!

I became entirely exhausted and had to stop work a few days. I'm going at it again today. I simply can't give you a date. It all depends on whether I get that very desirable spurt, that keeps you at the job ten hours at a stretch. If that hits, well and good. If it doesn't, it will be well into December before I can quite finish. So say a brief prayer for me. . . .

And please don't hurry me unless you have the best of reasons. I trust you so implicitly that if you wired me that it was absolutely necessary to finish the book in a week, I should believe you, and do it if it killed me.

Marjorie K. R.

34. To Maxwell E. Perkins

Hawthorne, Fla.
Feb. 11, 1935

Dear Max Perkins:

(We agreed that if you liked the next novel I would call you "Max.")

A thousand thanks for "The Adventures of General Marbot"[1]—it's magnificent. The pictures are the best Thomason has done. The style, increasingly firm and stirring.

Having read it and delighted in it, I'm doing a possibly ungracious thing—I'm giving it away, to a good friend, Major Otto F. Lange.[2] I've hunted with the Major this winter, duck, dove and quail, and shivering in a duck blind one winter day in the middle of Orange Lake, when the ducks had stopped coming over, somehow or other I happened to mention Thomason, and recommend him. And he said he had known him in France! He told me of a night when he and another chap were with Thomason in a cafe in Paris. Thomason drove the waiters and proprietors absolutely insane by drawing pictures with the burnt ends of matches on the tablecloths ——. Thomason's leave was up, and along with his companions, he was agreeably high. He was all for telling the whole war to go to Hell, but responsibility rode sternly in the other two—probably because their leave was *not* up—and they called a taxi and ordered the driver to deposit Thomason safely on his train. Thomason balked again and they bundled him head first through the taxi window. The taxi drove off and they returned to the cafe feeling nobly like *enfants de la patrie* etc. They were nicely settled with their drinks when Thomason appeared beside them—still indifferent to the war—still hell-bent on drawing pictures on the table cloth.

Major Lange's sense of responsibility has not been so high in relation to me. I was at his home in Gainesville for cocktails last Friday, before going on to a dinner party at the house of Dr. [John J.] Tigert, president of the University of Florida. Dr. Tigert is a prig and a fanatical dry, and the Major deliberately set in to get me high, saying that his ambition was to deposit me on the Tigert door-step and say, "Here's your guest." Then, he said, if Dr. Tigert asked me where I had been, I was to say, "I've been out with the Army." He accomplished his purpose. My dinner partner was an inoffensive preacher, and I disgraced myself thoroughly by asking my hostess what the devil she meant by putting me next to a parson, and announcing in a clear voice, "The hell with all preachers."

So on the handsome yellow frontispiece of "General Marbot," I have inscribed:

Pour Otto F. Lange—

Bon soldat, sans doute, mais homme méchant—

Meilleur ami de Thomason, soldat, que de moi, femme——

If I get my bear material together for the boys' book, do you think Thomason really would condescend to do the sketches? How much longer is his Washington hitch to last? If not long, do suggest to him that he run down here and make sketches on the ground—my old hunter living in the scrub can't live much longer. Major Lange (I don't know whether he was Captain then or Major) said Thomason might not remember him and our hunting season is over this week, but if Thomason likes fishing, we could give him deep-sea fishing or inland bass fishing and give him a swell time. Do suggest it, anyway.

Cosmopolitan is running me ragged on the shortening for them (the original 130,000 will have to come to 80,000 for them) but they're very considerate and aren't asking anything terrible. Shall I send you on the first quarter to third to get into proof? I can get you that at any time. I am trying to get the second installment off to them today. . . .

I'll write again when I get a breathing spell.

And again, many thanks for the new Thomason.

MKR

1. A book by John W. Thomason (New York, 1935).
2. Professor of military science at the University of Florida.

35. To Maxwell E. Perkins

Hawthorne, Florida
Oct. 15, 1935

Dear Max:

I hope your forced vacation wasn't because of your health. You have had your share of worries with authors-in-need-of-editing, and I should think sooner or later it would wear you down.

But Max, in spite of your great conscientiousness and honesty, you are too lenient a critic. You should simply raise hell with Thomas Wolfe, to make him do the artistic thing and not the chest-beating thing. You should *make* him understand that it is better to say a thing once, superbly, than to scream it hysterically half a dozen times. You have too much sympathy with the torment of the writer's mind. A writer was born to be tormented. It is his destiny. You should torment us still further, when you see, as surely, you must see, the inadequate thing emerging.

I don't blame anyone but myself for "Golden Apples" being interesting trash instead of literature. But you should have bullied me and shamed me further. I can do better than that and you know it. I wish to Heaven I could take the book as I now see it, and re-write the last half of it. There are two or three things I could have done to make a better book. One would have been to work out the story with only Luke and Allie and Tordell and the Doctor. Another would have been to have taken a much greater space to handle the latter part, so that there would not be that staccato and violent effect. To be as leisurely about Camilla and the freeze and so on as I was in the early part. That would have made a book probably in two parts; the two phases of Tordell's life in Florida. Actually, two books in one.

When I read the book the other day, from cover to cover, I was astonished. It never occurred to me it would seem so violent. The "story" was the last thing in the world that concerned me, yet the thing seemed solid "story." No quietness at all. And I had been afraid that it would be too quiet; that Tordell's struggles with his background would seem stupid and without eventfulness. If I had set out to plan a "plot" I could not have done it. The characters were to me all part of his struggle. Yet the book reads as though I had charted an artificial plotting. My only key to this, is my old difficulty with actual truth. When I use characters (like Camilla and the doctor and Claude) suggested, if ever so vaguely, by true characters; when I build on actual events (like the Big Freeze); I deviate somehow from Absolute Truth. Or else the fictitious groundwork I lay does not fit in with the previous true one. I may try, next time, to begin with a simple situation and one dominant character, and let it work itself out as it seems to want to, without any pre-conceptions— and see what happens.

I have only seen three or four of the reviews.

October 16.

A large batch of reviews came in this morning. I am astonished at their generosity. I should not have been nearly so kind with the book! It is amusing to see the reviewers contradict one another, isn't it? One says the book has an unsatisfactory ending, up in the air. Another says the ending is "too perfect"—managed. Henry Seidel Canby[1] comes closer than anyone, except Carl Bohnenberger[2] in the Jacksonville *Times-Union,* to understanding what I was trying to do. But Max, *no one,* (least of all your abominable blurb writer on the back of the jacket!) makes note of the one point that was important to me. That is the struggle of a man against a natural background. One paragraph is the key to it, the one beginning, "The relation of a man to a natural background was profound. It completed him as no other human could complete him. It was dispassionate and stable." The Englishman who wrote me some time ago is the only person to pounce on that. He called it the crux of the story. How can people miss it? I was afraid my "message" would be too blatant! Yet everyone is concerned with the characters, the plot, the technique, the "background," using the word in the theatrical sense. To me, that point dignifies and validates all the characters. Otherwise, it would be indeed, as TIME said, "dull melodrama." (I think the JEW on TIME who wrote that review got annoyed with Tordell mid-way and never even finished the book!). At least, this point, that is the one thing I have to say in most of what interests me to write, has gone so unnoticed that I shall dare to say the same thing again, with other characters! The prospect of that pleases me, for I have never been satisfied with the way I said it here. But for no one to give it a thought! It is beyond me.

I do wish I could talk with you occasionally. I need to spill out half-formed ideas, to be shaped later or rejected. I believe, from the reaction, I should go on with the Florida vein in one form or another, a little longer. One hates to be localized. Yet there is still much fascinating material here. And if real and true and honest characters can be made to move across a little-known setting, I suppose it is foolish for me to long for wider worlds to conquer. And I still think I shall write a good book some day——.

Do hope you're well. Hope the book sells to suit all of you who

have been so very good to me. Whitney Darrow[3] is a darling,
isn't he?

My best, as ever,

M.K.R.

P.S. Please return the Englishman's letter. He is the only
reader to get my point.

November 6

I just had a letter from Robert Herrick, whose reaction to the
book is much like everyone else's. He finds the simpler people
and the setting sound; feels a distaste for the "Hamlet" Englishman; does not find Camilla successful for the great reason, he
thinks, that she does not have a good chance in the book. He
asks, "Why not do a book about *her?*" Off-hand, having given it
no thought at all, it is an interesting suggestion. If I ever did
such a thing, I suppose a great deal of my own struggle would
go into it. It might have value for the reason that my response
to the terrain has value; it would be something thoroughly
understood by me. I do not think I shall ever be able to present
a convincing picture of anything from the outside. I never got
inside Camilla; never even tried to. I presented her as she appeared to other people. Why Tordell is not completely successful,
I do not know. I understood him thoroughly. It comes to me
sometimes that I violated the truth in having him achieve unity
with his background. I am almost afraid that his basic character was such that defeat was inevitable for him; perhaps with
understanding. I think it might have been better to do as I first
planned; have him go down in his despair; probably into death; with
a glimmer of vision before him. Letting Luke express the sound-
ness of union with the particular land.

That is the hell of publishing exigencies; of personal ambition, which makes you want to "produce." If I had put the
manuscript aside for a year or two, I might have made a more
artistic unit of it. But it annoyed me so, fretted me, and I could
get nothing else done with it in me. I took it for granted it
would not be quite right. And perhaps the inherent dishar-
monies were so great that it could never have been. In the end I

believe I shall learn a great deal from it; much more than
from the first book.

Don't bother about the reviews. As you say, I've seen the more
important ones. They were kinder than I should have been.
I'm not in the least interested. They said nothing I didn't know.
I am only pleased that after all there is as much stimulation
in the book as there seems to be.

As ever,

M.K.R.

1. Henry Seidel Canby, author, editor, and critic (1878–1961).
2. A Jacksonville, Florida, librarian and friend of MKR.
3. The vice-president in charge of business affairs at Scribner's.

36. *To Maxwell E. Perkins*

Hawthorne, Florida
November 5, 1935

Dear Max:

I'm glad to have the Wolfe book of stories.[1] The book form
means something a magazine never can, and I'm glad to have
the "Web of Earth"—one of my favorites—in permanent form. I
believe the reason Wolfe was so successful with that, speaking
so much to the point, was because he allowed his character to
absorb him. He was no more redundant than the old woman
would have been. It was truly her story—not Tom Wolfe perorat-
ing—and it had as great a reality as anything he has done.
Hemingway wonders, I believe, whether Wolfe would be a great
writer if he should serve a term of exile in Siberia. I do not
think Wolfe is tainted, as Hemingway is, by any shadow-boxing
with the sophisticated world. I do not think he is particularly
on the defensive. As a writer who has always had to fight over-
writing, it seems to me that his fault as an artist lies in in-
dulging himself in the deliciousness of piling word on word,
phrase on phrase, rhythm on rhythm. Used judiciously, his
cumulative effect is prodigious, of course. Over-done, it is like
too much poetry, or too much symphony music, or too much
passion—cloying; surfeiting. I have often been tempted to write

him, but being entirely inferior as an artist, it would be presumptuous, so I have never done so.

It would be delightful to meet you and Wolfe and Major Thomason at Chancellorsville. You can count on me at a moment's notice. I have been over several of the battlefields and there were no ghosts there. It seemed to me that the markers and the tourists had driven them all away. I tried to induce them with my own pity, but it was no go. I have always wanted to be there with someone who knew something about it. But are you sure I would be acceptable to your two historians? Can you convince them that I am not a "lady" author? You don't need to worry about the chaperon for me. I can't think of anything safer or more respectable than being with three men.

I have begun the "Tidal Highway."[2] I can't tell yet whether it will be usable or not. But if it isn't, it will serve to give you most of the story, which to me at least was fascinating. I hate to tell you, Max, but I am afraid that some time in the next three or four years I shall have to go to Alaska to spend a year or so and write a novel. A whole set of characters, a motif, suggested themselves to me, irresistibly, requiring that setting and no other. I had to fight staying there, to do it right then. You see, with the acute feeling I have for the relation of man to his natural background, that dark and forbidding and mountainous country offers a setting for the theme of betrayal. Human treachery is the most appalling thing. You have to learn to expect to be betrayed. Yet you must learn never to betray. So I give you fair warning, if things get too thick for me here, or too unhappy, I shall have to clear out for that part of the world. The story is already a unit.

Meantime, about the Florida vein, I don't know. Lots of short stuff waiting to be done. Just a matter of keeping myself at it.

I don't know what to say about the boy's book of the scrub. At present, I don't have the enthusiasm. Looking over my notes, and remembering all the bear stories of the northwest, my material seems very thin. There was a time, about two years ago, when I believe I might have done something with it, but the "Golden Apples" material was so deep-rooted it wouldn't let me alone. I'll have to let it take its course. My thought of a further Florida novel is vague. Yet the material is here. The old days of sugar cane, of timbering, are very stirring. I think a great deal about a character who opened up a large part of Florida with a railroad and so on, about whom I wrote a sketch for the "Life in the United States" contest, which was rejected because it didn't carry conviction.[3] A story could be built around that period. There is a story, too, in the period of the Indian Wars in Florida, but it leaves me cold, somehow. Just let me putter along this winter with the short stuff and we'll see. The boy's thing may hit me all of a sudden.

There is one Florida book that will surely be done, I don't know how soon. One I had thought would not be possible because I hadn't done it when the material struck me freshly. Yet mellowness, not freshness, is the requisite. It will be non-fiction, called "Cross Creek: a Chronicle." It will not be a confluent narrative, (for the reason that I do not wish to write my personal story), but made up into chapters. Some of the chapter headings are: "The Sixteen Acres"; "Old Boss"; "'Geechee"; "Black Shadows"; "The Pickers of Magnolia Leaves"; "Toady-Frogs, Snakes and Antses." It will be as quiet in tone as anyone could wish for! Some of the material is violent, but it will be interesting to tell it in a matter of fact and quiet way. It will not be a book to sit down and "do," but one accumulated. Some of the material has been done several years, needing re-writing, of course. Sketches, stories, narratives, essays, laid here at the Creek, done with no special use in mind. But all with a certain, what shall I say, out of the world flavor, catching, I hope, the quality that has made me cling so desperately and against great odds to this place. How it will fit into your publishing schedule, I don't know. It is possible it will be ready in a year or two and will fill in until I have a novel ready for you. Or it may be several years more before I feel I have caught what I want to. I thought I would speak of it to you, since I am sure you wonder what may be shaping itself in my mind.

1. *From Death to Morning* (New York, 1935).

2. Working title of an intended novel inspired by a boat trip with her brother, Arthur, up the Intracoastal Waterway from Seattle to Alaska. She later abandoned the project.

3. "Lord Bill of the Suwannee River," which was turned down by both *Scribner's Magazine* and *Atlantic*. It was published posthumously in *Southern Folklore Quarterly*, June 1963.

37. To Maxwell E. Perkins

Hawthorne, Fla.
December 18, 1935

Dear Max:

I am immensely puzzled by the fact that absolutely no mention is made of *Golden Apples* in either last Sunday's or this Sunday's Scribner advertisement in the N.Y. *Herald-Tribune.* The *Tribune* is the only New York paper I see and it is possible you have divided your advertising. Yet in a general listing I should think the book would at least be mentioned. If it had been a complete failure I could understand it, but with as many books as there are published, it seems to me that one that has held a place on the general best-seller list for two months, deserves more consideration, especially for Christmas gift-selling. The Magazine never carried an announcement of the book until a full month after publication. What is wrong? I have always felt that you have all been very generous with me, but this omission is really distressing. . . .

The writing has been going very badly. I have done several pieces of verse, but have finished nothing else. The "Tidal Highway" I do not think will work out. It is stilted and without value. After the first of the year I shall "take the veil" again—I cannot write, even short things, and do *anything* else—and get something done.

I went last week to the strange and remote place in the scrub, Pat's Island (a pine "island" in the heart of the lower scrub growth) where I stayed with the old hunter who was old man Payne in *South Moon Under.* The old man is dead, his wife moved away with her children—she was a second wife—and the house that he had lived in for sixty years is beginning to cave in under the pressure of that peculiar despairing frailty that seems to possess uninhabited places, as though the supporting breath had left the body of the house, along with the human occupants. I think I shall take some camping stuff and my typewriter and slip away over there without anyone's knowing where I am, to do the boy's story (based on material I got from the old man) in peace and quiet. The location is one of the strangest and most beautiful places I have ever seen. There is a moonshiner four miles away in one direction, a hunting camp four miles in another, and nothing at all for nearly twenty miles anywhere else. Does "The Sink-Hole" sound at all interesting for a title, or is it phonetically unattractive? There is a large sink-hole near the place, grown up in dog-wood and holly and bay and magnolias, that would have meant something very fascinating to a boy.

Robert Herrick is encouraging me strongly on the verse. I sometimes send him a sonnet I've done instead of writing a

Maxwell Perkins in the 1930s. Photograph courtesy of Charles Scribner's Sons.

letter, and of one lately he wrote that "the firm sure phrasing shows a master's hand." Shall I send anything to the Magazine, or is it just as well not to cross the track of my fiction there?

I hope you have a fine Christmas and that all is well. And do see if something shouldn't be done about my being dropped entirely from your list at this time.

As ever,

M.K.R.

"The boy's book of the scrub" (*The Yearling*), which had been working vaguely below the surface for more than two years, suddenly clicked into sharp focus.

38. To Maxwell E. Perkins

[Cross Creek
January 1936]

Dear Max:

The feeling for the boy's book, the particular thing I want to say, came to me. It will not be a story for boys, though some of them might enjoy it. It will be a story *about* a boy—a brief and tragic idyll of boyhood. I think it cannot help but be very beautiful.

It would be a long story—say, 50,000 words. But don't ask me about it yet. When I have begun to catch what I want, I'll send it on, or tell you about it.

M.K.R.

39. To Maxwell E. Perkins

[Cross Creek
ca. June 1, 1936]

Dear Max:

Wolfe's "Story of a Novel" is unbearable. I have just finished it. It's unbearable—its honesty,—its fierceness,—its beauty of expression. And for another writer——

There is no damnation for such a man. Don't be concerned—I know you are not—that he goes "completely off the reservation." He is his own torment and his own strength.

He is so young! When a little of the torment has expended itself, you will have the greatest artist America has ever produced.

My thanks and my gratitude for autographing the book as you did.

When all of us are done for, the chances are that literary history will find you the greatest. Certainly the wisest of us all.

Marjorie

40. *To Maxwell E. Perkins*

Hawthorne, Florida
June 18, [1936]

Dear Max:

I've had an unbelievably good time. It was somehow without reality. Even while I was being terribly happy, it seemed to be someone else who was being gay. I could live that sporting life forever, and love it, but I should never touch paper if I did it. My friend Robert Herrick—who, by the way, is desperately ill—once told me that if I were happy, the chances were that I shouldn't write. But why should torment be a pre-requisite? I find that Malvina Hoffman[1] first called her group "The Sacrifice," by the title "Sorrow is the Mother of Beauty." I can't quite accede to this. The exquisite sensitiveness which makes sorrow strike deep is of course necessary. Otherwise, I agree with Masefield when he says "The days that make us happy make us wise."

I was glad to meet Hemingway, and wished we could have had time for more than a brief talk. My hostess, Mrs. Oliver Grinnell, was the former president of the Salt Water Anglers of America, and she still works with people like Zane Grey and Hemingway on conservation. He came to call on her on her yacht, and she was privately furious that he talked far more about literary things than fishing! The man astonished me. I should have known, from your affection for him, that he was not a fire-spitting ogre, but I'd heard so many tales in Bimini of his going around knocking people down, that I half-expected him to announce in a loud voice that he never accepted introductions to female novelists. Instead, a most lovable, nervous, and sensitive person took my hand in a big gentle paw and remarked that he was a great admirer of my work. He is immensely popular with the anglers, and the natives adore him. The day before I left, he battled six hours and fifty minutes with a 514-lb. tuna, and when his "Pilar" came into harbor at 9:30 at night, the whole population turned out to see his fish and hear his story. There was such a mob on the rotten dock that a post gave way, and his Cuban mate was precipitated into Bimini Bay, coming to the surface with a profanity that was intelligible even to one who speaks no Spanish. A fatuous old man with a new yacht and a young bride had arrived not long previously, announcing that tuna-fishing, of whose difficulties he had heard, was easy. So as the "Pilar" was made fast, Hemingway came swimming up from below-decks, gloriously drunk, roaring, "Where's the son of a bitch who said it was easy?" The last anyone saw of him that night, he was standing alone on the dock where his giant tuna hung from the stays—using it for a punching bag.

A story, told and re-told in Bimini, is of Hemingway's knocking down a man named Platt, for calling him a big fat slob. "You can call me a slob," Hemingway said, "but you can't call me a big fat slob," and he laid him out. Now the natives have a song which they will sing to you if they are sure Hemingway isn't about—"The big fat slob's in the harbor."

There is, obviously, some inner conflict in Hemingway which makes him go about his work with a chip on his shoulder, and which makes him want to knock people down. He is so great an artist that he does not need to be ever on the defensive. He is so vast, so virile, that he does not need ever to hit anybody. Yet he is constantly defending something that he, at least, must consider vulnerable. It seems to me that there is a clue to it in the conflict between the sporting life and the literary life; between sporting people and the artist. That life on the water, with its excitement, which almost nothing that I have experienced can equal, is a self-containing entity. When you are a part of it, nothing else seems valid. Yet occasionally a knife would go through me, and I became conscious of treachery to my own, and when I put it behind me, I felt a great guilt. The sporting people are delightful. They lave your soul. You feel clean and natural when you are with them. Then when you leave them, you are overcome with the knowledge that you are worlds away from them. You know things they will never know. Yet they wear an armor that is denied you. They are somehow blunted. It is not so much their money, for some of them are not unduly prosperous, but their reaction to living. They enjoy life hugely, yet they are not sensitive to it.

Hemingway is among these people a great deal, and they like him and admire him—his personality, his sporting prowess, and his literary prestige. It seems to me that unconsciously he must value their opinion. He must be afraid of laying bare before them the agony that tears the artist. He must be afraid of lifting before them the curtain that veils the beauty that should be exposed only to reverent eyes. So, as in "Death in the Afternoon," he writes beautifully, and then immediately turns it off with a flippant comment, or a deliberate obscenity. His sporting friends would not understand the beauty. They would roar with delight at the flippancy. They are the only people who would be pleased by the things in his work that distress all the rest of us. He injects those painfully foreign elements, not as an artist, but as a sportsman, and a sportsman of a particular type.

Bimini caught at my throat the way the scrub does. The struggle there for existence is terrific. Last summer's hurricane swept it almost bare—most of the roofs, most of the coconut palms, the shrubs. Typhoid and malaria followed. A little white girl who followed me like a dog one morning when I got up before dawn to walk along the high crest of the island, told me that her whole family except herself and her mother had been wiped out by the fever. A six-foot West Indian nigger with a beautiful, tender face who caught our bone-fish bait for us, had not tasted meat for a year and a half. There are about five hundred blacks, and some thirty or forty whites. The whites, I think, are all a bit batty. There is a nightmare quality about their lives. And the beauty of the waters about them is incredible. The color close to the island, in full sunlight, is the palest jade-green. At a little distance, it is aquamarine. Across the horizon, it deepens into a purple for which I know no name. And when you are out on the deep water, it is the purest indigo.

Unless someone really good, like Hemingway, does something about it, I'd like to go and live there a while some day. There is a stirring novel there. I can see its outlines and most of its people, very plainly.

The Malvina Hoffman book [*A Sculptor's Odyssey*] was waiting for me. It is a magnificent document in every way. I am reading it slowly, not to lose anything. I remember being taken off my feet by the quality of the Pavlowa "Gavotte" in the Metropolitan, some years ago. I thought at the time it was in pink marble, but it seems to have been the colored wax. My deepest thanks for the book and for your thoughtfulness.

I couldn't have liked anyone as much as I liked Hemingway, without his liking me a little. So perhaps now he and his family will stop off with me some time on one of those long drives— I am most conveniently located for it—and perhaps you would be willing to come too, then, and see my part of Florida.

Thank you for sending the check. I came home to find my account overdrawn.

Always with my best,

Marjorie

1. Malvina Hoffman, American sculptor (1887–1966).

Now confident of her direction for the new book of the scrub, but seeking to know her material in authentic personal depth before trying to write, MKR resorted to the practice that had worked so well for *South Moon Under*. She had already made one additional stay in the scrub with the family of old Cal Long, who had since died. She arranged to visit with another old pioneer, Barney Dillard, who had another fund of stories and hunting lore and, best of all, had promised to take her out on several real bear hunts. She had her twelve-year-old boy clearly in mind, and by this time had decided that the book should be a full-length novel rather than the novelette she had originally intended, so that she could unwind the story at pleasurable leisure. Above all, she now knew that she must abandon the claptrap of romance which had flawed *Golden Apples*, and she felt free to "luxuriate in the simple details that interest me and that I have been so amazed to find interested other people."

41. To Maxwell E. Perkins

Hawthorne, Florida
July 31, 1936

Dear Max:

I can see that you're disturbed about my feeling that I had better take a full-length for the boy's book.

It will positively be as we both first conceived of it. I have in front of me your letter of October 27, 1933. You say, "I am thinking of a book about a boy.— — A book about a boy and the life of the scrub is the thing we want.— — It is those wonderful river trips and the hunting and the dogs and guns and the companionship of simple people who care about the same things which were included in 'South Moon Under'— —"

Until lately, I have had in mind one incident, almost, that would make a complete long-story in itself, about a boy. I wanted a bear-hunt in the story, for it fitted in with the other, and I have been prowling all over trying to find somebody who was actually bear-hunting, for I felt I had to see one to get what I want from it. By the merest accident, I met, and was taken into the confidence of, a perfectly marvelous old pioneer [Barney Dillard] living on the St. Johns river—the beautiful broad river I took the trip on, and which borders the scrub on the east side. This old man, a famous "bad man," but honorable and respected and at one time prosperous, too, took me bear-hunting twice, and in a few days I am going over to live a while with him and his wife and go hunting and fishing with him. So much material has come from my contact with him, and there is so much more there—anecdotes, hunting incidents, people—that I realized before I went to North Carolina that I had at hand a mass of stuff—and as always, the facts have suggested imaginary characters to me who fit in with the true ones—that couldn't possibly go in the simple 50,000 word narrative that I was ready to do. I had to resist constantly the thought of all these other things. . . .

The day before I left Carolina, I told just about this much—I didn't want to go very deeply into it with anyone—to Herschel Brickell[1] and said that I was going home reluctantly instead of on to New York to talk with you about it. He said, "I can tell you what any publisher would say. From a publishing standpoint, there's no question of choice between a short book, which has to sell at almost the price of a full one, and a full-length book. It is only the rare thing, like 'Good-bye, Mr. Chips',[2] that sells in brief form. People want to read about that scrub life you write about, and if you have the material, you would be very foolish to put out a short thing instead of taking all the room you need to tell a real story. And unless a short book happened to have a rare and enormous success, booksellers would not be enthusiastic, and you would harm yourself immensely on your next full-length book."

It was just one of those straws that settle a thing, for I had been having a battle to keep down the thought of taking more room to it.

He said, "See Max, or think it over very carefully before you pass up any chance to do a full-length thing with that wonderful scrub material."

I said, "it's all settled."

I don't want to write you about the actual stuff—I could talk to you for hours about it and not do harm. But if I try to express in a few sentences in a letter what I mean to do, it has a paralyzing effect—making the stuff *congeal* in a quickly-said form, when I want to take all those pages and pages of a book to say it. I can't sum it up like a review, without spoiling my pleasure in working it out right. But the short narrative I had in mind will make my culminating point—my climax and my point, and a very stirring point it is, too.

It will be absolutely all told through the boy's eyes. He will be about twelve, and the period will not be a long one—not more than two years. I want it through his eyes before the age of puberty brings in any of the other factors to confuse the simplicity of viewpoint. It will be a book boys will love, and if it is done well enough otherwise, the people who liked *South Moon* will like it too. It is only since *Golden Apples* that I realize what it is about my writing that people like. I don't mean that I am writing *for* anyone, but now I feel free to luxuriate in the simple

details that interest me, and that I have been so amazed to
find interested other people—probably just from the element of
sincerity given by my own interest and sympathy. . . .

I have a mass of animal material that will be fascinating to
anyone at all interested. I have to laugh at Carl Brandt. I have
told him again and again that the short thing I was ready to
do was not for any magazine. I wrote him that the short thing
would have to be full-length. He wrote back blandly, "Such good
news. *Cosmo* will be delighted." I refuse to tell Carl what I
have in mind, but what a shock it will be when all the stuff
about bear-hunts and so on comes before him!

I think I will burst sometimes at your not coming to Florida
and letting me show you some of the places that I shall use
for background. If Hemingway is at a place where he wants
you in the early fall, for Heaven's sake come down, and let me
talk with you on the ground. A few words here and there and
you will see just what I'm after. If you still won't, I'll come up in
say, October and show you what I have in hand and as much
writing as I may have done by then. If by any chance it wasn't
good I could still do the short narrative, but I don't see how
what I have in mind could fail me.

Of course, I am up against the technical problem now of working out "plot" and inter-play of characters, but once I have
decided on the people who will be in the book, I think the narrative will flow naturally of its own accord. The basic theme is
clear in my mind—the same as for the short thing—and it
should be very moving. I *cannot* write about it.

Yes, I read Hemingway's story in *Esquire.*³ It is *gorgeous*. It
stirred me deeply as story. Then I thought about it as autobiography and it was illuminating. Also most encouraging, for I
had the feeling of his having taken a hurdle, faced facts with
courage, and being ready to go. I can't tell you how glad I am
about the novel laid in that section. If he doesn't see the Bahamas as I saw them, someday I'll do you a book about them.

I'm feeling happier than in a long time. Desolation doesn't
strike so often or last so long; and I'm not being bothered, this
time of year, with the frivolous diversions that make life bear-
able when it's too black, but that interfere with me when I'm
ready or trying to work. I have two jolly new pets—and you can

always shut them up when you don't want them around, as
you can't do with your good friends!—a highly pedigreed and
marvelous pointer puppy, 6 months old, and a pet baby raccoon
who is great fun. . . .

Now please don't write me another of those restrained "You
must do it as seems right to you" notes. Tell me what is really in
your mind.

And I *must* talk to you not later than October, here or in
New York.

My best,

M.K.R.

1. Herschel Brickell, editor, journalist, and book-review columnist (1889–1952).

2. Novel by James Hilton (New York, 1934).

3. "The Horns of the Bull," *Esquire,* June 1936.

42. *To Ida M. Tarrant*

Hawthorne, Florida
August 5, [1936]

Dearest Aunt Ida:

I can't tell you how good it would seem to have you in Ocala. It
really seems to me the thing to do, if there is a comfortable
place at your price. My fear was of two things: your feeling up-
rooted again, and perhaps feeling unconsciously homesick for
the place you were brought up in; then the fear that the me-
chanical difficulties of the move might seem too great to you,
and perhaps the labor of packing and shipping make you ill,
bring on one of those attacks you had. I really think the second
is the only thing we need worry about. As you say, you have
no ties in Cincinnati, and there are more people in Florida this
minute who think a lot of you, than in Cincinnati. But you
must consider very carefully whether packing up will [be] too
hard a job. I don't like to promise too far ahead, but it might be
I could drive out and help you do it, and drive you to Florida.
I hope to be deep in the next book, but we might strike a gap
when I'd just as soon do it as not.

It may be difficult to find a suitable place in Ocala. The canal
boom capsizing has made rents drop down to normal again,
and there are plenty of small apartments, but most of them have

no furnace heat—just fireplaces or Heatrolas or something like that. You know what Florida winters are—much of the time very pleasant, but many mornings and evenings cold, even when the day is warm, and the trouble of starting your own heater in the mornings is something to think of. And while I never think of you as old, still your age is such that physical comfort should come first in everything you do. I hope to take a day this week and comb Ocala and then I'll write you what I find.

It would be wonderful to drop in on you once or twice a week, and I should often be happy to stay overnight. Then you could visit me here, and it would mean a great deal to both of us. As for your being a burden, I should feel much easier to have you close in case you were ill. If you were ever seriously ill or ill for a long time I should want to come to you, and having you at a great distance would be a real hardship, while if you were here I'd feel a lot better about it. The year-round climate here is certainly an improvement on yours. You think very carefully about the work of moving—I assume you'd want your own things—and I'll see what I can find.

Well, I had a great surprise. A very up-set note from Mother Rawlings, telling me Charles is getting married in New York City August 15. I didn't realize she really cared for me, but she must. She said the girl was 26 years old (Charles will be 41 this fall) gentle and lovable, with a slight limp, or drag of the leg, from infantile paralysis, very dark-skinned, tall and slim— was on the Times-Union in Rochester. She said she ought to feel good about it, but said, "It's you I want. You are still ace-high with your old Mother Rawlings." Said if she was interfering, she was sorry, but she had to follow her feelings. It was plain she hoped I still cared for Charles, and would do something about a reconciliation.

Well, did I have a thankless job writing her an answer! Tore up three before I sent one—then felt it was still too harsh. I couldn't be nasty when I realize I meant that much to her. Yet I felt I should let her know in no uncertain terms that I was sure-enough "through," for her own peace of mind if nothing else. I told her the girl sounded just right and I was very glad he was marrying. That it was perfectly possible he had matured and could act with ordinary civility and kindness in daily human relations, and that if he could act like a human being, the marriage should be an ideal one. Said that for myself, any change of heart in him (of course I don't think he has changed for one minute) simply came too late. Said I wouldn't be back in the hell of our life together for anything on earth. That I'd put up a lonely fight here, but that except for occasional moments of depression, life was again the beautiful and glamorous thing it used to be. Told her just to help Charles get a fresh start and forget the past without bitterness, as I tried to do. Told her not to worry about me, I was O.K. *Could not* resist telling her that one of the last things Charles said to me when he left was, "Of course, you realize you have no friends. Nobody likes you." And that once I was on my feet, the world had opened kind and generous arms to me, and the love and friendship of men and women and even children had come to me like a revelation. Told her to pass on to Charles my best wishes for success and happiness. Did I do right?

Well, I have my puppy! Six months old, and he looks so much like Mandy, and acts like her, that I said to him "Are you Mandy?" and he wagged his tail. He is highly pedigreed, and very valuable, smart as a whip, anxious to please me, learns fast, and I am certainly happy with him. Have had him ten days and it seems as if he'd always been here. Name is *Pat*.

Also am making a pet of a baby raccoon. Kate[1] feeds it milk from a baby's nursing bottle. It is cute as can be. Name is *Racket*.

Have spent a day and night over at the ocean at the lovely summer cottage of Mrs. Corcoran, the one who took us to the bird-man's place and then home to dinner in Palatka. Mrs. Tigert[2] and I spent a nice afternoon and evening alone together last week, supper down town and then the movies. Bob [Camp] and Cecil [Bryant][3] ate Sunday dinner with me, and I ate picnic supper with them last night.

Dessie [Smith Vinson] has been to New York again and back, looking very attractive and more arrogant than ever. Think she has accepted my withdrawal for she doesn't bother me any more. Gives me a funny look, but prefers evidently not to make an issue of it, which suits me, as you hate to come right out and hurt anyone's feelings.

Is it $20 or $25 that is your limit for rent? And have you been paying your gas and lights separately or is that included?

Loads of love,

Marjorie

1. MKR's maid.
2. Edith Tigert, wife of John J. Tigert, president of the University of Florida.
3. See letter 66, note 1, June 17, 1938.

43. To Maxwell E. Perkins

Hawthorne, Florida
August 27, [1936]

Dear Max:

I was glad to have your wire and know you liked the mule story.[1] I haven't heard from Carl [Brandt] yet, but any reasonable price will be all right as far as I'm concerned. I feel much better about Scribner's using it, for it really has a more substantial quality than a "popular" story. And it will be wise to have them all in the one magazine. I thoroughly enjoy doing that kind of story, and I imagine it's as much of a relief to most readers, after solemn fiction, as it is to me. The way Uncle Benny has been re-printed and talked of has amazed me, and yet it's understandable enough.

Max, I am going perfectly delirious with delight in my material as the boy's book takes shape in my mind. The most delicious people are in it. Wait until you see Grandma Hutto. A little impudent, infidel, sharp-spoken thing with gold circle earrings and Spanish or Minorcan blood who scandalizes the staid residents of the scrub and who tells the boy wise and impudent things. She doesn't want to go to Heaven because they live on milk and honey, and she likes a piece of fried mullet now and again. She likes music made from a harp and a bass violin and an octave flute, and she couldn't get along listening to just a harp. I intend to be careful about not over-stepping any boundaries, so that the book won't be spoiled for boys. But oh Max, the stuff is going to be grand. I've been spending a lot of time over on the St. Johns river, which is the eastern boundary of the scrub, if you'll remember. And the people of the east scrub have never even heard of the ones on the west side. I'll use the

St. Johns river a good deal in the story. You and I are going to
love the book if nobody else in the world reads it. I am very
happy and confident about it as it forms. None of the fear and
torment of "Golden Apples." Then the following book[2] will be
hell again. By the way, do you still have that map of the scrub I
sent you? I'd like it back, if you do.

I had a grand letter from Ernest Hemingway. I wrote him
how much I liked the "Snows of Kilimanjaro," and asked him to
stop off here with his family any time they passed through.
He said he would like to stop this fall late if he comes back then
to Florida. I can give him some good bird hunting of various
kinds then. I told him to try to get you here some time, that I
had been a miserable failure at it. But you might be disappointed, at that. Hemingway's letter was very remarkable—most
revealing in many ways.

My ex-husband has just married again, which takes a burden off my mind. I had a tragic letter from his mother, hoping
I'd do something about it while there was yet time. She wrote
that the girl (much younger than he, only 26) was very gentle
and lovable, but said "It's you I want." It was so hard to write
her that I wouldn't be back in the hell I lived in with him, without
hurting her, because after all, a son is a son, even though, as she
herself once said, "Nobody could live with him that didn't love
him." But it is a great relief to me to know he is taken care of.
I've never wanted anything at the expense of anyone else—
even peace.

I don't know yet whether I'll get north or not. If I can work
here when I begin the actual writing, I'd rather, but if the September heat is too bad I'll go to the Carolina mountains and
come to New York from there. I'd rather see you when I have a
start made.

Tell Whitney Darrow I love him even though I don't write
to him.

Had an amusing experience. I've spent a good deal of time
with the marvelous old pioneer [Barney Dillard] I've been bear-
hunting with. Several of his fifteen grown children raised a
howl about his telling me stories etc. He is a famous character
with a really brilliant but self-tutored mind, and they thought
of what he had to give me as something tangible, with a cash

value to him and to them—sheer illusion, of course. They thought I was working up his own life-story—which is of no use to me at all. One of his sons followed me around whenever I was at their house with the suspicious eye of a police dog. The other morning I was taking notes from the old man on the various herbs that were used locally for medicines and "remedies"—such stuff as "mullein tea," and dried pomegranate peelings brewed for fever. The son asked in amazement, (he seldom spoke to me directly), "She writing up sich as that?" The old man said, "That's just the kind of thing she's writing. She's not like you sorry, no-account things. She's interested in the old days and the old ways. Why, I never heard a woman cuss like she cussed this morning when we went to Juniper Springs and she found the government had cleaned out the Springs and put up picnic tables." The son said, "Well, I'll be dogged." When I left, he followed me rather sheepishly to the car and handed me a very handsome ram's horn. He said, "You get you some old-timer to put you a mouth-piece on this and polish it up, and you'll have you the finest blowing-horn in the county."

I have a pet baby raccoon that is lots of fun. He sleeps with the dogs and makes a strange, chirring sound that a damn mocking-bird has learned to imitate, so that we're always thinking Racket is lost in the grove! I don't know how long it will work, for baby that he is, he can bite like the dickens.

All my best,

Marjorie

1. "Varmints," published in *Scribner's Magazine,* November 1936.
2. A projected novel on Zephaniah Kingsley, a colorful Florida planter of the early nineteenth century. She never got beyond the planning stage with the book.

44. To Maxwell E. Perkins

Sept. 22, [1936]
Pinnacle Inn Cottage
Banner Elk, North Carolina

Dear Max:

A hurried note to say that I am here for a month at least. I simply could not get going on the book, although it was clear as daylight in my mind. Things were on my nerves—mosquitoes bad, heat sticky and depressing, grove responsibilities wearing, and a drugged lassitude besides. Decided just to bolt for the mountains to see if I couldn't take the hurdle that way. Saw my doctor before I left and found there was a very good reason for my being in such shape—full of malaria, and running a steady temperature of 100 all through the day. The doctor laughed when I said I couldn't work. He said no wonder, with a steady temperature. I'm on quinine, reached North Carolina last Friday and feel like a new person already.

After a search, found simply an ideal cabin and location. A new, attractive cabin of undressed white oak, hand made furniture, big fireplace, electric lights, bathroom, electric stove and water heater, and a gorgeous mountain view. A village within walking distance. Just enough isolation. Brought my Proust and my pointer—perfect company for work! Just got settled today, but can tell I'll have no further difficulty, more than the ordinary ones, with the work. Am having my mail forwarded, and hope there'll be a letter from you telling me your vacation did you lots of good.

My best.

Marjorie

Any book you want to send me, would love to have it here.

Late in September of 1936, while MKR was at Banner Elk in the North Carolina mountains working on the manuscript of *The Yearling,* Perkins wrote asking her if she would visit F. Scott Fitzgerald, who was staying at the Grove Park Inn in nearby Asheville, recuperating from a broken shoulder, from alcoholism, and from outrage at a sensational feature article in the *New York Post* which had pictured him in a jittery state of collapse and on the verge of suicide. MKR was none too anxious to get involved, but out of respect for Perkins' wishes, dropped Fitzgerald a note asking him if he would like to drive out with her to visit a pottery in the Pisgah National Forest. He politely refused, pleading a temperature, but suggested that she stop by on her way back from the forest. She left another note on her way through Asheville, saying that she would call on him later in the day. It was a fascinating encounter.

45. *To F. Scott Fitzgerald*

Dear Scott Fitzgerald:

I'm so sorry about the temperature—nothing tears you up so badly. One reason I came up here from Florida was to try to shake a malarial temperature that ran about 100° all through the day. I defy anyone to do any work with the system practically simmering.

I'm very much relieved you didn't want to go to Pisgah Forest, especially as I find the place I've been looking for is only a few miles out of town. I thought it was some distance away.

But I do want to meet you and hope you'll feel up to it when I get back early this afternoon. I've tried and failed to get a copy of *The Great Gatsby* for you to autograph.——I hope you don't mind, it's being my favorite of your things. It simply took me off my feet.

You have what must actually be a painful insight into people, especially complicated people. I don't understand people like us—and what little I do understand, terrifies me. That's why I write, gratefully, of the very simple people whose problems are only the most fundamental and primitive ones. I have probably been more cowardly than I'd admit, in sinking my interests in the Florida backwoods, for the peace and beauty I've found there have been definitely an escape from the confusion of our generation.

You have faced the music, and it is a symphony of discord.

It seems to me that you have a great gift as a social historian—something of Thackeray's feeling for a period—but having a finer literary style than Thackeray, you should do something very stirring before you're done.

Here I am rambling all over the [Hotel] Vanderbilt's stump-tailed stationery, when what I set out to say was that if you feel

like a bit of chat early this afternoon, but don't feel keen about getting up, why can't I talk with you just the same? Good God, I've
seen men in bed before.

I must tell you an awfully funny incident of my own, con-
cerning my one-eyed 'Geechee maid and my reception of a caller
in bed——

Hoping you're feeling better today—and I'll telephone
about 12:30.

Marjorie K. Rawlings

(It's "Mrs.")

46. To F. Scott Fitzgerald

[Banner Elk, N.C.]
Sunday night
[October 25, 1936]

Dear Scott:

I've just finished "The Great Gatsby" again——

I have no business trying to write you about it now, because
I'm all torn up again—much worse than when I read it ten
years ago—you were wise so young—I'm only beginning to
know some of the things you must have been born,
knowing——

The book resolves itself into the strangest feeling of a crystal
globe, or one of the immense soap bubbles we achieved as
children, if it could hold its shape and color without breaking——It is so beautiful, it is so clairvoyant, it is so heart-
breaking——

Please, how can you talk of security when the only security is
the loveliness of the dream? And you are right to think that
anything can be mended, and life can be cut to order, like a
diamond——But turn about is fair play, and you must give life
the same privilege—to mend and change you, and to cut new
facets—I suppose you know that nothing is wasted——The hell
you've been through isn't wasted——All you have to do, ever,
is to forget everything and turn that terrible, clear white Light
you possess, on the minds and emotions of the people it stirs
you to write about——That's your security——

I enjoyed myself unreasonably talking with you, and have no apologies for not letting you get the rest your nurse was having fits about—I think you probably needed that kind of talk as much as I did—only we kept darting up so many alleys—and a perfectly sane outsider would have thought we were a pair of articulate panthers, the way we took turns pacing up and down—you'll have to pace with me on my thirty-foot farmhouse porch this winter—we could pass each other comfortably— —

I was high from the really very decent wines and I suppose the talk, as far as Spruce Pine— — I got absent-minded once and found myself at the foot of Mt. Mitchell—a man told me I *could* go over the mountain—having been up it in broad daylight, driving myself and paralyzed with terror that I wouldn't admit, I about-faced shamelessly and retraced the fourteen erroneous miles— —

The reason I keep doing this—and this—is that the period broke off my typewriter a few days ago— — When I try to end a sentence in all decisiveness, I just get a blur, like this. There are always connotations in dashes, anyway—none in blurs.

So many thanks for your hospitality— —

I'm writing Max, who sounded to me a bit worried about you, a favorable report—and an honest one— — Good God, man, you're all right— — Don't let anybody hurry you—not that you would— — When you're sore through and through—I don't mean physically—It has to heal in its own way— — Don't I know— — If anyone knew how good my little '32 revolver has looked to me sometimes— —

Don't ever write to me politely, answering a letter—but anytime you really want to call me "obvious" or what else was it, I'd enjoy having you do it— —

Don't repeat to Max or anyone the small bit I told you about the book I have in mind after this one— — But I'm longing to get to it, and dreading it, for if I can say one-tenth of what I want to, it will be perfectly beautiful— — Then, when of course, it isn't, I'll consider the '32 again, or maybe do a Cross Creek Cleopatra with a rattlesnake— —

Again, thank you—

Marjorie

47. To Maxwell E. Perkins[1]

Banner Elk, N.C.
Oct. 26, 1936

Dear Max:

I had a strange answer from Scott Fitzgerald, refusing my invitation to drive to the Pisgah Forest Pottery, but saying with what I could only take as sincerity, that he wanted to meet me and hoped I could make him a stop when I did go through Asheville. So Friday afternoon late I wired him that I'd be in Asheville at seven that night, and I barged along. I ran into the most beastly driving, storms, and detours and those vicious mountain roads, and finally, thick fog for the last thirty miles into Asheville, I was all but babbling by the time I got in, alone, and I thought I'd have to climb in bed beside Fitzgerald and send for another psychiatrist. So it was almost with relief that his nurse's voice, and then his own, very faint, informed me that his arthritis had been bad and he had run a high temperature all day and couldn't see me. He was doubtful of his health the next day and I was very dubious about pressing the matter. But again I felt sure he really did care about a meeting. So the next morning I wrote him a very nice long note and said he needn't get out of bed if he felt badly but wanted a bit of chat, and I went along to the potter's and took care of my business there, came back to Asheville and telephoned him again at one o'clock. Something in the note must have hit right, for when he found I hadn't had luncheon, he insisted on my coming right over and having it with him in his room.

Max, we had a perfectly delightful time! Far from being depressing, I enjoyed him thoroughly, and I'm sure he enjoyed it as much. He was nervous as a cat, but had not been drinking— had had his nurse put his liquor away. We had only sherry and a table wine, and talked our heads off. His reaction to the N.Y. *Post* story had been to go to New York and kill the German Jew, Mok, until he decided that would be a silly gesture with one arm disabled. He was terribly hurt about it, of course, for he had listened to a sob story from him, to let him in at all, and had responded to a lot of things the man told him—possibly spurious—about his own maladjusted wife, by talking more freely than he should have done. But he has taken the thing very gracefully and is not unduly bitter or upset about it. He was also more forgiving and reasonable than I think I should have been, about Hemingway's unnecessary crack at him in "The Snows of Kilimanjaro." We agreed that it was a part of Hemingway's own sadistic maladjustment, which makes him go around knocking people down. Scott said that Hemingway had written him very violently, damning him for his revealing self-searchings in *Esquire*,[2] and Scott expressed the idea that it was just as legitimate to get one's grievance against life off the chest that way, as by giving an upper-cut to some harmless weakling. He resented Hemingway's calling him "ruined," and from other things he said, it was plain to me that he does not himself consider himself "ruined," by a long shot.

I am firmly convinced that the man is all right. I know just what his state of mind has been. The same kind of panic hits anyone like me with no one dependent on me. With an ill and expensive wife, a child brought up to luxury, and then one thing after another going wrong—all on top of the inevitable revulsion, almost, against writing—"the times," as Hemingway wrote me, "when you can't do it"—it was natural enough for him to go into a very black mood. It lasted longer and he publicized it more, than with most of us—I am always ashamed to let anyone know about mine—but I should lay a heavy wager that he's safely on the way out.

We disagreed heartily about many things, of course. Principally as to what we expect of life. I expect the crest of the wave to have a consequent and inevitable trough, and whenever I'm at the bottom, I know there will be an up-turn sooner or later. Then when I'm at the top, I don't expect it to last indefinitely— he said that he did—but know there will have to be less pleasant things coming along sooner or later.

He said, "You're not as much of an egotist as I am." Then he said and more or less correctly, too, that a writer almost had to be an egotist to the point of megalomania, because everything was filtered through his own universe.

His point of view lets him in for much desperate unhappiness and disillusion, because he simply cannot expect the consistent perfection and magnificence of life that he does, frankly, expect. But as a writer, except for the times such as this one has been, when his misery holds him up too long, his masochism will not interfere with his work. We talked from a little after one, until five-thirty, when his nurse came back and fussed about his not resting, but we never reached talk of our plans for the future in any detail. He did say that he had a plan—and he spoke with every sign of the secret pleasure that is an indication of work in the brewing.

He spoke of the autobiographical thing, but said he could not do it with most of the people alive. That he could only do it now in a pleasant way, and it wouldn't be any fun without a little malice.

I wrote him that I felt he had a great gift as a social historian, and I do—that he had Thackeray's feeling for a period, and that I thought he would someday do something very stirring as a record of our confused generation.

I feel I had no tangible help for him—he is in no truly desperate need of help—and our points of view are very different—but there is a most helpful stimulation in talk between two people who are trying to do something of the same thing—a stimulation I miss and do not have enough of, at Cross Creek. And I am sure that stimulation was good for him. I may be able to have another visit with him when I return to Pisgah Forest in a couple of weeks, if the dishes I ordered are ready before I drive home. He may go to a quiet place on one of the Florida coasts, this winter, and if he does, we shall have some good talks.

So certainly I can report that the contact was very pleasant. And I do not think you need to worry about him, physically or psychologically. He has thrown himself on the floor and shrieked himself black in the face and pounded his heels—as lots of us do in one way or another—but when it's over, he'll go back to his building blocks again. Have you ever felt what I call the cosmic despair? It's no joke. And if you slip a little too deep in it, as he did, it's one devilish job getting out again. But he's well on the way out and I think deserves lots of credit for getting himself so well in hand again. There will perhaps be relapses, but I don't think he feels the abyss so inescapably under him.

M.K.R.

P.S. When we had our sherry, we lifted our glasses, as you might know, "To Max."

1. MKR left three separate accounts of her meeting with Fitzgerald: the present letter; a long letter to Fitzgerald's biographer, Arthur Mizener, dated March 18, 1948 (letter 148 in this volume); and a prose sketch entitled "Scott." A conflation of these three accounts, including all details but avoiding repetitions, appears in G.E. Bigelow, *Frontier Eden* (Gainesville, Fla., 1966), pp. 29–34.

2. "The Crack-up," *Esquire,* February 1936; "Pasting It Together," *Esquire,* March 1936; "Handle with Care," *Esquire,* April 1936.

48. To Maxwell E. Perkins

Cross Creek
Nov. 10, [1936]

Dear Max:

The touchiness of writers and fixed ideas of publishing as a business must keep you constantly "on the spot." I knew the chances were that you had been a little misunderstood, but you are the logical wailing wall, you know, because you always understand.

What I am concerned about is that the forthcoming book should not be labeled a "juvenile," because I think it will only incidentally be a book *for* boys. I hope there will be nostalgic implications for mature people for we never *feel* more sensitively than in extreme youth, and the color and drama of the scrub can be well conveyed through the eyes and mind of a boy. I believe, I hope, that the book will be able to stand on its own feet. The only thing different I am doing with the market, or appeal, for boys in mind, is avoiding the psychological (usually sexual) involvements of maturity. But a boy's reaction to the mature world is a valid one, and has value for anyone. The adventure and simplicity, will carry it, quite secondarily, for boys' use. But it is important that no announcement ever be made, anywhere, that the book is a "juvenile." Walter de la Mare's "Memoirs of a Midget" is from the point of view of the midget but no one could call it a book "for" little people. He simply showed a phase of the world through a sensitive mind.

I run a danger, I know, ending up with what is neither fish, flesh, nor fowl, but I really feel I have that angle of the thing firmly in hand.

I reached home Saturday and found completely disorganized darkies, whom I had to fire. My vacations always cost me dear that way, but I consider it just part of the price. My place is in complete confusion and it irks me to have to stop and look after domestic details and break in 5 brand new grove men and 1 house woman, when I should like to sit down in tranquility and go ahead with the book.

I get so tired of carrying such a complete responsibility but my place here offers the only security that is at all tangible, so I cling to it.

I believe it will be a good orange year, and I plan to sell my fruit by Christmas, to be free of the anxiety about freezes.

I wrote a story while I was in the mountains that Carl sold to the Post but it's not a Scribner type at all, so you didn't miss a thing.[1] I think the new magazine is immensely thrilling.

Marjorie

1. "A Mother in Mannville," *Saturday Evening Post,* December 1936.

49. To Maxwell E. Perkins

Hawthorne, Florida
December 31, 1936

Dear Max:

I'm glad the mule story[1] was liked. The magazine was so generous in its display and illustrations, that I'm pleased that you had a response on it. Miss Ives did a difficult and creditable job in cutting it—but a certain leisureliness that was of value was inevitably lost, and I don't think I shall ever agree again to a cutting of a manuscript that I have myself pared down as far as possible. When I turned the story over to Carl Brandt, I told him, and thought I had told you, that I had a series in mind—humorous stories told by the same woman, Quincey Dover. They would have a definite continuity. Ordinarily a book of stories is poor business for everyone, I know.

I have had the happiest Christmas of many years, for my beloved brother has been here with me from Seattle, since the opening of hunting season. The duck-hunting was really magnificent. I have eaten duck until I am afraid that when I speak a drake will circle around me, recognizing the mating call. I can't hit them myself, but my brother did nobly. I had a perfect set-up—we used small frog-hunting boats and made our blinds, and I hired a man with a motor boat to circle about and keep the ducks in motion. I shouldn't say "hired" because all my arrangements with my Cracker neighbors are peculiar. I had loaned this man money to take his baby to the doctor, had fed his wife while she was convalescing from child-birth and so on, and I simply took out the debt in the duck-hunting. But anyway, everyone who hunted with us said we had the best duck-hunting in the state. Tell Hemingway for me that I thought of him when we were having such good luck. He passed me up cold in November, putting up nearby in Gainesville. I was sorry he didn't come out here, even if he had a party, because my place is wide open to people for whom I have infinitely less respect than for him.

We went for turkey last week, but they had left the island in the marsh where we had them located, evidently the day before we got there. We've had top-notch quail-shooting. I enjoy that the most of any of the hunting, probably because I can hit them.

My brother returns to Seattle Monday, and I shall be quite desolate. We are devoted to each other, and it seems silly for us to be separated by a diagonal line across the continent. Yet ties of one sort and another keep us in our respective sections.

Needless to say, the book, begun nicely in Carolina, stopped short. Not entirely because of his visit, but largely because I returned from the mountains to a pair of completely demoralized niggers,[2] whom I had to fire. My grove work and my household have been so disorganized that I have had to take responsibilities and do actual work that I usually delegate to my help. If things had been running as smoothly as usual, we could have put in part of each day hunting, and I could still have done some work—which we planned. I have stop-gap help now which will do for a while, and one thing the enforced separation from the book has done, is to make me terribly keen to be at it again. I may not be out any time in the end, because I shall sink myself in it completely. I hope that mid-Spring will see it done.

I haven't heard from Scott since I left Carolina. I want to send him a book I promised him. Do you have an address that might reach him? He spoke of Florida this winter, for work, but since he didn't go north at Thanksgiving, as he planned, he may have changed his whole program.

Why do you hope Hemingway won't go to Spain? A grand book might come of it. He writes with so much color of the terrain—he would lose himself in the situation there—and his writing is best when it is objective. If he's killed in the melee, what of it? He must go where his feeling impels him.

I sent you some of my oranges—still rather acid. If you use them much, I can send you some better ones a little later in the season when they're sweeter.

Thank you for writing me. There is always comfort in hearing from you.

Marjorie

1. "Varmints," *Scribner's Magazine,* November 1936.
2. MKR's attitude toward blacks ran a considerable spectrum. In her early years at Cross Creek, before she had had much experience of southern rural blacks, or sometimes in her later years when she was being ironic and addressing a familiar friend, her language could reflect conventional white bigotry. But on the whole her mature attitude was one of sympathy and understanding, and she became an outspoken advocate of the human and legal rights of black people (see, for example, letter 110).

50. To Maxwell E. Perkins

[Cross Creek]
February 25, [1937]

Dear Max:

Thanks so much for both books and the good letters. I don't think I could like anything Edgar Lee Masters wrote, "not even if it was good." And unless a biographer has a luminosity of interpretation to bring to his subject, so that the book itself is creative and stimulating, and can stand on its own feet as a thing of value, I resent a mere probing into the life and mind of a great artist. It is too much like worms feeding on a corpse.

"Dusk of Empire,"[1] on the other hand, took me off my feet. I could not put it down. If Williams is as thoroughly honest as the context would indicate, it seems to me the book cannot help but have an international effect. Certainly it should give this whole country a jolt. It saddens me, for I am one of those who rather tend to ignore painful facts, and I have been taking peace for granted. Williams leaves no doubt but that the vast percentage takes war for granted. Admitting that, there is probably no course for the United States but to acquire the whip hand. Among nations, tolerance and generosity and simple goodness, as with our negroes in the south, are not held a sign of strength, but of weakness, and are, slyly or boldly, to be taken advantage of. Williams' title is gorgeous.

The book filled in a vacuum of questions in my mind at this particular moment, for I found it waiting for me on my return from a week-end at Rollins College, where I appeared on the Animated Magazine. The program was keyed by Dr. Hamilton Holt, a lifelong and patient League of Nations advocate, as you know, to the international flavor. Our own Thomas J. Watson[2] was a noble representative of American altruism, and I burst with pride over his fineness. The other two principal guests of honor were Lord David Davies,[3] who persisted, with superlative diplomacy, in labeling himself a Welshman, "a citizen of a very small country," and Dr. F. H. F. Van Vlissingen, of the Netherlands, president of the international Chamber of Commerce, and head of the international rayon industry. Lord Davies made precisely the charming and irresistible appeal for British-American cooperation that Williams warns us against, unless we are prepared to give ourselves to it wisely. He went so far as to use the old Wilson shibboleths, and asked whether, having helped fight to preserve democracy, we meant to go back on the job now. He said, "Federalism is the child of the United States. Instead of holding aloof, you should be going up and down the earth, preaching the worth of your progeny." The thought came to me, even in my ignorance of, and actually, indifference to, world matters, "England, speaking through the poise and calm of that man, is frightened to death. They are on their knees, begging us to fight with their gang." So you can imagine what a revelation the Williams book was for me.

The Hollander spoke with a magnificent detachment. He was thoroughly sincere, and he was fighting for free trade. There is of course nothing objectionable in an honest statement of aim. It is only hypocrisy that offends. There was on the face of the man the mark of sorrow, of tragedy. He may see, probably must see, Holland as Williams sees her—the next Belgium. I should have given my orange grove for a long talk with him, for he interested me more than any man I have ever met. I am writing you with a thoroughly broken heart, for while I had a most delightful contact with both Lord Davies and Thomas Watson, Van Vlissingen bowed politely—and was unaware of my existence.

About "The Yearling." I am on the point of exploding with frustration. The work stopped short, as you know, on my return from the mountains, because of my beloved brother's visit. That was worth while. Then servant trouble prevented my getting at the book again. I am peculiarly at the mercy of reliable help. I don't in the least mind doing all my own work, even to feeding the chickens and milking the cow and driving the truck on grove-work, but there is such a mass of detail here on the shabby old lovely place, that I simply cannot do it and do anything else. My nervous energy burns fiercely about so long and then the current just stops. There are at least six hours of hard work here every day, aside from the grove work. And a new or incompetent servant requires all my time and effort to break in. The Lord sent me, or so I was fatuous enough to think, not long ago a most capable and settled woman of intelligence, clean, hard-working, a good cook. She came to me at the time I had a houseful of flood refugees from Louisville—a dear friend and her children.[4] They left on Tuesday, and I prepared to settle back with a sigh of delight, forswearing all human contact. I took the woman to the doctor yesterday and find she has either a tumor or, more likely, a cancer, and operative work is necessary at once. Humanitarianism requires my seeing her through, but leaves unsolved all over again the question as to who shall do the manual labor while I write. It will all work out in the end, but I shall go mad if I can't soon have peace in which to do concentrated work.

Scott Fitzgerald told me that Hamilton Basso[5] was a charming person. His "Cinnamon Seed," which you sent me at time of publication, infuriated me. There is a taint in his viewpoint which I haven't quite analyzed, but he does write well. I had the feeling in the "Cinnamon Seed," of a good picture's being under a dirty blanket. The thing was definitely *muffled* and a little soiled.

I hope to have better news when next I write.

Marjorie

1. A book by Wythe Williams (New York, 1937).

2. Thomas J. Watson (1874–1956), president of International Business Machines.

3. Lord David Davies, British industrialist and Liberal member of Parliament (1880–1944).

4. A friend from college.

5. Hamilton Basso, American novelist and biographer (1904–64).

51. To Ida M. Tarrant

[Cross Creek]
Friday
[March 12, 1937]

Dear Aunt Ida [in Ocala, Florida]:—

I may see you before you get this note—

I had told Mary[1] I would take her to Fairfield tomorrow, Saturday, to spend the afternoon and evening at her father's. If this goes through, (if you don't see me today), rather, I'll pick you up Saturday afternoon and we can do our marketing together then have supper together. If it's a nice evening we might drive some pretty place & have supper.

Why I say you may see me today is that crazy Mary just started for the front gate & asked me the name of my neighbor who owns the cow we're milking. I told her, & asked her what she wanted of him. She said, "I want him to take me home." I said, "Don't you dare go to my neighbors for anything. I'll take you home any time you want to go. What's the matter?" She said "Nothing. I just want to go home." I said "To stay?" She said "Yes." I said, "You can pack your things any time you're ready to go. I don't want anybody working for me who doesn't want to work for me."

She is getting dinner now, perfectly quiet, so don't know what will come of it. No reason at all. Work all caught up, no company, nothing.

She is really crazy as a bed-bug. The next move is up to her. If she does pack to go, I'll just have to take her. In that case, I'll come on to Ocala today. If it blows over, I'll be in tomorrow (Saturday) afternoon.

Lots of love

Marjorie

1. MKR's maid.

---

52. *To Maxwell E. Perkins*

[Cross Creek
March 1937]

Dear Max:

I had a sheet of paper in the typewriter ready to finish a paragraph, when your welcome letter came. I was beginning to have visions of Hemingway's dragging you about, packing cartridges and guns and bandages. I am glad you are reconciled to his going. It is one of those inevitable things, and, death for him, or no, is somehow right. I only hope for myself that if I ever become too firmly entrenched in a meaningless safety, that something as fatal and as luminous will drag me out.

I am one of your duties, you know, Max, and you really must write to me at least every couple of weeks. Sometimes a letter from you is the only thing that bucks me up. When everything else fails, I can know that it really matters to you whether or not I get a piece of work done, and how well.

I had to discard everything of "The Yearling"—which we may call it for the time being—back to the first chapter. I had to go a little farther back, to give it cohesion. My first thought had been to plunge into more or less exciting events. Then I realized that they were not exciting unless the boy, and his father, and his surroundings, were so real, so familiar, that the things that happened to him took on color because it all came close home, in its very familiarity. Just as the Louisville flood meant nothing to me until I found that the factory and beautiful home of my dearest friends were under water, and I was unable to contact them. The whole sweep of water and devastation became at once a true and unbearable thing. That is perhaps the whole secret of fiction. When the people written about move in reality before our eyes, touch us, then anything they do becomes vivid and important.

I shall perhaps send you a few chapters after a while, just to give you the flavor of the book. It is terribly slow going. The worst of my interruptions are behind me, but even with all my time and energy given to it, it goes slowly for the very reason that I have to visualize, to feel, with great clarity, every moment, allowing no looseness, no unawareness, in order to show the boy's world through the sensitive medium of adolescent being. If it is not dull, or of too limited an interest, I still think it may be something beautiful and moving.

You didn't send me an address where I might reach Scott Fitzgerald with the book I promised him, Granberry's "The Erl King."[1]

Thanks for writing.

Marjorie

1. A novel by Edwin Granberry (New York, 1930).

53. To F. Scott Fitzgerald

Cross Creek
Hawthorne, Florida
[March 1937]

Dear Scott:

How are you? I decided not to send you Granberry's "The Erl King" because you wouldn't like it.

I've had a fiendish winter, entertaining people I loved dearly— my brother from Seattle—friends from the Louisville flood— but who stopped short—in completely delightful fashion—the work that was going smoothly in the mountains. When anything is bursting to be done, interruptions make you seethe. I curse every car that stops at my gate. I begin to loathe the human face and voice. I shall probably go to the Bahamas for two weeks at the end of April, with Bill [Mrs. Oliver] Grinnell, because I am homesick for sea and islands—and I shall suffer the torments of the damned until I get back again. God, I wish I were beautiful and dumb!

Here's a laugh for you—

My agent, Carl Brandt, wired me the other day that Cosmopolitan was in straits for a serial and insisted on seeing what I had done on the book—which I had assured Carl was unsuitable for them. I wired back there was no use in anyone's looking at the manuscript—the story was about a twelve-year-old boy in the scrub—there was no love interest. In desperation I finished, "All women characters past the menopause."

The telegraph operator at the village station adjusted his spectacles and began to count the words. "—47. 48—now this word here—." I thought, "Of course. Damn the Western Union."

"This word here—menopause. Is that all one word?"

Let me know some day how things are going with you. I really liked you.

Marjorie K.R.

In early summer MKR took a nearly completed manuscript of *The Yearling* to New York for Max Perkins to look over. She stayed out on Long Island at the estate of a wealthy socialite friend, Mrs. Oliver Grinnell (see letter 40, June 18, 1936). Since Thomas Wolfe was also in New York City at this time, Perkins took the opportunity to bring his two authors together for an extended evening of drinks, dinner, and talk, which ended with an early-morning visit to the Fulton Street fish and vegetable markets.

54. To Maxwell E. Perkins

[Bayshore, Long Island]
Sunday
[June 20, 1937]

Dear Max:

When you do your memoirs, I should suggest for title, "The Perils of an Editor; or Days and Nights with the Authors." And I hope a brief chapter will include Tom Wolfe plowing his way among the vegetables in a drizzle of rain at four o'clock in the morning, while you and I followed like pieces broken off from a meteor in transit. I shouldn't have started the argument about suicide in the Chinese dive if I'd known he would take it so personally! I have always found suicide a delightful abstraction for discussion, but when I found that he thought I was urging him to do it, and refused at the top of his lungs, "even to satisfy his publishers," I wished I had argued about something simple, like transcendentalism. But it was grand, and I wouldn't have missed it. I should love to feed him some time. If I go to North Carolina, and you go down to see him, I'll drive over to his cabin and cook you both a Ritz dinner.

The outlook for work here is not, at the moment, promising. I can work here as far as adaptation and surroundings are concerned. I am writing now in my room, isolated in the center of the house, overlooking a broad lawn full of flowers and birds, with seven miles of blue bay beyond, and Fire Island just visible across it. But in spite of Mrs. Grinnell's earnest intention to do for me exactly what I may need or want, her social demands are impinging. Her friends are finding that she is at home, and my hope that she would go ahead and play with them and leave me to work, is fading a bit. As a guest, I am helpless. But I'll keep an open mind a few more days. I should love to stay awhile, but I dare not stop the work too long.

Mrs. Grinnell will come in for cocktails with us anytime, as desired, but she has an alternative suggestion, an invitation which seems infinitely more pleasant to me, and I'm hoping that it will to you. She wishes me to ask you to come out here for a brief respite from heat and confusion, either during the day, or to stay over-night. I told her I didn't think it would make you happy to stay away over-night, and she said I must never take too much for granted what would make anyone else happy or unhappy.

Her place is huge and old-fashioned, the house itself not artistic, but solid ease and freedom, with acres of grounds and gardens. There would of course be no one else here while you were here. There are two morning trains leaving the Pennsylvania Station at 10:30 and at 11:30, getting into Babylon, where her car and chauffeur would meet you, an hour later. There are trains returning to New York in the afternoon at 4:56, at 5:49 and about every hour through the evening. Mrs. Grinnell thinks it might be most comfortable for you to come in the afternoon, giving you practically your whole day for work, taking, say, a train from Pa. Station at 3:45 P.M. or 4:47, having dinner and the evening here—which is very beautiful on the water—and taking any of the many convenient trains back in the morning. But if you will come, it is entirely up to you to say what time appeals to you.

Will you drop me a note or 'phone me?

A long wire from a most considerate friend at home informs me that everything is all right there, including the live stock.

Selfishly, I hope you will accept Mrs. Grinnell's invitation. But don't come if you don't really want to. I can give you enough misery with a manuscript, without making you go places and do things you don't want to. I have an infinite capacity for abnegation.

Marjorie

phone 766

55. *To Ida M. Tarrant*

122 S. Penataquit Ave.
Bayshore, Long Island
Wednesday
[June 23, 1937]

Dearest Aunt Ida:

Your good and welcome letter received this morning. That air-mail certainly makes good connections, doesn't it? The Langes must have been thinking of me, or I of them, for I was writing her a note the very day they came to see you. I didn't want the poor little thing to think I had forgotten her entirely. I wanted to give them your new address, too, but they evidently already had it. I read your letter to Mrs. Grinnell and we had a good laugh together over the picture you drew of the Major blossoming like the rose after his beer. I hope you and Mrs. Grinnell can meet some day. She said she knew from your letter she'd like you.

Yesterday we had a delightful time in New York City, and I was able to do a little something for her, for a change. She hasn't allowed me to so much as pay for a movie. She will probably have a book about the fishing at Bimini some day, and I realized she would like a contact with the Scribner people. So I took the president, Charles Scribner, and her to lunch together at the Ritz. What a swank! We dolled up in our best and her chauffeur drove us in. She put on a fistful of diamonds which she doesn't usually wear, and when she said to the chauffeur, "To the Ritz," I thought, like the nigger, "Do, Jesus!"

Don't ask me what my bill was——. Then in the afternoon I had my editor, Max Perkins, and a newspaper man friend of mine [Ernest L. Meyer], to cocktails at Chatham Walk to meet her. She was very much pleased to meet all of them and I was glad there was something I could do for her on her own territory.

I have worked hard today and got quite a bit done on the book. Mr. Perkins told her to keep me if she could, that he thought I needed the change. I shall really try to get some work done, but I'll tell you frankly, I put in several days just lately being ridiculously homesick! I felt better when I got your letter. I have been missing you terribly. I certainly am perverse.

Tonight we are going out to dinner with friends of hers, and tomorrow night in to New York to the famous French Casino. She told Mr. Perkins she had deliberately kept me occupied with social things for two weeks, but now was trying to leave my days clear for work, with something pleasant doing at night.

I am so glad the little house is working out all right. Don't keep anything from me if anything is not right, though. I miss Pat, too, and hate to think of him in the kennels.

Norton [Baskin][1] scribbled a note on the back of your letter—said he was going to Washington and New York, leaving Florida on the 2d. Would I still be here. I don't know, but probably will. Mrs. Grinnell said to invite him out. I'll write him as soon as I know my own plans.

Keep me posted, because I do worry about you lots. Lots of love

Marjorie

1. MKR and Norton Baskin were married four years later.

56. To Maxwell E. Perkins

Cross Creek
August 22, 1937

Dear Max:

I was tempted to wire you "You have my sympathy in your great sorrow," but I was afraid it might not, at the moment, strike you funny. It seems to me the honors are all Eastman's.[1] Hemingway very definitely proved Eastman's contention. I have found that all truly big people are gentle, because they can

afford to be. I know how you must have hated being mixed up
in it.

Mrs. Grinnell sent me clippings on the fracas, with this amusing and trenchant comment:

"There are many more versions, but these mention your beloved Max.

Does he have a time with his men and women? He DO. First
he takes a woman off the streets in the early morning to the
quiet sanctity of his home—then he has to separate two beef-
eating bulls to decide if the hair on the chests is genuine or
false—and incidentally to raise in my childish mind the question of what constitutes manliness. I never would have dreamed
of asking any gentleman to show me the hair on his chest before I labeled him as a man and a gentleman. Well, all this
comes of being old-fashioned and not keeping up with the speed
of the world. I am to meet a gentleman from Washington tonight whom I have admired greatly—but I will have nothing to
do with him until he shows me whether or not he has hair on
his chest. I will NOT be behind the times."

My silence does not mean that I am not progressing. The
work, by the grace of God, has gone forward with a slow steadiness in spite of many obstacles. I found the grove in good shape, everything as it should be. The book will be finished by the middle
of September. I think two weeks will do for revision. There
will be very little editing necessary on the new portion. I have
swung back into the tone for which I aimed. If the POST does not
take it—and no one else would want it—we can count on winter publication—possibly we can anyway.

Marjorie

1. A reference to the notorious fisticuffs in Max Perkins' office between Hemingway and author-critic Max Eastman.

57. *To Edith Tigert* [*in Gainesville*]

Hawthorne
Wednesday
[October 1937]

My dear:

Thanks so much for your note. I'm not drowned, but have
been a bit jittery in spite of myself, thanks to just too many

snakes. Had a close call twice from cottonmouths, one right by my front steps. Got so every stick looked like a snake. Came back to the porch yesterday from going over my young grove, checking up on aphis and what-not. Saw this thing by my table. Said to myself, "Now you just stop this monkey-business. Go and pick up that stick." And by God, it was a snake. Just an oak snake, but you really don't want them in your lap.

Would love to knock off work, but am so close to the end that the only answer is to keep at it. The book is running much longer than I expected. I reached on schedule the number of pages that I thought would have covered the tale, and found I wasn't anywhere near the end. My beloved editor wrote, "You will have at least one reader who will not object no matter how long it is."

I haven't been in because I'm not fit human company. And I'm so exhausted by night that I've been going to bed about 7. I make myself take a four-mile walk at the end of the day, and between punishing my thin brain and my fat body, have nothing left by sunset but a swell set of cuss-words.

Dave Newell[1] is flying out to join Arthur [Kinnan] in Alaska Oct. 18. How I'd love to go. Arthur thinks there is a real future in building up a system of guided hunting and fishing expeditions up there. He is using his own small yacht and has a 100-foot yacht under charter as well. He'll probably end up with a million, if he'll quit marrying.

Mr. Ransom's[2] comment on the books was disagreeably patronizing—as he meant it to be. To say that he admired them as regional or local color novels, was to deny them all merit on any other counts. If I thought my stuff didn't have something more than local color, I'd stop writing. I have no very high opinion of my own things, and could crack down on them with more violent criticism than anyone has ever made—from angles no one has ever mentioned!—but each piece does have something definite to say, that could have been said against any of several other backgrounds. *South Moon Under* of course comes closest to being what is called, I believe, a genre novel, but even there I was saying—as Doctor John [Tigert] recognized— that man is at the mercy of invisible forces. The people in that particular book faced their destiny in their particular way, which happened to be an unusual and primitive and very courageous one, and the setting certainly was most important. But the same sort of story could have been laid in other locales, and stands on its own feet as a story, with living characters.

If I were interested, as I may be some day, in doing a "social" novel, I should show urban people swept along by the same invisible forces, but facing them hysterically and with little understanding and often with little courage. That does not much appeal to me as a subject, because I hate ugliness and cowardice.

I had a praying mantis for Miss Mary,[3] but it died. It was a wicked creature. It bit me and was the most pugnacious thing I've ever seen. But I'm sorry it died, for they are interesting to study.

My dear, could you—would you—get me a copy of that wonderful Florida bird book that the University put out? They are scarce and it may be hard to wangle one. They'd *have* to give you one. I need it now both because so many strange birds are visiting here, and because I need to check on several birds that I mention in the book I'm working on. I think they charge 75¢ for it, because it must have been very expensive to print. This would be a huge favor, as I cannot leave during the day to come in about it. I slave until 5:30 or 6 every day and live on food from Citra.

Love to all,

Marjorie

1. A journalist and artist.
2. John Crowe Ransom, American educator and poet (1888–1974).
3. Edith Tigert's mother.

Early December of 1937 saw *The Yearling* manuscript completed and sent off for Perkins' reaction. In a couple of weeks he sent MKR an enthusiastic response, telling her that he was ordering a larger format than usual for the book to give it a distinctive appearance and was commissioning Edward Shenton, one of Scribner's preferred artists, to do the illustrations.

58. To Maxwell E. Perkins

Hawthorne, Florida
December 29, 1937

Dear Max:

The overwhelming relief of your liking the book [*The Year-ling*]— —. And with no criticism that involves re-arrangement. The liberation is so great that my habitual winter catastrophes seem entirely trivial.

I am delighted that [Edward] Shenton is to do head pieces. His stuff will have exactly the quality that I meant to express. I hope he will do the cover, too. The jackets of the other two books made me very unhappy. I should like to have the boy and the yearling deer side by side, the boy's arm across the young deer's neck, the two looking out with the same expression of big-eyed wonder, and behind or over them the type of vegetation, of forest, that Shenton does so beautifully. Perhaps only a magnolia tree, with its big stiff leaves, rather stylized. I think this type of illustration for cover would in itself illuminate the title. It would certainly indicate at least that the yearling in question was a yearling deer and not a yearling bull, as might be otherwise supposed. And the connotation might register that the boy was a yearling, too. It seems to me too that black and white, or black and white with, somehow, a luminous April green, would be effective. I know I am supposed to have nothing to say about this angle of it, but I did suffer over the other jackets. And I can see so plainly what Shenton could do. I had meant to beg that either Shenton or the wood-cut artist, J.J. Lankes, do such a cover. And Shenton has a certain mystic quality that would be revelatory. . . .

My feeling about the hunting incidents is that their inclusion or elimination should be determined solely by the answer to the question: Does the reader recognize the beginning of another hunting episode with pleasurable anticipation, or is he bored at thought of another, and impatient to be on with the narrative? Everyone's reaction would not be the same, and we can ask that question of the several people who have already read the manuscript.

I have not heard yet from Carl [Brandt] about the Post's

reaction. But that needn't slow us up in any way, however it comes out.

I have waited to see whether the POST was interested, to ask for an advance, because if money should come in that way, I prefer to let royalty payments all come later. But I actually cannot get along without money more than another week. I had picked and sold not much more than a hundred dollars' worth of my citrus—and my crop was short this year, too—when that vicious freeze came in. I fired my young grove two nights in succession. It was very beautiful. There was a fat-wood bonfire in the center of each square, that is, one fire to each four trees. The light from the fat pine is a rich orange, and the grove seemed to be full of bivouac fires, as regular as a geometric design. They illuminated the sky to a Prussian blue, with the palm tops against it. Facing away from the fires, the light gave my low rambling house, the orange trees and palms around it, a flat silver-gold wash, most theatrical. The cold sky was absolutely sequined with stars. It was so beautiful that it was almost worth what it cost me. Then the next two nights I was ready to fire, but at four in the morning knew I did not have to. I was up with my crew of nine men the four nights. I kept them in food and coffee and liquor, and two of the boys sang almost all night long. I saved the young grove, raising the temperature from three to seven degrees. At first all of us in this section thought our mature fruit was not injured to speak of, but as the days passed, the damage became increasingly obvious, and just before Christmas the inspectors condemned carloads of fruit, including some of mine, and inspection is now very rigid. It is hoped that within a week or two the frozen fruit will rot and fall from the trees, and the good fruit be left on for profitable picking. But sometimes it all clings tenaciously, and there is no way to ascertain the damage without cutting the individual orange. So the winter funds that I had counted on drifted into that cold night air— and the Golden Apples money has long since gone with the wind! Finances don't worry me much any more, but I must have money within a week. We can wait and see about the POST a few days, then if there is no sale—and I almost wish there won't be—I must have an advance, much as I dislike it. I actually need a thousand dollars, for I have notes of eight hundred to be met, and a few other bills. And since I have no money to go on just now, I really should have fifteen hundred. My fruit salvage at best will not be more than two or three hundred dollars.

All kinds of small unexpected expenses have popped up. A transient worker split his foot open with an axe while cutting wood for me, and since he had nothing, and I could not let him die, and since he had lost so much blood by the time they got him to me, and I was afraid of the time it would take to get him entered as a charity case at the hospital, I simply took him to my own doctor for the necessary surgery, X-rays and dressings, and have paid the bills myself. This sort of thing does not bother me, for I have increasingly the feeling that nothing tangible belongs to us. I have supported, with work and assistance, several poor neighbors, all summer and fall, people who are too proud to go on relief and anxious to work, and it seems to me that it doesn't make a scrap of difference whether the few hundred dollars involved are in my pocket or theirs.

There will be a chapter on the freeze in the grove, and the firing, in the book I shall do some day, CROSS CREEK: A CHRONI-CLE. I have accumulated quite a few chapters. I write up things from time to time with that in mind. But that will be several years away.

The freeze is why I sent you grapefruit instead of oranges. With their thick skins, they are not injured by our cold. And oddly, here and there tangerines, for all their delicacy, were not hurt.

I have a more hopeless feeling about Fitzgerald since his story recently in *Esquire*,[1] about himself, of course, and the bitter refusal of his publisher to think he is done for. He seems sunk in subjectivity. Egoism, rather. His very laughing at himself is unhealthy.

Thank you for your good letters. Yes, the book did take a prodigious effort, and I can't understand it, for I knew just what I wanted to do and where I was going. But I thought I should never get it out. Toward the end, I was a little insane. But I feel marvelously now in every way. It seemed a waste of time at the moment, but I believe that going to New York when I did, and making a fresh start, was a life saver.

Marjorie

1. See letter 47, note 2, October 26, 1936.

59. To Maxwell E. Perkins

Hawthorne, Florida
January 23, 1938

Dear Max:

I have finished corrections on the proofs, and now I am going back over them again with as cold an eye as possible, to eliminate as much as I can of the flaccid quality to which you and I are both so sensitive. Isn't it odd that a writer can put down things that he would not tolerate in another's writings?

But in reading the whole thing as a unit, I realize that the quality, almost an indefinable one, is pervasive of the complete book, for the reason that that quality was actually a salient ingredient in my own feeling. And to a certain degree, I intended that quality, and meant to do it that way. What actually happened was that the boy became a very real boy, and less of a symbol of the transition from childhood into manhood, which was the thing I wanted to express. The first chapter, which is idyllic, is keyed as I intended, originally, to key the whole thing. I was disturbed when I found the boy becoming so actual, fearing disharmony. Whether the quality of actuality is more valuable than the idyllic quality, is perhaps a debatable question. But I do see the story, within myself, poetically, and I am afraid there is no getting away from it, even when there is too much of it. But there are many places which need a greater stiffness, and I shall supply it whenever I can.

Oddly, the two spots that you pointed out, at my request, I intended humorously, especially the boy's saying that his mother was "purtiest" with a dish in her hand because I meant to portray her as anything in the world but a pretty woman! I never intended him to think she was pretty. But if the effect is

as it was on you, that settles it. Out it goes. But I was amazed
to have you pick out what I meant facetiously, as instances of
the thing we are agreed should be eliminated.

I shall have to take an extra day, too, to go to see the old
hunter, the only one alive of the two old men who gave me so
much valuable hunting lore, to check two or three technical
matters.

Unfortunately, I have to take Tuesday off to go to St. Petersburg, where I am giving a short talk at the meeting of the
Florida Historical Society on the use of Florida historical material for creative writers. I felt obligated to accept the invitation, as I expect to use the Society ruthlessly in gathering material, if I do the book I have in mind.[1]

But I can promise to have the complete set of proofs in your
hands next Monday morning, January 31. Would it be of much
advantage to have me send on the galleys as I go over them
again? Because of my trip to see the old hunter, only a couple of
days would be saved.

I have no new photographs, but will try to have something
taken in St. Petersburg. I never got around to having any done
in New York. Why plaster a woman's face over very much of
the advertising, anyway? It's not that I'm modest, probably the
opposite, for I like to think that my work is more attractive
than my face—certainly than my figure. So few writers express
in their faces the best of their work.

I can't emphasize too strongly the necessity of the jacket's
revealing the meaning of the title. Once the book has been read,
there's no question but that "The Yearling" expresses it exactly, and with a desirable over-tone. But beforehand, it doesn't
register any too well, I'm sorry to say. One man, an English
professor, who inquired the title, asked if I wasn't afraid it would
seem to indicate a yearling bull, which people think of first.

Shall I see the Shenton drawings? I can't help wondering
what he will do about suggesting the type of vegetation, which
is so peculiar to the section. And since I have been at great
pains to be accurate about physical details, any foliage or trees
used, as Shenton uses them so beautifully, should certainly be
true to the locale. He may know Florida, but it is different in
different regions, and the vegetation of the scrub is like nothing

anywhere. I can't help feeling uneasy, on that account only.

Marjorie

1. The Zephaniah Kingsley story.

60. To Maxwell E. Perkins

Hawthorne, Florida
Feb. 6, 1938

Dear Max:

I cannot understand your not having received the last galley proofs by Friday noon. They went out Thursday afternoon air-mail special delivery on a train that connects easily with the N.Y. mail plane that gets into New York at 8 the following morning. If you do not have them, wire me at once.

The Shenton drawings are very lovely. I like particularly the heading for the second chapter, and the one showing Ma Forrester among her sons. Jody looks too dainty for my conception, and of course the sink-hole isn't quite right, but it would be impossible for Rembrandt or Corot to please me completely without having seen the country, which is too unique to be done from the imagination, or from any second-hand knowledge. But I am sure no one but myself could find any serious fault. The deer, somehow, doesn't look like a Florida deer. The ears and tail aren't right.

But the quality of the drawings is everything exquisite. Certainly it is better to have them so beautiful, than to have mere factual sketches. I can only wish Shenton could have come down. He could have made the trip itself for $50 to $75, and then been my guest. He would be immensely stirred by places I could have showed him. However, nothing is too seriously wrong.

The jacket sounds fine, if the fawn is recognizable as such.

The flamingoes are far-fetched as even before they became almost extinct in Florida in a wild state, they nested in the Bahamas and only came to the southern part of Florida in the summers to feed. However, ornithological reports record the killing of a flamingo in Volusia County (the county of the book) in 1876, so if anybody in Florida complains, there is a comeback. White herons or white ibises (curlews) would have been better. I know you think I'm needlessly fussy about my use of fact in fiction, but after all, nobody would put a Baltimore oriole in a drawing of Alaska. And while the book is (we hope) literature, and straight fiction, the details and the setting are true, as I think they should be. The Florida Historical Society has put both my other books in their library, which is amusing when you remember the howl first made of my "libelling" Florida when "Cracker Chidlings" appeared.

I left an unraveled end in Grandma Hutto's admirer, Easy Ozell, and am enclosing a brief insert to take care of him.

I have formed what I hope is a real friendship with Robert Frost and his family. They are in Gainesville for the winter. I spent the day with them yesterday, and I was shocked, as he had been, at the news that Thomas Wolfe went to Harper's for a large advance. No wonder you thought me capable of coming to New York and not coming near you! I didn't realize how truly I spoke when I snapped at you that you must have known some very strange authors. Robert Frost and I both take it as a very menacing sign for Wolfe himself.

No advance could make up for losing you as an editor and critic. Then the damned advance has to be earned, and that's like paying for a dead horse. I did hate to have to ask for one, myself, for that reason. And after all Wolfe owes you——. His artistic future certainly hangs in a perilous balance.

The weather is heavenly, the orange trees just coming into bloom, and the yellow jessamine all over the woods, red-birds singing——. I'll be glad when the book is really out of the way and I can get on the lakes and rivers and in the woods, with a free mind.

I do think the physical make-up of the book is very impressive.

Marjorie

61. To Edward Shenton

[Cross Creek
May 1938]

Dear Edward Shenton,

I meant long before I met you, to tell you directly how happy I have been over your drawings for "The Yearling." They prove how profoundly the spiritual and emotional quality transcends fact. I should not have believed that the feeling of the Fla. country could ever have been conveyed by one who had not seen it. I really think that the good sales of the book owe an enormous am't to your appealing characterizations. Jody became increasingly the Jody I had in mind as the chapter drawings progressed. I loved particularly Penny & Ora riding into the wilderness, Ma Forrester lost among her sons and Jody cajoling his implacable mother.

I can't begin to thank you for the loveliness you contributed.

If you ever come to Florida let me show you that country.

Aren't literary teas awful? There were 2 or 3 of you there (actually it was a very delightful affair) whom I should have liked to have dragged off and really talked to.

Cordially & gratefully,

[MKR]

62. *To Maxwell E. Perkins*

Hawthorne, Florida
May 14, 1938

Dear Max:

My secret fear about "The Yearling" has just been allayed. I was so afraid the old-guard hunters and woodsmen would find flaws. I know you think I put too much emphasis on the importance of fact in fiction, but it seems to me that this type of work is not valid if the nature lore behind it is not scientifically true in every detail. I saw a letter to the old man who told me so much, from the hunter who was with us on several of our hunts and prowls, and who knows his lore backward and forward. He wrote the old man that the book was a masterpiece, and that he not only read it but studied it. He said it made him so hungry for the scrub that he was ready to throw over his job and get back to it; that he could almost see old Slewfoot's tracks beside the branch. So now everything's all right.

People's response to the book amazes me. I am getting the most wonderful and touching letters. Readers themselves, I think, contribute to a book. They add their own imaginations, and it is as though the writer only gave them something to work

on, and they did the rest. It is fine to have the book stirring
as many people as it seems to, but as I wrote Whitney, the so-
called "success" seems to have nothing to do with me.

I haven't been able to get down to work yet. I was really tired
at the end of my trip.

That was really noble of Mrs. Boyd to write to the *Nation* so
forcefully. I want to write her. I don't know when I have liked a
couple as much as I did the Boyds.[1] I almost stopped off in
Southern Pines on my way up, to call on them, but was afraid it
might seem an intrusion.

I was tempted to jump on Lewis Gannett for questioning
my *provable* nature incidents in his otherwise very generous
review, but I don't think a writer ever gets anywhere with any
sort of protest, no matter how right he is. It's a different matter when someone else does it, like Mrs. Boyd.

I'm glad the Hemingway play is good, and that he seems to be
maturing. If someone could only wash out his mouth with
soap, now, he might become the truly adult artist he should be.
If he only knew the real he-men who object to his little-boy-
dirtiness. Of course he is an adult artist, a magnificent artist,
but he has that funny defensive, arrogant quirk, that expresses
itself in a completely unoriginal and puerile offensiveness.

Mrs. Grinnell is in Bimini on her yacht, and I expect to join
her for a week in June when she cruises the Bahamas in general just for pleasure. I saw a careless fishing article of hers in
some Miami publication, and she really writes awfully well. If
she will ever do something about fishing, or Bahaman lore, it
ought to be worthwhile. The Bahamas tempt me, too, as material. The poor people on some of the islands are up against
the same primitive struggle as the scrub people, except that the
sea and the wind are the adversary, instead of the land. I like
to see people bucking something solid, instead of their own
neuroses. Of course, neuroses have become something to reckon
with——. I suppose it is too late for humans to turn back to
the basic simplicities, the soil, the prehistoric struggle for food,
and so forth. The answer is probably an advance outward, toward a cosmic perception, so that on the ultimate day when the
earth burns out, or freezes solid, there will be a natural mi-

gration to some other planet, and some way of life more psychic, more electrical, than our unsatisfactory dependence on the physical.

I want to write Louise[2] a very nice letter soon. She is very sweet and a little pathetic, and I understand her. You are so much wiser than she—you must not be intolerant. The Catholic Matter will probably fade away. I don't mean to be presumptuous in speaking so. But you know that.

Marjorie

1. James L. Boyd, American novelist and essayist (1888–1944).
2. Max Perkins' wife.

63. *To Townes R. Leigh*

Hawthorne, Florida
May 20, 1938

Copies to DR. TIGERT
and to DR. LYONS

Townes R. Leigh
Dean, College of Arts and Sciences
University of Florida
My dear Dean Leigh:

I am profoundly shocked by your communication of May 17, informing me that salaries "recommended" for teachers for the 1938 Summer Session are subject to "scaling down" if the income from fees proves less than "estimated."

I most certainly refuse the position proffered me "under the conditions as stated above."

I have associated myself with the Department of English at figures that are a fraction of what I should ask anywhere except the University of Florida, out of personal friendship for Doctor John Tigert and Dr. Clifford Lyons.[1] But I cannot be a party to so shady and unjust a proposition, as that teachers should be subject to salary cutting according to the enrollment. Such a thing might be conceivable at a private institution, but all public institutions within my knowledge make an honorable guarantee of fixed salaries, and any deficit within those institutions is borne by them, and not by the employees.

I should recommend such an arrangement to President Roosevelt as an ingenious scheme for balancing the national budget. I can scarcely recommend it to anyone planning to teach at the University of Florida.

The matter is closed as far as I am concerned. But I am wondering, since you say "I am instructed to make clear to you," who is responsible for this evasion of responsibility.

Yours truly,

Marjorie Kinnan Rawlings

1. Chairman of the English department at the University of Florida.

64. To H.L. Nevin

Cross Creek
Hawthorne, Florida
May 30, 1938

My dear Mr. Nevin:

How good of the Juniper Club[1] to write me about "The Yearling," and so generously. I trembled in my boots for fear the old-guard hunters would find too many flaws. I'd rather please the people who know that life and section, than all the New York critics rolled together.

It will be fun to come to dinner with you at the Club next winter.

No, I kept missing Mel Long, and don't know him, but I'm doubly sorry, if he is that much like Penny Baxter. I knew Cal Long, and lived a while with him and his wife about five years ago, before his death. "Baxter's Island" is of course his clearing, geographically. Old Cal was rich in stories and in lore. So is old Barney Dillard, at Astor. And the boy Jody is something of a composite picture of a boy, evoked in my imagination by the memories of these two fine old men.

I'm delighted to have the marked map of the Club territory, which includes so many of the places I used. It's grand country, isn't it? If they'd only keep the damned CCC [Civilian Conservation Corps] out of there——.

I visited your clubhouse with Cal Long years ago, in the

summer season. It will be most pleasant to visit it again with the members present. All my thanks.

Marjorie Kinnan Rawlings

1. A group of Louisville businessmen who owned a large hunting preserve in the Ocala Scrub on the west shore of Lake George.

The Yearling had been published in February 1938 to an immediate and growing fanfare of acclaim. The Book-of-the-Month Club chose the book for its March selection; Carl Brandt, her literary agent, sold movie rights to MGM for $30,000; the book went to the top of the best-seller lists, where it remained for months. MKR was now something of a national celebrity and on the way to becoming rich. Then right in the midst of all this, her chronic physical ailment, diverticulosis, flared up in a severe attack, and she decided to accept the advice of a physician friend to undergo major surgery. Before she went into the hospital, she sent Perkins a somber letter, implicitly bidding him a final farewell and naming her brother, Arthur, as her heir and executor. Fortunately, she was persuaded to seek other medical advice and avoided what might well have been a fatal operation.

65. To Maxwell E. Perkins

Hawthorne, Florida
June 8, 1938

Dear Max:

I'm in for a rather serious operation that may sound like bad news, but that actually should prove to be a fortunate thing, for after a series of X-rays, I have finally run down the source of a condition that has kept me half-sick all my life. To explain it briefly, a section of the lower intestines must be removed. If the surgeon finds no inflammation, he will finish the whole job at the time and I'll be out of the hospital in two weeks. But he thinks it probable that it will be impossible to close things at once, and in the latter case I shall have to be in the hospital between three and four months. My appendectomy six or seven years ago—(you may remember that I was ill when "Cracker Chidlings" came out, and while I lay on my porch, convalescing,

Harry Barnes' mother drove up and down all day, sending word that she was coming in to whip me to death—) took out a perfectly good appendix, just because no doctor had ever found the source of my attacks, and the peritonitis I had at that time proves now to have been caused by the intestinal condition— with which, as a matter of fact, I was born. There is a mass of twenty-five or thirty diverticulae, they call them. The immediate danger is of a peritonitis that might get out of control. The ultimate danger would be of malignancy setting in.

I go into so much detail so that if I am laid up a long time you will know why.

I sha'n't mind the thing in the least. I shall be in competent hands, and I have so much vitality, with nothing else wrong, that there is no reason for anything but quick and complete recovery. If by chance I should not come out of it, I do wish I could make it clear to you and to everyone else interested in me for whatever reason, that it would be the sort of death that would not matter. Some deaths do matter. The death of a young and promising person, the death of a young mother, seems unjust. The death of one of two devoted lovers, matters. But in my particular case, I have lived so full and rich a life, with so much more than my share of everything, that I feel indebted to life, instead of life's still being indebted to me. The next book that I have in mind is an uncertain proposition, as I have warned you. If I am big enough, I can make something of it. But the material itself is treacherous. The ultimate book, "Cross Creek: A Chronicle," will be a beautiful book, for its substance is both sound and profound. It is the only thing about which I should feel that something was undone.

To be completely practical, for there is no point in being ostrichlike in the face of any possible danger, my brother is my heir and executor. He is Arthur H. Kinnan, 403 Fourth and Pike Bldg., Seattle, Washington. In case of my death, he would go over all my papers, with authority to dispose of them as he wished. But I can assure you that I have nothing that you would want saved. Even the sketches for the "Cross Creek" are in the unpolished form that can be so bad with me, as you know. There is nothing there ready for publication.

I'm going to St. Joseph's Hospital, Tampa. I have every confidence in my surgeon, also a personal friend. A close friend, Norton Baskin, Marion Hotel, Ocala, will have charge of my affairs if I am in for a long siege. If I should not be able to scribble to you, you can get word of me at any time from him. I am not letting my brother know anything, as he leaves tomorrow for his Alaskan trip to make colored films, and there's no point in his being worried about me, when I am more than likely to be dancing on the fourth of July.

I go into the hospital this coming Monday, and [the doctor] will operate on Wednesday the 15th. I'll ask Mr. Baskin to drop you a note toward the end of the week giving you news of me.

I should be able to go ahead with the *South Moon Under* dramatization most comfortably while I convalesce. I can't work on the story I had in mind, as I needed to do some more prowling and go to some backwoods cock fights first.

I'm missing my trip to the Bahamas with Mrs. Grinnell. She wired me last night to join her at once, but of course I couldn't make it.

I'll be glad to have you write me one of your good notes now and then. St. Joseph's Hospital, Tampa, until further notice.

Marjorie

66. To Maxwell E. Perkins

Hawthorne, Florida
June 17, 1938

Dear Max:

Well, I got out of a devil of a mess by the skin of my teeth. I can't be positive of being through with it, but a reprieve is something. The three musketeers who are like brothers to me,[1] got together and practically refused to allow me to go ahead with the operation without a corroborative diagnosis. I put up a fight, for the X-rays looked incontrovertible, and if I don't make up my mind quickly and stick to a decision, I suffer too much in vacillating. But I gave in at the last minute and they took me to Jacksonville, where the head of a fine private hospital, also a friend,[2] put me through everything again.

The diagnosis was confirmed, but three good men there
agreed that operation was the last thing in the world to try, that
it should be done only as a last resort or in an emergency, as
could occur. It seems the mortality for that particular operation
is 40%. Even if it is ever necessary, the Jacksonville man said
there was no one in Florida competent to do it, and that I should
go to Johns Hopkins or to Dr. Abell in Louisville, president of
the American Medical Association. But they believe that a rigid,
though not at all unpleasant diet, will remove the toxic condition, and the danger, and make me feel all right.

The Jacksonville doctor friend said that the Tampa surgeon
had made utterly inadequate preparations. The restricted diet
should come first in any case, and in the second place, my blood
should have been typed and two donors ready the moment the
operation was done, as transfusions are invariably necessary. So
with the mortality so high even when a top-notch man does it,
I can see that the Tampa man was going at it blindly, and the
Jacksonville man was probably right, when he dismissed me
yesterday, saying, "If you'd done it, you'd have been cavorting
with the angels just about now."

So it was really a pretty close call. I wasn't at all afraid, but I
did have the feeling that I probably shouldn't come out of it.

What I regret is getting several of you disturbed about it. I
usually don't speak of difficulties until they are over, but expecting to be laid up so long, at best, there seemed no alternative
but to communicate with you and two or three others who would
have no explanation for my not communicating later. But I
am sorry to have worried anyone. But we can only do what
seems wise at the moment.

Sam Byrd[3] is coming to Florida next week and we will go over
the South Moon Under dramatization plans.

Marjorie

1. Norton Baskin, Cecil Bryant, and Robert Camp.
2. Dr. T.Z. Cason, brother of Zelma Cason, who was later to sue MKR for "invasion of privacy."
3. Sam Byrd, American actor (1908–55).

67. To Maxwell E. Perkins

Hawthorne, Florida
September 21, 1938

Dear Max:

I have grieved for you ever since I heard of Tom's death.[1] I grieve, too, for the certain loss of the work he would unquestionably have done, for his very touching letter to you shows a chastening and mellowing of that great half-mad diffusive ego, that would have been a guarantee of the literary self-discipline we all so wanted for him. It seems that each of us can go only so far in wisdom and in insight, and then for one reason or another we are done. And no one can take up where another leaves off. No one can profit by all that Tom had come to learn, with so much torture to himself and to others. Just as civilizations never learn from other civilizations, but must build up agonizingly, making the same mistakes over and over, with never any *cumulative* progress.

I know how glad you must be that you never withdrew your personal goodness from Tom, even when others were bitter for you.

It is strange that so vibrant and sentient a personality as Tom knew or guessed that he had come to the great wall. He must have felt far beyond most of us that withdrawing of the cosmic force from his individual unit of life. I felt the thing this summer for myself, knowing—and I still know—that if I had done the thing I planned I should not have come through. I felt the reprieve, too, and I am still puzzled. It is like the hurricane scheduled for the Florida coast the other day, that suddenly swerved from its path and swept on elsewhere. It is all accidental and incidental, and yet why is it so often one knows in advance?

I have thought of you a great deal since hearing, and I hope it is something you can accept without too much pain.

Marjorie

1. Thomas Wolfe died September 15, 1938, in Baltimore.

68. To Beatrice H. McNeill

Hawthorne, Florida
Jan. 9, 1939

Dearest Bee:

My dear, I thought I had sent you a copy of The Yearling in April. Since you speak as though you had a copy, by way of novelty I'll send you the English edition. I think it looks very shabby beside our own, and without Shenton's lovely drawings, but I understand the English think our book-jackets very noisy. Besides England, it is being published in Norway, Sweden, Denmark, Poland, Finland, Germany and Italy, and is being pirated in Holland. Margaret Mitchell wrote me that the Dutch firm that stole Gone with the Wind, and whom she is suing in the Dutch courts, had announced the Yearling. Wonder what those furriners will make of the book?

Bee, the square flower-holder is simply stunning. If you could only see my farmhouse, you'd know how perfect any of those green-blue or blue-green shades are in this setting. I've had tiny yellow button chrysanthemums in it, and now short sprays of the red Turk's cap, a relative of the hibiscus. My garden will soon have African daisies, gerberas, schizanthus, snapdragon, pinks, baby's breath, forget-me-nots, pansies, larkspur, fluffy-ruffle petunias, calendulas, Queen Anne's lace, lupin, bachelor buttons so I can use all kinds of combinations in the new vase. I just love it.

We're having a lovely mild winter so far. The red-birds are thick in the yard today.

Somewhat to my distress, Chuck came by to see me a couple of weeks ago on his way to the Gulf Coast for a month or so. He looked just the same, but his face rather lined. Don't know what he's done with his second wife. He was at his mother's cottage outside Rochester all summer without her, and he had only a dog with him as he came through here.

Well, angel, have to go to the city to the hospital to see how my colored hired man is doing—he very carelessly got shot by another darkey. My colored girl had been trying to trap a husband, largely so I would have a man on the place, and she finally landed this one a couple of months ago. His name is

Charles Rawlings, about 1940.

Sampson, so since he got shot naturally we are calling her
Delilah.

All my thanks for the lovely vase—just perfect for me, style
and color—and as always, my love.

Marjorie

MKR's active sense of humor extended at times to the ribald.

69. To Norton S. Baskin

[Cross Creek
Spring 1939]

To Whom It May Concern:

This is to certify that Rear-Admiral Norton K.O. Baskin, B.B., being desirous because of advancing years to devote the remainder of his active life to a broader field of action, is of his own volition withdrawing from the service of her Majesty the Queen. His time of service has been long and arduous, and his efforts noble and unflagging. With no gain or profit to himself, spurred only by an unfailing sense of duty, making untold sacrifices, he has never let the Queen's sheets be furled by any hand but his own. Not even the crashing of bedsteads in the thick of battle has caused him to lower his colors or to drop his flag.

Her Majesty discharges him honorably and reluctantly, and by this document does set him free of the royal will. In commemoration, this day shall be known as Baskin Day, all shorts to be lowered at sunset to half-mast.

In testimonial thereof, we do hereby give our sign and seal.

Signed,

Dora Regina[1]

1. MKR's Jersey cow was named Dora.

Following the great popular success of *The Yearling,* MKR turned to a pleasant task which she had been considering for several years, converting her first novel, *South Moon Under,* into a play. At the University of Wisconsin she had been active in theatrical affairs, acting in several plays and having a hand in the writing of at least one musical, and she had found these activities so congenial that at one time she had seriously considered a career in the theater.

In the fall of 1938 she began active work on the dramatic version of her novel with some enthusiasm, but before she got very far with it she was deflected by other things, among them several severe freezes which posed serious threat to her citrus grove. She also began serious research into the life of Zephaniah Kingsley, an eccentric Florida planter of the early nineteenth century who had taken as his legal wife a full-blooded African princess.

Much in demand now as a speaker, she made a lecture tour through several midwestern cities. In January 1939 she was elected to the National Institute of Arts and Letters, then in May received the Pulitzer Prize for fiction.

70. To Norton S. Baskin

[Cincinnati
May 1939]

Hello, darling:—

We had a good trip, but I was furious to find we missed the mountains! Went through Atlanta at 4:15 p.m. Sunday, and stopped for the night at Blue Ridge, Ga.—500 miles in all!

Headed for Knoxville, thinking of course we got the mountains, but they were just "funny old hills."

By pushing, we made Cincinnati at 11 last night. I had every intention of taking Aunt Ida direct to her friends, but nobody could direct us to what she called "Northside"—nobody knew her section by that name, and she knew no other! It is probably ante-bellum. We wandered through one slum after another and agreed it was hopeless, so I found a good taxi driver who knew her street, and sent her out. Fell into bed at the Gibson [Hotel] more dead than alive. Blew myself to a $4 "single" (reduced from $5 because they have a convention and were out of what I wanted) and the damn room is big enough to have a party in. The Gibson comes close to being the hotel man's dream. My coffee came in an individual glass Dripolator with Sterno heater under it, and a pack of Pall Mall cigarettes "with compliments." But there are no bed lights, and the paint is peeling off the radiator, so Heaven must lie further afield.

Mean to rest and think up what I'll say tonight to a thousand "Christian-hearted sons of bitches," & will pull out for Columbus early in the afternoon. After the affair tonight, will begin to enjoy myself.

Darling, I miss you painfully. I'm not going to ever leave you again. Well, hardly ever. Maybe just often enough to make you glad to see us come home. I despise being away from you. You see, I enjoy you anywhere.

I do love you.

Marjorie

Saw the Pulitzer announcement in my morning paper. I'm glad for Scribner's sake. Publishers get an awful kick out of those things. I really thought I'd already had as much luck as I deserved on one book, and I sort of hate to think how blue the unsuccessful candidates are feeling this morning, when I wouldn't have minded particularly.

71. To Norman Berg¹

Hawthorne, Florida
June 14, 1939

Dear Norman:

It would be a serious mistake for the Hoodlum Club to bow stiffly from the waist, for it would give me too good an opportunity to plant a wallop on its rear.

It would be impossible not to take a certain pleasure in the Pulitzer, but it's also impossible to take any of those things too much to heart. An award over a bunch of mediocre books doesn't mean very much—and where should I have been if The Yearling had come out the same year as Grapes of Wrath? My God, what a book. Of course, it's so much more than just a book. The experience of reading it is a hell of a nuisance for an escapist, for all the social consciousness, and conscience, that you've been ducking for years, rolls over you in an appalling wave. And Steinbeck is the answer to those, and there are many, who have been complaining that our male and virile writers are totally without tenderness. How clean and natural his dirt seems! Hemingway's makes you mad, Faulkner's makes you sick at your stomach, but Steinbeck's is entirely right.

Aunt Ida and I had a good trip, but I was crazy to combine business with pleasure. Things were too hurried and I was under too much tension, though the Derby weekend itself was lots of drunken fun. We went through Atlanta at unreasonable hours both ways, trying to make long-distant objectives and I didn't think it would be fun for anyone to contact you. I hope

Norton and I can get up for a good spree with you. You'd better
work on him. But if we come, I WON'T APPEAR AT ANY BOOK-
STORE!!!!! We come for fun only. There was no Pulitzer dinner, so
I didn't have to go to N.Y.

Marjorie

1. Norman Berg was representative in the Southeast for Macmillan and Co.,
publishers.

72. To Beatrice H. McNeill

Hawthorne, Florida
July 20, 1939

Dearest Bee:

It was just about this time several years ago that I was
setting out for my visit with you. What a swell time we had.
Well, we'll do it again some time. And what about our trip to
Japan?

I'm staying here all summer to get some work done, but am
going over to the Atlantic Ocean at St. Augustine beach for the
month of August, where I mean to combine lots of swimming
with the work. Am taking my pointer dog with me, the best
company in the world. He has a lot more sense than I do, and if
I can teach him to use the typewriter, think maybe I can train
him to write my books for me.

I nearly fell over when I got Sam Wright's wedding announcement. I was sure he was a confirmed bachelor, sipping the
nectar here and there without having to take any responsibility.
Arthur [Kinnan], for some reason, is disgusted with him, said
he was so hopelessly selfish he had lost interest in him. Sam
must have invited him to a twenty dollar dinner and then let
him pay the check!

I finally read "Tortilla Flat," which you urged me to read long
ago, and loved it. Grapes of Wrath, of course, took me off my
feet. It's not only the most important social document of our
time, to my notion, but a beautiful work of art from the literary
standpoint.

The last I heard, MGM planned to go into production on
The Yearling next spring, to get the fawn sequences right. Victor Fleming will direct unless plans change. We hope they

will come here to do the backgrounds, but don't know. They took lots of stills here when their company was doing the new Tarzan picture here—that is, the underwater scenes.

Well, honey, this isn't a very newsy letter but better letter than never! Hope you're feeling all right and not overdoing. I think of you and love you lots.

Marjorie

73. To Ida M. Tarrant

[Crescent Beach]
Thursday
[August 3, 1939]

Dearest Aunt Ida:

. . . I went crabbing yesterday afternoon and got five, more than enough for me, in just a few minutes. They aren't as big and fine as the Salt Springs crabs, but of course the flavor is about as good. The way I crab here is off a private dock on the river where I have permission to go. I take a chunk of raw beef, the riper the better, and tie it to a heavy string long enough to reach the bottom of the river. I hang it down, and I can tell by tugs on it, or by seeing the string move away, that a crab has hold of it. Then I ease the string up very gently, and the crab will hang on tight until he and the meat are almost to the surface of the water. I dip down under him then with a very long crab net with a wire mesh, and scoop him out. The trick is to get the net under him before he is out of the water, when he lets go, and before he is aware of the net. It is very hard to manage it alone. It really needs two people, one to manipulate the crab and string, and the other to get the net under him. I damn near fell in the river several times. Came home and cooked my crabs and had them with fresh mayonnaise, which it took Meade[1] 40 minutes to make, but is the most delicious I ever had. I heard him beating and beating, and knowing that Adrenna[2] often has to make several starts, thought maybe he wasn't getting it, or didn't know how and wouldn't say so. So I called to ask if he was having trouble, and he said No, he was just taking his time.

This morning when Pat[3] and I went for our walk and swim

before breakfast, I came across the most amazing trail. It had come up out of the ocean at high tide, and gone to the foot of a sand dune, made a shallow mound about five feet across, then turned and gone back into the ocean. It looked like the track of a small tractor, about four feet across, and then when I saw a narrow flat trail right in the center of it, I realized that it was the track of a deep sea turtle, one of those huge ones, that had come out of the sea on the full moon to lay its eggs. I dug and dug in the mound, but there were no eggs. I seem to remember that they come out about three times before they actually lay so I shall watch carefully each morning now. The eggs are round, about half the size of a large hen's egg, and are a great delicacy.

Yesterday I finished up the last of my back correspondence— about sixty letters—and am ready for work.

Hope all goes well.

Much love.

Marjorie

1. MKR's handyman.
2. MKR's maid.
3. MKR's pointer.

74. To Norton S. Baskin

[Crescent Beach]
Thursday
[August 10, 1939]

Dear Norton [in Ocala]:

I not only despair of making you understand me, but I have a great embarrassment in attempting it, for it comes to me that you really do understand, and have only pretended to be puzzled, since you didn't see things the way I did, and it is something that is very hard to bring out into the open. When a woman has wanted more of a man than he has wanted of her, it puts him on the spot to talk about it, and is very humiliating for the woman. But I want to try to give you a clear statement, so that at least, if your not understanding has been genuine, you will know the conflict in my mind.

All the time of our close relations, I have not wanted less of you, but more of you. It was dreadful in the early days, when you seemed actually afraid of me, and showed no desire to be with me very often, and came moseying out once a week at eight or nine o'clock at night after you had fooled around with miscellaneous people. I came so close to putting an end to everything, just out self-respect, but something told me you really did care for me and things would work out. Things did work out, to a large extent. We reached a greater understanding and closeness. You came to trust me and to trust my affection for you, which you certainly did not in the beginning. And as time went on, my mere hunch about you, ever since I had known you at all, was verified: that you had a wonderful quality to give a woman, and there could hardly be a more lovable companion.

So: what did I want? Frankly, marriage. You did not. You said once that you did. You said once also that you had nothing to offer me. Let me try to give you my idea of marriage. I am not concerned with the legal or social or ethical aspect of it. It is just that I am convinced that the greatest good can be had of life when a man and a woman who love each other and are happy in each other's company, live it together.

I loathe living alone. I need more solitude, more privacy, than most women, but even I can get all I want in the course of a day. My work does not satisfy me as the end and aim of my life. It is something I have to do, but it does not fill and complete my life. Neither am I satisfied with what might be called weekend love, romantic and charming as it really is. I want the quiet satisfaction of living with a man I enjoy.

I certainly am not appealed to by a very usual type of marriage, where it seems as though the poor man and woman were handcuffed together, and neither could move an inch without the other. Loneliness—and week-end love—are much better than that. But I want the solid base of a joint life.

All right. Where does that put us? First of all—and the thing I resent so deeply, and makes me flare out at you in my ill or drunk unguarded moments—you not only do not want that kind of life, but you have very obviously avoided it. You have a deep and actual horror of it. You have changed a great deal in your feeling about me, and are much closer to feeling about such things as I do, than you used to be. But I think it is very deeply rooted in your nature. All right again. Supposing that in time you came to want the same sort of life I want. Your profession seems to me to make it impossible. I not only could not live the hotel life, but I think there are very few instances where a wife fits in it. When I was younger, I could have adapted myself to a man's life, whatever it was. Now certain aspects of life are as necessary to me as love.

I am torn most of the time between my real love for you, and my desire for a type of man and woman life that I think is impossible for us. If I could accept my loneliness and just go ahead and enjoy you when we are together, as you enjoy such an arrangement, all would be well. If I could make up my mind to break with you entirely and set out on a deliberate and some-how shameful man hunt, I would not be so tormented. But I love you too much and appreciate too much the large measure of happiness that we do have, to be able to do it. Yet our life together is not what I want and it does not complete or satisfy me.

It is poor sportsmanship for me to subject you to my feel-ings, when there seems to be nothing, according to the circum-stances of your profession—which is as right for you as writ-ing is for me—that you can do about it. I made up my mind some time ago that at least while our relationship was close, I would keep my torment to myself. But when my guards go down for one reason or another, I'm not strong enough to do it. I am terribly sorry not to make you easy in mind and entirely happy with me while I'm at it.

Now I have done my very best to be frank, although it em-barrasses me, and to try to make you understand what is back of my apparently meaningless fits. I know that you love me very much in your way. But it makes me feel cold and ugly sometimes when I stop to think that you don't want of me what I wanted of you.

I can't begin to tell you what a cruel thing that was for you not to come to see me Saturday when you could. You had told me that you would not be able to come over for a long time, because of Floyd's[1] going, and it never occurred to me to ques-tion it, when you called me. If you had been here to stop my

damn work for a while, and give me the comfort and release of
your companionship, I don't think I'd have gone down for the
count the way I did Monday. I told Edith I was desperate, so
she and Verle² got a friend and came down Sunday evening to
play bridge.

Now I do hope I have made you understand.

Love,

Marjorie

1. One of Norton Baskin's employees at the Marion Hotel in Ocala.
2. Edith and Verle Pope were St. Augustine friends of MKR.

75. To Norton S. Baskin

[Crescent Beach]
Wednesday morning
bright and early
[September 6, 1939]

Dear Honey:

Was lying on the floor listening to the early war news before going out for a pre-breakfast walk, when I heard a tap on
the door. It was nigger Will and of course I had visions of Cross
Creek in flames, or Adrenna returned with ten men, or what-
have-you. He had a little package for me that Martha¹ had
forgotten to put in the car. It was half a dozen small cheap
napkins——. I could have bought their duplicates in St. Augustine for fifty cents. Counting Will's time, it costs about three
dollars for the truck to make that trip. But the sense of virtue
with which Martha must have dispatched him to bring me the
damn things——. And we are in the midst of the grove fertiliz-
ing and need both truck and Will there——. Have put him at
cutting the grass while I write you, so he can mail it on his way
home.

Drove over in a terrific rainstorm. Could hardly see most
of the time. The rain was actually attacking the cottage—
had driven in under the front door. It was so beautiful over
the river, had to open the door to watch, then run for the mop to

keep from getting flooded. It would have been very cozy and wonderful with you here. It was cozy, actually, but not wonderful——. Your bathing suit, the radio, the two reading lights, and so on, made me very homesick for you. I don't know why, but this seems more your place than Cross Creek.

The weather cleared about seven at night and Pat and I walked to the mile and nine-tenths house and back. The sky and sea were gorgeous—salmon and deep violet. The pools of water on the receding tide were violet. As we got back to the cottage, met the Popes. They visited a while, then we went riding on the beach and Verle cast the cast-net for pompano. He got only mullet but plenty of that and it looks fun. Billions of donax, but I thought, "Well, as Norton says, I don't *have* to gather them."

My clean typewriter fools me—I don't get the usual timing.

Have got my mental kinks straightened out again. Am wondering if salt air is all I need for my aberrations. And thanks for your patience. After spending all your life with sane people (or don't we count the Baskins?) you must wonder how come you now to be hanging on trapezes etc. I insist that I'm good for you. And I know you're good for me.

Realized you probably had planned to go direct to Jacksonville and stop by here on your way back, as you'll be in a hurry to do your business on the way up. My errand doesn't need doing at all—have to do some other things in the neighborhood when I go up the 9th, that no one else could do for me—so don't bother about it. Will hope to see you on your way down again.

Well, will send Will on now. God, when I look at that little package of unneeded napkins——. You know, if the niggers get turned loose, it will be awful, but won't it be funny? Just a little sense is worse than none at all.

Lots of love, my sweet.

Marjorie

1. Will, Adrenna, and Martha were all members of the Mickens family who from time to time worked for MKR and lived in the tenant house at the orange grove in Cross Creek.

76. To Norton S. Baskin

[Crescent Beach]
Thursday
[September 7, 1939]

My dear:

It certainly was good to find a parcel of mail in my box just now. Curtis sandpapered out the "Poole" and I painted "Rawlings" in very droopy-drawers black letters and the postman came across.[1]

Sorry you've been hot—it's been divine here. The cross ventilation here is marvelous. There's always at least one place that's breezy and cool.

Put in an infuriating day yesterday. Was all set for hard work, total abstinence except for one small drink just before dinner at night, a slimming diet, lots of exercise. Had just gotten turned around after Will and the truck left, when he popped up at the door again. The truck had broken a spring about two miles across the river. Had to hustle around and get the garage at Dupont Center to tow the truck in, go to town for a new spring, etc. The truck wasn't done until nearly six o'clock. It discouraged me so that I just collapsed with the bottle, ate like a pig, read two books and wondered if I would ever write another word.

This morning all is well again, have had a walk and a marvelous swim—the water is rough now, but then was flat and smooth on the low tide—and think I can hold my appetite down and my typewriter up.

Am going in to Edith's for supper and female bridge, and I enjoy a day's work when I have something to look forward to at night.

In my mail was an express notice of what is almost certainly Julia's [Scribner][2] rye, though would imagine two bottles weighed more than 5 lbs. Am enclosing the notice, and will write the agent that you will call for the package. Assume you won't mind so pleasant an errand. You may even peek.

Phil May[3] wrote me warning me that I am to be introduced in Jax. by Marcus Fagg, from one of whose addresses to a Baptist Sunday School, Mencken quoted as an incredibly priceless bit of Bible Belt Americana. Afraid I had better not tell Leo-

nard's Christian-hearted sons-of-bitches story——.[4] Though I
may never have a better target——

Tuesday morning I went to the bank and talked with Clyde
Long. Got my information there O.K. and found the postal savings had so little interest difference, so low an amount deposi-
table, so much red tape etc., so just went ahead and opened a
$20,000 savings account at the Commercial. No objection made
to the amount.

Will hope to see you soon.
Lots of love,

Marjorie

Total cost of upkeep on pink napkins (original cost 50¢)
    Cash $14.95
    Total loss—1 temper—1 ambition
    Gain—2 lbs. weight

1. MKR had just purchased an oceanfront cottage at Crescent Beach, Florida, a
few miles south of St. Augustine.
2. Daughter of Charles Scribner (1890–1952), president of Charles Scribner's
Sons.
3. MKR's friend and attorney, who later was to be in charge of her legal defense
in the so-called "Cross Creek Trial."
4. See letter 19, April 1933.

77. To Norton S. Baskin

[Cross Creek]
Friday morning
[October 1939]

My sweet:

   . . . Can't say I've had much rest. Didn't really need but one
night, anyway, and feel pretty good. Found a pile of work waiting for me, including proofs on both the New Yorker and the
long Post stories. The dirt that I thought was bothering the New
Yorker, they left intact and the dirt I thought very funny and
wouldn't disturb them, was out with a vengeance. They had re-
arranged a sequence to eliminate it, and I had to admit it carried just as well as the original. Had some fun with the Post. I
had Quincey Dover say she blazed up higher than the fire in
a Presbyterian hell, and they queried the "Presbyterian," so I

just put: Author's note: Fix the fires of hell to suit the Post's religion.

So far, Jeff[1] and I split 70¢ as the return to date on our squash field. But there has been frost to the north, so we think from now on we will do better. The hard-working creature has cleared a quarter-acre of land ready for the Cornell lettish [lettuce]. If the original Jeff Davis had worked as hard, the South might be free.

It would take some mighty fancy plans to tempt me from home tomorrow.

If you come in time for dinner, you might have lamb croquettes. At three in the morning, however, it will have to be just minced lamb on toast. Not that I'm luring you from your duties—but a choice is always a choice.

Will go in to Aunt Ida's tonight, but won't call you unless I get in very early before you go to your game. Until tomorrow, my love

M.

1. Jefferson Davis, with whom MKR planted truck crops on shares. She provided the land, seed, fertilizer, and tools, and he provided the labor.

78. To Mark Ethridge[1]

Hawthorne, Florida
October 22, 1939

Dear Mark:

I maintain not only that the War Between the States was primarily a conflict between an urban civilization, with the Puritan taint, and an agrarian civilization, but that the conflict still rages. To go directly from Louisville's spiritual warmth, to the cool aloofness of Chicago, was to reach home licking my wounds. Was it Luke Breckenridge in "John Brown's Body" who said he didn't much care which side he fought on, long as the Kelcey's took the other side? I am all ready to oil up my old muzzle-loader, if I can fire the first shot against Chicago. Or, on the other hand, if Louisville ever needs a water-girl—or, more usefully, a gal Ganymede—you can count on my support. I left Louisville feeling like the Queen of Sheba, and crawled out of

Chicago feeling like the lowliest of Sheba's slaves. In contrast to
the *Courier-Journal*'s welcoming box of flowers, corsage, etc.,
Chicago didn't come across with a sprig of mignonette. Instead
of offering the warm hand, extending a cold julep, Chicago
peered from under its Eskimo parka and grunted.

I did have a good time with the audience at Mendel Hall. The
hall was full, and the icy breath that lifted from it was like
the air from a super-size Norge refrigerator. I began the formal
address that I know they expected, as erudite and informative
as my limited wisdom allowed. Then a wave of pity came over
me, and I thought, "Why, you poor frozen bastards, you've had
the living hell educated out of you," and I made my technical
points hurriedly, swapped the bread of information for hyacinths
for the soul, and went to town. When I finished, they applauded generously, but didn't stir. I sat down beside Percy Boynton, the
introducer, and waited for them to leave. They just sat there. I
said to him, "Your customs are very different from what I'm
accustomed to. Do they remain seated until I leave the platform?" He said, "Why, I don't know." So I got up to leave and the
Eskimos clapped their fur-mittened paws together again. He
mopped his forehead, and said, "Why, this is unheard of. They
usually go. Why, they want some more. Please do something."
So I went back to the microphone and talked some more, and
still they sat. I finally told them I wasn't going to tell any more
stories, and they might as well go home. In all seriousness, I
don't believe the University had had a human being on the
lecture platform in the memory of this generation. It was pitiful.
When the president's secretary gave me my check, I said that
I had some personal bills at the Blackstone, and would pay those
myself. She said, "Well, you know we agreed to furnish entertainment." I said, "Honey, you don't know what entertainment
is," and I went back to the Balinese Room at the Blackstone
and got tight all by myself, and charged it to the University of
Chicago, Educational Dept.

All nonsense aside, you spoiled me for any other public
contacts.

I wired my friend who met me in Montgomery, Ala., "Left
Louisville with regret. Leaving Chicago with joy and relief."
When he gathered up my luggage, he said, "But where are the

twins, Joy and Relief? And what have you done with poor little Regret?"

Thanks for everything——

Marjorie

1. Editor of the Louisville *Courier-Journal*.

79. To Ida M. Tarrant

[New York City]
Tuesday 6 P.M.
[November 28, 1939]

Dearest Aunt Ida:

Have kept quite busy and happy yesterday and today, but
came in late this afternoon to the hotel for a rest before going
out to the theatre tonight, and got caught with that twilight
forlornness that we feel without any good reason. Your letter
was waiting for me, and it cheered me right up.

I am indeed ashamed when I allow myself to feel lonely, and
much of the pleasure I would otherwise get from the city is
upset for me by running into obviously poor and unhappy people, and when I pass them in my fur coat, with my stomach full
of expensive food and drink, and my purse full of money, it
seems to me that it is wrong for anyone to have either an *under*-
share or an *over*-share of comfort and security. An old, old
woman selling 5¢ bunches of lavender outside the theatre last
night—not right.

Remind me to tell you of the interesting Thanksgiving sermon
I heard Sunday.

My aunt [Wilmer Kinnan] wants to take me to the very
best of the new shows December 6, the earliest she could get
tickets, so I am staying through the sixth and leaving here the
seventh.

Lots of love,

Marjorie

P.S. It was very cold Saturday and Sunday—Central Park
ponds frozen over—but it warmed up yesterday and is very
pleasant now, just crisp and good, my taxi driver today was slow

in seeing the signal for him, and he said, "It's such a glorious day, I guess I was day-dreaming!"

80. To Norton S. Baskin

St. Moritz
On-the-Park
Fifty Central Park South
New York
Monday morning
[December 11, 1939]

Honey,—

Well, the worst is over, and I think from now on I can come closer to enjoying myself. The National Council affair[1] went off with very little suffering as far as I was concerned. I made my proposition to let them publish the essay and just talk, and they burst into grateful applause, so the officers had nothing to say. They were a grand audience, 2 or 3,000 and I had a good time.

Went alone to Hellzapoppin' Friday night and it was so insufferably lousy that even tho' my seat had cost me $3.30, I walked out on it at intermission. I'd have paid another $3.30 not to be compelled to go back. The woman sitting next to me whispered, "I wish I could go, but I'm with a party and don't know how to get back to my hotel." I heard another woman say, "It's very discouraging to know that the human family would support this for nearly 2 years."

It was the tackiest kind of burlesque, not even enjoyably dirty, and as un-funny as possible. New Yorkers are the biggest *hicks* in the world. They stand in crowds watching a silly electric sign.

I put in a God-awful week-end with Auntie [Wilmer Kinnan]. After the Saturday luncheon, she said, "Now there are two things that will rest you," and I said, "They are both a drink." I had made up my mind I would do anything she wanted except suffer for a drink. She sighed and said, "That would be no. 3 or 4." But I ploughed ahead to a bar and she drank ginger ale in great martyrdom while I had a couple, and it certainly ruins the pleasure to drink with anyone like that.

Then she took me to "The Little Foxes" and it was so swell

I'll wait to tell you about it when I see you. Tallulah is *marvelous*, and the whole cast was grand.

Yesterday was *awful*. Wilmer took me to *church* in the morning (a big new thought church), then to a Health Food restaurant for dinner, vegetarian, where I ate baked potato and steamed broccoli that wasn't done. I thought working on my soul and on my stomach would do for one day, but she had only begun. She took me at night to one of a series of lectures she is attending, and this one was "The Rejuvenation of the Face." It was the damndest *medicine show* I've ever seen perpetrated, a bunch of fake "chemistry" ideas, and then they sold all this trash— "Malanite"—very rare, and they have almost the world's supply cornered—so rare that you get about a half-pound package for a quarter. That is to cleanse the capillaries, I believe. Something

Norton Baskin, about 1940.

else removes wrinkles in one preparation, etc. etc. The audience was the most incredible hags, all looking for miracles—
which were promised them. As a pièce de résistance, they took
an old gal from the audience who was a double for Ma Fiddia,
and made up her face. When they were through, she looked like
a monkey in a pink and white mask.

I did insist on drinks after that, and fell back on Wilmer's
preacher, who had said that while human beings were individu-
alizations of God, that material things were God's thoughts.
So I told Wilmer liquor was one of God's thoughts, and in my
opinion, one of the best ideas He ever had.

She plans to study jiu-jitsu, and thinks I should, too. She said
that if you studied it, "A man simply could not get a grip on
you." I said in that case I didn't want to know even the first
principles.

Lots of love,

Marjorie

1. On December 2, 1939, MKR had addressed the National Council of Teachers
of English on "Southern Literary Regionalism."

81. *To Beatrice H. McNeill*

[Cross Creek]
January 4, 1940

Dearest Bee:

You do think of the loveliest and most unusual things to do.
I am simply enchanted with the Chinese pajamas and got into
them the minute I opened the package. My first glimpse of the
width of the trouser tops was a blow to my vanity. I wondered
if you had remembered me as THAT big. (I have lost quite a bit,
thank goodness, since I was West). It is great fun to adjust
them as you directed, and so far they seem to hold up. I think I
may end up though with an elastic arrangement. I think it
would spoil the lines to have the top cut down. The outfit is
really very becoming and I am already enjoying it heaps. I do
like to sit at my work in loose clothes, and wear housecoats and
slacks a lot, especially in warm weather. . . .

I recently bought a small but modern cottage right on a

high dune above the ocean (Atlantic to you) south of St. Augustine. I was in New York in early December to give two lectures, and bought the furnishings for it. The walls are paneled wood, and the living room walls are a soft mulberry color—an artist friend calls it egg-plant, but it hasn't that much red in it—and all the wood part of the furniture is to be pickled pine—davenport and love seat upholstery has lots of true aqua—two large deep armless chairs in a soft coral—and cotton chenille rug is in a lavender so imperceptible it is almost French gray. My large bedroom that looks out on the ocean, is panelled in a dull green and dusty rose or peach will be used there—the chaise longue covered in dusty rose with huge white magnolia blooms. Guest bedroom with twin beds in marine blue and white. Dining in a corner of the living room—glasses are in Mexican glass, aqua color, dishes, Swedish modern in a soft gray. It is small and simple but think it will be very attractive. A great contrast to my very old-fashioned rambling farmhouse in the grove, and it will make a good change in climate, especially in summer. I do most of my work in the summer, and the ocean is delightful, while it is quite bad inland. Temperatures never unduly high, but a long steady humid heat.

Saw Helen Knowlton in New York, and Jerry Ochsner came to a small party Adelin Briggs gave for me after my lecture at Columbia University. Adelin is married to a nice plump jolly archaeologist at Columbia University. Jerry put on the Federal Project dance program last year in New York. She had hardly changed at all—even, alas, to her complete absorption in Jerry![1]

Saw lots of plays in New York—Helen Hayes—the whole thing rather a disappointment—they say the play is nothing, and she carries it—but she is having a good *loaf* in it—a dozen actresses could have done it as well as she—much as I love her work. Gertrude Lawrence in "Skylark"—perennially coy. The fashion in plays is for just a series of half-dirty wise-cracks. *Adored* Katharine Hepburn in "The Philadelphia Story." Had never much cared for her on the screen, but she won me completely. Never saw such vitality. Sat in the second row center, and long as she has played it, she got so worked up there were tears in her eyes at one dramatic point—and not glycerin either. Liked best the utterly insane Saroyan "Time of Your Life" with Julie Hayden. Went with Skip Clark and his darling wife, and Skip and I alternately shrieked with laughter and wept bitterly. Terribly moving if you're a bit cracked and feel sorry for just people, and you can't make sense out of it to save you. "The Man Who Came to Dinner" is as good as they say, which is something. A perfect riot. Was also mad about Paul Muni in Maxwell Anderson's "Key Largo." Anderson gets too damned long-winded philosophical toward the end, then saves it by a quick dramatic gesture. I am an ardent Paul Muni-ist, and he was *lovely*. Sat close, and he too wept at one point.

Of the musical shows, liked "Too Many Girls" and "Yokel Boy" (with two of our pet Floridians, Buddy Ebsen and Judy Canova.) Walked out on "Hellzapoppin." It was worth another $3.30 not to have to sit through it. Couldn't get in everything in my ten days and had to miss "Life with Father." Was in New York alone, and longed to have you with me for the shows.

Haven't had but a note from Arthur [Kinnan] since he got back from Alaska, but his first expedition was successful, and he is all set for next year. So glad it has worked out, as he is crazy about the life and the Alaska country.

Am working now on the editing of my short stories, for a book collection scheduled for spring publication.

I don't have anything to do with the movie version of The Yearling, although the research dept. writes me pitiful laments that they can't get any "visual" material for their technicians. All I can tell them is that the Florida backwoods people didn't take photographs in 1870, and the best I can tell them to do is to read the damn book——.

Well, angel, I think about you lots even when I don't write you. We'll have another good fiesta one of these days. Loads of love, and my best to Bill [McNeill].

Marjorie

P.S. Went to Atlanta for the premiere of "Gone With the Wind." Vivien Leigh is *perfect* as Scarlett, the technicolor is lovely, but I thought the thing as a whole was a disconnected *mess;* no continuity at all, and to me, the magic of the book just wasn't there. Clark Gable wasn't even top-notch Clark Gable—and anyway, after seeing and hearing Mickey Rooney's parody of him

in "Babes in Arms," I can never watch him make love again
without having the giggles.

1. All persons mentioned here were friends from college.

82. To Norman Berg

[Cross Creek]
Feb. 3, 1940

Dear Norman:

How dare you pull a stitch out of my heart, all neatly sewed
up with catgut, and fast healing? How dare you appeal to my
maternal instinct? How *dare* you make me cry? That damn
Steinbeck quotation——

Of course you're right. There is no alternative but wanting
the moon and catching fireflies. But it is one hell of a nuisance.

If They aren't going to let us drink from the golden cup, They
oughtn't make us want to——.

If I ever establish a religion, it will be of a God-and-Devil
irrevocably mixed. Man, of course, creating God in his own
image——.

Odd, the different things different people ask of life. The poor
ask to be fed and housed and clothed. When they get that, are
they satisfied? I suppose most of them are. Or are they? Those of
us who have that, and are capable of asking for something
better, catch the fireflies, sip from the moon—and are still hungry and thirsty. I myself have held the moon in my hands,
and I have a whole bottle full of fireflies—and I still beat my
hands against the cosmic Wailing Wall. It is our blessing and
our curse.

I spent a little time the other day with James Branch Cabell.
Edith Pope had tried to get him by himself, but his loving
spouse so snaps the whip, we had to give her a drink at the
same time. It is amazing to contrast his writings about women
with the discipline he has accepted—and very gracefully—
from his wife. I told him how long and how much I had admired
his work, and said that of course women had a great deal to
forgive him. He said "I'm tired of hearing that. I have compli-
mented women." I said that the compliment was this: that no
matter how disillusioned his Jurgens become about women, how
often they have their ideals slapped back in their faces, they

go on searching! He said, "Men are more capable of living a violently romantic life than women," and I said that the sensitive man was certainly more capable of it than the average woman, but that the beyond-average woman looked for the same thing the sensitive man looked for—and the irony of life was that a man and woman with the same viewpoint seldom got together. At this point his wife, across the room, sensing our pleasure in discussion, arose and said, "James, it is six o'clock. We shall be late. We must leave at once." He said, "Mrs. Rawlings and I have begun a discussion about the intelligence of men and women. It will take us about two weeks to finish it. Of course it is time to go. We must not be late." And off she dragged him. But he did say that we should talk again, here or at the St. Augustine cottage. I have no personal designs on the man— the wife is not even interested in abstract talk—a very fine and worthy and pleasant woman, I am sure—but how can I get him by himself?

It is still beastly cold. The freeze damage to the grove will perhaps be only about 50%.

Norton is down with the flu and feeling very abused and forlorn. It is a very depressing germ. I took him "The Convent"[1] to read——.

Dave Newell, a Florida sport writer, just stopped by, leaving behind the story about the cannibal. He was walking in the woods with his wife and passed his mother-in-law——. . . .

I enjoyed having you and Carl[2] with me so much. I hated not being able to make you comfortable, but was selfishly glad to have you here, especially as I should have been most unhappy alone with my lovely oranges freezing under my eyes. . . .

Marjorie

1. Novel by Alyse Simpson (New York, 1940).
2. Possibly Carl Carmer, a writer.

83. To Ida M. Tarrant

Hawthorne
March 15, [1940]

Dear Aunt Ida [in St. Augustine]:

. . . Julia [Scribner] got off Monday. I miss her, but have been busy doing garden work. Yesterday I hoed the vegetable garden and Martha and I set out tomato and eggplant and Bell pepper plants. This morning I cut half of the lawn grass, and will do the rest tomorrow. Can't get a man for love or money. It is not too hard if I take it in easy stages and is wonderful exercise.

Sunday afternoon we started out in the car to go to Gainesville, and around the bend in the road, while I was still going slowly, a runaway mule crashed right into the car. It killed the mule almost instantly and mashed the whole front of the car into pure junk. The windshield was shatterproof, and while it cracked into a million pieces, it did not break out. We were not hurt, because of my low speed. Julia had a small bump on her forehead and a slight bruise and scratch on one knee. Monday when she went to the train in Ocala, I towed the car in with the truck. I drove the truck and Julia steered my car. The garage is not sure they can get a new hood, but other parts, radiator etc. can be replaced. Am covered by insurance. May possibly be able to trade for a newer car while I am at it.

Am stuck meantime with nothing but the farm truck, so don't know just when I can get to St. Augustine. Will come soon if I get a car.

Am feeling fine and enjoying the wonderful weather.

> Much love,
>
> Marjorie

84. To Norman Berg

[Cross Creek]
March 18, 1940

Dear Norman:

I'm more than perfunctorily sorry about the family cataclysm.[1] I know too well not only the hell you've been through, but the hell you're in for. There is a time in youth when rootlessness is necessary and beautiful. A few seem to continue to want it, or to be unable to accept anything else, but for most of us, maturity requires a certain fortification of ourselves against the loneliness that is, as James Boyd said, "the terrible discovery of maturity." Of course, the fortifications, whether of place or person, are treacherous, through no fault of their own, but the need to establish them is very great.

When the first attempt, made in such good faith, fails, as it did with you and with me, one is more conscious of the lack, the need, than before. Freedom from the pain of the daily un-happy living is relief. It is also a vacuum. Out of that emptiness, the most appalling mistakes seem reasonable. What happens, I think, is that we who are idealists read into others the quali-ties that we long to find. Then when the truth hits, we have a fresh sense of betrayal and frustration. Search—the illusion of discovery—rejection—it is a disturbing business.

However, it is all to the good that you made the break be-fore more futile years had gone by, and life will have infinitely more meaning without the steady torment of bad home condi-tions. Good luck.

Is your schedule at all flexible? Malvina Hoffman, the sculp-tress, and a friend are going to be stopping here for a day and over-night, on their way north, and I don't know yet exactly when. It would be too bad for you to over-lap, for I don't imagine you're in any mood to be polite to strangers, and besides, I wanted to take you to the beach cottage. If you could change your dates by a day or two, if necessary, on a couple of days' notice, give me addresses where I could reach you by wire the rest of this week. If you can do that, I'll just wire you the dates they are to be here—their dates will be fixed once they start—and you can know that I will be free any times except those dates.

Norton is away this week on a trip for the hotel, being polite to other hotels so that they will route the tourists this way on their way north.

Had a lovely two-weeks' visit from young Julia Scribner. One of the grandest youngsters I've ever known.

Cheerio and be seeing you.

Marjorie

1. Norman Berg was in the process of divorce.

85. To Maxwell E. Perkins

Hawthorne, Florida
May 14, 1940

Dear Max:

The Gilkysons[1] came by, and had Sunday dinner with me. He is just as jolly as can be, and I enjoyed them a lot. Bernice explained the Scribner proof-reading system to me, and it does explain why there is so much trouble. As I understand it, it is really no one's particular business, that the editorial department does not have a definitely assigned proof reader. In future, unless this gap is filled meantime, I shall simply take responsibility for the proofs myself.

I should love to have the cat book. I like them almost as well as dogs.

I am delighted that the reviews of the stories[2] are so kind. I had been dreading "Time," and it was grand to have them say that the book had good claim to being a better book than "The Yearling." I should think that would be desirable for quoting, considering its source.

Had a lovely note from James Branch Cabell, whom I met in St. Augustine, sending me a copy of the rare pamphlet he wrote as a portrait of Ellen Glasgow, signed by her "With tremendous admiration." I was overcome. In the pamphlet, he said that she admired only two women writers, one of them Jane Austen, and the other he agreed with her about. You don't suppose it could possibly have been "The Yearling" he was speaking of, do you? The pamphlet was written in 1938, but the month was not given. He embarrassed me when I met him by asking, "How does it feel to be a great writer?" and I couldn't tell whether or not he was pulling my leg. He told me that when I was elected to the National Institute of Arts and Letters, he had never known such unanimous accord on an election, and that the man who proposed my name said, "Of course, you realize that this woman's work will be known after everyone in this room is forgotten." Cabell is so frightfully sarcastic, and a bestseller must seem such a horrible thing to him, that I felt dubious about his feelings.

Did I write you that I met Thornton Wilder[3] in St. Augustine and he came down to my cottage at the beach and had lunch with me? He is a grand person and coming up against his mind was tremendously exciting. We seemed to begin talking where we had left off. But such scholars make me feel positively illiterate. If I manage to stick life out, I shall devote my old age to my education.

Marjorie

Your family is increasing so that some day I expect to see one of those immense group photographs of Sire Perkins and progeny——

1. Walter and Bernice Gilkyson; he was a novelist, she a poet and an editor at Scribner's.
2. MKR's collected stories, *When the Whippoorwill* (New York, 1940).
3. Thornton Wilder, American novelist and playwright (1897–1975).

86. To Norton S. Baskin

[Cross Creek]
Wednesday
[June 1940]

My dear:

I hope you aren't as heavy-hearted as I am this morning. The Barclay's quarrel was of course all my fault. I cannot understand how I could have developed a chip on my shoulder, for I was so happy to have you and Cecil [Bryant] with me. Of course, the chip meant nothing at all. My ugliness never does mean anything, which makes it all the uglier.

Any ugliness from you is so rare that it is a different matter, and no matter how I have provoked you, I feel that you mean it. The terrible thing you said, that all I wanted was a man—did you say "a little man"—to dance attendance—must have come from a profound mistrust and resentment of me. It explains the wall I often feel you put up against me—the withdrawal—the lack of any desire or need to be with me as much as I like to be with you—which haven't fitted in with the affection I know you have had for me. I have wanted something so much closer than you have wanted and have had an awful struggle to accept the fact that what meant closeness to me, meant something irksome and "regimented" to you. I have a great respect for and understanding of, a self-respecting man's need of freedom, and have tried my very best not to let my loneliness make unreasonable demands on yours. I am sorrier than I can tell you, that you have interpreted my pleasure in being with you, as only the vanity of a predatory and arrogant woman. That you are both wrong and unjust doesn't help the situation at all, for there is nothing more I can do about it. If I thought that the only thing that stands in the way of our having the closeness I have wanted is your mistrust of my nature, I should just go on loving you patiently, as I decided to do last summer when I ran away to the cottage to make what adjustment I could to the shock of your feeling of regimentation. But I am awfully afraid that the thing goes deeper than that. I am afraid that we simply ask different things of a very lovely relation. What I ask would give you everything I have. What you ask, leaves me still lonely. You feel that I ask too much of you. I feel that you do not ask enough of me. Many times I have thought that the wisest and best thing for both of us was to call it all off, and I haven't done it for two reasons. One is that I have cared too much for you and enjoyed you too much to give you up if it wasn't necessary, and if I could make the adjustment to your point of view. The other is that I have been afraid that once it was over, you would realize the potentialities we have for something close and beautiful and permanent, something that would end my loneliness—and that then it would be too late. Your psychology and your way of life—with people all the time—sharing your bedroom with someone you are fond of—so that I represent, not your whole life, but someone you go to as just a pleasant adventure—make me unnecessary to the inmost core of you.

I know that my own psychology as well as the typical female psychology have a great deal to do with the difference in our requirements. But there are men who feel and know that the only complete unity in the world is that between a man and a woman—between the right man and the right woman. My misfortune, like the misfortune of most such men, has been in not getting the proper combination together. Your misfortune in not feeling this way is also your good fortune. You simply do not feel this need. It takes much less to satisfy you than it does men who want the same thing I want. You will probably always be able to find what you need to satisfy you. The only danger you face is as you grow old or older, and I can foresee for you the same loneliness that I have felt for many years. But the way you look at this is probably safe and wise for you and I can't run the risk of upsetting what is right for you. I have evidently cramped your style, without meaning to. You'll just have to take my word for it that it has been only because I preferred being with you to being with anyone else—not because I wanted you "dancing attendance."

I am terribly afraid that we've done something that can't be fixed. The revelation you gave me of what you think I am is too painful. I don't think anything has ever hurt or shocked me more. I'd suggest that we not see each other for a while. Then if we find that our mutual trust and affection are strong enough we'll try again. It didn't seem to me that I was making any demands on you, but you evidently can't be with me three or four days in a row without feeling coerced. It's possible that I'm asking of a man that he act as a buffer for me against the strange despair that hits me and that I can't seem to lick. Only I've hoped that a man I could care for would be glad to help me. But I suppose there are some battles that we always have to fight alone.

Well, cheerio. I'll probably go alone to the cottage today and stay there until I come home next Thursday to entertain Aunt Ida's friends. Think it would better if you don't come over even if you want to, for seeing things as you do, you'd feel I was just putting it over.

Please understand that I have no criticism of you in any way. You are the sweetest, kindest, most generous person I've almost ever known.

Marjorie

87. *To Ida M. Tarrant*

[Crescent Beach]
Saturday morning
[July 5, 1940]

Dearest Aunt Ida [in Ocala]:

Well, Pat [MKR's pointer] and I are getting along fine. I am working and he thinks he is. He simply torments me to go on the beach with him. He loves it, but wants somebody with him.

It is marvelous without a nigger drooping around! I only have to brush up every other day as there is no dirt, and my dishes are nothing.

Have been in to St. Augustine one evening to play bridge at the Popes. We heard the Republican Convention on the radio nominate [Wendell] Willkie—hope you heard it—it was very exciting. We were all Willkie fans and are sure we helped to nominate him. Actually, I was so afraid the Convention would shame the country by nominating one of that bunch of small fry that I sent telegrams to the Chairman of the Florida delegation and of the Wisconsin delegation, urging support for Willkie, and was thrilled when both delegations finally switched their support to him. I would vote for Willkie over any candidate except Roosevelt, and may even vote for him anyway. He is big stuff, has held a lot of Roosevelt's progressive and valuable theories, but simply has the practical common sense not to go hog wild over anything unfeasible. He would balance Republican practicality with Democratic progressiveness.

Hope you have not suffered with the heat. A note from Norton said it had been very hot there. Edith Pope said that in St. Augustine itself it was stifling, but on the beach here it has been grand except for a couple of hours yesterday afternoon. The ocean has been mostly calm and have enjoyed swimming.

Hope to get a lot of work done.

Be lazy and take care of yourself. Will watch my chance to invite you over for two or three days.

Lots of love,

Marjorie

88. To Ida M. Tarrant

[Crescent Beach]
Wednesday
[July 31, 1940]

Dearest Aunt Ida [in Ocala]:

Am getting low on writing paper and know you won't mind a letter on my work paper. Was so glad to get your letter this morning. Glad you had the new permanent. Straight hair is an awful nuisance in hot weather. As I imagine Norton told you,

I planned to come in Sunday evening, then we had a scare at the Creek about an escaped negro and my folks were afraid and didn't want me to leave. Decided I had better get on over to the cottage Monday and get down to work. Couldn't understand why your phone didn't answer at noon time, but the beauty parlor was the explanation.

Your warning about overdoing the exercise came two days late. My first evening here walked too far on the sand, barefooted, and bruised and blistered one foot so that I can't walk! Have been able to get down to the beach for a swim, so far, but have really put the quietus on myself. It is nothing, and will be all right in a day or two. Have plenty of food in the cottage and a little boy comes twice a day with the paper and to do odd jobs so can send for anything by him. Was tempted to wire to have Will bring Martha over in the truck, but after the couple of days of real usefulness, she would be terribly on my hands.

My sweet friend Edith Pope remembered my birthday and wants to have me there for dinner, and have you and Norton. Told her I usually had my birthday at your place, and didn't know whether Norton could come over or not, but we'll see how it works out.

It is delightful here at the cottage, a cool breeze every minute. The bride and groom left everything in very good order, the kitchen especially was as clean as could be. Norman[1] also left a very grateful note. The bride doesn't know the rudiments of manners and of course didn't even put a postscript on it. Have an idea Norman cleaned the house himself. Edith Pope saw the light and came in one evening while they were here and said Norman was doing the cooking.

Think Pat got his feet sore on the sand, too, for he limps and except for a short run night and morning, is quite content to stay in the house with me. He is the most wonderful company over here.

Had better end this, as the laundryman is going to stop on his way back and get my letters and mail them in town for me. Everyone over here is so kind and accommodating.

Much love, and take care of yourself.

Marjorie

Al Smith's swing to Willkie will take a lot of Democrats with him. Think Roosevelt is sunk.

1. Norman Berg had remarried and had been staying at MKR's cottage for the honeymoon.

89. *To Maxwell E. Perkins*

Hawthorne, Florida
September 19, 1940

Dear Max:

I can't tell you how relieved I am to hear from you, and to know that you don't consider the material hopeless.[1] I shall wait to do any more work until I hear from you at greater length, for if you have hit on any better approach, I should prefer to make a fresh start. My mind is very open on the matter, and I shall be most receptive to anything that occurs to you.

However I handle it, the material is such that I can work through interruptions, as I cannot with fiction, and I look forward to settling down to a long good autumn and winter.

I remembered that I never answered your question about the radio use of "The Yearling." Anything that you considered desirable would be all right with me, but I have an idea that you will find the movie contract quite restrictive about such things. Carl [Brandt] will know about that.

I enjoyed Julia Scribner's visit immensely. She is most unusual and very mature.

My trip to Madison, Wisconsin will be a brief one just for the one lecture for the benefit of the Alumni Scholarship Fund. I am going at my own expense. It seems little enough to do for one's own college. I think I shall go by train instead of driving so that it will not take so much time.

Needless to say, I am most anxious to hear from you in detail, but because I do want your reaction in detail, please take your time.

We had an unexpected and very jolly meeting here with Ernest Hemingway and Martha Gellhorn.[2] I was entertaining over the week-end for Julia and our party was at Marineland at dinner. I recognized Hemingway at a nearby table and spoke to him. They joined us for drinks and then came up to the cot-

tage and stayed much later than was wise for them, as he was
trying to make time going west. He is obviously in a much
better frame of mind than when I met him in Bimini, and we
all liked Martha immensely. Do send me as early a copy of
the book as you can. He spoke as though he might be coming
through here in the fall and I offered him the use of the cottage,
as I shall only come over here, after October first, for occasional week-ends. If he speaks of it, tell him the offer was not
just drunken hospitality, and I should be glad to have him
and Martha make a stay here. They would not be bothered by
anyone.

Marjorie

1. MKR had been working on a draft of *Cross Creek*.
2. Ernest Hemingway's third wife.

90. *To Maxwell E. Perkins*

Hawthorne, Florida
[January 1941]

Dear Max:

Had this sheet in the typewriter ready for making the ninth or
tenth beginning of "Cross Creek." I still don't know why I
can't find the right approach, but it will surely hit at any
minute. I have torn up pages and pages. There is some key to
coordination that I have not yet stumbled on, but it will come,
and when it does, I know the work will go fast, because it is all
piled up, dammed, ready and waiting to pour out. I shall be so
happy when I really get going. The introduction, or preface, is
still approximately right. The "light" approach proved very
wrong. Or did I speak of that in a letter I began to you, and
mislaid and never sent. I was writing you about some of the
books you had sent. Please send me anything you can.

The news about Scott[1] made me very sad, though his life was
more tragic than his death. The tragedy came, I think, from
having a spectacular success too early, and on top of that, valu-
ing the wrong things in living. It is difficult enough to be
happy when one takes satisfaction from the simple and infallible
things, but it is an R.S.V.P. invitation to disaster to depend on

the quicksands of the treacherous things that to him represented the "gloria mundi." But as you say, it was not fair to attribute to him personally all the shallowness and stupidity of the people he wrote about. The very fact that he could write about them with that bitter irony, put him beyond them. But people in general are totally unable to detach the personality of a writer from the products of his thinking.

The holiday season has been a round of more or less asinine parties that I felt obliged to go to, because of many visiting friends. I'm hoping things will be quieter now, and I am getting a bit more ruthless about dodging people. And my perfectly grand well-educated new colored maid makes everything domestic very pleasant and easy for me, so that when I do have company I enjoy it too.

My good colored man came mournfully yesterday morning to give notice. It seemed he had sat down, quite unlike the average darky and checked over his year's progress and decided there just wasn't any. When he got sympathy over such a sad but common state of affairs, he cheered up at once and poured out his year's sorrows, which consisted mostly of discouragement over having all his wages go to pay his fat lazy wife's doctor bills. The last doctor told her she needed more exercise and less laxatives, so under the unexpected, I presume, stimulus of my understanding, he decided to plant a cash crop for himself in one of my vacant fields and make his wife work in it. We agreed that this stood a good chance of bettering both their conditions, and he has been so happy today over the new hope that he has almost run me out of the house by piling joyous and unnecessary wood on all my hearth fires.

I continue to get a flood of literature asking for money and cooperation for everything connected with the world's mess— China's Children, Exiled Writers, Committee for Aiding the Allies, Committee for Keeping Us Out of War, Hoover's Committee to Feed Europe, somebody else's committee to block such feeding. I send checks to a few and just tear up the rest of the stuff. If a creative worker needed any lesson in minding his own business, he would find it in Edna Millay's new book of so-called poetry, "Make Bright the Arrows." Of all tripe——. If an artist wants to do something practical like giving money or doing nursing, well and good, but he serves no purpose by so abandoning his art.

Marjorie

1. F. Scott Fitzgerald died December 21, 1940.

91. To Maxwell E. Perkins

[Cross Creek]
March 3, 1941

Dear Max:

No, my silence comes not from progress, but from being stopped again.[1] I had a quite a good deal done, when it seemed to me that it was still coming in too episodic a form. I began all over once more and the type of re-creation, of re-visualization of the life and people and happenings, went so slowly because of the great concentration necessary—and I still could not tell whether it would work out that way—that I went into a tempo- rary paralysis and thought it best to leave it alone a while. I am going back to both manuscripts in a day or two and hope that I will know, on re-reading, what is right.

It is difficult to explain the problem, but it is one principally of *time*. If I tell a direct, almost, in a way, day to day narra- tive, so many of the details of the stories of the people have no interest and no meaning. That is, it may have taken many of the years I have been here for enough details, with point to them, to accumulate about any one person or family. Their stories are sometimes only valid as completed stories. Doing it this way, as I was, it was necessary to write as of the moment, looking back to something completed. As I said, this seemed to me to make a choppy narrative. It also damaged that flowing sense of following a scene or a person, so that the reality is *immediate*. This is very important. It is not enough for good anecdotes to be told, either humorous or moving. The sense of knowing a particular place and people with a deep, almost Proustian deepness and intimacy and revelation, with my own feeling about things back of it, is what I want. Also, the way I was going, it went too glibly. It was easy to fall into a superficial narrative style that was almost journalistic. To do it as I have begun the last time, is more like doing hard creative fiction. I can call less on facts and true details, and must project myself painfully and slowly into years and scenes and feelings that I have actually forgotten, and must re-create. I would say that I cannot do it, except that I know by working hard enough, it is possible. And there is always that problem of making something of trifles that are not in themselves interesting, but must lay the ground for the point of incidents, to be resolved and completed long later.

Does this help make you see the peculiar difficulty? We cannot talk of illustrations or any publishing matters. The book can only be done right, no matter how long it takes. If it is right, it will be good and if it is not right, it will not be worth publishing.

Marjorie

1. MKR was still working on *Cross Creek*.

92. *To Norton S. Baskin*

[White House
Washington, D.C.]
April 1, 1941

Dear Norton:—

I should probably be doing something more serious, here at Lincoln's desk, than writing you, so may the shade of Lincoln forgive me.

The usher showed me into a room somewhat larger than your dining room, and asked me if I thought the room would be large enough! It is the Lincoln room—and Lincoln's bed—and I simply don't feel good enough to sleep in it. Do you suppose he might possibly have liked "The Yearling"?

The vast room is comfortably shabby, and the draperies are almost a duplicate of my English material that is on my davenport—and there is dust on the marble-topped center table—so I feel almost at home — — And the help has as easy a welcome as Martha [Mickens]—

I haven't met Mrs. Roosevelt yet, but was told to appear for tea at five in the West Hall. All the newspaper women here simply worship her. And it is not that they are being diplomatic,

for they say the most indiscreet and disreputable things about
the great and the near-great.

The luncheon today was nice—Margaret Mitchell[1] was there,
and Sella Warren, who shocked me by being the spitting image of Phil May!

I went to a British cocktail party yesterday afternoon, and
had dinner with my friend Sigrid Arne—Jim Rawlings' old girl.
She had with us such a jolly Australian girl, who used to be a
champion swimmer, Pat Jarrett, and is now living at the Australian Embassy, covering the U.S. for the big Melbourne paper.
And she is Dessie's [Smith Vinson] double! Voice, manner-
isms, and all.

The dinner tonight promises to be a delightful brawl. All
kinds of women, from Clare Boothe Luce and Mary Martin, to
Eve Curie.[2] And by the way, a funny thing happened about the
luncheon at Pierre's today. Mrs. Herrick, the hostess, told the
head waiter that Margaret Mitchell and Marjorie K.R. were
coming, and he hustled about nobly. Then later he said to her,
"You said it was Mary Martin coming, didn't you?" and when
she said no, he lost all interest.

It is pouring rain—Washington at its typical spring worst—
but still warm.

Wednesday morning

Ashamed to report that I am suffering from a hang-over in
the White House——. It's a long story, but I did your trick of
being the last one at the party—Mr. and Mrs. Eugene Meyer[3]
and I had a grand time together and ate and drank at two in the
morning after everybody else had gone.

I have been quite an orphan at the White House. It was, of
course, just a gesture from Mrs. Roosevelt, in thanks for my
cottage gesture. I must say I'm happier where I know I'm really
wanted! I'll have to see you to tell you everything.

Love,

Marjorie

Back at the hotel to pack my other bags to be moved over
to the White House. Just after I finished my letter there to you,
I called Miss Thompson, Mrs. R's very jolly secretary, and asked to

see her. I told her I'd never been as lonesome in my life as at the
White House! Mrs. Roosevelt took an early plane for New
York this morning, and I had heard her very gay voice and
laughter, going off. Miss Thompson and Mrs. Helm, the social
secretary, came into my room and we had a grand visit, and I
stopped feeling like an orphan immediately. I even felt that I
was wanted as they told me Mrs. Roosevelt had looked over the
Press Club guest list and picked out the ones she wanted to
stay in the White House. Eve Curie and Genevieve Tabouis[4]
were the others, so I didn't feel so much that I was just the
victim of courtesy—Mrs. Helm insisted on my staying on at the
White House, so I am checking out here at the hotel. I could
have a good time here for days, but will go home either tomorrow or Friday arriving in Ocala 10:49 a.m. either Friday or
Saturday. I had a note from Miss [Ellen] Glasgow[5] and will stop
over to see her in the afternoon.

You *could* have had a note for me here.

I'll let you know my definite plans, later.

Love,

Marjorie

1. Margaret Mitchell, American novelist and journalist (1900–1949).
2. Eve Curie, French musician and writer (1904–   ), daughter of Pierre and
Marie Curie.
3. Eugene Meyer was a college classmate of MKR.
4. Genevieve Tabouis, French journalist (1892–   ).
5. Ellen Glasgow, American novelist (1874–1945).

93. To Helen Hastings

Hawthorne, Florida
April 28, 1941

Dear Mrs. Hastings:

I am so sorry that you were disturbed by not hearing from
me. I have been away from home three days out of the past
week and the rest of the time have been very busy, with many
interruptions. I brought the Williamson day book into Ocala last
Friday to bring to you, but did not have time to leave it after
all.

I myself found the book in the attic of the abandoned house at

Lake Kerr. I cannot remember the exact date. It could have
been any time between 1933 and 1938. I was on a fishing trip
and was either with Ed Hopkins[1] or Dr. and Mrs. Vinson. We
stopped by the old house hoping to find a well with water. The
place was of course in great disrepair and wide open. We went in
and remarked that it must once have been a fine homestead
for that section. We prowled about and went up into the attic
which also was wide open. I don't even remember there being a
door.

There were no trunks there, nothing at all but old newspapers and farm magazines, and these of a rather recent date. I
am always interested in old records, so looked at the papers to
see if they were old. In among them was the old day book, and
I had no qualms at all about taking it away with me. There was
nothing else there but the day book and the papers.

It may interest you to know that I drew on the type of
shopping list in the day book, as a model for the list of things
Ma Baxter in "The Yearling" drew up for the Forresters to buy
in town for her. The day book was very valuable to me in indicating the types of materials and supplies used in that period,
which was only a few years in advance of the date of "The
Yearling," 1870–71. I was of course always alert for any records
that would give me intimate details of the life of the period I
was writing about.

After I finished "The Yearling," it seemed to me that the day
book had a real historical value and that I should not keep it
as an individual. I approached the Florida Historical Society
about it and they said that they should consider it a valuable
addition to their library. I had inquired here and there about the
Williamson family, and I believe that Nettie Martin remembered the family being at Lake Kerr, but I did not know there
were any descendants who might be interested in having the
book.

I should not have kept the copy so long, as the Historical
Society only sent it to me to see. It has been on my conscience. If
you don't mind, please return it to Florida Historical Society,
St. Augustine, instead of to me when you have finished with it.

I consider six dollars a very reasonable price for copying this
record. It must have been a long and tedious job, especially as

the old book itself was in very bad shape, water-stained and with pages and sections missing. I hope you will look at the original some time when you are in St. Augustine. I am sorry I did not know at the time that there was someone connected with the family that might have liked the book, yet I think you yourself might have felt that it should be part of the state records.

I think this answers your questions. As to the vandalism in the old attic, it must have been completed many years before we were there, for as I said, everything was wide open and there were no such things there as trunks or boxes, nothing but the papers.

Genealogical tracings are really fascinating, and I am glad that this old record has come to your attention.

Sincerely,

Marjorie Kinnan Rawlings

1. A Cross Creek neighbor.

94. To Norton S. Baskin

[Crescent Beach]
Thursday
[June 1941]

Dear Norton [in Ocala]:

Well, I am on my feet instead of my back today, to my amazement. I had my initiation into floundering last night, and Verle [Pope] darn near killed me. My only satisfaction is that he must have ruined himself, too. He invited the [Frank] Harrolds (the banker) to go with us, for they are flounder fiends, too. Fortunately Edith [Pope] decided to stay home. She could never have stood it. We set out at nine o'clock at night, at low tide, and parked the car down one of those roads that lead toward the ocean, on the island here, up where you're so crazy about the cedar trees. (If that is a clear direction.) Verle carried a big gasoline lantern and we all had gigs. We walked along in the shallow water for about a mile before we got the first flounder. The place is one of those sort of bays, with a strip of marshy land between it and the ocean. The floundering itself is fascinating. You can barely see them, for they take on the color of the sand, and are sometimes almost buried, so that you just see the shape. They don't move when the light is on them, and you joog them with your gig, then reach under them and somebody puts them on the string. I don't know how far we walked, all in the water. All of a sudden even the men admitted they were tired, and we had all that way to go back again. Verle over-does things like that terribly. We must have gone about three miles then. Meantime, the tide had come in and was close to high, and everything looked different. We walked and walked, and all of a sudden we were lost. The lighthouse was on the wrong side and so was the moon. We thought we'd passed the car and worked back, then decided we hadn't come far enough. We walked and walked, and there were deep creeks and sloughs where there had been dry land. Sometimes things would just drop from under us and we were in over our waists. That was plenty spooky. Verle left us to reconnoiter and then couldn't find us again! We could see his light, but he couldn't see us. We called and whistled and the sounds were deceptive and we could see the light go off the other way. At last we got together again and walked and walked, pushing through the deep wa-ter. We could hardly put one foot ahead of the other. Mr. Harrold had played 18 holes of golf and hadn't had any dinner, and I had been fool enough to take Pat for a three-mile walk! We found the car at 2 o'clock in the morning, having walked stead-ily for five hours. We had to deliver the Harrolds back in town, divide the flounders—we got twenty—and get my car, and I reached home at three-thirty, hardly able to crawl up the steps.

When we set out and didn't get any flounder for so long, I said snootily, "So this is floundering." Then we caught a lot fast and I said with enthusiasm, "So *this* is floundering!" As we struggled in at the end, I said bitterly, "So this is *floundering*."

I was so wet and sticky and muddy and shelly and achey, I soaked in deep hot water, and am all right today.

The work has me chewing off all my nails, but it goes steadily.

Verle told me last night about the deal,[1] and said he wouldn't be willing to have you pay more than $22,000. Said you were running into danger past that, counting what you'd have to put in for fixing and fixings, and much as he wanted you over here, he didn't want to see you get into trouble. I thought that was pretty white of him and it made me feel better about him.

The war looks worse again, doesn't it.

The ocean is rough, the way you like it, but it scares me. The undertow was awful yesterday and I didn't dare take my feet off the ground.

I had a swell time over the week-end, too. We'll do it again any time you say.

Much love,

Marjorie

1. With MKR as business partner, Norton Baskin was negotiating to buy a mansion in St. Augustine, which he was to convert into the Castle Warden Hotel.

95. To Beatrice H. McNeill

Hawthorne, Florida

June 24, 1941

Dearest Bee:

I would have sworn I wrote all about my Madison visit. It seems to me I even remember writing that Jo would probably send you clippings. At any rate, it was an absolutely perfect experience. The old school did everything but turn out the band. There were so many more old friends there than I expected, and it was like picking up my youth where I had left it behind me. I accepted every invitation and did everything; even went Saturday night "jooking" with some of the kids. Had Jo come to my rooms at the Union for lunch so we could have a visit alone. She is a wonder, and some man certainly missed a bet.

I had two beautiful rooms at the Union, overlooking the lake, with oak and maple trees in full autumn foliage. The week I was there had divine warm fall weather. I was never so scared in my life as before and during the first part of my lecture in the new theatre. I could see Gertrude [Johnson] on an aisle seat patting her foot, and I thought, "Oh God, here I go." As I went on, it was all right. We cleared about $750 for the scholarship fund. I went at my own expense and without a fee, but the Alumnae insisted on treating me to my elegant quarters. I

talked to Gertrude's classes, and got a swell revenge on her by
telling tales on her and taking her off. I met Sinclair Lewis
and the artist Curry[1] and altogether had the most wonderful
week of my whole life.

I had another couple of days' fun in April. I went to Washington for the Women's Press Club annual dinner and met such
fascinating women—Daisy [Mrs. Averell] Harriman, Mrs. [Wen-
dell] Willkie, Lady Halifax, ambassadresses and so on. I was
invited to stay at the White House, and of course got an immense thrill out of that. I got very high at the Eugene Meyers'
big brawl after the dinner, staying alone with the Meyers until 2:30, and rolled in to the White House in a taxi about 3 A.M.,
waking up in the Lincoln bed next morning with a dandy
hangover. They run the White House like a hotel, and unless
you are asked for some special meal, you have a tray in your
room or are free to do anything you want to. I had tea with Mrs.
Roosevelt, and she left for New York the morning after the
party. She is one of the most charming people I have ever met in

MKR with the artist John Steuart Curry.

my life. She asked me to stay at the White House, not because she thought I was "somebody," but because she almost borrowed my beach cottage for her spring vacation. The contact was made through the new Mrs. Ernest Hemingway, who had been at my cottage and thought Mrs. R. would love it. She had a snooty friend though who wanted to go to Miami Beach for the night life. I had arranged to lend her my maid, and had begun to work out menus, when at the last minute she wrote that her friends wanted to go to Miami.

I do wish I could move Idella[2] back to the time you spent with me. I have had her since October and she is the answer to a prayer. Not only a marvelous cook, but doesn't drink, isn't interested in men, borrows my books, likes the same movies I do, and adores having company and protests when I pay her extra after a heavy week. Her cheerfulness and efficiency are balm after the wounds Martha and Adrenna [Mickens] inflicted on me. She was in her last place in Palm Beach 5 years, and only left because her mother and family live just a few miles from here and she wanted to be near them. I leave her at her home once or twice a week on my way to Ocala, and she seems perfectly happy. I had ten men to dinner at the cottage Saturday and I wanted to get help for her, but she said she'd rather handle it alone, and it went as smoothly as if we'd had two butlers.

I am at the cottage most of the time, just come to the grove for a day or so every couple of weeks to check up on things.

I am working hard and steadily on my book and should have the first draft done by the end of August. I'll go to New York for a conference with my editor then.

Well, the movie business certainly turned out a mess. They spent half a million dollars here, seemed to have a perfect set-up, and suddenly cleared out at a moment's notice after a week or so's work. Nobody seems to know just what was the trouble. I was only on the set twice, and I could tell [Victor] Fleming wasn't satisfied with Anne Revere or the boy. He was very nervous, taking sleeping tablets, etc. and felt he could handle things much better on the Hollywood sets. The wind registered on the sound track, not sounding like wind at all, etc. The boy Gene Eckman, in looks and personality, seemed quite all right,

On the film set of *The Yearling*, at Salt Springs.

but the sound man had me listen in, and it was true, as he complained, that the boy was not enunciating and his lines were not registering. [Spencer] Tracy was bored and morose, Anne Revere is not Ma Baxter as I visualize her, but had a fine pioneer look and I thought she was all right, but she didn't seem to "put out" emotionally in the one scene I saw her do. We do know that there was much internal dissension, labor trouble etc., and I am told that Jerry Bressler, a son-in-law I think of [Louis B.] Mayer, made a lot of trouble, keeping everybody stirred up against everybody else. At any rate, Fleming is out as director and King Vidor in, Anne Revere and Gene Eckman out, and the word is that the picture will be shelved, whether permanently or not I don't know. John Marquand[3] was in Hollywood and said Vidor was drafted after Fleming had a nervous breakdown, but Marquand thought Vidor would do a lovely job. I for one don't care if they never do it at all!

I still can't believe that I didn't write you about Madison.

Norton is as sweet as ever, Aunt Ida as chipper, Pat goes his arrogant way and has made Idella his slave, and all goes well. My health is slowly improving, tho I still have those attacks slip up on me, but at longer intervals.

Loads of love and my best to Bill [McNeill].

Marjorie

1. John Steuart Curry, American artist (1897–1946).
2. Idella Parker, MKR's new maid.
3. John Marquand, American writer (1893–1960).

96. To Ellen Glasgow

Crescent Beach
RFD St. Augustine
July 19, 1941

My very dear Ellen Glasgow:

I had such a vivid dream about you last night, that I must write you—which I have been meaning to do ever since our delightful brief visit together. The reality of a dream can never be conveyed to another, but you came to live with me. I was away when you came, and on my return, to one of those strange mansions that are part of the substance of dreams, you were outside in the bitter cold, cutting away ice from the roadway and piling it in geometric pattern. I was alarmed, remembering your heart trouble, and led you inside the mansion and brought you a cup of hot coffee. You had on blue silk gloves, and I laid my hand over yours, and was amazed, for my own hand is small, to have yours fit inside mine, much smaller. You chose your room and suggested draperies to supplement a valance. The valance was red chintz and you showed me a sample of a heavy red brocade of the same shade. I told you that from now on I should take care of you, and you must not do strenuous things, such as cutting the ice in the roadway. James Cabell came into the room and asked what the two of us were up to. (As of course he would!)

My memory of my time with you is quite as vivid as the

night's dream. I have thought of you oftener than I can tell you. So often a personality is detached from writings, and the two in fact seem to have nothing to do with each other. You as a person have the vitality, the wit and the irony of your work, but I was not prepared to find you so warm and so beautiful, in spite of the devotion of your friends, which would indicate those things in you.

I am at my cottage on the ocean, and have been working very hard on my book, so hard that I put myself in the hospital for a week. It wouldn't seem necessary to tie oneself into knots to get out a few ideas, but while I *feel* at the drop of a hat, thinking is terribly hard work for me! The first draft of the book is nearly done. Much of it is very bad indeed, and after Max Perkins has seen it and given me, I hope, some of his marvelous suggestions, I shall go at it again.

I am wondering if you went to Maine, and if there is any chance of your visiting Florida this winter. I do hope you are strong again and that I shall see you here.

With much affection,

Marjorie

97. *To Norton S. Baskin*

[Crescent Beach
ca. September 1, 1941]

Dear Norton:

I have no intention of making any mystery of what I am feeling. The street was simply no place to have it out. And I don't think it can be had out in any case.

You gave me a first class shock when you turned on me after my sputtering and said that you hated people who had fits. Your face was appalling. You really hated me. You changed instantly from my sweet Norton to someone with whom I could not possibly be close. And since you are capable of feeling that way toward me, if only for a moment, you don't want to be close to me either.

I make no excuses for my "fits." I am ashamed of them. But I exercise as much control as is possible for me, and when I make a trivial fuss, as in that case, or really boil over, I simply

cannot help it. My temperament is what it is, volatile and
high strung—and you may use any other adjectives you want to.
My virtues—if any—come from exactly the same temperament as my faults, and each is a part of the other. I couldn't
write books, I couldn't have a warmly emotional nature, if I
were a placid pond. A man who was right for me would never be
upset by my fits, and certainly would not hate me for them.

When we have stepped on each other's toes before, my heart
has been like a lump of lead. Now it is just a chunk of ice and I
don't even care. You aren't Norton any more. Your sweetness
has been the happy aspect of a passive nature, and without the
sweetness I don't want you. I certainly am not going to make
myself liable to spells of being hated. Probably you don't care to
be annoyed into hating.

Your charm is devastating, as nobody knows better than
you, and I don't know whether I am permanently immune. In
any case, I want to say that regardless of our future personal
relations, the hotel deal is still a business deal.

Marjorie

98. To Maxwell E. Perkins

[Crescent Beach]
Sept. 15, 1941

Dear Max:

I expressed you the first draft of "Cross Creek" on Saturday,
and it should reach you today. I consider it only a draft, and I
did hate to send it when I am so dissatisfied with many aspects
of it. But it was making me so nervous not to have it in your
hands, and I knew you must be anxious, too, that it seemed
better to send it on without making any further effort at the
moment to get it right. If you have not already finished reading
it, I feel it will be better for you to do so *before* you read the
following questionings.

The first and perhaps the most important question is whether
there is even approximately sufficient fluidity of narrative.
Now that you have the material in hand, I think you will understand why it seemed to me *impossible* to provide *straight nar-*

rative. There was no one hook on which to hang anything
approximating a *story*. There was not even the movement of a
travel or adventure story, such as in Peter Freuchen's Arctic
adventure, or even my "Hyacinth Drift." I did not want to tell a
story of myself, particularly. I did not want anything like an
autobiography of these past thirteen years. I wanted the thing
objective, the only subjectivity consisting of my personal reaction to the Creek, its natural aspects and its people. I came as
close as possible to a thread, in more or less dealing with the
growth of my knowledge of place and people. If I had tried to use
Martha [Mickens] as more of a hook, for instance, I could not
use much of the subjective material that seemed to me important. Also, to use her that way would be spurious, for I have
exaggerated her importance as it is, just to keep a thread moving through the whole thing.

Now perhaps you may see a way in which I can make a
stronger thread of the growth of my knowledge. I myself can not
see one.

It seems to me that much of it carries along fairly well as
something of a consecutive chain of events. Up to the chapter
that I called "Residue," it does not seem to me too spotty. I have
the feeling that that chapter, in spite of its uniting theme, is
terribly episodic and jerky. The individual character studies are
not woven into anything at all. I am hoping that you can see
where they could be worked in more smoothly. I think on further
consideration I might be able to use some of those people in
that chapter in a less thrown-at-your-head manner.

Now for other questions.

Is Martha sufficiently interwoven into the episodes, after my
initial claim for her of something of a dusky Fate?

I wanted to avoid all reference to the family life that preceded my years alone at the Creek, yet I was not there alone at
the beginning, and it seemed to me I needed some indication
of the other life, so mentioned briefly the three brothers "for
whom the pattern proved within a year not the right one," this
in the chapter "The Magnolia Tree." Does this seem valid to
you, and not offensive to the "three brothers"?[1]

Now I have used true names in practically every instance. I
have tried not to put things so that anyone's feelings would be

hurt. These people are my friends and neighbors, and I would not be unkind for anything, and though they are simple folk, there is the possible libel danger to think of. What do you think of this aspect of the material?[2]

Do you consider it bad taste for me to have mentioned my books and stories by name as I have done? In so many cases

Will and Martha Mickens.

they were a part of something I was telling and I did not see
how to avoid it. Yet it is very necessary not to seem to be blow-
ing one's own horn, as it were. I also raise this question of
good taste about my mention of kindnesses I have done for
people at the Creek. There is a danger there of setting a reader's
teeth on edge.

There is of course the very serious question of when details
are interesting to others and when they are not. You will have
to judge that.

Do you think it is desirable or otherwise to use chapter
headings? In some cases the heading clarifies the material, but
on the whole it may be that it would accentuate any possible
jerkiness or episodic quality.

I find that there is a sharp variance of style between the
serious nature of philosophical portions and the humorous incidents. I think I have too flippant or facetious a style in dealing with the humorous things. I can take care of that myself to
an extent, but I wish you would check on the manuscript the
places where the style is offensive.

There are places where I get too "preachy"—please indicate
the places where you feel this, too.

I think the actual ending is nauseating. After giving a picture
of struggle and strife, suddenly to go into the cosmic love angle is revolting. That passage just happens to be a favorite of
mine, and I wound up with it, but I think it is out of keeping. I
think things could end with the "there are only people" idea,
phrased better.

As a minor detail, in the "Winter" chapter, I think the death
of the mule should precede the Old Boss episode. It is absurd
to grieve over Old Boss' dying wife and then follow with a dying
mule.

There is really no reason for me to talk with you personally
in New York about the material, for we do just as well by letter,
but I need a change and plan to come up anyway, perhaps the
end of this week or the beginning of next. I want to go to Medical Center or somewhere for a physical check, for I have had
more trouble than is reasonable with my insides. I will probably
be here at the beach until Thursday, then at Hawthorne from

Thursday to Saturday. Please give me a wire on your general
feeling about the possibilities of the book.

Marjorie

Through Thursday wire *Western Union*. Phone Crescent
Beach 4, St. Augustine. After Thursday, Island Grove.

1. Charles Rawlings and his two brothers, Wray and James.
2. This concern about a possible libel suit is noteworthy in view of the suit
brought by Zelma Cason two years later.

99. To Norton S. Baskin

Harkness Pavilion
[New York City]
Wednesday afternoon
[October 1, 1941]

Dear honey:—

And what an afternoon! Gorgeous! Wish to Heaven I'd come
directly here. Have the most divine HOTEL room on the 12th
floor looking out over Hudson and the Palisades. The food as
good as Longchamps. Darling nurses. A bathroom big enough for
Badminton. Feel rested enough already to whip Hitler single-
handed.

Well—JOKE on you and Edith [Pope]. The first doctor to come
in is an eminent psychiatrist! Hate to think they signed me
up at once as nuts.

Actually, he is the coordinating diagnostician. They get all the
physical data together, and he tries to see the whole picture.
He said, "Emotional disturbances may be causing most of the
trouble." Of course, I knew that nervous tension had a direct
effect on both stomach and colon. Anyway, he said he wanted to
go into the mental and emotional angles. He said, "I may or
may not give you any advice at all, but I have to get a picture of
the patient as a person." You should be here to tell him!!

Have had just the routine things checked today. The resting
is divine.

Forgot to say that the psychiatric diagnostician is an intimate
friend of John Marquand and Stephen Benét.[1] He knows you
don't get books out of contented cows.

Had to have my vulgar fun, of course, with somebody. The

intern doing the blood pressure etc. took himself pretty seriously. The nurse turned down my bed jacket so that my bosom
was exposed for something or other, and the intern had a 6-inch
ruler in one hand. I said, "You don't need to measure. I'm a
rather droopy 36."

Only the nurse and I thought it was funny.

Evening

Julia [Scribner] came up to see me this afternoon, and that
was grand.

Maxwell Perkins sent me books later yesterday evening by
messenger. There has been no mail from you. Perhaps a letter is
there now and Max will send it up late as he did the books.

Can't see how you can let me be away without wanting to
keep contact. If there's nothing by tomorrow afternoon, when
Dr. Atchley begins our probing, I'll just have to tell him my man
doesn't love me—and what can a psychiatrist do about that?

I will be through here Saturday afternoon. If Julia is ready
to head forth then, think I'd rather do it than fool around in
town.

Saw "The Corn is Green" Monday night, alone. A mess! Like
something out of the Ladies' Home Journal forty years ago.
Nothing much in town very good. We'll see "Arsenic and Old
Lace" sometime.

Will drop a line as we go along. Weather suddenly cooled.

I love you, but I think it's awful for you not to write to me.

Marjorie

1. Stephen Vincent Benét, American poet (1898–1943).

100. To Norton S. Baskin

Harkness Pavilion
[New York City]
Saturday morning
[October 4, 1941]

Dear Honey:—

Your sweet letter of Wednesday just came, forwarded by
Max.

I am hoping that the time is past, or soon will be, when I snap at you so. Had a long session with Dr. Atchley yesterday, and he identified the cause and source of my unreasonable rages— which I told him about—so simply that I can't see why I couldn't have figured it out for myself. But he said that an outside, disinterested, objective point of view is absolutely necessary—no one can get the perspective on his own picture for himself. The rages, as I suspected, have nothing to do with you.

It's a long story, and I'll have to see you to tell you all about it. But there is one thing I want to tell you now so that you'll have a chance to be thinking about it by yourself before I come home.

I presented my immediate problems to Dr. Atchley—principally our considering the matter of marriage, and the way I am torn at the thought of giving up the Creek way of life—wanting to be fair to you, and not wanting to worry if it would mean I went on rebelling. I just had to tell him the cute thing you said about the Will o' the Wisp.

Well, honey, he is perfectly certain that you are Willie. He said, laughingly, "What the Hell are you waiting for?" He said I needed exactly what you are, as I described you. I didn't go into any intimate detail, of course, but I had to tell him about you, as I feel at a crossroads in my life.

I gave him an outline of my life, and the things that I could identify as having disturbed me. He clarified so many things for me. Will have to tell you when I see you, as it's a long story.

Anyway, we'll have to talk things over, and so I'm giving you the chance either to run like everything or to propose to me![1] My heart ached a little about the telephone and cottage business—I thought what a wonderful time for you to suggest the other alternative—of your really taking me under your kind wing, permanently.

So you think things out from your point of view, decide what you *really* want, and we'll figure from there.

My dear, I do hate to have you think for a minute that I wanted the cottage. That never entered into it. I just hate New York alone, had such a lousy week-end at Princeton, and was dreading getting into the doctor business. Once I was here, as you will know by my last letter, I have been completely relaxed and happy. Am *still* content to lie in bed and watch the Hudson. The nurse said this morning, "Well, your temperature is almost normal." So must have been running one all along.

Dr. Atchley won't know until he has gone over all the tests, by this afternoon, how long I am to stay here. Neither Julia nor I is in any hurry.

1. MKR and Norton Baskin were married October 27, 1941.

101. To Ellen Glasgow

Castle Warden
St. Augustine, Florida
Jan. 17, 1942

My very dear Ellen Glasgow:

I have thought of you much, even when I was too swamped with detail to write and say so. The completion of my book [*Cross Creek*] left me exhausted at the beginning of October and when I followed the manuscript to New York I collapsed gratefully at Medical Center. A week there and a week driving through Vermont and New Hampshire put me on my feet and I am as good as new. On my return to Florida I was married. The last of the book's page proofs were back this week. You can see that the minutiae to fill this outline would be considerable.

In my memorable, to me, visit with you, I was about to go deeper into the man question when your watchful and wise guardian of necessity took me away. I had told you of the great relief of being free of an oppressive and almost entirely hideous marriage. After the nearly fifteen years of that nightmare came eight years of being entirely alone. I was alone in the large rambling farmhouse and there were many months at a time when there was not even anyone in the tenant house at the far side of my grove. The stark and complete loneliness, never filled by casual friends or the grove work or even the writing, was punctuated by emotional entanglements. From much of your work I know that you must be familiar with the pain of these.

My marriage, to a man whom I had known for eight years and who had been my dear close friend for nearly four, was something of a gamble, and there are few to whom I could or would admit this. Long independence, and above all, the peculiar mental independence of the creative worker, is not the best of bases for a successful marriage. Yet the circumstances are such that I feel the odds are in its favor. The man too is accustomed to independence. And his nature is so generous, so tolerant and so tender, and we care for each other in so deep and quiet a way, that being with him is like coming into harbor after long storms.

The conflict, for me, lies not in any adjustment to him but in the pull of the isolated rural life against the more or less sophisticated and urban life that we must share. He is a hotel man, and loves it, and this summer he bought a charming old gray stone showplace in St. Augustine and will open it next week as a small good hotel [the Castle Warden]. We will have an apartment on the top floor, overlooking the bay and ocean. The place has large grounds filled with huge old live oaks and magnolias and is everything attractive. Once things are in running order, I think I shall be able with a clear conscience to spend a part of almost every week at my grove. At any rate, I believe that great happiness is probable. Wish us luck.

It was good to see the Cabells. They are having their difficulties in comparatively small quarters, as there is inevitable intrusion on his hours of work. He asked me please to tell his wife that he is not being peculiar in being unable to work with two people and a dog walking in and out of the room where he is working!

We are having a most pleasant winter, and they wish, as I do, that you would come to St. Augustine for the rest of it. The town has everything that you would love, and it is only two days' comfortable driving from Richmond. Actually, I believe that you and your good companion would be very happy at our Castle Warden. It will be quiet, with as much of privacy as anyone wants, entirely comfortable, with sun porches and the lovely grounds for getting out of doors. And what a good time we should all have together.

Mr. Cabell says that you are considering following Roy and Stanley[1] a little further. The idea is fascinating. Did you know that a list of the ten most evil women in literature included Stanley?

"The First Gentleman of America"[2] is a gorgeous piece of work. It will of course set St. Augustine completely on its ear.

My book, "Cross Creek," will be published March 16. I'll have an early copy for you.

I do so hope that the heart is behaving reasonably. And consider St. Augustine seriously.

Affectionately,

Marjorie

1. Characters in Ellen Glasgow's novel *In This Our Life* (New York, 1941).
2. A novel by James Branch Cabell (New York, 1942).

Like *The Yearling, Cross Creek* was a true labor of love, and like *The Yearling,* it had a spectacular success, both critical and popular. It went through numerous editions in the regular trade version; it was published also in a special armed forces edition and was read by thousands of servicemen around the world; it was once more the choice of the Book-of-the-Month Club. MKR was now one of the most widely known writers in the United States.

102. To Maxwell E. Perkins

Castle Warden
St. Augustine
[ca. March 30, 1942]

Dear Max:

I feel as though I had lost you. All the business of the book publishing has so little to do with the book itself. But it is gratifying to have such a generous reception for so queer a book [*Cross Creek*]. I still wish, in a way, that I had done an entirely serious book with the "classic" touch—but the human stories were irresistible.

My colored maid Idella finished the book when we were at the Creek last week. She came to the door and twisted her apron, and said, "I had a speech all ready to say to you about the book, and now I've forgotten it." I said, "Never mind the speech. Just tell me what you thought of it." She burst out, "Oh, it's a beautiful book! When I read it, it seemed to me we ought to come back to the Creek to live."

I am slowly making an adjustment to the life in St. Augustine, but it is difficult. I had thought—and hoped—that perhaps I had wrung dry the backwoods section and living, but there is something there from which I cannot seem to tear away. My husband is so completely lovely a person, and it grieves me to see him grieved when I simply have to clear out and go back to the Creek. Actually, there is a whole new literary field before me in the old town of St. Augustine, and I really hope that in time I shall be able to sink myself in it.

I know that Whitney [Darrow] must be deep in his new marriage plans, which seem to me very nice and wise, so will ask you please to have sent, with compliments of the author, a copy of Cross Creek to Mrs. Sigrid Undset,[1] Hotel Margaret, Brooklyn. Also copies to Edward Lawrence

Frank Whitbeck
Spencer Tracy
Victor Fleming

all care of
Metro-Goldwyn-Mayer
Culver City
California

cards, compliments of the author

Marjorie

1. Sigrid Undset, Norwegian novelist (1882–1949).

After her marriage to Norton Baskin in October 1941, MKR tried hard to live and work in their apartment in the Castle Warden Hotel in St. Augustine, of which Baskin was now owner-manager, but she was often drawn back to the beloved old farmhouse at Cross Creek where, even if life was not always a pastoral idyll, she felt that the writing went better. She still felt more at home and at peace at the Creek than anywhere else, and after fourteen years of residence there (and even though she was now something of a national celebrity), she was no longer looked upon by her cracker neighbors as a Yankee newcomer but very much as one of themselves. She loved the feeling of being part of the community and had a relish for becoming involved in local disputes and intrigues, as the following letter illustrates.

103. To Norton S. Baskin

[Cross Creek]
Tuesday afternoon
[April 1942]

Dear honey:

It's a good thing I didn't try to go to Jax with you, as it took me two and a half hours to do my various errands and I didn't reach the Creek until 3 p.m. as it was. And no Idella![1] And she has not come yet. I knew that transportation from Reddick here was most difficult, but it seems as though she should have been able to hitch hike by this time. And if something went wrong, she has had time to notify me. If she doesn't show up in the next two hours, will go to Reddick, much as I hate to use the gas.

I had been in the house about five minutes when Mrs. Williams (Brice's daughter) and Doug Whidden, whom they had called on to help in the rumpus, came up. Mrs. W. had a contract that a lawyer had drawn up, whereby Tom Glisson leased his right of way and paid for a cattle gap, and Tom was making objections and wouldn't sign it. The contract seemed extremely fair to me in every way—and it was up to me to get Tom to fall in line. Tom had telephoned me to St. Augustine just before I left, asking when I was coming, as things were getting worse. To make an involved story short. Armour Brice and I went with Tom to the controversial land this morning and worked out an arrangement satisfactory to all. To swing it, I am paying for a second cattle gap and one line of fence myself, for I felt Tom would balk at paying out any more, and it is well worth a hundred dollars, say, to me, to have everybody feel all right about it. Armour and I walked down the road together, and I said, "Do you remember what it says in the Bible? 'Blessed are the peacemakers, for they shall see God'." He said, "That doesn't promise anything but seeing God. I'm afraid they'll let us have one look, and then throw us out again." Anyway, the contract is signed.

I also had it out with Doug Whidden and we both felt better about it.

Found a week-old letter here from Marcia Davenport, saying that she and her husband (who recently had his appendix
out) were going to Hobe Sound, and would I like to have them
spend a day or two at the Creek on their way back. Wired her I
was delighted, and am now wondering what the hell if anything of any sort has happened to Idella. Anyway, hold up on
asking anybody else to come over with you. If they come, it will
be between May 1 and 3, and it would be fun if you could
come over. You'd enjoy them both very much, especially him.
Will let you know what I hear.

Mrs. Cason has absolutely no claim on the 64 feet of Chet's
[Crosby] property. She sold the land 30 years ago to Ed Johnson,
Ed owned it 20 years and sold to Chet's uncle who owned it 10
years. Now Zelma is going around saying she (Zelma) is going
to throw Chet out, and is foreclosing right away. She or her
mother has no more legal right to foreclose on Chet than on me.
She has an appalling nature. Chet said the gist of it is that
she told him if he would take her to Gainesville to check on the
records, she would allow her mother to sign the quit claim
deed. Knowing they had no claim, Chet refused. What she
wanted to do, he says, was to make it appear that she was doing
him a big favor, so that he would feel obligated to her!

Twelve bi-motored bombers, several towing gliders, just
flew so low over the house they almost touched the pecan trees
across the road. Spooky. . . .

It is a gorgeous day, but the Idella situation has me
depressed. Feel sure there is a reasonable explanation, but am
only afraid somebody, perhaps she, is seriously ill.

Am getting ready to bake my own soy bean bread. Have the
sponge "raising" now, but it doesn't look very promising at the
moment. Had to guess at a suitable recipe. The soy flour seemed
of the consistency of cement.

My 21 rose bushes are dead as door-nails. Martha said they
were that way when they opened the package, but Will planted
them and kept them well watered anyway. So that Texas company just isn't any good. They were probably a long time on the
road, and probably dug days before they were shipped.

Well, wish you were here. And hope you can come over. Only,

of course, if it is convenient, for otherwise you wouldn't enjoy
it.

Loads of love,

Marjorie

1. Except for MKR's maid, Idella Parker, and Marcia and Russell Davenport,
who were friends from the New York literary world, all the persons mentioned in
this letter were Cross Creek neighbors.

104. To Ellen Glasgow

Castle Warden
St. Augustine, Florida
April 14, 1942

My very dear Ellen Glasgow:

I was horrified to hear in a note this morning from James
Cabell that you had not received a copy of my "Cross Creek,"
signed for you nearly a month ago. Having no word from you, I
was afraid you had been too ill or busy to read it—or, horrible
thought, that you hadn't liked it and wouldn't say so! I had
mailed out a dozen or more copies, and when I had James' note,
I rummaged under some piles of papers—we have been using
one hotel room until our apartment should be ready—and here
was your signed, and sadly unmailed "Cross Creek." I'm so
distressed to be late with it.

We can move into our apartment on top of Castle Warden in
another week or ten days, and I shall feel much less like a
wildcat in a cage. The pull of Cross Creek is still strong and I
have to go back every week or two. It would be so sensible to
wean myself away from it altogether, but after you've read the
book I think you will understand the almost unreasonably deep
roots there.

I feel itchy at not working, but I comfort myself with your
wonderful remark in the Prefaces about needing to let the well
of the subconscious fill up again between books.

I am down at my ocean cottage on a totally un-springlike
day—the sky and sea gray and angry, and big tankers sliding
along as close as they dare to the shore, to evade the subma-
rines. They are hellish times and take one back to an old Mil-

tonian sense of definite Good and Evil in conflict. Not that
Our Side has been any lily, but I don't really think we deserve
what we're getting.

I do hope that with winter over you'll feel stronger. I think of
you often.

> With my love,
>
> Marjorie

105. To Norman Berg's pointer, Patrie

> [St. Augustine]
> July 7, 1942

Dear Patrie:

In all my long four months of life, I have never had a greater
shock than for you to write to that Topper Baskin[1] instead of to
me. I know that I shall never be anything more in the world
than a rough country fellow, while Topper is the glamor boy of
Castle Warden—but Patrie, you must surely know that you
cannot judge the heart by long silken red ears and feathered
paws and tail. I think you should know, for your own good, that
Topper did not pay you the compliment of burying your note
decently with his morning bone, but dropped it indifferently on
the marble floor of the lobby for all to see. I have carried it
away in tender teeth and hidden it under a coontie palm, cher-
ishing it for your sake, even though it was for Another. Believe me, in revealing Topper's nature, I am not being a dog
in the manger. It is only that I can see the pitfalls ahead for
a girl of your *impressionable* temperament. You are with the
Army—you will know temptation—there is a fate worse than
death—you could become a *camp follower.*

Enough of these sad warnings! As to family matters, the
Mister has been having a good many brides and grooms and
wedding parties at his Inn. I might mention in passing that
Topper usually tries to crowd himself into the wedding pictures,
and, of course, sits up and begs shamelessly for chicken sandwiches at the wedding breakfasts. Tammy has spoken sharply to
him about it, but you can't change a leopard's spots or a spaniel's appetite.

The Missus had a most interesting caller yesterday, by invi-

tation, and my feelings are rather mixed about it. It was the
Florida negress, Zora Neale Hurston, who has done some really
superb work. She is at the Florida Normal School and will teach
there this winter. She is a lush, fine-looking café au lait woman
with a most ingratiating personality, a brilliant mind, and a
fundamental wisdom that shames most whites. She puts the full
responsibility for negro advancement on the negroes themselves and has no use for the Left Wingers who consider her a
traitor, nor for the "advanced" negroes who belong to what she
calls the fur-coat peerage. She says she doesn't like spirituals
"with their faces lifted," and wants to establish a Negro Conser-
vatory of Music that would depart entirely from white tradition, and develop negro music from its own roots. She tells a
marvelous story to make her point about the folly of negroes'
being imitative. A railroad engineer had a pet monkey that
he took with him on all his runs. The monkey was fascinated
with the affair and watched everything. One day the engineer
left the cab and the monkey in delight pulled a lever and seized
the throttle and the train "high-tailed it down the mainline."
The telegraphers sent out word, "Clear the tracks! Monkey on
the line." The train reached an open switch and crashed into a
string of box-cars and that was the end of the monkey. She
said dryly, "A lovely monkey, but a damn poor engineer."

She says that both "advanced" whites and "advanced" negroes make a mistake in handling "the negro problem" with
kid gloves, each afraid of the other. She says that the negro is
America's "sacred black cow." She discussed lynching with the
Kleagle of the Ku Klux Klan! Remarked to him that the individual didn't matter—a man has to die sometime—but a wise
and practical system of law was built up by the Greeks and
Romans, taken to England, from England here, "and when you
go against that you're undermining something valuable that
has taken thousands of years to build." She said he took his feet
off his desk and said, "Zora, there's something in that."

The Missus has had quite a jolt and feels rather small. By
all her principles, she should accept this woman as a human
being and a friend—certainly an attractive member of society
acceptable anywhere—and she is a coward. If she were on her
own, she would do it. She feels that she cannot hurt her hus-

band in a business way. But her pioneer blood is itching——.

The airplane spotting has become very lively. Sunday morning
there were four heavy explosions at sea—the report was made
to Naval Intelligence at Jacksonville, who queried N. excitedly
in detail, but there has been no word as to what had actually
happened.

Idella is on vacation, and a tie-tongued darky is substituting.
She asked, "Ih ah ohhing oo oot ou o e i?", which meant, apropos of some rat poison in the bathroom, "Is that something you
put out for the mice?"

You and your family are very much missed. We all speak of
you often and hope you will be home on furlough soon.

> With love and forgiveness,
>
> Moe Rawlings

1. Norton Baskin's cocker spaniel. Moe was MKR's new pointer.

106. To Maxwell E. Perkins

> [Crescent Beach]
> July 23, 1942

Dear Max:

. . . Florida has been having a heat wave, and it was 100 in
St. Augustine yesterday, and 104 in some other Florida cities—
the hottest weather for Florida in 59 years. It has never been
over 83 at the cottage, where I am working, and many days
during the hot spell has been 72 when it was 90 in town. I tried
to work in our apartment at the hotel, but just could not.

This part of the coast has become practically a military zone,
and now passes are necessary to use the ocean road that leads to
the cottage. I have black-out shades, and it is rather creepy
alone here at night, with no traffic on beach or highway, convoys
going by, bombers overhead, and the thought of the saboteurs
who land on isolated beaches. Twice a submarine has been seen
from the airplane spotting post where Norton and I do duty,
but the sub was gone by the time planes could reach the spot.
We hear mysterious explosions out at sea, and never know the
cause.

I have suffered over the requests of the Treasury Board and the War Writers' board, on which I agreed to become a member, and tried to write things, but have decided two things: the forced "Americanism" is both disgusting and unnecessary (the simplest people are aware of the danger and the need for concerted action); and I can do no more than write as I always do. A basic Americanism is implicit in what I write, and the inferred is always more effective than the obvious. An astonishing percentage of my letters about "Cross Creek" is from men in the service. I may have written you what one man in the Army said: "You are writing about the simple things for which we in the Army are fighting." A flier wrote from Cairo that space was at a premium in his duffle-bag in leaving for Egypt, and he was tempted to leave "Cross Creek" behind, but did not, as it meant something valuable to him that he wanted to hang onto. I *cannot* turn out the sort of thing that Wrigley's chewing gum and Pepsi-cola use on the radio for "morale."

A week or so ago I had a call from a private with the Texas Division, a young chap who had been a clerk in a large bookstore. He was an aesthete, almost a sissy, but with such a receptive mind that he was finding Army life fascinating. He said that he had roamed over old St. Augustine, alone, and said to himself, "Well, this is worth fighting for." You don't need "propaganda" when people feel that way. And the other day when Norton and I were doing our airplane spotting, a very tough and drunken soldier borrowed our binoculars and talked with us. He said, "I'm raring to go. I'm ready to shed my life's blood." Now that sort of thing could be "worked up" into a radio skit or bit of newspaper propaganda—but it shouldn't and needn't be.

Marjorie

The chapter on food and cookery in *Cross Creek* evoked such enthusiasm among readers that MKR decided to expand the material into a full-size volume entitled *Cross Creek Cookery* (New York, 1942).

107. To Maxwell E. Perkins

Box 550
St. Augustine
August 21, [1942]

Dear Max:

I'm so glad that you find the *Cookery* good reading. I'll fix the details you mentioned. I too dislike the word "drooling" and used it almost unconsciously because so many of the letters to me, from plainly very nice people, used that word.

I am getting *so many* letters from men in the Service. Some ask where others of my books can be bought. One asked if I had any of my "old books or stories" I could send, as the library was meagre. Now, can you find out how many libraries there are for both soldiers and sailors? If there are not too terribly many, I'd like to send copies of my books to all of them.

Almost every letter I have had in connection with the Digest's condensation has said that the reader now intended to buy the book, so I guess it is as you said, that it helps sales.

I have had four very vicious letters, two anonymous, calling me a low evil woman for writing about the disgusting sex relations of animals, but they were plainly from the kind of peculiar Puritan who, himself or herself, has the dirtiest kind of mind. The other letters have been simply beautiful. Several from ministers, two of whom used bits of the book as texts for sermons. One used the part, "Sift every man through the sieve of circumstance, and you get the residue," etc. Also had a four-page dictated letter from an executive of the Aetna Life Insurance Co., who said he had handled $100,000,000 of mortgages of the "Okies," and trying to explain the capitalist's point of view! He said that "powerful writers like you and Steinbeck, whose written word is taken as law, should at least know the other side of the picture." Evidently something I said about property got under his skin! . . .

One of my old maid aunts, about whom I have told you many tales, wrote me, "I just don't know what to think about your writing a *cook book*. Somehow, it doesn't seem at all *classical* or *literary*."

Norton has just had a fine business "break." The Coast Guard has just taken over the huge Ponce de Leon hotel in St. Augustine as a training school, and probably the two other good hotels, the Monson and the Bennett. Norton's Castle Warden had too few rooms for their purpose, and the Lieutenant Commander who looked at his place told him he was lucky, as his place was much too nice for such a purpose. It means that Norton is bound to have a splendid business, both from visiting families, officers, and the St. Augustine elderly Old Guard who come for the winter and just sit—since his will be the only good hotel open to private business. I am enough of a cynic to believe it will probably mean that now he is all set in a business way, he will be drafted! He applied for the officers' training

With Norton Baskin, spearing blue crabs at Salt Springs (1941–42).

school, but is not a college man, so was not eligible and will just wait for the draft.

My friend General Lange told him that if he is drafted, he will certainly be put in a place where his particular experience will be used. I think he could easily be entered in the officers' training school for draftees, as he is widely read and passes intelligence tests about 40% higher than I do!

We had a delightful week-end at Cross Creek. We had as guests seven army doctors, Majors, who have been coming from Camp Blanding to his place and have had their families there. They are Boston men, who organized their own unit of 50 so that they will go into action as a group—top-notch surgeons, plastic surgeons, brain surgeons, etc. We went to Silver Glen in the scrub Saturday, fishing for blue crabs. Sunday we had dinner at the Creek, baked sherried grapefruit, Crab Newburg, also plain crab with mayonnaise, raised rolls, guava jelly, carrot souffle, tomato aspic with artichokes, Dora's peach ice cream and orange cake. I didn't have enough good white wine for that many people so served a good Burgundy, and it went very well with the Newburg. One of the men said, "This meal was a symphony." Another said, "I don't know about that, but it's the best Goddam dinner I ever ate." So in spite of Auntie's qualms, there is certainly artistry in a perfect meal.

Marjorie

One of the most dramatic and harrowing episodes in MKR's later years was the so-called "Cross Creek Trial." In all her Florida writings, she showed the most scrupulous concern for accuracy of detail and factual "truth," and in some stories like "Jacob's Ladder" and in *South Moon Under* the events and the characters were often thinly disguised versions of real life. In one of the sketches in "Cracker Chidlings," she used a young man's real name in an uncomplimentary context, which so incensed the man's mother that she stalked up and down in the road outside MKR's house (MKR was recuperating from her appendectomy at the time) and threatened to come in and give her a horsewhipping. So she was well aware of the problem of using real names when she came to write *Cross Creek,* and she queried Max Perkins once or twice for an opinion (see letter 98, September 15, 1941), but he thought the tone of the book so friendly and cordial that he turned the matter back to her, saying that she knew the individuals involved better than anyone else and could therefore make the decision better than anyone else. She actually went out and asked one or two of her cracker neighbors if they would mind her using real names in the book and was assured they would not. But she didn't ask Zelma Cason (whose brother, T.Z. Cason, had been friend and physician to MKR for several years), assuming that she "would be all right." It turned out to be a costly assumption. On January 8, 1943, Zelma filed suit against MKR for libel, asking $100,000 damages. Her complaint was that several passages in the book had caused her severe pain and humiliation, one in particular:

> Zelma is an ageless spinster resembling an angry and efficient canary. She manages her orange grove and as much of the village and county as needs management or will submit to it. I cannot decide whether she should have been a man or a mother. She combines the more violent characteristics of both and those who ask for or accept her manifold ministrations think nothing of being cursed loudly at the very instant of being tenderly fed, clothed, nursed, or guided through their troubles.
>
> [*Cross Creek* (New York, 1942), pp. 48–49]

Most people who knew Zelma thought this to be an accurate description and, in context, a complimentary one, but she insisted in her brief that it defamed her character and held her up to ridicule and scornful abuse, particularly the reference to her use of profanity.

Zelma was represented by two lawyers from nearby Palatka, Florida, Judge (his first name) Walton and his daughter Kate Walton. MKR was defended by her friend and attorney, Philip May from Jacksonville, and by Sigsbee Scruggs of Gainesville, who had a considerable local reputation as a trial lawyer. The nature of the suit was so ambiguous that a year and a half of legal negotiation was required to determine if legal grounds for suit existed. The case was taken finally to the state supreme court, which ruled that grounds would exist if the charge was changed

from libel to "invasion of privacy," a phrase which turned out to
have its own ambiguities. Then more than a year and half of fretful preparation elapsed before the case was tried in the circuit
court at Gainesville in May 1946. The trial itself lasted an entire
week, and was played out like high drama before a packed court-
room, with MKR starring in a two-day testimony. The jury found
for the defendant in less than thirty minutes, and at the verdict
the audience broke into a spontaneous ovation; but the case was
not over. Zelma appealed, and after further delay the case went
once again to the state supreme court, which two years later reversed the lower court and found for the plaintiff, awarding only
nominal damages of $1.00 and costs ($1,050.10), though the cost to
MKR was much higher than this would suggest—more than
$18,000 in legal fees and more than five-and-a-half years of worry
and frustration that caused a major distraction and hindrance to
her writing, which went badly during the entire period.

108. To Philip May

Castle Warden Hotel
St. Augustine, Florida
Feb. 5, 1943

Dear Phil:

I think the Declaration[1] is one of the funniest documents I
have ever read in my life. I laughed out loud all by myself,
which I seldom do. The particular grievances and the way they
are phrased make me feel that our so-called "defense" is infinitely simpler than I expected. Zelma's statement that she
had always "consciously avoided all conduct and behavior that
would or might make her conspicuous or warrant general public
interest in or curiosity about the private and social aspects of
her daily life and the normal development and manifestations of
her personality" is a riotous one to come from a woman who
cusses a blue streak in front of assorted people, and in a voice so
loud that she is famous for its carrying quality.

I feel that she defeats herself in her very claims; for whereas
no one aside from her own friends and acquaintances could
possibly have connected "my friend Zelma" with Zelma Cason, a
femme sole, of Island Grove, she now seeks to bring on herself

a nation-wide notoriety and curiosity as to her personality. And she admits herself that the portrait is "clearly recognizable" to friends and acquaintances—which it would not be if she did not answer the description.

Of course, her charge of maliciousness on my part is an outright lie, and no one knows it is a lie better than she. Aside from my witnesses, etc., I know that my word would carry against hers, for I am a great believer in the recognizability of truth in the human face and voice.

She would scarcely have trotted out photographs of her niece and niece's baby for me to admire, if she thought I entertained malicious feelings; she would not have joined with me in an embrace at the time I gave her an affectionately signed copy of "Cross Creek," when she had seemed to get it off her chest that she was offended; I should not have been a welcome caller on her mother if it were a fact that I meant her harm.

Incidentally, I presented her with the copy of "Cross Creek" in St. Augustine, at the place on Anastasia Island where she lives. Her work is out of St. Augustine, you know, and she goes to Island Grove about every other week-end. Actually, except for the inconvenience to Norton of having to leave his work here to go to Gainesville, I think it really makes very little difference whether the case, if it does materialize, is before a Gainesville or a St. Augustine court. The only possible advantage would be that in St. Augustine a jury would be remote from local factions around Island Grove. If you secured an objectively-minded jury at Gainesville, it would be all the same.

Chet Crosby voluntarily put himself at our disposal. Incidentally, Judge Murphy [Murphree?] at Gainesville is a good friend of his. He says he is a swell person.

Your best, and certainly most delightful and entertaining witness, will be Fred Tompkins, of Citra.

He said, with an engaging twinkle in his eye, "On the witness stand, I'd be obliged to tell the truth. And the truth would be, I always figured Zelma was *proud* of her cussing."

He would also be a delightful witness in the matter of "selling a personality" and violating privacy, for he is the "Uncle Benny" of "Benny and the Bird Dogs," a story that has gone into editors' anthologies and high school and college anthologies

all over the country. He has always felt that it was an honor to
be interesting enough to be written about, and would say so
on the witness stand. He would delight in engaging in repartee
with you on the subject. He would prove that an entirely delightful and *normal* person takes such an attitude, whereas it
takes a combination of exhibitionism and greed and unwar-
ranted touchiness, to take the attitude Zelma has taken.

I have not broached the subject with him as yet, and would
like to wait until later to do so, but I think that the most
estimable citizen at Cross Creek, W. R. Brice, "Old Boss," who
was written about in the book at length, and in not too favorable
terms when it concerned his defense of the shooting-negro,
Henry, would be willing to take the stand and testify to the
same reaction as Fred Tompkins'. I think that Zelma has carried
out her threat, which was reported to me, to try to stir up
Cross Creek, for Mr. Brice's daughter was cool to me last week
when I dropped in for a visit, as is my habit. At the same time,
Old Boss put his arm around me, an unusual gesture for him,
and I felt a tacit support in that gesture.

The only indication of the type of attack I expected Zelma to
make comes on page 2 of the declaration, paragraph 6, where
she speaks of the period of intimacy when "defendant" was "then
neither wealthy nor famous." If anything is made of this in
the trial, if it comes about, Walton will undoubtedly try to
contrast her simple way of life and poverty with my rise to
wealth and fame. I meant to bring this up when I talked with
you. I went through years of poverty and hard work exceeding
anything Zelma has ever known. I did all the housework, cleaning, cooking, washing, ironing, for a family of four, and tended
vegetable gardens and worked on making the old farmhouse
habitable as well. At the time of my divorce—and in case she
introduces anything of this, the facts are only that Chuck Rawlings, as a newspaper man and urbanite, could not stomach
the hard rural life, whereas I felt my life and destiny were tied
up with the simple way of life—I was left with an overdrawn
account at the bank and subsisted for some time only on what I
could raise and grow myself. I came very close to actual hunger. When my Florida books brought me prosperity, my first
move was to pay off the mortgage on my grove, so that I might

be assured of living that simple life that I loved, among the people I loved. And the Florida books brought me prosperity, for the sole reason that the reading public responded to my own love of the country and the people and felt a sense of sharing in that love, as the letters I have will show.

I call these elements to your notice while they are in my mind.

Norton made the point that Zelma contradicts herself. She claims on the one hand that the sketch etc. of her was "colored and distorted and only true in part," and on the other hand that I "sold her personality." Only one or the other can be true.

I am pretty certain that Zelma lied about her age, in claiming to be 46. I am 46 and am sure Zelma is considerably older than I. If Mr. Scruggs (if he is acting for us in Gainesville) can see her birth certificate there, it would be worth checking, for if she lied about her age (about which she has always been very touchy) it is a minor point to prove her undue touchiness. It would also show that calling her an "ageless" spinster (by which I meant that she looks the same now as when I first knew her) I was kinder than in giving her actual age. If she objects to the word "spinster," the Feb. 8 issue of TIME describes Margaret Woodrow Wilson, p. 50, as "a spinster." I consider the word kinder than "old maid."

I don't know whether she would be willing to testify against her, but a mutual friend here in St. Augustine, Mrs. Grace Bugbee, (Lowland Florists) has always deplored Zelma's unkind way of speech, and violence of speech, and told Mrs. Tarrant (Aunt Ida) that Zelma was in her shop one day and was saying dreadful things about some man at Moultrie who had angered her. Mrs. Bugbee told Aunt Ida that she "would never have said in the presence of the late Mr. Bugbee, the things that Zelma said in front of a strange man who was in the shop at the time."

It may not be a useable point and is a trivial detail, but Aunt Ida also reported a conversation she had with Zelma apropos of Aunt Ida's landlady, Mrs. Reginald White, very much of a gentlewoman. Mrs. White had taken a paid job as supervisor of a free nursery school in St. Augustine, operated under the WPA. Zelma said, "She'll have to take her checks from the WPA, and that'll take some of the pride out of her." Mrs. White being a lady obliged to make her living, there is no reason for her to be humbled, and it only shows Zelma's resentment of well-meaning folk. . . .

My conversation with Milton Carr of the United Press at Miami was very pleasant. He said, "Personally, I don't think a thing will come of it, except that you'll sell a lot of copies of the book."

Mrs. White (I speak of things as they come to mind) said to Aunt Ida, "Miss Cason is not well-thought-of here." She might be able to direct you to a useable witness who would testify to the very way in which Zelma makes herself conspicuous, refuting her picture of herself as a shrinking violet.

I enclose a few letters that in one way and another seem to have special relevance and helpfulness. The one from Ross Allen[2] speaks of being thrilled at appearing in the book. Zelma might claim that he was not written of "maliciously," but when it comes to "selling a personality" and details that evolved out of the privacy of friendship, Ross has more reason to feel aggrieved than she, for he could have written and sold the story of our snake-hunt himself and received good money for it, whereas it is I who has made the fabulous profits from selling him, and now he cannot make use of the material. Yet he is pleased to be a part of the larger pattern.

I have been unable to find the note I made at the time of Zelma's commenting on the destruction of wild life by the local commercial hunters, in what I considered vivid and pertinent terms. However, I mean to question some of my friends, such as Nettie Martin of Ocala, for I seem to remember having spoken of this at the time, as I thought it a delightful and searching comment.

The note from the *Atlantic Monthly* seems of value, for this dispassionate source calls "Cross Creek" "such a friendly book." Norton also pointed out that Zelma (or rather, Walton) might claim that there could be no objection to the book in general (though she does say it is only a compendium of gossipy and scandalous items) and that they object only to what they consider the maligning of her. The answer to that seems to me to be that when the world in general considers the book a friendly and generous one, the author could plainly not be capable of malice. Which God knows is true!

The letter from Maxwell Perkins dealing with the matter of libel and my consulting with Mr. Martin to make sure he would not be offended, would seem to prove that I had in mind the desire not to offend any of my friends and neighbors. If I had had any idea that what I wrote about Zelma would offend her, I would plainly have consulted her in advance, as I did Mr. Martin. Incidentally, Mr. Martin is proud to be in the book, and I think we could call on him. One advantage of having the "trial" in Gainesville would be that my local friends would not be inconvenienced by appearing there, whereas if they were called to St. Augustine, it would interfere with their business.

There are many items I can take up with you in the "declaration," but others can wait. For instance, page 6, paragraph 4, she speaks of descriptions "colored to suit a gross and depraved imagination." I think the bulk of letters I have received show that the imagination in question not only is not gross and depraved, but is humanitarian, kindly and generous.

I shall probably take off for New York Tuesday or Wednesday. When Norton takes me up to meet train or plane, I shall wire you, so that we can meet and talk over any details. At that time I shall bring to you several envelopes of letters that you can cull over for items useful to prove both my lack of maliciousness, and the sense in the general reading public, including many men in the service of our country, that they have had a feeling of spiritual uplift in the book—which would not be possible if there were any taint of unkindness in the writing.

If Walton attempts to disbar such general reaction as irrelevant to the specific so-called "slandering," I am sure you can prove the relevance to the case, and present this vital material to judge and jury.

As I have said to you before, if it were not that losing the case would harm my poor misguided friend financially and mentally, I should welcome a public airing of the matter.

I thought in the beginning that poor Zelma's reaction was one of exhibitionism and venom, but as I read the declaration, I think that the hope of "collecting" is the main motive. . . .

Marjorie K.R.

1. As an opening maneuver in the lawsuit, each side sent to the other an Interrogatory, which had to be responded to under oath. In this letter to Philip May,

MKR was reacting to the answers made by Zelma Cason to a recent Interrogatory sent by Mr. May.

2. Ross Allen, American herpetologist (1908–81).

109. To Mr. Mixon[1]

May 1, 1943

Dear Mr. Mixon:

I am sorry to be so many months in answering your interesting letter, but I am just out of a long siege in the hospital. (Now fully recovered.) I too wish you might describe your environs, but guess that will have to wait until after "the duration."

As to Martha's [Mickens] disloyalties, you must realize she is motivated by flattery and tips. A friend of some Army doctors Martha and I entertained here stopped by in my absence, and having heard of Martha's "spirituals," asked if she wouldn't sing for him. Martha said demurely, "I gen'rally gets fifty cents for singin'."

I haven't been bass fishing in some time, but while bass are legitimately and properly taboo commercially, my fishermen friends sometimes find them past hope of life on their catfish lines and bring me one, and then I have chowder. I must tell you a story somewhat along this line. I overheard two negro grove workers talking, one of them the Raymond I wrote about in the Black Shadows chapter of Cross Creek. Raymond has always had woman trouble, his wives deceiving him or walking out on him. The other negro was an older man, Will, who has had several faithful and good wives. Raymond said, "Mr. Will, I sure would like to know what you does to get and keep a good woman." Will said, "Well, Raymond, you's been with Cap'n fishin. And you's seed him make a cast, and a big swirl come, and the line go tight, and Cap'n pull in a great big fish." "I sho' has." "And other times, you's seed Cap'n make jus' as good a cast, and a big swirl come, and the line go plum limp, and Cap'n cuss like hell, for he's lost the fish." "I sho' has." "Well, Raymond, it all depend how you get the hook sot."

With best wishes,

Marjorie Kinnan Rawlings

1. Mr. Mixon was a serviceman stationed somewhere overseas. During World War II, MKR received dozens of letters from men in the armed forces who had read her book, and she tried to answer each one personally, as here, even though it drained off literary energies she could ill afford to lose at the time.

110. To John Temple Graves[1]

[1943?]

Dear Mr. Graves:

I am afraid that it is utterly futile to try to make you see the point of view of a Southern "liberal" who goes so much further than you in interpreting Southern liberalism. But I must speak my piece. I know how sincere you are, I know of your integrity, I know that you are convinced of your broad-mindedness, and that you must feel you have gone a long way since your early prejudices. To a degree, you are indeed fighting the good fight, and I applaud you.

Yet in a recent column, you urge "justice" and "opportunity" for Negroes, while insisting on the pattern of segregation. This is where we part company.

How can I say it, how can I open your mind and heart, to the psychological and actual fact that "justice" and "opportunity," however far they extend into education, politics and economics, are a cruel and hypocritical farce, as long as the artificial barrier of "segregation" is maintained. Don't you see, can't you see, that segregation denies a man or woman something more important than "justice" or "opportunity," and that is self-respect, freedom from being made to feel subtly inferior, from being, after all, and finally, an outcast. Most of us now know enough of psychoanalysis to understand the devastation worked on even the character of the dominant white Nordic male, the top-dog in the world of today, when he is made early to feel inferior.

You have been honest enough to admit that part of your own timid psychology, and that of such semi or pseudo-liberals as Hodding Carter,[2] derives from a preponderance of Negroes in certain sections of our mutually beloved South. I do not remember your ever having said so, in so many words, but I assume there is an unexpressed fear that if segregation disappeared, for one reason or another, the masses of Negroes in their heavily populated districts in the South would "take over," with appalling results. I have no idea of your age, but this fear amused me, for I am of an age to remember the Suffragists, or Suffragettes, picketing the White House to try to get "Votes for Women." The great argument against "Votes for Women" was that once allowed "equality," women would "take over," men would become slaves, and the country ruined. It is not only obvious, but shameful, that since women were given "equality," they have not even done their proper share toward solving national and world problems, to say nothing of "taking over." I prophesy that the same thing would happen among the Negroes if there were no segregation, they would go on about their own affairs as before, and would do very well indeed if they took a greater interest than before in government and general problems.

As to "social equality," no one has given a better answer to that than Eleanor Roosevelt, who said quietly, "Why, that's something that can't be legislated. It is something you have with your own friends." And as long as we have our blessed democracy, we can all choose our own friends. There are circles in which I should not be welcome, there are folks I should not invite to my home, not because of "race, color or creed," but because we have nothing in common. This will hold good forever.

I myself began with an acceptance of segregation, I took it for granted, coming of a preponderantly Southern ancestry. I can only tell you that when long soul-searching and a combination of circumstances delivered me of my last prejudices, there was an exalted sense of liberation. It was not the Negro who became free, but I. I wish and pray for your own liberation. It is almost a religious experience. No man is free as long as another is enslaved, and the slavery of the spirit is more stringent than that of the body.

[MKR]

1. A columnist and editorial writer for the *Florida Times Union* in Jacksonville.
2. Hodding Carter, American editor and author (1907–72).

111. To Norman Berg

The Gotham
5th Ave. at 55th St.
New York City
July 6, 1943

Dear Norman:

Things have moved so fast I haven't had a chance to thank you for the most welcome books and the new drake, who has "taken over."[1]

Norton volunteered for the American Field Service—was accepted—had about 16 shots in 16 days and Saturday had a wire to report with equipment at headquarters here this morning. I came up with him on the chance that it might be a week or two before sailing, and because I wanted to be with him as long as possible. But it looks as though he could leave much sooner than that. He doesn't know where he will be sent—could be India—could be the Middle East—could be anywhere at all where the British Army is, for though it is an American unit, it operates under British officers. Imagine you know about it—a volunteer ambulance service. They work in the front lines and in the last war their casualties were twice the ratio of regular army casualties—which of course makes me feel just swell. But I wouldn't stop him if I could—it is what he wants to do, and a man has to make his own decisions about things like that. I think it is infinitely more heroic for a man of Norton's temperament to do such a thing, than for most kinds of men. And he will do a calm, good job, no matter how he suffers inside. Am being a good sport *now*, but shall quietly collapse after he goes!

Will write again.

Marjorie

1. MKR had a flock of mallard ducks which lived wild in her yard and nearby grove.

112. To Edith Pope

[Harkness Pavilion
New York City]
Bastille Day
[July 14, 1943]

Dearest Edith:

Just a facetious touch—not meaning to indicate the storming of any gates or the falling of any guillotine.

You might know I couldn't get out of New York without a sojourn here [at the Medical Center].

Norton sailed *very* soon after we arrived. We scrambled to get his equipment together in time. We both developed a variety of bronchial flu. Norton had a temperature of 103. I called Dr. Atchley frantically and he prescribed by phone. I all but held up the St. Regis Pharmacy to get the necessary codeine to relieve his cough. He had so little *time,* but I got his temperature *under* 100 by the time he just disappeared into the void. I wasn't supposed to know, and he said he was sure it would be the *next* day, but I knew damn well he would not be back again. But it was really easier to say good bye with *some* elements of uncertainty.

My dose was not as bad as his, but after he didn't show up that night, I came up to the hospital, as it was no more expensive here than at a hotel. Got rid of the germ and cough and went—*fortunately*—right into one of my diverticulosis attacks. Dr. Atchley has been experimenting with the proper timing and dosage of belladonna and luminol, and it works *divinely.* I will be able to get over the attacks *quickly* and *without pain,* at home. But it had to be worked out in a hospital. So it was time *well spent,* although it irked me. . . .

As things look now, I will be home the end of *next* week.

I hope to get right to work on a book, and want some conferences with Max. Have three other people to see, and probably won't be out of here until the end of this week.

My wonderful Idella chose this time to leave me, 6 weeks ago. She is in New York—"gone Harlem" but did telephone me rather tearfully, so after she has a belly full she may come back some day.

You will be interested to know that at Norton's parting with
Miss Gray,[1] she said, "Dear boy, I just want to tell you something. There's a very difficult time in marriage for a year or two,
but if you'll just stick it out for about ten years, nothing can
separate you." He said, "What on earth are you talking about?"
She said, "Well, you know what people are saying—that you're
going off like this just because you're so desperately unhappy."

He and I were both so mad we could have spit. When his
motives are of complete altruism, and I am being a good sport if
it kills me, it is infuriating to find I am the bitch who is *driving* him to war!

Julia reports that Scribner's is much pleased with your book.[2]
God, I'm thrilled. I haven't seen Max yet. If they offer you a
10% royalty, ask for a clause making it 15% if the book sells over
5,000.

Will hope to see you. And hurray to Verle [Pope] for the
captaincy!

Much love,

Marjorie.

1. A St. Augustine acquaintance.
2. A novel entitled *Colcorton* (New York, 1944).

113. To Maxwell E. Perkins
Note summer address: Crescent Beach, Star Route
                                        St. Augustine, Fla.
                                        Aug. 2, 1943

Dear Max:

Home again, after a more or less satisfactory hegira. I got
along fairly well until I headed for Florida, then have been
increasingly depressed at coming back to—no Norton. That's one
trouble with having an almost perfect husband—anything
that happens is too awful. I was delighted to find two letters
from him, mailed en route. It seems possible that he is on the
Queen Mary. Each man in the unit has his own cabin and private cabin boy, and he was enjoying everything immensely. He
said that the first night out he heard three torpedoes swish by
and just miss the boat. In the morning he found out that it was

someone flushing the toilet——. He wrote: "We all talk like Hemingway characters. Now and then an eight-letter word creeps in, but then you realize it is made up of two four-letter words." His sense of humor will be a life-saver through the mess he is going into. He said he was by far the oldest of the unit, "but they show me no respect." He is crazy about all the men but one, who is a stinker, loathed jointly by all the others.

"Aunt Ethel" [Riggs] proved a fount of knowledge of the rich days on the farm, and had in her possession, to boot, the most fascinating family letters dating back as far as 1822. I spent most of my time reading them, box after box, and studying the old ledgers and account books. It was intriguing to re-create the personalities from the correspondence. Great-aunt Elsie, writing to my great-grandmother, wrote the best letters of the lot, and was up on all current movements and ideas. She asked in 1869 what her sister thought about the woman's suffrage convention, the first one ever held. She wrote, "On this subject, I myself am greatly in its favor, and mean to exercise every privilege offered me."

The information I got on my own grandfather, the prototype of the principal character in my book,[1] did not fit in with what I plan to do. My grandfather was much better educated than I realized, much more articulate. This need not throw me off from my original conception of the character I have in mind. I found that he was passionately devoted to music, especially the violin, but was not allowed by his fanatically religious mother to study the instrument. He kept a violin in the hayloft and slipped off there to play by himself. I shall probably use this angle, as it fits in with my idea of a frustrated artist and man of thought. I was amused and a little shocked to find that both my great-grandmother and her sister, who married my great-grandfather after my great-grandmother's death, were inveterate writers of poetry. I had thought that all my annoying urge-to-expression came from the intellectual Kinnan side, but find I am doubly damned. Out of the welter of religious poetry written by my great-grandmother, there were some telling phrases. Speaking of her own weariness, she wrote, in a verse, "The Savior's heart and hands were weary, too." And she wrote to a grieving sister, "Do not let your sorrow drink your blood"—which is vivid enough for anybody!

They may not enter in my scheme—as I haven't decided yet how far back I shall take the story—but there were marvelous letters from my grandfather's brother, who died in the Civil War. He had a brilliant mind and gave a picture of the war from the Northern angle, and all its implications, that Douglas Freeman[2] could well have used. And great-aunt Elsie, the politically minded one, wrote my great-grandmother in 1864, I think it was, that prices were high (inflation), and that the copperheads were saying that if Old Abe was elected again, things would be worse. "What do you think of that for sound reasoning!" she wrote.

You will remember that one of the keynotes of my book was to be the consciousness of the principal character of the cosmic set-up. I all but fainted when I found a receipt among my great-grandfather's accounts for a book on astronomy, which my grandfather must have read in detail. I am putting in an order with the Argus Bookshop (Chicago), which has gotten me many rare books, for this one, for it will give me just the slant I want on the principal character's thoughts along cosmic lines. It does seem a strange coincidence, doesn't it? I feel more than ever that what I want to do is "a natural." Yet I know that my bones will have to go through a duck-press to squeeze out the essence of the thing I want to do.

Edith Pope has been spending the week-end at the cottage with me. Entertaining her proved no problem, for a box of new books was delivered, and we have spent our time at opposite ends of the davenport, reading up a breeze. Please send me any reading matter you can lay hands on.

Marjorie

1. MKR had begun work on her last novel, *The Sojourner* (New York, 1953).
2. Douglas Southall Freeman, historian and biographer (1886–1953).

114. To Henry Seidel Canby

Hawthorne, Florida
October 26, 1943

Dear Mr. Canby:

The candidates proposed for the Gold Medal of the Institute for Fiction, seem to me unusually satisfying, and at first glance it is difficult to make a choice. We are asked to state our opinions, and these are mine:

Much as I admire his work, I feel that Hemingway should be eliminated for perhaps the sole reason that he is still a young man, with work ahead of him. I feel that a choice should be made among the older writers, for such an award is an accolade, to my notion, for a more nearly completed *body* of work.

Eliminating further, I feel that [Theodore] Dreiser's work does not stand the test of time as does that of the remaining three, Miss [Willa] Cather, Miss [Ellen] Glasgow and Mr. [Sinclair] Lewis.

I should now eliminate Mr. Lewis, though the mass of his work is impressive and has had a great influence on our time, for the reason that I consider him more the satirist than the creative writer of fiction.

Between Miss Cather and Miss Glasgow, I should choose Miss Glasgow, though the quality of their work seems to me almost equal, largely because of the greater body of Miss Glasgow's work, of consistently, almost classically, high standard.

Sincerely,

Marjorie Kinnan Rawlings

115. To Philip May

Cross Creek
Hawthorne, Florida
Jan. 12, 1944

Dear Phil:

Excuse the newspaper stationery, but your letter came as I was working on my book, and I do my first drafts on this paper.

My reference to the way in which we use "bastard" and "son of a bitch" is on pages 156 and 157 of "Cross Creek."

You asked me to describe to you my feelings in writing about Zelma when I included her in my story of my life at the Creek. When I wrote the first draft, I was concerned with the census-taking itself, (which, as I said in the book, revealed to me the countryside I so loved but to which I had been a stranger), and was a means of making me feel at home. I had mentioned

Zelma only as the medium of this wonderful introduction, with no description of her. My editor at Scribner's, Maxwell Perkins, wrote me, "Zelma is a wonderful person and we must have a description of her, and more about her," so I set in to interpolate a description of Zelma, who had been a real friend to me and of whom I thought in most admiring terms. She and Ed Hopkins and Leonard Fiddia, the latter the prototype of the hero in "South Moon Under," had done most in introducing me to the backwoods of Florida. At the time I wrote "Cross Creek," Zelma and I were not as intimate as we had been in earlier days, partly because the circumstances of our lives had separated us quite naturally, as happens with many friends, partly because she herself seemed to have no desire to be intimate. I attributed this to her disapproval of some of my other friends, especially "Dessie," of "Hyacinth Drift," and to the fact that after the two unmarried younger brothers of my husband, Charles Rawlings, who had been her close friends before I came to Florida, left the state, my lonely life at the Creek did not hold the same attractions for her. But I considered us still friends, we were always glad to see each other when we met, I made regular visits to her mother in Island Grove, four miles away, after Zelma left to do State Welfare work in Gainesville, Palatka, and St. Augustine, and I turned my health problems, which were serious, over to her brother, Dr. Cason, at the Riverside Hospital and have been in his hands, for two operations and many periods of treatment, until this last year, when Zelma brought suit against me and I was forced to question the good wishes of her family.

When I came to describe Zelma, as requested by my editor, I remembered the engaging combination of her ministrations to the sick and the needy with her blustering manner to them and her "bawling out" of them in no uncertain terms when they had been negligent in some matter of health or economic common sense. I was intrigued in attempting to give a picture of her as a vital personality, as profane as I, as interested in people as I, and felt happily that I had done so. I took her an affectionately signed copy of the book with every expectation that she would be pleased with her share in my picturization of our simple but good and vital life.

The rest you know, and the shock to me when I found that she had taken offense, or pretended to. I do not know what more I can tell you in answer to your question.

Sincerely,

Marjorie Kinnan Rawlings

116. To Ida M. Tarrant

Hawthorne
Jan. 21, [1944]

Dear Aunt Ida:

If I suddenly end up with cussing, and a pencil, it is because my new typewriter ribbon just came loose, and I tried to fix it myself. I have small hopes of its holding. Norton's address is:

Vol. Norton S. Baskin
AMERICAN FIELD SERVICE
A.P.O. 465
c/o Postmaster, New York City

He wrote me an account of his Christmas Eve that was a nightmare. He had not received a single one of his Christmas packages, had had no letters in more than a month, was in a jungle full of Japs and tigers, had been living for days on bully beef and tea, and was sleeping on the ground in a small tent without lights or a seat to sit on. There are three other men with him at this remote outpost. Christmas Eve they went to bed—on the ground—and sang Christmas carols. His Christmas day was better, as some British officers stationed about twenty miles away invited them to dinner. But even so, Norton had to make an emergency run with his ambulance Christmas afternoon. He doesn't mind anything, he says, except the horror and the waste of war. Think I wrote you that he has been in action about two months, making a five-hour trip each day with his ambulance. It is hard to imagine him in such surroundings and doing such work, but under that superficial gayety, there is all the staunchness and courage in the world, and I have always known he could and would do anything that was necessary.

Thelma[1] was buying turkeys on the route much cheaper than

the stores, so I asked her to get one for me, and when I picked it up Wednesday, it weighed 24 lbs. I immediately wired for company, and thank goodness they couldn't come, for this morning when Idella lit my bathroom heater, the box of matches exploded in her hand. I saw the flare and knew at once what had happened, dashed out of bed to my medicine cabinet, and had a wonderful ointment, Butesin Picrate, on her hand in a few seconds. It must have been horribly painful, but she never made a sound. The ointment is so good—something Dr. Fred Tarrant[2] told me about—that I think it will save her from a really bad burn. But I am certainly glad we are not faced with company. Yet she scolded me when she found I had made my bed and tidied up! She seems just the same Idella, and I hope is here to stay. She has turned up the hems on the living room curtains, washed and ironed and put them back, and every day does some new job of cleaning up after months of Martha and Sissie, without my having to speak of a thing. I someway do not believe there was ever a husband at all. I think she just did not want to be stuck here on the old domestic wages, and that the pay was the principal thing involved. It is perhaps a good thing for both of us, for she has found that New York is not Heaven after all, and I probably would have been horrified at paying her so high if I had not gone through such punishment without her.

She told me of an amusing experience on her $35 a week job. She said that she didn't think a day passed that she didn't speak of me or of the Creek. One day her mistress ordered broiled liver for dinner and said it must be rare, not well-done. Now I never had broiled liver, as I prefer it quickly sautéed in butter, and Idella was stumped. She just whisked the liver through the broiler and it was not rare, it was plain raw. The woman was furious and stormed out to the kitchen and asked sarcastically, "Will you kindly tell me just what you people ate at this Creek?" Well, time passed, and Idella's employers were going to a buffet supper in one of the apartments at the Waldorf, and were to take a baked ham as their contribution. The mistress looked through cook-books and said she knew there was some way of simmering it first, and finally asked Idella sharply if she knew anything about it. Idella said she knew how to do it so the ham was left to her. Now I am famous for my hams, simmered with wine and spices and honey, and baked with a crust of bread crumbs and brown sugar and sherry, with whole cloves inserted, and the ham proved the hit of the supper at the Waldorf and the woman complimented Idella. Idella said she turned away carelessly and said, "That's one of the little things we people used to eat at the Creek."

It is certainly wonderful to have her back and I think she is happy to be here.

My bronchitis is much better and if it ever warms up (it was 32 here this morning) it will be all right.

Love,

Marjorie

1. Thelma Shortridge, daughter of Fred Tompkins, of Island Grove, Florida.
2. Aunt Ida's husband.

117. To Maxwell E. Perkins

Hawthorne, Florida
May 3, 1944

Dear Max:

I just had an amusing (to me) letter from my wild friend Dessie, the young woman who took the St. Johns River trip with me. She is a lieutenant in the WAC, quite the perfect place for her, and she informed me that I was failing in my duty, not particularly to my country, but to literature. She wrote, "Kid, you're making the biggest mistake of your life, not getting into the war. You were able to write about Florida and the Crackers with such understanding, because you lived the life. You must get into the war, so that you'll understand all that is at stake, and then you must write about that." She stopped to see me a few weeks ago on her furlough, and damn near had me, Idella my colored maid, and Moe my bird-dog, in the WAC. She worked on me to join, and I said laughingly, "Oh, I couldn't leave Moe and Idella." She pointed out that Idella could join the colored WAC, and something could certainly be done about Moe. I have been expecting her to show up with an order from a General, designating Moe as a WAC mascot, leaving me no exit. It will be almost impossible to explain to Dessie that I should never write about war, except as an incidental influence on the people I should fictionalize.

Edith Pope arrived at the Creek from Colorado when her husband left to go overseas. The bus she arrived on, which I met in Gainesville, was four hours late, having blown its tires and caught fire, en route. The first day she was here she wandered out in the yard and called to me, with her slow drawl, "Marjorie, what sort of snake has black and yellow and red bands? Goodness, it's pre-e-etty!" I answered casually, "Probably a ribbon, or garter, snake. If by any chance it has a black nose, it's a coral snake." Edith is completely near-sighted, and I went out to the yard. She had her face with its beautiful big brown myopic eyes, practically in the face of—a coral snake. I called Idella to bring my gun and shot its head off, and it was not only the largest coral snake I have ever seen, but the first I have seen around here in several years. The next evening we took a walk up the road, and she investigated a piece of rubber tubing that proved to be a small cottonmouth moccasin. I told her she'd better go home, as she was too dangerous to have around!

She has just had a cable that her husband has arrived safely— almost certainly in England. She is now in St. Augustine.

Max, I have never taken such a beating as in the last few weeks. I put in more than two weeks, not knowing whether Norton was dead or alive, and it almost floored me. I have heard from him directly, and he was one of the American Field Service men who drove his ambulance through to an isolated forward British post. He got out by the skin of his teeth, with his ambulance loaded to the roof, and lost all his personal belongings. He wrote that he wondered what little yellow so-and-so was wearing the Tibetan lama's brocaded robe he had bought for me, to use as an evening wrap! On his furlough, just before the near-encirclement, he had been up near Tibet, in sight of Mt. Everest. His sense of humor, thank God, is still rampant, and in his last letter he said that after his day's run he had been playing poker at the base, and set out for his ambulance, half a mile away, "for censorable reasons," in the bright moonlight, gaily swinging two bottles of American beer that had been issued. He said that the guards just now were very much on the alert, and he was suddenly halted and found himself looking down a rifle barrel. He couldn't remember the pass-word, but said, "This is a friend, friend. I can't remember the pass-word, but will two bottles of American beer do just as well?" The British Tommy guard said, "You're damn well right they will," and Norton said he continued on, still gay, but swinging nothing.

I had no sooner caught my breath from his narrow escape, when I was called to St. Augustine. A disastrous fire swept through one wing of the Castle Warden, killing two women—the woman in whose room the fire started, where presumably she fell asleep with a lighted cigarette—and a dear friend of ours who was using our pent-house apartment. I wouldn't go through such a week again for a king's ransom. One other friend and I had to take care of all details for the friend who died, and I had to keep the hotel manager, who was devoted to our friend, from going entirely to pieces, and had to take care of insurance details etc. It was a nightmare.

I suffered as to whether I should write Norton about it, but the A.P. sent the story all over the country, including New York and Chicago, and I was afraid someone would mention the catastrophe to Norton, in writing him, in such a way as to upset him worse than the truth, so I wrote him the details.

My lawyer wrote me that he was uneasy as to not having a decision in Zelma's law-suit from the Florida Supreme Court, and it seemed ominous to him, but his partner, a much older man, said he was sure the Court had already given us a favorable decision, and that the Judge assigned to write the verdict was engaged in producing a literary masterpiece in keeping with the literary tone of the suit! Well and good, but he could just as well be engaged in producing a literary masterpiece against us!

If life ever calms down a bit, I still think I can go ahead on the book. It is entitled, tentatively, "Earth and Sky." That title will probably not stand, but at the moment it covers my theme.

Please tell Whitney [Darrow] and Charlie [Scribner] how thrilled I have been to see the good ads for "*Colcorton*," and I hope and believe they will pay off.

I think I was right in feeling that while Norton is a born narrator, he could not write consciously—or self-consciously. He

had a story in the India publication of the Field Service, and
while it was not bad, he would have written of the incident to
me with much more natural vivacity. The other day he enclosed
a story for me, of an experience of his youth, and it was so
bad that I was embarrassed. I wrote him that, so help me God, I
should quit him if he came home writing stories. I said that it
was hellish enough to be burdened with the delusion that *I*
could write, without having him get off the boat, bringing, like a
rat carrying the Bubonic plague, the delusion that *he* could
write!

Marjorie

118. To Ellen Glasgow

Hawthorne, Florida
May 24, 1944

Ellen, my dear:

I should have written you at the time I sent the oranges,
saying for God's sake not to thank me! Letters, tokens of friendship, are lovely to receive, if one is not obligated to acknowl-
edge them! I get many letters from strange men overseas in the
Service, and I answer them all, then could fair swoon when
answers come in within ten days from the Aleutians and the
South Pacific, saying, "Hope to hear from you soon."

I know from the Cabells that you had a bad winter, and was
so sorry, and thought of you often. The burden of the war is
inescapable, I think, and a great pressure from it seems to
weigh on whatever else one is battling, mental or physical.

I thought that I was all ready to begin a book when Norton
went to India as a volunteer ambulance driver, but I have been
totally unable to work, great relief though it would be. I made
two forced beginnings, so bad that I was appalled at my delusion
that I could write! But I shall go back to it again, and probably find no loss in the waiting.

Transportation of any sort is so difficult that I am imagining
you will not go to Maine this summer.

Because of the help shortage, my grove has not yet been
tractored, and the dense summer growth has taken it over, so
that all sorts of small creatures draw no line between my yard

and the jungle, and I have been over-run with possums and raccoons and rambling turtles and squirrels and an occasional snake. I am obliged to kill the possums, for they eat not only the eggs, either fresh or under setting ducks and hens, but the biddies.

They are not wasted, for old Martha puts them promptly in the pot. One night I shot a possum and caught an enormous turtle, whose meat is delicious, and by seven the next morning Martha and her family had cooked and eaten the turtle, cleaned the pot and had the possum cooking. Most of the snakes are harmless and need not be bothered, though I do have to dispose of the chicken snakes, who also eat eggs and biddies. The summer heat is setting in, and I shall soon go to my cool cottage on the ocean. (And I hope, to work.)

I'll write you now and again, but you must not try to answer, for I know you must save your strength, and I think one needs more health for correspondence than for scrubbing a floor!

All my love,

Marjorie

119. To Edith Pope

Crescent Beach

St. Augustine, Florida

June 18, 1944

Dearest Edith [in Colorado]:

. . . I almost *missed* the news of the invasion. There was nothing about it, of course, in the morning's rural-delivery Jacksonville *Times-Union,* and the mail-man said nothing about it, and I did not turn on the radio that day. Chet Crosby happened to come out late that afternoon in the wake of the tractor and mentioned it. I laughed at the way you and I figured busily on the phases of the moon, completely failing to take into account the several hours' difference in time! We should never do as Generals.

I was outraged by the craven and hypocritical turning of the nation to God, at this late date. Why we should expect Him to pitch in on our side now, I don't know, when we should have been praying long ago for guidance in discerning what is important in life and what is not. If the world had anything remotely approaching a divine or Christian understanding of values, wars would automatically be impossible, and we should not need to flop to our fat knees and cry, "God, please direct our gun-fire."

I am just emerging from a minor intestinal attack, brought on by struggling with a 2500-word article for the Writers' War Board, to go into an English magazine called "Transatlantic." American writers are doing articles for it about various aspects of the U.S.A., and I was asked to cover every angle of Florida for people who knew little about it—in 2500 words. The result was as dull as ditch water. I had planned to go into St. Augustine this evening to mail it, as there was a June 20 deadline, but Idella's sister and some friends from the Florida Normal College came down to visit her, so will send it in by them.

We moved over to the cottage last week, with an addition to the family—Sissie's four-year-old Martha, the smart one. Sissie let us take her for the summer, and in the fall will decide whether we can keep her. I think by that time she will be perfectly willing. Little Martha asked Idella when we were going back to the Creek, and Idella was afraid she was homesick, but it turned out she only wanted to recount her adventures to her sister. Idella heard her reciting to herself the complete account of our trip over, the wonders she had found here, ending, "Then us all went swimming. Me too." She does not miss a trick, and remarked to Idella that every day Mis' Baskin read and wrote. I heard Idella correcting her grammar, from "When us get ready to go," to "When we get ready." This rather touched me, for Idella's last grocery list (after a year of so-called college) had "lemmons," "Wisson oil," "dry creale" (which proved to mean corn-flakes for little Martha's breakfast) and "landry sope"— which shows the inadequacy of the Negro education.

I had a sad experience along this line. Christopher La Farge on the Writers' War Board had asked me to do a 150-word bit as part of a series to be syndicated by NEA, on a war theme close to my heart. I promptly sent off a true story, of my asking a soldier sitting next to me in the diner on my way to Michigan last summer, when a Negro lieutenant entered amiably with white lieutenants, "How does the Army feel about fraterniz-

ing with Negroes?" He said, with a drawl, "Well, Lady, I'm from
the South myself, but all I can say is, if a man's good enough
to die for his country, he's good enough to live with it." La Farge
wrote me a few weeks later that NEA had rejected my item
as being "too controversial." He said the War Board almost
gave up its project on this account, but would try it out for six
weeks, and would I come across with something else. I wrote
him that I could not possibly contribute any starry-eyed plati-
tudes, as the American stand on the Negro question to me inval-
idated the whole war, for it could not be considered a moral or
spiritual crusade when we set out merely to stop other nations
from doing the very thing that we planned to keep on doing
to the Negro.

Mail has been coming in a bit more regularly from Norton. He
had been suffering for more than two weeks from dysentery,
attributing it to the diet, and I hope it is that, and not the tropi-

At the Crescent Beach cottage with Moe, in the early 1940s.

cal dysentery caused by a bug, for the effects of that are, I understand, life-long. He finally received my letter giving details of
the fire and felt a trifle better, realizing the true fatality of it.
He said he had had a letter from you, "obviously intended to
bolster my morale, but as such it was a great success." Ruthie's[1]
death has stopped the wise-cracks, except that he did say, of
the ubiquitousness of the Japs (the British would be told that 50
Japs were in the section, would kill 80 by actual count, and
the next morning there would seem to be as many as before),
"We have decided that they are breeding in their fox-holes."
Each morning the British clean out night-laid land mines and
snipers, and in the afternoon lay a smoke screen so that the
ambulances can get through to pick up the wounded. One of his
A.F.S. friends was wounded on a run, and a patient killed. Yet
he insists that he is "perfectly safe." He did pass on another
wise-crack, in speaking of his dysentery, when he said that if it
did not stop, he was going to the base hospital and have them
apply a tourniquet.

I had been at the cottage a day and a half when I had a wire
from old Martha, "My baby Hettie (who was all of 50) died in
Salisbury, Maryland. Please come at once." I could not see what
good I could do at Cross Creek with baby Hettie dead in Maryland, so wired Chet to handle the situation. Idella said, "She just
wanted you to come home to tell her what to do."

You and I are failures as comics, for Norton saw nothing
funny, either, in my account of our trip to the Deaf and Dumb
home. He said, "Do you suppose they have been there long?"

Much love,

Marjorie

1. Ruth Pickering, who died in the fire at the Castle Warden.

120. To Edith Pope

Barbizon Plaza Hotel
New York
Tuesday, Oct. 31, [1944]

Dearest Edith:

I am so confused and running in such circles that I do not
remember to save me when I wrote you. Anyway, if it is repetition, it is good repetition in a way.

Norton reached Miami on Sunday, via Army hospital plane, was popped into a government hospital there, and phoned me from a wheel-chair before he was put to bed. He had a relapse on the way over and is quite ill. To make a long story comparatively short, there was an apparently insuperable wall of protocol and red tape about getting him to New York as a private and civilian patient, to go into Harkness.

Nov. 8

All that seems irrelevant now—Norton has been in Harkness a week and is enormously improved. I am in his room—one of those lovely front corner ones, 1216, overlooking the river and the bridge—and he is having the last of his X-rays. At the moment it seems that all he needs is building up. The amoebae are definitely dead and gone, and while one intricate test showed that there had been damage to the liver (there are only 3 laboratories in the world that can make that test) that seems to be about over with too. His weight nadir was 112 lbs. and he is now up to 124. He will be here from one to two weeks longer, then if he is strong enough we hope to have a few days at the hotel to take in some shows. He told me (I finally had to call on Gen. Somerville again to get him flown from Miami) that when the most cooperative colonel at the Miami hospital came in to tell him he was flying up the next morning, other men in adjacent beds called out "How come?" Norton said icily, "My wife called up." The nurse came at 7 A.M. to tell him to get ready and he said "I haven't had any breakfast." A G.I. rose up in his bed and yelled, "They damn well better get him some breakfast. His wife will call up."

Dr. Atchley has been wonderful and Norton swears all anyone needs for a cure of anything is just to arrive at Harkness. I had Sunday dinner with the Atchley's and Norton said as I left, "Now don't smoke too much, remember to tell your hostess you had a nice time, and above all don't swear."

Well, two women came in in the afternoon and the talk turned to Dr. Damon and his charm. Dr. Atchley said to me, "Have you ever met Damon?" I burst out, "Met him? Hell, he took out my uterus."

I slunk back to Norton.

There is no question but that the Chef was drunk. Also, he was *consumed* with jealousy that Norton had called Doug[1] and had not talked with him. That is probably why he got drunk. Norton called him personally from the hospital here, so all is probably well. Norton was in a state of complete exhaustion when he reached Miami. The St. A. telephone exchange paid no attention to a wire I sent the supervisor, saying that Norton would try to call me at the cottage and please to move the call on to the Barbizon. So when Norton did call the cottage with his last scrap of strength and merely got no answer, he asked for the hotel. He had no energy with which to go further.

Edith, now that Verle's flying has come out, via a decoration, I just must say that I have seldom been so shocked as when you told me you had made him promise not to fly. It simply did not sound like you at all. Verle was bound to be obliged to fly. Surely you know that a man's integrity to say nothing of his maleness, is more important than sparing the little woman any worry. Asking that promise of him is the most Victorian, perhaps the only Victorian, thing I have ever known you to do. It is infinitely better for a man to be killed doing what he wants to do, than to play it safe. Yes, I know—I have Norton safely home and it is easy to talk. But I felt that about him all the time. You would have despised Verle in your heart, a little, if he had toddled home and reported, "I could have flown over Berlin and Stuttgart but I remembered that you didn't want me to." I hope you will apologize to him for having asked anything so *quaint*.

I have seen Julia [Scribner] two or three times a week. I had lunch with Max and he looks very badly. If you are going to need his help on the next book, don't fool around too long.

I am having dinner tonight with Hamilton Basso.

I reach the hospital about eleven every morning and leave at nine at night. I didn't dare give up the double room at the hotel for fear of not getting another.

Poor Idella has a severe case of stomach ulcers but will be home ahead of us, though on a strict diet for a year.

Love,

Marjorie

P.S. Thinking Norton might get in, the hotel moved me on Saturday to a very nice double room on the 15th floor. It overlooks Central Park and the *expensive slums* along its edges. I am much happier.

1. Douglas Thompson, who was managing the Castle Warden in Norton Baskin's absence.

121. To Philip May

Hawthorne, Florida
Feb. 10, 1945

Dear Phil:

Norton and I are going in to Gainesville Monday for lunch with Dr. and Mrs. Tigert, and I will phone you from a pay station there at twelve noon or twelve-five. There is no place anywhere around where everything I said would not be passed on.

I can manage the gas to meet you and take you to Gainesville and bus etc. Cannot see how the Ration Board could deny supplementary gas for legal business. You can be prepared to tell me over the phone exactly where and when you want me to meet you Saturday morning the 17th. Unless you prefer your first conference alone with Scruggs, I should like to join you.

I shall bully Mr. Scribner into getting you the data you want. However, records of my "achievements," as you put it, would, alone, play right into the hands of the opposition, for if I am not mistaken they will say, Yes, this bold publicity-loving woman attained fame and fortune, spread her words to the four winds, at the expense and misery of this mousy, retiring little lonely woman, this violet by a mossy stone, who did not ask fame and fortune of life, but only to live with her usual modesty and sweetness unnoticed by the brutal public——.

I know Zelma will play dirty pool, and it seems to me that we shall have to be ready, at least, to show that she is a loud-mouthed busybody whose privacy could not possibly be invaded.

Marjorie

122. *To Philip May*

Hawthorne, Florida
Feb. 27, 1945

Dear Phil:

. . . Now you asked me to search my memory for anything
in the past indicating that Zelma had expressed a desire for
literary privacy. There was such an incident, which she will
probably try to distort. . . . I cannot remember this precisely, but
the gist is:

I believe it was just after the publication of "South Moon
Under." Either she said, "Now Marge, don't you write a book
about me," (the hero of South Moon had his prototype in a mutual friend, Leonard Fiddia), or I said, jokingly, "I'm going to
write a book about you," in which case she said, "Don't write a
book about me," though I believe it was the former. Now in
any case, knowing her vanity, I took it as I take so many coy
comments from women particularly. Perfect strangers say to me
at gatherings, "Don't you write about me," when what they
mean is that they would give their eye-teeth to be written
about. I had no intention of writing a book about Zelma, for
there was and is not enough interesting material to make a
book. *She did not say at any time that she was never to be mentioned in my writings.* From her cooperation in helping me
trace material and in taking me to local people who, she thought,
might have stories for me, their own or others, I had no reason
to believe that she would object to brief mention. And as I say,
she is so vain, that I felt she would be immensely pleased by
favorable mention, which I thought I was giving her in "Cross
Creek" and which the Supreme Court felt I gave her. If I had
written untrue paeans of praise, calling her a saint on earth,
and had *at the same time* drawn an unfavorable picture of Dessie, whom she hates and of whom she has always been jealous, she would have gone up and down the land urging everyone
to read "Cross Creek." She was vain enough to believe that
she rated a full-length book.

In your outline of your plea, for Scruggs, you omitted one
point that seems of major importance to me—the fact that she

was mentioned only by her first name, and that no one outside her immediate circle of friends and acquaintances would have placed her as Zelma Cason of Island Grove, Florida, if she had not herself broadcast the fact. I imagine that she will try to claim otherwise, and will probably cite many instances where newly-met people asked, "Are you the Zelma in 'Cross Creek'?" If she does cite such instances, I could guarantee that she herself first gave the clue.

Before she had any thoughts of sueing me, aand shortly after I had taken her a copy of "Cross Creek," signed, "To my friend Zelma, with love," she bragged to some women she had just met in Palatka (one of them Frank Harrold's wife) of the effect her displeasure had on me. As I have told you, I found that she had already read the book and she greeted me at the door with, "Well, you made a hussy out of me and a lady out of a hussy." (Meaning Dessie.) I was so shocked and unhappy to find that she had taken offense, that I wept. The meeting ended with our embracing tenderly, and as far as I knew, she forgave me any encroachment on her feelings. She bragged to these women, "I certainly made Marge cry. I haven't seen her cry like that except when Mandy died." Mrs. Harrold mentioned this to me, in order to ask me who Mandy was, as she thought I might have lost a little daughter of whom she did not know! As a matter of fact, Mandy was a bird-dog given to me by Zelma!

Now as to the sales figures on all my books. I feel very strongly that it would not help us to use these figures, as no one not familiar with the publishing set-up could believe how relatively little I have received in money from such large sales. The bulk of these sales was from the Book of the Month Club, which took "South Moon Under," "The Yearling" and "Cross Creek." They pay a low royalty to begin with, and this royalty is split 50-50 between the publisher and the author. Add to that the fact that on all these books, I received, because of the Book of the Month's one-issue arrangement, all royalties inside of one year, so that the government took nearly half of the total. Over the twelve years since my first book, (this is just between you and me) I estimate that roughly $200,000 was paid me, and after my modest living expenses over those twelve years, and the income tax, I have myself saved almost exactly $100,000, and while

that seems like a great deal of money to me, it is not a high
figure in relation to the actual sales of the books, and if I never
have another successful book, as can easily happen, you can
see that the low income one now gets from investments does not
make me rich by any means. One-fourth of my savings are in
War Bonds, which pay a little over 2%. But without going into
all that detail, as I say, no one would believe that I had not
made so much but that I could well afford to come across with a
large sum for a chiseler. Also, on the large sales of the Armed
Services editions, I get, I forget which, about ½ cent or 1 cent,
royalty, and I am making arrangements to have even this modest sum turned back to some Army and Navy service, as I do
not wish to profit by these particular books. So do give this
angle some thought.

I am wandering all around, but have to speak of these things
as they come to me:

One major reason why Zelma asked me to accompany her
on her census-taking trip, was that she thought I could get a
great deal of literary material from it. I don't know why I haven't
remembered to speak of this to you earlier, but it does seem
most relevant to me. I always appreciated Zelma's interest in my
work and her helpfulness in running down material and people with stories to tell.

Also, in your outline to Scruggs, you did not raise the question as to what is to happen to all biography and especially
autobiography, if a writer can not tell his own life story, as I
did in "Cross Creek." And one cannot write his own life story
without mentioning, short of libel, others whose paths have
crossed his own. This is certainly in the realm of unquestionably
legitimate writing.

> Well, phone me.
>
> Marjorie

123. *To Edith Pope*

> [Crescent Beach]
> March 7, 1945

Dearest Edith:

. . . I was most disturbed by your report on Julia's intended,

Tom Bigham. She's terribly in love with him, and says they have such a rare understanding and are so much alike, that they can often tell what the other is thinking. She says he is shy and does not make a good first impression, so let's hope that was what you took for stuffiness. It would be too gruesome if he was using Julia as a step up. If he disappoints or fails her or breaks her heart, I shall see that he meets his maker years ahead of schedule. One can't help wondering how satisfactory a husband, from the sexual angle, a 33-year-old rector will make. He is likely to be inexperienced to say the least. It would be pleasant to think that God would take care of an Episcopal clergyman in any emergency, but I think in such matters God leaves every man pretty much on his own.

I had a note from Laura Benét,[1] asking me to contribute to a fund for Mary Carolyn Davies, who is now "ill and penniless." Being "ill and penniless" is somehow as Victorian-sounding as being a "fallen" woman. I shall send something, of course, but just what *should* be done for very minor poets who fall on hard times? It wouldn't be sound for the government to subsidize or pension very minor poets, for their already large numbers would multiply like termites.

I am writing at the cottage, while a colored man and woman finish the housecleaning that two other fly-by-nights began yesterday. I feel so baffled in my long attempt to live graciously and, certainly, cleanly. I can keep an impeccable house when pressed, with no help at all, but as you know, you can't do that and do anything else. I have done one story that still doesn't please me after three complete re-writings, but decided to send it on anyway—and just haven't had time to copy it.

My Louisville friend, Lois Hardy, arrives today to spend a couple of weeks with us. We will go to the Creek, which is heavenly now, with the orange trees in full bloom and my flower garden, including some new rosebushes, beginning to produce like mad. . . .

Norton & I went to Rollins for the Animated Magazine. Mabel Granberry had a cocktail party after the program, and asked us to stay to supper, too, and she was *all graciousness.* I think perhaps her bitchiness came from financial worry. Edwin [Granberry] is doing plot and dialogue for a comic strip and told me he is getting very high pay and will soon be able to leave Rollins. He turned his play into a novel, which is almost finished. Something will probably still come of the play, as Thornton Wilder & the Lunts were crazy about it, but all said it needed *something*—but *not* what a professional playwright would give.

As I think I wrote you, Norton plans to take over at the Castle in a couple of weeks, and I still move to the cottage in April.

I am just back from a trip to the Florida A & M (colored) college at Tallahassee, where I spoke on a program honoring Mary Bethune. It was a fascinating experience and I am more than ever ashamed of the people who try to hold the Negroes back.

Love,

Marjorie

1. Laura Benét, wife of Stephen Vincent Benét.

124. *To Maxwell E. Perkins*

Hawthorne, Florida

April 11, 1945

Dear Max:

It was good to hear from you—and please don't ever not write for fear I'll feel prodded. No one knows better than you, except another writer to whom it does not come easily, that sometimes one cannot be hurried, no matter how long the delay in getting to work.

In the winter, I made still another start on the book, and it was wrong, too. Part of the trouble, of course, is that something is still not right with my conception, and I shall never force a thing like that again, as I did with "Golden Apples." I woke up last night with something of a new slant, and while I rejected it, I had the feeling that I was coming closer to the road out.

I am moving to the cottage on the ocean at the end of April, and since Norton has taken over the management of the hotel, as the manager is leaving, and will be gone all day and sometimes evenings, too, I think I will have enough peace and privacy. I am staying alone at the Creek for a couple of weeks, and am hoping that I may be able to make my start here. I think that once I feel I have begun properly, I can work even with a few handicaps. I'll let you know.

No, I didn't know about Martha and Ernest[1] until you wrote
me. I have heard a little more about it since, but none of it
makes too much sense. I was amazed that apparently it was
Hemingway who strayed, for I had thought that he would not be
able to hold Martha, and that she would be tired of him first.
It is so expensive and so nerve-racking for a man to keep *marrying* women! And I do not see why he takes on another woman
presumably deep in her own work. A man like Hem admires a
woman who can hold her own with him intellectually, but he

Julia Scribner Bigham, MKR's good friend and later her literary executrix. Photograph courtesy of Charles Scribner's Sons.

also likes a domestic establishment run for his sole benefit!

I gather that Julia's approaching marriage to the young clergyman [Thomas Bigham] has been a bomb-shell in the family. I know it has to Vera [Scribner], who is selfishly putting Julia through a big formal wedding, which she hates. Edith Pope did not care for the man, and neither did a most attractive friend of mine of whom I had hopes for a romance with Julia, also an Episcopal clergyman, but a lieutenant-chaplain in the Navy now. They felt he was a bit of a stuffed shirt and had his eye on the main chance. However, I do trust Julia's judgment, for she has been cold to so many suitors, and she is very much in love and says that she and the man have a rare understanding.

You did not say how you are feeling, and whether you are taking care of yourself? ? ?

Norton is reasonably well, though he tires easily and is upset by things that never disturbed him before. He does complain mildly that I have spoiled my dog Moe in his absence. He said that while he, Norton, is a scion of an old Southern family, and Moe is undubitably a son of a bitch, he thinks that I tend to confuse them — —.

Infinite thanks for the new [George] Santayana.[2] It is all and more than one would wish for from him. I can only hope there will be at least three more volumes. I felt I could not get enough of it, and was desolate when "The Middle Span" ended. I must go back to the first volume, which seemed dull. Yet it does seem to me that in the second one he felt more free, and allowed himself to make delicious philosophical observations, was objective, where in the first he was too absorbed in getting down rather meaningless items about his childhood and schooling.

Thank you, too, for the Ray Stannard Baker,[3] whom I know and admire very much as a person, but whose story, especially by the side of Santayana, is worthy and dull—as Hemingway said to me of the women who go in for game-fishing.

My best,

Marjorie

1. Ernest Hemingway and his third wife, Martha Gellhorn, had recently been divorced.

2. *Persons and Places* (New York, 1944).

3. *American Chronicle* (New York, 1945).

125. To Philip May

Crescent Beach, Star Route
St. Augustine, Florida
July 2, 1945

Dear Phil:

. . . Mr. [Hugh] Williams[1] brought up a point that he felt I should pass on to you. He said that I am generally considered a Yankee, and that the Waltons might attempt to prejudice my case with a local jury by denouncing me as such. As a matter of fact, I have always considered myself a Southerner. When I gave the facts to Hugh, he said it might be a good idea for you to work them in before the Waltons do any damage. Anyway: I was born and brought up until college age in Washington, D.C. and Maryland. At college in Wisconsin I was known as "the little southern girl" and I belonged all through college to The Dixie Club, composed of dyed-in-the-wool Southerners. My ancestry was half Southern. I had two great-grandmothers who lived in Kentucky, both slave owners. One sold her slaves and that branch of the family has always been well to do. The other "got religion" and freed her slaves, and that branch, the Fishers, which is my most direct line, has always been poor as church mice. My grandmother Kinnan lived in South Carolina a good many years of her life, and I visited her there with my father when I was a small child. My father used to tell me I was "the sweetest thing in Posey County," which as I remember is the Charleston county. Grandmother lived south and east of Charleston, somewhere near Beaufort. Anyone calls me a Yankee at his peril. My life for a few years in the North was a penance. . . .

Marjorie

I would have phoned you this information this morning, but one of the neighbors listens in on *every* call, and I didn't dare.

1. A Cross Creek neighbor.

126. To Norman Berg

Crescent Beach
St. Augustine, Florida
July 18, 1945

Dear Norman:

Well, I enjoyed your letter, and you sounded very light-hearted, and you did not mention the war at all. So you're writing a story! Well, it will teach you at any rate how hard it is to do. I hope it is good, though I feel that you are a born critic, in the broad sense, rather than creative. I do not think one could be as keen and demanding an analyst as you, and do creative work. The artist may contrive, being an artist, to be more or less objective, but he is seldom an analyst. He is emotional rather than intellectual.

Indeed, you and Julie may have the cottage for your second honeymoon, even if I am using it at the time. I never told you, but when you asked for the cottage before, "if I wasn't using it," I was using it most strenuously, getting going on "Cross Creek." However, you were my good and dear friend, and I felt it was more important for you to get a good start with Julie, than for me to be uninterrupted. I WAS upset, though, after I had cooked all sorts of good things for you both, for you to report later that you were perfectly willing to live on toast!

I have made the seventh, I think it is, beginning on my book [*The Sojourner*] and have done five chapters, which are unbelievably bad. I simply cannot hit the proper *style* for my subject. But I am plodding ahead, hoping that I will hit the key, in which case I can always go back and get the first parts in line.

I have done several short stories recently, about which Carl Brandt was enthusiastic, and he has been unable to sell a single one of them. The *New Yorker,* the logical outlet, I thought, for most of them, said that they thought what I was doing was "terribly experimental." This rather revived me, as I felt the stories might possibly be good. They are sad, ugly stories, and after I have done a few more, I intend to send them to Max Perkins. If he likes them, there will be enough for a book. The title should probably be "Gall and Wormwood." I don't know out of what sadistic, frustrated depths they come, and they are not pretty, though I hope they are telling.

Norton gets down to the cottage very seldom. His help comes— and goes—and he sticks with his damn hotel. Of course, I get more work done, but I am not happy. He is the most delightful companion I have ever had, but without that companionship, it is not a perfect marriage. I am probably better off than I know, for I do need a great deal of solitude. I imagine that Nor-

ton secretly feels that I should follow him and live at the
hotel with him. It is simply too late for me to follow a man into
a life utterly distasteful to me. Ten years ago I could probably
have done it, certainly fifteen or twenty. I cannot now. This, not
because I have any exalted ideas about my work, for with the
rejection of my stories and my own knowledge that the book of
the moment is not good, I am more than humble. But I am in
my late forties, and in the long years of loneliness, with the
dubious solace of lovers, working alone, I have become unable to
share in a commercial, gregarious life such as that of a hotel.
Yet it is the right life for Norton.

A Cross Creek neighbor of mine, discussing my still pending
law suit with "my friend Zelma," said that if anything defeated me with a local jury, it would be the popular idea that I
was a Yankee, as you suggested was probably Margaret Mitchell's reaction to my urging of a true democracy.

As I told my neighbor, and as I managed to write Peggy [Mar-
garet Mitchell], apparently casually, I am of mixed ancestry,
more than half of which was Southern and slave-owning. My
father was a Republican, and went every four years from the
District of Columbia to his last residence in Michigan, to vote,
and though I adored him, I remember as a very young girl,
standing up to him and arguing for Free Tariff.

I don't know, of course, where you are, but if you ever run into
a Chaplain, Lt. Bertram Cooper, on the U.S.S. BOUNTIFUL, in
Pacific waters, he is a good friend of mine, a scholar, a profound
thinker. He was in love, in a soul-saving way, with Julia Scribner,
wanting to make her happy and take her out of her dreadful
environment. Julia has recently married another Episcopalian
minister, assigned, fortunately for her, to a professorship at the
Union Theological Seminary in New York. Her last letter to
me does not sound too happy. Bert Cooper and I have agreed to
axe her husband if he does not please her.

Do write me, and tell me about the story, and how war cor-
relates with human decency, and what-not.

Love,

Marjorie

P.S. Edith Pope and her husband are in St. Augustine now (he

is a Major and has a Presidential Citation, the Air Medal, etc.
and does not know whether he will be sent on to the Pacific or
released) and Edith reports that Julia is radiantly happy, and I
am so glad. . . .

M.

127. *To Sigrid Arne*

Crescent Beach, Star Route
St. Augustine, Florida
July 21, 1945

Dear Sigrid:

I was so relieved to hear from you. And so glad you didn't
have to have the operation. Maybe it won't be necessary at all.

You must have had a heavenly time in San Francisco. I
haven't seen your by-line for a long time. Where would your
stories be?

The book sounds wonderful, and I bet it will sell like hot
cakes. The galleys *are* exciting, and you never get used to them.

I can't remember when I wrote you last, but shortly after you
were here, Norton volunteered in the American Field Service,
and drove an ambulance in India and Burma for a year and a
half. It was a great experience for him and he enjoyed most of
it. The Japs had them completely encircled and isolated for a
couple of weeks, on a mountain overlooking the Manipur plain,
and after that, every morning there was a road block, the British
would go out and remove mines and as many snipers as possible,
then would lay a smoke screen in the early afternoon and the
ambulances would dash through to pick up wounded and dash
back again. The closest call Norton had that way, was when
a Jap bomb knocked the initial off his finger ring! He was so
fascinated with the dog-fights in the air over the Manipur
plain, that he insists he was never scared—but he did get goose-
flesh over the roads themselves. They were one-way tracks
cut over the mountains, mountain on one side, often with land-
slides, and on the other, nothing but several thousand feet of
space. At one place, the ambulance had to *back up,* toward the
precipice, to get around a curve, and Norton had to take this
several times at night, with almost no lights. He said he really

minded that. He was crazy about the British. The AFS served entirely with them. At one time, Norton and another man had a first-aid post on top of an isolated mountain. Supplies were dropped to them by parachute. The post was dug in, two underground rooms, one for the aid station, the other living quarters. The Jap artillery was on one side and the British on the other, criss-crossing. The other man acted as cook and Norton as dish-washer. He wrote me, "Here I am between shot and shell, and all I will get will be dish-pan hands."

Well toward the end of his period of service, he got amoebic dysentery, but drove a couple of months with it, then when it was complicated by a never-diagnosed fever, he was flown out to a British hospital and eventually to one in Calcutta—where he was stuck for two and a half months and damn near died. At one point, the doctors cleared everybody out of his ward and then began moving in other cases. He found out from a nurse that they were all hopeless cases, and during the first night one man died beside him of spinal meningitis, and one on the other side of typhoid. You can imagine what that would do to your morale! About that time, his headquarters in N.Y. relayed to me a cable from India, that his condition was serious, and they would keep us informed. Well, I knew he would just naturally die if he was kept there, and I felt he had a chance if he could get home, so I phoned a dear friend of ours in Washington, who had had the good sense to marry Gen. Brehon Somerville a couple of years before, and Bree cabled the commanding general of the China-Burma-India theater, saying he would appreciate having Norton put on the next Army hospital plane for the U.S. Norton was home in ten days. I was waiting for him in New York, with an ambulance at the airport, and he went to Medical Center and was there a month. He had lost 50 pounds. As it turned out, he had been cured of the amoebae, and had had an abscess on the liver, but they fought the fever and general debility.

I took him home to the Creek for the winter and spring, and he is only now beginning to look like himself. He took over the hotel management two months ago, and of course is having the usual help problems. I am at the cottage, and he only gets down a couple of evenings a week.

I am working on a book and it is lousy. I begin to think I don't
have a story there, after all. I have done half a dozen short
stories that my agent was enthused about, and they have all
been rejected——. The New Yorker, the logical outlet, I thought,
for most of them, said they thought what I was doing was
"terribly experimental," which gives me the private hope they
may be good. If you can pick up the Dec. 9 New Yorker, there is
a story of mine in it you might like to see.[1]

I feel very low of mind about it all, but as you know, when
you are doomed to write, you can't stop.

You remember my little old adopted aunt, Aunt Ida? A friend
of hers has a son in the Pacific, and Aunt Ida told me that he
was safe, as he wasn't at the front. "He's in a fox-hole," she said.
She went on with pleasure to report that he has found a buddy, an
older man, who covers him up each night in the fox-hole with a
blanket, saying tenderly, "Warm enough, chicken?" I didn't
like to tell Aunt Ida that he is in great danger in more than one
way. . . .

Love, and write when you can.

Marjorie

1. "Shell," *New Yorker*, December 9, 1944.

128. To Maxwell E. Perkins

Crescent Beach
St. Augustine, Florida
Aug. 17, 1945

Dear Max:

No, I most certainly do not think advertising people are
wonderful. I think they are horrible, and the worst menace to
mankind, next to war; perhaps ahead of war. They stand for the
material viewpoint, for the importance of possessions, of desire, of envy, of greed. And war comes from these things.

J. Walter Thompson was polite only because we played into
their hands. We should not have done it, for profoundly moral
reasons. Though the use of wine in cooking is beneficent rather
than harmful. It doesn't particularly need advertising. There
are people who try to cook well, and they know wine or will

discover it; and there are people who do not try to cook well, and all the wine ads in the world will not change them.

I do not see how I can send you what is done on the manuscript. It is too very bad. But I am still plodding ahead, and if I don't burn it first, will eventually send it on to you.

Carl Brandt sold one of my "queer" stories.[1] One of the stories that was rejected was, of all things, a Quincy Dover story.[2] Carl and Bernice Baumgartner were enthusiastic about it and were amazed when the *Sat. Eve. Post* turned it down. It did not have a typical happy ending, which to my notion was its salvation, for I did not care for it, but evidently that was enough for the *Post*, horrid sheet. They told Carl that the Quincy Dover angle was fine, but the rest of it did not ring true—and "the rest of it" was the true story of my friend Dessie, of "Hyacinth Drift," except for the ending! This only proves what I tell young writers, that the truth is artistically fallacious.

Well, the last time I was at Cross Creek, I was depressed by the condition of the place, the house not clean, since old Martha can only keep up with the stock, making butter, etc., the yard a jungle. And the toilet would not flush. I used it for about eighteen hours, and Martha went to the bathroom to clean. She called out, "There's something in the toilet." I said yes, I knew, it wouldn't flush, and did she have any idea what it might be. "Yessum. A cottonmouth moccasin." It stuck its head up when she sifted in the Dutch cleanser, and stuck it up again when I peered in. I slammed down the lid and blocked the crevices with bath towels and went to Ocala on business. I had hoped to find Ross Allen, Florida's leading herpetologist, to come out and "bring it back alive." Ross was out of town. When I reached home, my good friend Leonard ("Lant" of "South Moon Under") had been out to see me, and laughing like a hyena at Martha's and my predicament, had speared the moccasin with an ice pick, hauled it out and killed it outside. It was four feet long, and thick enough in the middle to have blocked the toilet. He found a break in the drainage tile where it had gotten in, and fixed that.

Oh, when I told Martha how sad I was at the state of the place, and the moccasin showed up in the toilet, she said, "Sugar, this is the wind-up."

This morning Idella found a small snake under the head of my bed at the cottage. I am reasonably sure it was harmless, though it had a black mask and was not familiar to me. I killed it with a poker.

Marjorie

1. Probably "Miriam's Houses," *New Yorker,* November 25, 1945.
2. An unpublished story entitled "Donny, Get Your Gun!"

129. To Norton S. Baskin

[Cross Creek]
Friday evening
[September 1945]

Dear Honey:—

. . . About Sara's[1] helping you out in this emergency (wish you had told me what happened, so I could "get the picture"). I can see her of great help in many ways. If my guess is right, that Mrs. Huston[2] went to pieces and made a scene, etc., etc., Sara could tide things over while Mrs. Huston takes a much needed, in fact, I think, a NECESSARY vacation. Also the chef and others would accept Sara because she was your sister, whereas the Chef in particular might raise Hell with an outsider.

If your rooms are being pretty well kept full, having Sara would be expensive for you, for the cost of an otherwise rented room-and-meals would be added to whatever you paid her. But if you do not expect to be full, that would not be a consideration. Why don't you ask your mother to come with her? It always does her good, and if Sara comes anyway, it would seem like the ideal time. That is, if you have a double room free.

Just to be frank and to go on record, I don't think it would be a good idea to make such an arrangement with Sara a permanent or long-term one, because everybody agrees that in-laws living together is never advisable. Sara is as touchy as I am, in some ways touchier, and there would be an inevitable choice between our having to be a threesome all the time—which I should not like—or leaving Sara out of things—which would hurt *her* feelings—and we'd both be right. But in your present emergency, I do think it would be a fine idea, and all the better if your mother could come, too.

Now honey, feeling that our love for each other is a tragedy is putting it too strong, and I didn't mean to go that far. But as far as I'm concerned, it is a misfortune and a hell of a nuisance that I have exactly the man I want—and can't accept his way of life.

But if you are willing just to make allowances for my eccentricities—and to admit that a large part of my objection to your way of life isn't eccentric at all—and will go on being sweet and patient and let me come in to your roost when I feel like it and take off again when I feel like it, I still think we can work it out.

We are no worse off, and I think a lot better off, than in the last couple of years before we were married, when we saw a lot of each other in the winter and you could only come to the cottage every 3 or 4 weeks in the summer. As soon as the gas rationing is over there will be no problem at all.

When I see you next, I want to go into all this very thoroughly. We never have. You take an aggrieved attitude, and dismiss me as just plain nuts, and I get completely inarticulate.

I have "read a book," and found out the KIND of nut I am. It isn't as bad as it might be! And I am not completely nuts, and there is some excuse for me!

Anyway, I am extremely fond of you, and nobody else can have you. I mean to keep our lives together in some way. All my love,

Marjorie

1. Norton Baskin's sister.
2. The housekeeper at the Castle Warden Hotel.

130. To Ellen Glasgow

Crescent Beach
Nov. 9, 1945

Dearest Ellen:

I had a note from James Cabell, and he tells me that you haven't been able to do much work for some time. How I suffer with you, for it puts one into an acute state of melancholy and frustration. Being obliged to write is a strange curse. With the impressive true literature to your credit that you have al-

ready, it would seem that you could rest on your laurels, but I
know that you must be chafing at the bit. I understood that
you have been working on something of an autobiography. You
MUST finish it!!!!! Your prefaces are of course a most valuable
piece of autobiography, but you MUST do more, giving more of a
personal nature. Not that you should "tell all," but posterity
must have more of what you have thought and done and how
your mind and emotions have functioned.

I am in a dreadful state of mind, from being unable to do
anything with a novel that has been long on my mind, and on
which I have made eight or nine beginnings. In one version, I
did about a quarter's book-length, and was so depressed that
one night I tore it all into irretrievable shreds. And felt much
better. But the new beginning is no better——. I don't know
what's wrong. The characters, the setting, the general theme,
are clear as crystal to me—and it emerges as pure tripe.

But your work is so much more important than mine, that I
pray you will find strength from somewhere to go at it again.

James said that Miss Bennett[1] feels that you could stand the
trip to St. Augustine for the winter. Let me beg you to come.
You would have here a kinder climate; lovely places in which to
walk; people who know and appreciate your art and would
give you as much companionship as you wanted—or have the
grace to leave you alone when you didn't want to be bothered;
other writers, not only James and me, and forgive me for including myself in your, and his, genre, but all sorts of interesting
stray writers who pass through here. It might be just the right
stimulus to put you at work again. And even if it didn't, it
would do you a world of good physically.

I am turning my ocean cottage into a year-round home, as
Norton just can't get far away from his hotel. I am adding a
large studio work-room with fireplace, a dining room, another
bath-room and dressing-room, enlarging kitchen and maid's
quarters.

One writer here who worships at your feet is Edith Pope,
author of "Colcorton," which ran second for the Pulitzer prize a
year ago. She is a lovely person, aristocratic in somewhat the
way you are (though no one can quite touch you) and I know
you would enjoy and love her, as I do.

Please, dearest Ellen, do come to us. Do you recall my dream of you, in the cold, with the red curtains? I feel somehow that I, we, can give you some warmth—and you, of course, can always let us warm our hands at your fire.

With great love,

Marjorie

1. Anne Virginia Bennett, Ellen Glasgow's companion.

131. To Philip May

Crescent Beach
Dec. 31, 1945

Dear Phil:

I begin to see where a good lawyer earns his money! . . .

I must tell you of an amusing evening I spent with Mrs. Cason, Zelma's mother, the Thursday before Christmas. I decided that you were right in suggesting that there was no reason why she should not have her usual gift from me of Christmas whiskey. I had bought a case of Calvert's designed mostly for gifts, stopped at Mae DuPree's[1] to deliver one, took in another bottle and Mae and I had a couple of Yule-tide drinks. It was about seven-thirty or eight in the evening and I drove on to Island Grove and turned in at Mrs. Cason's when I saw a light burning in the back of the house. She was ready for bed, wrapped warmly with a sort of parka over her head, for there is absolutely no heat in her bedroom. It was a bitter cold night.

She greeted me warmly and said, "Let's go into the bathroom. It's the only warm place in the house." A small gas heater was burning in the bathroom. There is a fireplace in her living room, but it must be quite a chore for an elderly woman, in her late seventies, I think, to keep up with wood in cold weather. Anyway, there was no sign of fire having been there recently. She has always liked to go to bed early when she has finished milking her cow or cows etc., and read her morning paper then. It was too cold for her to attempt it.

I gave her the quart of Calvert's wrapped festively and she thanked me with real gratitude. I had taken in the open bottle Mae and I had had a drink from and Mrs. Cason brought in two jelly glasses and we each poured generous measures. She sat on the toilet and I sat on a low stool and we enjoyed our drinks and a long chat. I said, "I was sorry not to get you your Christmas liquor last year," and she said, "Marge, I understood."

We got expansive, and I said that my feeling for Zelma had never changed, that I should always feel the same affection, and that I felt that behind and beyond everything Zelma still loved me, too. . . .

Make of it what you wish! Under all circumstances, however, Mrs. Cason is to be protected in the trial. She is a *genuine* friend and must not be hurt or embarrassed.

As I was leaving, she mentioned that her birthday came two days later, so I dashed to the car and brought her another bottle of Calvert's for a birthday present. She said, "Oh, Marge, you shouldn't do that much," and took it happily. She said, "Come see me," and I drove off rather loopily.

It does seem rather incongruous for a daughter to be sueing me for invasion of privacy, while her elderly mother sits on the john and drinks a half-jelly-glass of whiskey with me.

Marjorie

1. A friend in Citra, Florida.

132. *To Norman Berg*

Hawthorne, Florida
Feb. 22, 1946

Dear Norman:

I wrote you a scrawled penciled letter, probably quite unintelligible, when I was ill at the hotel in St. Augustine and Norton was much more ill in the hospital. I had ordinary flu but Norton's went into pneumonia. Now I can't even find that letter—or I may even have mailed it or had it mailed. Anyway, I remember writing how glad we are that you are home safe and sound, that we are most definitely not separated or separating, and who the hell ever started such a story. Husbands like Norton don't grow on trees, (wives like me, MOST fortunately, don't either) and while the disparity between our professions and our ways of life can not be surmounted, at least for the present, we both accept that and make the best of it and have a wonderful time when we are together, and Norton would get away from me over my dead body, and he feels the same way about me.

At the moment, due somewhat to having been ill, I am fearfully harassed with accumulated detail, and almost every day brings a reproachful wire from some Writers' Conference or Committee or what-have-you asking for an answer. I have also been *swamped* with winter company, most of it welcome, but all of it making me think wistfully of that last resort, a secretary—which for me would mean quite the finish of any creative work. Since the so-called creative work is still going very badly, I am on the verge of taking up my mad friend Dessie, of "Hyacinth Drift," on a similar though much more dangerous trip of two or three months into the Alaskan wilds. Dessie gets out of the WACs in March, will testify in my law-suit which goes to trial in Gainesville in April, and if I can't get down to real work by then, I may go with her in sheer desperation. She wants to drive to Alaska, complete with sturdy boat, two motors and guns, ammunition, fishing equipment and food and camping supplies, and I quote, "get off the highway by plane or river and follow some of the streams." Now it is thirteen years since I trusted myself to Dessie on the placid St. Johns, and I just don't know whether I am still man enough to take the punishment into which I think we would inevitably run. Why Dessie wants a sissy like me, I don't know, except that she loves to eat and knows I can whip up a good meal on the Sahara or the Siberian tundra. Also, she can boss me. If she is going to do anything so crazy, she should have a man along. I know from what my brother has told me, and what I saw of Alaska when I was there with him, that the unknown and uncharted streams are bound to call for portages, and how two women could manage that with a boat heavy enough to carry all that stuff, is at least a question, even though one of the women is strong as an ox and the other is simple-minded enough to tackle anything. . . .

Now in spite of all the company, do stop by if and when you come to this section. And when you and Julie are ready for a week at the cottage, let me know.

Marjorie

133. To Philip May

Hawthorne, Florida
March 21, 1946

Dear Phil:

I feel that Scribner's is being very small indeed, in leaving it up to Mr. Edward Perkins[1] to send me a personal bill. I am reasonably sure they must use his firm on a retaining basis, and it seems to me the least they could do was to "count me in." I think I shall write Charlie Scribner, addressing him as "Dear Mr. Shylock Scribner."

I could probably have bought off Zelma for a thousand, which would have given her a moral victory, and by offering a hundred to each and every of the ten, say, other people most likely to dream of a little rake-off, could have cleared the board without these three years of annoyance and for no more than your entirely reasonable fees. But I felt I could not stop short of complete vindication where so vital a principle was at stake.

I did not understand that you needed Chet [Crosby], but there will be no difficulty about that. He made it clear long ago that while not what he would choose, he would give us whatever assistance we needed. I'll see him.

I enclose the Riverside [Hospital] list for you to copy. I remembered after I wrote you, the occasion for my last call there. It was a couple of months after my marriage and I went for a pregnancy test, hoping there would be a little Baskinnan. It proved a false alarm, and P.S., the test killed the rabbit——. I am sure that I had a talk with T.Z. [Cason] also, at the time, as I always did whenever I had an appointment with my good friends Dr. Merritt or Dr. Peyton or Dr. Jelks, and that I reported in friendly fashion on what I had been told at Medical Center about my intestinal condition and treatment. . . .

I do not have a copy of my first Florida sketches "Cracker Chidlings" but they appeared, I am sure, in the Jan. 1931 old Scribner's Magazine and there is probably a copy in your Jacksonville library. The two sketches based entirely on stories Zelma told me, and which she knew before publication I was using, were "Georgia Money" and the one about the preacher who gave his farewell sermon before leaving as chaplain at Raiford. It was in the latter that I used a true name which caused trouble, when the mother . . . of the boy who had robbed the Citra bank and was in jail when I wrote it, but was killed in a gun-fight with the Jax sheriff after escaping before publication, threatened to whip me. I have told you of this, of my being convalescent at the Creek after the Riverside appendectomy with Zelma nursing me in great kindness, and of Zelma's driving me in and making the peace for me, and explaining that I had meant no harm and was deeply grieved to have hurt the mother's feelings. A couple of years later, the mother indicated that she blamed Zelma for giving me an unkind picture of her son, saying, "You'd have liked Harry if you'd known him." I think this incident is important.

I have seen Mrs. Cason twice this week, once to take her some fresh-killed pork, once to take a mutual friend I picked up on the road, headed there. The first time, Mrs. Cason slapped me playfully on the leg and said, "Where have you been? Why haven't you been to see me?" I hadn't been for about a month. . . .

Snow Slater[2] came by this morning to borrow my wire stretchers and ask if I needed anything, and asked "When is your little business coming up? I couldn't remember whether you mentioned a date." I thought that was a good sign, that he should call it "my little business." . . .

Now about Monday night. I *think,* but am not positive, that my two Kinnan aunties will still be here. I gave them the two comfortable bedrooms with baths, and am sleeping myself in the tiny room back of the living room, so unless they have gone by Monday night, you would not be comfortable in the remaining room with double bed, for lack of access to a bathroom. If they leave on Monday, I shall wire you to that effect and you can still cancel your reservation. Otherwise, it is best for all that the hotel room appear on my next bill for expenses.

In any case, I shall expect you and Lillian for dinner Monday evening. Dr. and Mrs. [Clifford P.] Lyons were here for dinner last night, Mrs. [John] Tigert and Mrs. [Raymond] Weaver[3] are coming for lunch tomorrow, and the aunties are enjoying that sort of company no end, and would enjoy you and Lillian, and I think they will tickle you, as they are really *cute.*

I am catching it on the money end, as Mr. Davis[4] has decided that I owe another thousand dollars for 1942——. I cannot see how———. Anyway, we can revise the $30,000 to $29,000, which doesn't sound so bad, or does it? I was telling Dr. Lyons about Chet's reaction to the amount that you and I felt was so far below the . . . expectations of Kate and Zelma, and he told me of the anger of some fishermen who run a camp on the Suwannee where he goes, against the man who runs the wholesale fish truck around there. Mrs. Odlum said, "Why, he *admits* that last year he made *two thousand* dollars." It is all so relative. Margaret Mitchell, who has made so much more than most successful authors, told me that she would be perfectly content if her receipts ever reached half a million.

I think I have covered everything you brought up.

It is inevitable (I have your letter and note of March 20) that all this gets on my nerves, but you can count on me not to fail you, and to rise to the mark. In spite of Mr. Crawford's[5] feeling that the suit is won or lost by your examination of Zelma, I am hoping that my sincere statement of my aims and motives and attitude will be a valuable factor.

Marjorie

1. A lawyer retained by MKR to take depositions in the Zelma Cason suit from several persons in the New York literary and publishing world.
2. A Cross Creek neighbor.
3. Raymond Weaver was dean of the College of Architecture at the University of Florida.
4. MKR's accountant.
5. Philip May's partner in the firm of Crawford and May.

134. To Philip May

Cross Creek
Apr. 18, 1946

Dear Phil:

. . . Now, I must tell you of something so utterly weird, that, as I told Norton, I would not be surprised if you threw up your hands and relinquished the whole damn case———. Day before yesterday, Tuesday the 16th, I came in to my beach cottage after having been to the Welch Convalescent Hospital to give a talk to the wounded veterans, at the request of the man in charge of such things (without a fee, of course) and found a note from Clare, (T. Z.'s daughter), saying that she and Terry (her little

boy) had walked past my cottage and seen the door open and
had come in, and were so sorry to miss me, and they were
staying at Spenser's, and would hope to see me. Norton had
supper with me at the cottage, and I said I'd like to drive down
to the Spenser cottage to ask Clare to come up for a chat. I
have always been devoted to T. Z.'s children. We drove down, and
since I was in a house-coat, being worn out after my talk to
the veterans, Norton went up to the Spenser cottage to see
Clare. She came down to the car, and said they were just about
to eat supper, and we talked a bit, and then she said, "Please
come on up and have a drink with us. There isn't a soul there
but Aunt Zelma." Realizing that she must have called by my
cottage with "Aunt Zelma's" knowledge, love nor money could
not have kept me from going up for a drink, and Norton said
later he felt the same way. So we went up, and I apologized for
my house coat, and Zelma apologized for her bare feet, and we
had a drink of whiskey, and Zelma fed Donac broth to Clare's
little Terry, while Norton egged him on by saying that if he
didn't eat it by the time he, Norton, counted ten, he would take
it, and Terry laughed and ate the Donac broth, and so on and
so on. Zelma showed us Clare's baby girl, asleep in a crib . . .
and said to me, "Marge, you'd be just crazy about Terry if you
knew him," and I said, "Well, Zelma, you remember, you and I
always did prefer little boys," and Zelma gave me the hardest
and most friendly poke in the ribs, and said, "Yes, Marge, we
always did like little boys."

Norton came away shaking his head. He said it just did not
make sense for two women who were at each other's throats, to
chat so amiably about Cason family matters, and I reminded
him that *I* had never been at Zelma's throat, and was actually
glad to see her, and she certainly seemed glad to see me.

Clare had left word with Idella at my cottage (one reason I
went down to see her) that her grandmother, Mrs. Cason, had
been very ill. Clare told us first, and then Zelma later, that what
happened to Mrs. Cason was this: the whole Cason family was
at Island Grove, having a mint julep, and did not fix anything
for Mrs. Cason, and she was sore about it, so they poured her
out a slug of gin. She did not drink it that night, but drank it
the next morning, then had her usual breakfast of a glass of

port wine and a raw egg, then took another slug of gin, went out
to feed her chickens and fell flat on her puss and had to have
a doctor— —.

Now the whole goddam business is ridiculous— —.

I still say, that when I have not given in and offered to settle
out of court before the suit goes to trial, I think it more than
likely that they will call quits. This may be just wishful thinking, but it seems to me that T. Z. must certainly wake up sometimes
at night with the heebie-jeebies at the thought of the costs, if
they lose. They cannot be *that* sure of winning. . . .

I had a fine audience at Welch, about 200 men, and they
seemed to enjoy my Florida yarns.

I was also taken after my talk to meet the librarian Miss
Swan Martin. She said she used to teach school in Island Grove.
Since I came home, I have been thinking, and I believe she
may be the missing school teacher that Zelma got fired. Miss
Martin, a most attractive young woman, said school teaching
had cramped her style, that she couldn't have a smoke, and if
she went to a jook, there was sure to be one of her pupils there,
or a pupil's parent. I shall write her and ask if I may have a
talk with her the next time I am at the cottage, week-end after
this. I would hardly dare tell her what I want, by mail, in
case she was a friend of Zelma's after all—but I have a strong
hunch she is our gal. Maybe the Lord will provide, after all. It
would be only fitting that the anguish I go through in giving a
public talk, should be rewarded with such a find. Please indicate just how I should write her. Would like to save myself the
trip if she is not the one.

Marjorie

135. To Norman Berg

Hawthorne, Florida
May 14, 1946

Dear Norman:

I'm sorry you found me in one of my black moods. I go up
and down, you know, like a barometer in the Caribbean. One
would have to be an idiot, or a saint, I think, to be always
happy, and I hope I am neither. What happens is that a great

deal of the time I am in contact with something, quite indefinable, but possibly the cosmic warmth or the cosmic vitality. As long as the strong current flows through me, I can work, I am *aware*. Then suddenly the lights go out. I am lost in despair.

This is a common condition, of course, a type of "neurosis," with a fancy name for it. It is also much more. The same thing is implicit in the ancient Biblical cry to God, "Withhold not Thy countenance from me."

I enjoyed your visit so much. You are a true friend.

I drove to the Scrub yesterday at sunset, through a terrific thunderstorm and downpour. I had never been there in that sort of weather, and it was wonderful. The thin pines were like sea-weed in an angry sea, yet it all seemed safe, as the bottom of the sea is safe. The Fiddia family was having supper in the twilight kitchen of the cabin, old Miss Piety eating biscuits and honey with the slowness of age, Leonard talking of the bear that is eating all his hogs, and he can't take time to lay for him, his wife quiet, ladling out beans and venison on the children's plates when she saw them empty, and the three children as lovely as flowers. The baby, Gracie, and I fell in love, and she clung to me, and a little black kitten kept patting her bare toes with its soft paws. Moe, of course, peeking in the door from the breezeway, wanting to come in, too.

A gray day this morning, and I think it will rain again. We are having high water, and the snakes are moving up to dry ground. We killed a rattlesnake in the afternoon, coiled in the corner between the dining room and the bathroom. I *don't* like them to *live* with me. He was doing no harm at the moment.

Marjorie

136. To Maxwell E. Perkins

Hawthorne, Florida
June 5, 1946

Dear Max:

I have read the book you sent me, "I Chose Freedom,"[1] with profound interest. I began it some time ago, and it sounded "ghost-written" to me, and I dropped it. Then the other night three professors from the University of Florida were here, and

we were arguing about Russia, and capitalism, and so on, and
one, who had been an administrator in Germany after the end of
the war, until very lately, quoted the book. His thesis was that
we are ignorant of what is going on in Russia, and of Russian
intentions, that is, of the intentions of the Soviet regime, that
they are utterly dangerous, and that book gives the true picture.
So I read it. I have been an apologist for the Soviet system, in
total ignorance. If this book is true, the picture is so different
from what we honest liberals have imagined, that it is most
alarming.

I have been thrown off the track, like many others, because
of the type of people who for the most part have damned the
Soviet system, in ignorance equal to mine. I have considered
these people, not only capitalistic but *materialistic,* which is both
different and worse, as dangerous to the world, to humanity,
as it is possible to be. They are the people with an over-large
and quite *unearned* share of material things, placing too great
an emphasis on material things, and frightened to death that a
world revolution would deprive them of trips to Palm Beach,
etc. etc. etc. I still consider them dangerous, but they seem like
small fry indeed in comparison with the menace this book
portrays. I hope this man will be able to go further and give
some idea of what can be done, in a tangible way. Of course,
exploding the myth is of primary importance.

Thank you for your wires about the trial. I had begun to feel
that I had been thrown to the wolves from the sleigh, so that
the other occupants of the sleigh might make their escape.
There was apparently nothing about the suit in papers outside
of Florida, and I am amazed at this, as it would seem to me
obvious to all concerned with writing in any form that if I lost
this case, no writer could be truly free. I know that I could have
bought Zelma off for infinitely less than it has cost me, but I
felt I should be betraying all writers if I took the easy way out.
A thousand dollars at most, I am sure, would have stopped
her and her lawyers, and it has already cost me about $4500,
with the final lawyers' bills not yet presented. Phil May has
charged me reasonably, but it has been going on over three
years, and he did not leave a stone unturned, in case we had
to go to the Florida Supreme Court. As it turned out, we did

not need the expense of the New York testimony, but he was taking no chances. He did read to the jury your testimony, Dr. Canby's and Bernice Baumgartner's. It came at the end of a long hard day and the jury was exhausted, and he was tempted not to use it, as he felt the jury had already decided to vote in my favor, but he was afraid not to get it into the record. (James Branch Cabell wrote me that, knowing juries, he would personally be afraid of a conviction if accused of killing Julius Caesar.) Phil and I were gratified to have the jury listen to that literary testimony as avidly as to the enemy's reading aloud of what they called "lewd, lascivious, lustful and salacious" passages from "Cross Creek." The enemy used Whitney's [Darrow] testimony for their side! They also entered Norton as their own witness, to his utter confusion and horror, but did not call him. I think they were just prepared to use Whitney's statements on sales, and to ask Norton about his finances, if my financial answer did not suit them. I was obliged to announce my net worth in money, from the witness stand.

After my experience, hard as it was, I think Tom Wolfe and any other writer ought to fight any such suit. Perhaps Tom was getting old grievances off his chest, and so really had something to fear. It was clear to all that I had no grudge or malice in my brief writing of Zelma.

The charge of malice against me took equal place with the charge of invasion of privacy, and the very fair judge was obliged to instruct the jury that if malice was proved, there must be extra "punitive" damages against me. The trial was utterly vicious. We kept our side of it on as high a plane as possible, and even that was thrown in our teeth by the opposition. Because critics had written that what I wrote was literature, because I was in "Who's Who," because I was the only woman and only the second person ever to receive three honorary degrees from Florida universities, they said "Is there to be one law for the rich and famous and another for the poor and humble?" They said that only my vast wealth had enabled me to call fifty-one witnesses from the environs, and take depositions all over the country. This proved a boomerang, as the good but extremely average jury could recognize that every person who testified for me, personally or in absentia, was motivated by genuine friendship.

Zelma had approached some of the Cross Creek people to help her, saying that if she won, they could sue, too. They were already perfectly aware of this. Tom Glisson spoke for them all when he told her, "Friendship is worth more to me than any amount of money."

The trial vindicated, to me, two things: the democratic system, for I felt that if that most commonplace jury, none of whom had ever read anything I had written, could not see that something important was involved, there was no hope; and the loyalty and friendship of all the people, their integrity, of which I had written so many years. There was an ovation in the court-room when the jury's verdict of "Not guilty" was announced.

But why, why, did the newspapers outside of Florida not understand what was happening?

The opposition ended their address to the jury with saying that it was exactly as though Joe Louis, the Negro champion, had stalked into Gainesville and knocked down a private citizen without provocation. "He might have done it with great finesse, gentlemen of the jury, as we admit that this woman handles language beautifully, but is that any reason for the public to applaud such a malicious attack?"

One of the most amusing incidents of the trial, to me, was when Zelma's lawyer was cross-examining me. I could see the petty pit-falls he was trying to lay, and could anticipate him. He had asked me an inane question, and I said, "Now do you mean so and so, for the answer in that case would be one thing, or do you mean thus and so, in which the answer would be quite different," and so on. He floundered around, and Phil May jumped up and said, "Mr. Walton, what are you doing?" Walton said most plaintively, "I'm answering her question." Phil said, "Mr. Walton, you don't have to answer her question. She has no right to ask you questions." The court-room and the judge all but had hysterics.

Well, it is over, and I hope to get down to hard work. I still think it will have to be the book I have torn up so often.

Marjorie

1. Victor A. Kravchenko, *I Chose Freedom; the Personal Story of a Soviet Official* (New York, 1946).

137. To Sigsbee Scruggs

[Cross Creek]
July 23, 1946

Dear Mr. Scruggs:

Mr. May has forwarded to me a copy of your letter to him, on the subject of your compensation in the Cason suit. I should have written you before this, but I am ashamed to say that I had a nervous let-down after the trial, and have only begun to feel like myself, since the motion for a new trial was denied. More than three years is a long time to have had this hanging over me.

There is no need for "arbitration" or for any further discussion. I enclose my check for the additional $1,000 requested by you, and with it, my thanks for your very fine help during the trial, and your splendid argument to the jury. In spite of the strain I was under, I realized that you were giving more time than originally contracted for, and I had the thought of asking you if you would accept an extra amount.

I must admit that the rate of payment you receive for your professional work is higher than the rate I receive for mine. However, I suppose that, like a doctor, you feel obliged to handle so many cases for poor people, who can pay only a minimum, or nothing at all, that you must necessarily make it up on those who can afford higher fees.

Your rate of payment is also infinitely higher than Mr. May's in this case. I understand, of course, that the suit meant two entirely different things to you and to him. For you, it was a routine piece of business—though I do think you became as interested as the rest of us, as the case went on. For Mr. May, as for me, it was a battle for a strongly-felt principle. He told me, both early in the suit, and again shortly before the trial, that he felt it his duty to warn me that I could buy off Zelma and the Waltons for a great deal less than a trial would cost me, in money and in nervous energy. He would have been greatly disappointed in my integrity if I had done so. And, too, he has been a close friend of mine and of my husband for many years, and for that additional reason, I am sure, has cut his own fees drastically.

One wonderful thing to come out of the expensive mess has been the affirmation of friendship among my neighbors for miles around. Many of the poorest of them wanted me to take back their mileage and witness checks. It all made me know more deeply than ever, that my instinct was right, so long ago, in casting my lot with them, and in giving my heart to them and to the section of which I wrote with so much happiness.

With appreciation for your good assistance,

Cordially,

Marjorie Kinnan Rawlings

138. To Norman Berg

Hawthorne, Florida
Dec. 9, 1946

Dear Norman:

Norton joined me from Wed. to Sat. in New York and we reached the cottage yesterday. Your good letter was among my waiting mail.

I know only too well what you are going through with your book. I could not conceive of your getting any work done at Summerhaven.[1] There were too many people in that small place. Too much coming and going and what-not, aside from a lack of privacy. You could manage the necessary mental isolation in quite a small place with just Julie, if you had a room where you could close the door, not *against* her, but inward *toward yourself.* For the books come from so far inside.

I know, too, what you mean by not wanting your principal character to be too autobiographically *you,* yet if that character is representing deliberately what you want most to say, it is right and proper that you put your thoughts in his head and your words in his mouth. In editing and revising later, you will probably see where you have been perhaps a little untrue to the created character, by being too much yourself. No actual autobiography, even, ever is truly the individual. In writing of ourselves, we shade ourselves almost as much as we do an imaginary character—often quite unconsciously. For instance, I gave a false picture of myself in "Cross Creek." Readers think of me so much as The One Friend, and my flesh crawls when they approach me, which would never happen to The Friend.

I agree with you that solitary confinement would be ideal for work, and have sometimes longed to satisfy my wilder impulses to smash things and raise hell, and as a result be placed in a nice cozy little cell alone. We should probably not be allowed a typewriter, or perhaps even enough paper——. It may be best, after all, to behave——.

I present you the gun, with pity for your perverseness. It is a bitch of a shotgun, as you have found. I had it cut down for me, and perhaps you could add another rubber pad. You are MORE than welcome to it.

Remember, "There are only two kinds of sound—conversation and noise." When it is not good conversation, (someone said, "A man is known by the conversation he keeps") it becomes noise. I have often seen you sit among dull people like an unfriendly cat, switching your tail. However, I have found the stupid people sometimes the most pitiful, and I try to reach out a kind hand to them, with a few words in the palm. In the play "Dream Girl" which Norton and I saw in New York, someone says, "She was clad in her thoughts. Poor naked creature."

I am surprised that you use the word "friction" as existing between Norton and me. I should, rather, call it "tension," of a subtle and unidentifiable kind. There is no question but that he is acutely sensitive to my moods, to the constant tempest in me. Neither he nor I knows what to do about it, and he is unwilling to probe into the deeper thoughts and emotions. He bore alone for so long the burden of weak brothers and sisters, and still does to a certain extent, that he has schooled himself never to let any sort of distress or conflict come to the surface. I can talk *anything* out, and he cannot. He suffers so dreadfully when I try to get at roots and sources, that I have given up inflicting the punishment on him. And when I talked of some of these things with you, I felt as *unfaithful* as though I had gone to bed with the ice man—simply because I knew he would hate it.

As I grow older, I do think, or hope, that I learn more and more the *relative* values, and that I may eventually attain the necessary balance. If I find that I do not, that the battle becomes more difficult, I shall have Dr. Atchley at Medical Center send me to the best possible psychiatrist to trace down the origins of the scar tissue that aches whenever the wind changes!

You put your finger on one very true thing—that I am afraid of a complete giving—and there is surely some simple reason for that. Or is there? It seems to me that there is something endemic in withdrawal for the writer. How else would the work get done?

I had one evening of true conversation, at Marcia Davenport's, with Jan Masaryk[2] and Robert Sherwood.[3] Masaryk has one of the most magnificent minds and spirits I have ever met.

My love,

Marjorie

1. A beach community at Matanzas Inlet, a few miles south of MKR's cottage, originally settled by members of the Mellon family.

2. Jan Masaryk (1896–1948), Czechoslovakian foreign minister; shortly afterward he died in a fall from a hotel window.

3. Robert Sherwood, American playwright (1896–1955).

139. To Norman Berg

Cross Creek
Feb. 21, 1947

Dear Carney:

I am at the Creek to *stay,* for two or three months, or until I really get my teeth into a long job of work. I'll go to the cottage every week-end or every other one, according to how the work is going.

I wish to report that my status at Cross Creek and environs is quite unchanged. I have already been *embraced* by five of my women friends in the neighborhood, usually most undemonstrative, and had my hand pumped by as many or more men, all expressing joy that I am "home." You see, they all *know* that this is home to me, and understand that my being away is due only to the accidental misfortune of having fallen in love with a hotel man. These people don't change. When they accepted me, it was for better or for worse, and I should have to outrage them dreadfully and peculiarly for them to grow cold. They *sympathize* with my absences, instead of condemning me for them. Although we have little of what is commonly known as "social contact," we are true friends. They would do anything in the world for me, and I for them, and we all know this.

You disturbed me with your charges of arrogance and

Cross-Creek-alienation-of-affections. I was sure you were mistaken, for all you know of the relationships here is what you
read in the book "Cross Creek," yet I wondered if by chance my
friends might be as touchy and querulous as you, and did feel
that I had betrayed or abandoned them. They do not.

Many thanks for the books. "The Wanderer"[1] is an exquisite
thing, and I am grateful to you for not having missed it. You
said you could get another copy, so I'll keep mine. I'll send you
back the hard-to-get "Lonely Plough."[2] This has wonderful descriptions of English country life, and handles natural and human catastrophe with a great deal of power. It is also sometimes very sentimental, as only the English can be, and has an
acceptance of the English class system that sets one's teeth on
edge.

I re-read "Handful of Dust"[3] with even more pleasure than
before. Haven't yet read the [E.M.] Forster.

Phil May and his wife just left. He has been working in the
Gainesville Law Library, getting ready for Zelma's appeal on
April 10. He wants to meet you, and I told him I'd ask you to get
in touch with him when you are in Jacksonville. . . . He was
one of Carl Bohnenberger's best friends, you know, and Carl had
spoken of you. Phil is a nice little fellow, solid integrity, with
such an *eager* mind. If you meet his wife, don't let her air of
affectation throw you off. She has a bad inferiority complex, the
rather touching kind, but is solid gold. . . .

The Hugh Williams down the road, and I had a good laugh
yesterday. They were telling me about a woman who had passed
through Cross Creek and "felt" my "presence," though she
didn't know it was C.C.; got to Ocala, asked questions, came
back again, and talked a long time with the Williams at their
fruit stand. They said, "She thought you were next to Jesus" and
I said, "My God, I hope you kept your mouths shut." When
they were over their hysterics, Hugh said, "We let her get away
in the same dreamy state in which she arrived."

One gay angle of our relationships here, is that we can laugh
at one another. Tom Glisson was telling me that an "outsider"
had remarked to him that he heard Mrs. Rawlings did a lot of
drinking. Tom said, "I told him, 'Why, yes, she's real fond of it,
and she's got more sense drunk than most people, sober'." Now

Tom and I BOTH thought that was funny. And he felt free to repeat it to me.

Well, it is Balm in Gilead to be here, and I try to put out of my mind the picture of darling Norton going into a cold, empty cottage at night, and leaving same in the morning! Once I get my book *going,* I can work anywhere, under any conditions, and then I can write and still be A Good Wife. And I am going to stop *whining.* It is absurd to want EVERYTHING, when I have so much.

Marjorie

1. A novel by Nathan Schachner (New York, 1944).
2. A book by Constance Holme (New York, 1936).
3. A novel by Evelyn Waugh (Boston, 1944).

140. To Maxwell E. Perkins

Cross Creek
April 30, 1947

Dear Max:

I am delighted that you may publish Zora Neale Hurston's next book. I feel that she has a very great talent. You really should read her "Moses, Man of the Mountain." She has not only the Negro gift of rhythm and imagination, but she is proud of her blood and her people, and presents her stories from the Negro point of view. I am very fond of her. And will you send me her address? I have been wanting to write her, but didn't know where she was.

I was just ready to go to work on Calpurnia[1] again, when I wrecked my car seriously, myself and maid rather lightly, considering the fact that we turned over twice. Our road at the Creek had been oiled, without my knowing of it. It was raining hard, and we skidded. My only damages were beautiful multi-colored bruises, but Idella broke two ribs.

The delay will probably be to the good in re-writing the story, as I do need the perspective you suggested, of not trailing after Bob Camp's very engaging pictures. He made them all, before I had begun work, and they did have a great deal of influence on me. He and I had been talking about the book for several years.

I can't help wishing, in spite of the very high remuneration, that Carl Brandt had not sold that movie story[2] to the POST. When I wrote it in narrative form for M.G.M., I really never expected it to appear in print of any sort. I read the first installment of the serial, and could have died of shame. It is even worse, from a literary standpoint, than I remembered.

My beloved friend Edith Pope is certainly rubbing it in. We were at a party with Owen D. Young [see page 296], and he asked her if she had read the first issue. She had, and gave him such a wan, comprehensive smile! Norton reports that the next night she and her husband were at his Marineland[3] for dinner, and she asked Norton if he had read it, saying, "DON'T." I told Norton that I didn't mind Edith's high-hatting me about it, as I deserved it to begin with, and it might have a good effect on her, by making her think twice before she put down something sub-standard. But I am most embarrassed about it all.

I'll go back to "The Secret River" now, and we can only see what comes of it.

My best,

Marjorie

1. Referring to "The Secret River," a story published posthumously (New York, 1955).

2. "Mountain Prelude," which ran serially in *Saturday Evening Post* beginning April 20, 1947.

3. Norton Baskin at this time held the restaurant franchise at Marineland, south of Crescent Beach.

141. To Norman Berg

Hawthorne, Florida
May 1, 1947

Dear Carney:

When you do come down, can't you bring with you the young writer whose letter you read me? I am still in such a stymied state on my work that I probably couldn't be of any help to him, except that talk is stimulating.

And when I wrote you that half a dozen of your friends were likely to pop off before you, I came close to making a prophet of myself. I went and wrecked my car, and Idella and I didn't

miss the Grand March by much. I'll hasten to say that I was
only gloriously bruised and shaken up, while poor Idella, equally
bruised, broke two ribs. The road department had oiled our
normally safe gravel road at the Creek, which had never been
done before. I could not notice the oil, as it was raining hard—
we skidded around a curve and turned over twice. I owe somebody
about forty feet of fencing and posts. And oh man, you should
see the car! I am more devoted to the Oldsmobile than ever, as
the body is really tough. In Norton's convertible, there wouldn't
have been a chance. There were four wrecks on the road within
a few days, one of them very serious.

I hired a car to take Idella to the doctor, and home (where
she was headed anyway, claiming she was sick. I didn't think
she was, still don't think so, but she sure as hell became so!) I
didn't think I was hurt at all, and when Tom Glisson drove me
to Island Grove to 'phone my insurance agent and Norton, I
told Norton I was all right. He said he was too busy to come
over, then he got to thinking about it and decided perhaps I
didn't know what I was talking about, and drove over and insisted on taking me to St. Augustine. A good thing, too, as the
next morning I couldn't *move*. Anyway, I'm all right now. I went
to see Idella yesterday and she is getting along nicely, and
can come back in about two weeks more. I'm taking her to the
doctor again tomorrow.

One side of my face, including the eye, was such an assortment of color that Norton of course came in for a lot of kidding.
He said, "The fact that I am alive proves I didn't lay a hand
on her."

He brought me back here Monday, and to Ocala to borrow a
car. I am promised a new Olds this month.

Having been invited months before, two of my dreadful old
maid aunts chose to accept our invitation to come to Marineland,
a couple of days after the accident. They are so peculiar and
touchy I didn't want to tell them not to come, so I got a substitute maid, got nobly out of bed, and had them to lunch at the
cottage, having to do the cooking myself. I had a letter from
them yesterday, saying they were worried about my *health*, that
I just didn't seem *well* to them. Because of my rainbow appearance, I had been obliged to tell them lightly of the acci-

dent, and now I am resisting the temptation to write them that when one's eye meets one's ass, one really does not look one's best.

I wish Julie could come with you, too. One of the things I wanted to talk with you about, was giving Julie a gayer time. I don't mean night clubs, but taking her to the sort of places she enjoys. You have proved so right about her in every way that I should probably not say so, but my feeling is that she does not care about worldly or literary success for you. Her utter happiness in the fishing at Cove Tavern, even while living in that crowded dump, was a thing to see.

Love,

Marjorie

Among MKR's most cherished friends in the St. Augustine area were Owen D. Young, former president of General Electric, and his wife, Louise, who wintered at Washington Oaks, an estate located a few miles south of MKR's beach house. Mr. Young was a great admirer of MKR's work, and when he heard that the writing was going badly on her intended novel of the northern farm country (*The Sojourner*), he offered her the use of a cottage located near his summer home in Van Hornesville, New York, in countryside closely resembling the setting of her novel. She found this country so lovely and so congenial that she bought an old farmhouse in the area, had it renovated, and used it as her summer working place, going north each spring and staying on until bitter weather in early winter drove her back to Florida.

142. To Norman Berg

Brown's Hollow
Van Hornesville, N.Y.
June 22, 1947

Dear Norman:

Norton and I reached here quite late Thursday night, and found the Owen D. Young's waiting up for us, insisting on our spending the night with them—and giving me a telegram from

Charlie Scribner saying that Max Perkins was dead.

My first feeling was of unspeakable grief at losing the man himself, and then one of utter frustration that I had made this long trek to begin a book that he would never see and on which he could not save me from possible pitfalls. I felt inclined to return to Florida. Then I realized how horrified Max would be by such an attitude, for to him only the book mattered.

A further irony is that this place is perfect for working. It is a little old house deep in woods, above a trout stream whose rushing sound, day and night, is much like the susurrus of the wind in pine trees. To the south lies an open field golden with buttercups, where the deer come. A wood peewee is sitting on five eggs in an exquisite nest on the porch. A flag-stone terrace overlooks the stream. There is a huge fireplace and modern conveniences. Roses and day-lilies will soon be in bloom, and a wild raspberry thicket already has tiny nubbins of fruit. If I cannot write a north rural book here, I cannot write it anywhere.

Moe and Benny[1] and I were at home instantly. Benny brings me his catch of small garter snakes each morning. He picks them up by the middle, the head and tail waving on either side of his mouth like a Mandarin's whiskers, and he will do that with a Florida rattler just one time——. I think he is due for a short life but a merry one.

A book came for me from Macmillan that I thought would be the Tarbell[2] biography of Mr. Young, but it proved to be "Patterns for Living," which used excerpts from "Cross Creek." I told Mr. Young that you were sending me the Tarbell book, and he said it was a poor affair, that it was an insensitive eulogy instead of an appraisal. The more I see of him, the less I see how any biographer could "appraise" him except in eulogistic terms.

I gathered wild columbine and wild forget-me-nots yesterday, and when I took my bath, I was covered with flower petals, and as I wrote Norton, felt like a nymph, if a nymph was ever of Rubenesque proportions. I do want to trim down this summer, but the Van Hornesville cream, really necessary on the strawberries, is an obstacle.

It was good to see you and yours, even so briefly.

With my love,

Marjorie

1. MKR's dog and cat.
2. Ida Tarbell (1857–1944), biographer of Owen D. Young.

143. To Charles Scribner

Van Hornesville, N.Y.
July 3, 1947

Dear Charlie:

Any author who could be lured away from you because Max is gone, would be overlooking a vital factor: Max would always have been Max, but only with Scribner's would he have had such a free hand, with the integrity of the house backing up his own integrity. The almost indefinable quality of your firm is as important to a writer as Max's rare editorial judgment. This is safe at least during your life-time and that of young Charlie.

For myself, I feel that I shall only have to work harder, to be even more critical of my own work.

I need your opinion on an immediate problem.

I don't know to what extent Max discussed with you the child's book, "The Secret River," to be illustrated by Bob Camp. Max gave me his usual valuable criticism on my first draft. I think I asked him not to show the manuscript to anyone else. Bob and I planned the book together several years ago, about a little colored girl in Florida. He showed up with delightful paintings and drawings before I did my part of it. Bob had evinced so much imagination in the art, that I told him I thought he could do the text, and then the whole book would be his, but he insisted he could not, and that the story must be mine. I did actually shape part of my text around his illustrations, and Max objected to this. He wrote me that the story must come first, and the pictures must then illustrate it. The story as it was first written, fell between pure fantasy, or faery, and realism, and Max felt I should swing it further to the side of realism, while keeping a certain "magical" quality I had tried for, and which he said was definitely there. He told me from the beginning to let the story have its head.

No more than a week before he died, I wrote him a rather fretful letter, which he may not ever have seen. I said that I saw no reason why the text might not fit in with the already-done pictures, and that I was afraid he expected me to do something much more creative than I had planned. I said I had lost interest in it, which I realize was not true. I think I was trying to make sure that he didn't have any illusions that if I went deeper into the story, I might come up with a sepia "Yearling."

Now some day I might possibly do a full book with a colored hero or heroine, but this story is not it. I don't think it would take me very long to re-write it along the lines Max suggested—and I did and do agree with him—and since I have been catching up on odds and ends and have not begun my book yet, I thought it best to check with you on publishing schedules.

Would you prefer to have such a child's book come out in time for the Christmas trade, and if so, is it too late in the summer to plan for it this year? Or doesn't that make much difference?

The book (the novel) is going to be a long and anguished business, and a little more delay in getting at it won't matter, if you want me to go ahead and finish "The Secret River" first.

Carl Brandt wants to come up here and see me in late July or early August, but I think I'll put him off. I certainly won't have enough done to care to have him see it, (Max was the only one you could *bear* to have see things while they were naked) and I am afraid Carl thinks that with a book *begun,* he could talk me into signing that profitable movie contract—and I'll be damned if I'll do it. I shouldn't touch one of the filthy things until a book is nine-tenths done, at least.

I get awful qualms sometimes about our not publishing the Post story, "Mountain Prelude," as a book. I have had the most terrific number of letters about it, saying the most touching things. I wish now I had taken more time and written it more creatively, so that I needn't be ashamed of its lack of literary quality.

I am extremely happy here.

With love,

Marjorie

144. To Bernice Gilkyson

Van Hornesville, N.Y.
July 9, 1947

Dear Bernice:

Your comforting letter was forwarded to me here. I had been trying to find a place in the Carolina mountains for beginning my book, and Mr. and Mrs. Owen D. Young offered me the loan of a cottage near their summer home. I got my new Oldsmobile two days before we had to leave, and Norton drove me up, with Moe and Benny. He could only stay one day, as he had a new Chef coming, but he fell in love with the place as deeply as I did, and I think he will come up again during the summer.

The night we reached here, going to the Young's home, Charlie's telegram about Max's death was handed to me. I felt like turning right around and going home again, as it seemed the last straw of impossibility to try to get the book going, without Max. It was startling to realize, as you said, how much we wrote *for* him, and certainly with his judgment constantly in mind. I dream about him often and wake up in tears. In one dream, I went in to his office and said to him, "I have terrible news for you. Max is dead." He smiled, and I said, "But you are Max. You know better than anyone what this means to all of us."

Edith Pope hasn't answered my letter to her, which is unusual, and I am afraid that being right in the middle of a difficult book, she is crushed, too. Max did the most enormous job of straightening out her first jumble of "Colcorton."

Well, I for one shall have to work all the harder.

The little cottage where I am staying is enchanting. It is in "Brown's Hollow," deep in the woods above a rushing trout stream, old, furnished with antiques, but with modern conveniences. I have no help, except for one of Mrs. Young's maids who comes once a week to clean, but I am getting along without any trouble at all. I am reveling in the flowers and the wild strawberries.

AND, tomorrow I go to Cooperstown, fifteen miles away, to pay the enormous sum of $1200 and acquire the deed and the key to the *loveliest* little house, with several acres of good land and woods and a divine view! The house was General Sullivan's headquarters during the Revolution, is in splendid condition, and needs only re-plastering and papering, and plumbing and electricity, to be ready to move into. The electric line is close by, and Louise Young has a good man and crew to put to work as soon as they finish a place of hers, and she thinks $1000 will do my whole job. She and Mr. Young have bought up several fine old places that were falling into ruin and fixed them, and have made Van Hornesville a little gem of a village. Norton is going to be upset, I'm afraid, both because it is so far from Florida and because it means he will be abandoned for longer periods, but I couldn't help myself. The second time I saw the place, I knew I *had* to have it.

Couldn't you drive up, or over, some time this summer, especially if Norton comes? There's a cute guest room here.

With love to you and Walter,

Marjorie

145. *To Norman Berg*

Van Hornesville, N.Y.
Aug. 22, 1947

Dear Norman:

By all means go by Cross Creek and sleep there and assure the old house that it is not forgotten. I think it was in "South Moon Under" that I wrote something to the effect that "human habitation keeps a house standing." The roof will leak all over you, but the first large bedroom with the mahogany bed, my room, is the dryest. My dear friend Leonard ("Lant" of "South Moon Under") has messed up his whole summer waiting to put on a new roof for me, and now I find that it will be from 3 to 6 months before the St. Joe Lumber Co., the only people we could locate still making cypress shingles, would have enough to fill our order. I just don't know what to do. I am afraid the farmhouse will collapse if there isn't a new roof before then. We don't need an entirely new roof, as Leonard put some on new in 1933 (and cypress is good for at least 50 years) and I wonder if the cedar shingles that I used for my little house up here would weather to the same lovely gray color, or whether I'd better settle for asphalt shingles. Mr. Young put a new roof of

them on an old church here and they really look well. As you
see, I am just thinking out loud——. . . .

I get more excited every day about my house. I have the
strangest feeling that some day I shall live here most of the
time, spending the other months at Cross Creek. In consequence,
I am doing over the house better than it really needs to be
done. Aside from my own desire to have it practically perfect,
the lovely little house deserves to be made right for another
hundred years. The workmen are all interested in its restoration, and the plumber told the nice girl who comes to clean up
for me at Brown's Hollow, that while when he first went into the
house, he thought it was hopeless, now he thinks it will be
the most beautiful house he has ever known. . . .

Julia Scribner and her husband spent a week with me. I like
him, but am afraid I did your trick of arguing too vocifer-
ously—no, I don't mean that, I am not at all afraid of what I
said. We got into a deep theological discussion, and I merely
insisted that if *I* were going to be a man of God, or give myself
to the Church, I should go all out on it. His position is that
"the Church needs administrators as much as it needs saints."
This left me cold and I said so, and I don't think he likes me
any more. Julia will come up again later, alone, while Tom
"makes a retreat," which is so High Church as to be almost
Catholic, and it seems silly to me when he is not at all a mystic.

Having begun my book again, and shocked by the bit I did, I
have been writing verse. One sonnet needs re-working but is
not too dreadful, another needs tearing to pieces, and so on. Did
you see Edna Vincent Millay's strange poem in the last *Atlantic Monthly,* "To a Snake"? It is wonderfully *vigorous.*

Marjorie

146. To Beatrice H. McNeill

Van Hornesville, N.Y.
Aug. 27, 1947

Darling Bee,

. . . It would be marvelous to have you come here for a visit, except that I should hate such a short one. Which appeals to you
most, coming now while my house is a mere stripped-out shell,

or next summer when I am living in it? It is not the house I am in. Mr. and Mrs. Owen D. Young loaned me a little place called "Brown's Hollow" for the summer. The place I bought is too enchanting for words. You would be full of ideas for it, and could go antique-ing with me, for it just has to be furnished with old things.

It is small, a perfect little gem, over a hundred years old, I haven't checked yet just how old, with lovely architectural detail, 8 acres of land, a divine view that includes, in clear weather, the upper end of Otsego Lake, James Fenimore Cooper's "Glimmer Glass." I bought it for $1,000, plus rather high lawyer's fees for clearing the ancient title. The new shingled roof is on, three fireplaces will go in, new plastering, two bathrooms, one downstairs and one upstairs for the *single* large bedroom, an electric line was nearby, so putting in lights will not be bad, and I took out lots of partitions to turn tiny little unuseable rooms into: a very large studio work-room that I think will end up as the "parlor"; a combination country living-and-dining room;

MKR's house in Van Hornesville, N.Y., before restoration.

kitchen; (a grand pantry with beautiful old pine shelves is already there); and a large upstairs bedroom with sort of an alcove at one end, formed by an added closet at one side (there was hardly a closet in the place) and the bathroom on the other. Upstairs fireplace. At the far end of the long studio or parlor, I plan to put what will look like a long deep comfortable couch, but will actually be two box-springs and mattresses on legs. This end of the room has a door into a downstairs dressing or powder room, which in turn opens into the downstairs bathroom, so that when I have guests, I can still sleep two. If they, he, she or it, is just for over-night, the downstairs will do. If for a week or longer, I'll give them the upstairs, especially if Norton is not here. Poor Norton, he has really caught it this summer. I simply abandoned him. While I am away, he is enlarging the beach cottage, adding a studio for me and another bathroom and fixing a useable terrace. He has also been so busy, firing and hiring chefs, that it was a good time for me to be away. . . .

I must tell you about an amazing coincidence in connection with my darling new house. It stands on part of the original Gen. Philip Schuyler grant, and I mentioned this at an antique shop in nearby Cooperstown and asked jokingly if they had a portrait of Philip Schuyler. They didn't, of course, but the name rang a bell, and out of an upper store-room they brought down the most charming American primitive portrait which they had bought many years ago from the old Schuyler mansion near Albany. It was of "Maria Bogardus Schuyler and daughter Catharine." I almost fell over, as Bogardus is the name of my father's first ancestor in this country. I told them to hold the portrait while I investigated, and after corresponding with my Kinnan auntie who keeps track of the family lines, it is definite that the woman in the portrait is either an aunt greatly removed or a cousin greatly removed. My ancestor, William Bogardus, oldest son of Anneka Jans and the Reverend Everardus Bogardus, had a daughter named Maria, and so did his younger brother Pieter, and there are records showing that the first ancestor of Philip Schuyler married in Renssalaerwyck, N.Y., where the Dominie Bogardus married Anneka Jans, and also records of Anneka Jans selling some land to a Schuyler. If you do come, when you come, and I meet you in Albany, I'll find out exactly,

as Anneka Jans Bogardus is buried there and the Historical
Society will be able to trace things.

Norton didn't mean a word of what he told Neal Smith about
refusing to travel with his animal trio. He is the most patient
man in the world with all of us, and really likes us. He wishes
Moe wouldn't wake him up every morning by pushing his wet
nose right into his face, and he wishes Benny wouldn't jump
from the window-sill above our bed right on his stomach in the
middle of the night, and as for my traits—I phoned him from
the Young's the other night, as I hadn't had a letter from him,
and I explained that I was afraid he might be depressed. Mrs.
Young asked "What would depress him?" and I said, "Me."

He doesn't know it yet, but I plan to stay here until the middle of October. It will take the workmen that long to finish my
house, and I want enough furniture in it by then so that I can
go right to it next year. I shall paper the bedroom and dining
room and haven't decided yet about the "parlor" which will have
Aunt-or-Cousin Maria's portrait over a lovely old square rose-
wood piano that I bought with the house, and everyone says the
new plaster should go through the winter before papering.

I have done nothing about maid's quarters. Idella up and
got married this spring, after I went on paying her regular
wages while she recovered from our automobile accident. I had
also bought an expensive combination bed-davenport for her
new *suite* in the tenant house at Cross Creek, so she could have
a guest. And she had known for months she was going to leave.
Now her husband is in an Army hospital with stomach ulcers,
Idella is lost without her own money, and not at all happy. We
may possibly get together for the winter. But a colored maid
would be impossible up here for more than a couple of weeks, as
there just are no Negroes here. Any help I have would be a
white girl who would come in each day. Behind my little house
is a huge old hop-house, and some day, if I ever make any
more money, I should like to convert it into a studio, guest-suite
and maid's quarters. I have rather enjoyed doing my own
cooking this summer. An awfully nice young woman comes in
and cleans up.

The place where I am is a dear little fixed-over old house deep
in the woods, no view, theoretically a perfect place for work—

and my book still is not started. I began it once again and it was so awful I just went out and picked wild strawberries. Mrs. Young is "mothering" me like all get-out, makes me go to parties, is reducing me, and my soul is not quite my own. I am really enjoying it, and the change of climate or something has made me over. I don't think I will be behind in the end.

Benny loves it here, especially the steep little old stairs, and he races up and down them and plays at being a tiger behind the banisters.

If you can't come *both* this year and next, which I should love, decide carefully which would be the most fun for you. If you decide for now, and need to wire me, a wire should go c/o Owen D. Young, Richfield Springs, N.Y. (we have no Western Union in Van Hornesville.)

> Loads of love,
> Marjorie

147. To Norman Berg

> Cross Creek
> November 4, 1947

Dear Norman:

I am back in this enchanted place, but like a bird in passage——

Martha was expecting me, and had the front of the house clean, and spider lilies for me, and the house seemed ready and waiting, and not abandoned or unloved at all—— The place knows that I am doing the best I can, and that some day, somehow, we shall be truly together again——.

I have ordered a new gate, and cedar fence posts, and a lightweight wheelbarrow for old Will, and my friend at Baird's is combing the state for cypress shingles for the roof.

Martha's Bible from you and Julie was among my unopened mail, and she was more than happy about it—there was a hushed awe—her first Bible——. Since she can't read, it had never occurred to me to ask if she owned one—— She wants me to read a bit from it to her before I leave today——It was a

lovely thing for you to do for her. She is disappointed that you
didn't return for a stay and some fishing.

Norton came to Van Hornesville where we had a fine week,
with gorgeous weather, and he loved the Yankee house, too. We
stayed a week in New York City, then drove on down with
Moe and Benny and reached St. Augustine last Wednesday
night. I was *shocked* by the new size and elegance of the erst-
while "cottage," and by realizing that it must have cost Norton
his entire profits for the year. He said it was more than worth
it if it made me happier and more comfortable. As a matter of
fact, the new studio, with its complete privacy, will be a great
place to work, and I shall love it, and work very hard. I made a
beginning on my book that I can let stand at least long enough to
go ahead.

I have to return to New York in a few days for an operation. A
routine check-up in New York revealed a condition that will
probably prove simple to take care of, but that should not wait
for attention, almost certainly *not* a malignancy, but Dr. Damon and
Dr. Atchley said I must not wait until my normal return to
Van Hornesville in the Spring. So we are getting it over with at
once, and there will be a letter at St. Augustine having the
day I am to appear at the hospital.

Idella has come back to me, only because an opening for her
husband unexpectedly came up at Norton's bar. They will both
live in the new nice garage apartment at the cottage.

Write me news of you and yours.

My love to you all————.

Marjorie

In this letter to F. Scott Fitzgerald's biographer, MKR describes
her visit with Fitzgerald at the Grove Park Inn in Asheville,
North Carolina, some years earlier. That visit is also discussed in
her letter to Perkins (see letter 47, October 26, 1936), but she here
includes so many additional bits of information that it seems jus-
tifiable to include this one as well.

148. To Arthur Mizener

Crescent Beach
St. Augustine, Florida
March 18, 1948

Dear Mr. Mizener:

You are one of the few who "realize that it is an imposition" to ask writers to write letters—and to provide material for the books of others! You dis-arm me.

I have known so many of the best modern writers, often at critical periods of their lives, that I have had it in mind to do a series of sketches about them. Scott Fitzgerald was to be one of them. However, there would be no reason why I could not now give you what material I have, for your purpose, and still use the same material later, myself.

I had one brief but rather spectacular meeting with Fitzgerald. Aspects of it were revealing, for all its briefness and limitations, and I shall give you a blow-by-blow report. I ask only that you let me see what use you make of it, before publication, and with the understanding that I may make corrections.

Consciously or unconsciously, our magnificent mutual friend and editor, Maxwell Perkins, played off his authors against one another. He knew the stimulation to a writer of knowing what other writers were both doing and failing to do.

Max had the strange idea that I was "wholesome." I was staying alone in a rather remote cabin in the North Carolina mountains during the summer of 1936, I believe it was, beginning the actual writing of my book "The Yearling." Scott was ensconced at the elegantly Victorian Grove Park Inn at Asheville, recovering from a broken collar-bone or shoulder or whatnot, and presumably from alcohol. Max wrote me that Scott was only a hundred miles away from me, and would I go see him. He thought I might have this dreadful "wholesome" influence on Scott——. I answered that I was certain that was the last thing in the world Mr. Fitzgerald wanted or needed, that missionary work was out of character for me, that I was working hard and it would be a long mountain drive to Asheville. Max persisted, and evidently wrote Scott, too.

I had an errand in Asheville, and I wrote Scott, saying that at

Mr. Perkins' suggestion, I should like to call on him. He wrote
that he was not well, but that if I would telephone him when
I got into Asheville, he would be willing to see me, and suggested a certain evening. I was delayed by storms through the
mountains, and 'phoned him from the outskirts of Asheville one
evening about seven o'clock. His nurse answered, and after
consultation, reported that Mr. Fitzgerald was having a bad time
and could not see me that night, but would I 'phone again the
next day. I felt rather outraged, as all this was none of my doing. (You see, my personal record enters into this account!) I
decided to do my business and leave Mr. Fitzgerald to stew in
his own juice. The next noon, as I was ready to check out of
my hotel, I relented and did telephone him again, and he answered in person. I said that I was just leaving, but did want to
follow Mr. Perkins' request that we exchange greetings. He
became very excited, and insisted that I must join him for luncheon before I left. Because of Max, I agreed.

Scott's nurse met me at the door of his room. Scott introduced us and dismissed her. She was fishy-eyed and most dis-
trustful. He began talking eagerly, saying that the last nurse
had left because they had become intimate and she was terrified
of becoming pregnant, and that the present nurse was devot-
ing herself to keeping him from drinking and from any other
malevolent influences. Whereupon he 'phoned and ordered
a bottle of sherry. We drank the sherry, he ordered luncheon
served in the room, and after luncheon he ordered port. And
again, port, and again——.

He was exhilarated. He talked of his own work. He was modest, but he was *sure*. He said that he had made an ass of himself, that his broken bone was the result of his having tried to
"show off" in front of "debutantes" when he dived proudly into a
swimming-pool, that he had gone astray with his writing, but
was ready to go back to it in full force.

He talked a great deal about Hemingway. He told me most
intimate details. He said among many other things, that Ernest
had written much as he did, because he couldn't play foot-
ball. He talked of the caste system at such places as Princeton
and Harvard, and I realized that a great part of Scott's writings
and personal difficulties came from a sense of insecurity, of

inferiority, in the face of such a collegiate system. My impression of him was of the true artist, who had been conditioned to false values, and that while he understood that the values were spurious, could not disassociate himself from them.

I remember being impressed by the affection with which he spoke of Hemingway and of two or three other writers—I forgot who they were. He also spoke of Hemingway with a quality that puzzled me. It was not envy of the work or the man, it was not malice. I identified it as irony. It is of course the most valuable quality in his writing. At times he turned this irony on himself, quickly, and away again, as though he swung a flashlight on a dark thicket into which he had no intention of penetrating deeply. This was not for cowardice, I felt, but as though he intimated that it was enough for one to know the darkness was there.

He was looking very well at this time. He was not interested in me as a writer or as a woman, but he turned on his charm as deliberately as a water-tap, taking obvious pleasure in it. The irony was here, too, as though he said, "This is my little trick. It is my defiance, my challenge to criticism, to being shut out."

The quantities of wine had little apparent effect on him. He maintained a consistent animation for the eight hours, as I remember, that we talked, and effortlessly. I think he was anxious for me to report to Max Perkins that he was truly himself. There was also the excitement and satisfaction of an interested audience, not to "show off," but because he had been too long without mental stimulation. I kept suggesting that I must be tiring him, that I must leave, and he insisted frantically, "No, no. You can't go yet."

I said that someone had borrowed and not returned my copy of "The Great Gatsby," my favorite of his books, but I meant to get another copy and read it again. He dashed to a cupboard and from a box of books brought out a new copy for me. I asked him to sign it for me.

He said, "No, no, that won't do at all. I'll sign a copy of our luncheon menu and paste it in the book. I'll check the dishes we had."

I was both touched and embarrassed. The idea seemed so

"collegiate," like marking a Prom program. Yet it was a boyish thing, naive and eager, and it seemed to me that the adult artist was bound irrevocably to the college lad who had never felt quite secure. Now the successful man of letters was in a position to tie the two together, as a favor for me. I should have allowed him to "check the dishes," but I said that there was no need, I should remember. I looked at the menu, pasted in "The Great Gatsby," not long ago, and of course had no memory of what we had eaten.

Scott's wine had had a devastating effect on me, and in the night I found myself half-way up the highest mountain in North Carolina, quite off my path home to my cabin. The next day I re-read "The Great Gatsby," and was again over-come by its high quality. I wrote Scott with inordinate enthusiasm, and had no answer. Some time later I was with Maxwell Perkins in New York, and mentioned that my contact with Scott had ended with what was perhaps too lyric a letter [letter 46, October 25, 1936].

Max smiled his wry smile, and said shyly, "Of course, Scott thinks that all women are in love with him."

I was offended at the moment, but have come to understand that this, too, was one of Scott's defenses.

Well, Mr. Mizener, you have my permission to cull from this account whatever suits your purpose. With the stipulations afore-said——.

I believe that there is a letter from Scott to Maxwell Perkins, after Max sent him a copy of my book "The Yearling." This may or may not be, pertinent.

Marjorie Kinnan Rawlings

MKR was not able to enjoy for long her triumphant 1946 acquittal in the $100,000 invasion-of-privacy suit brought against her by Zelma Cason. Zelma's lawyers appealed the verdict immediately, and two years later the Florida Supreme Court reversed the lower court's finding. MKR, still convinced of her innocence, and convinced that she should defend the right of authors to use autobiographical material in a semifictional book, seriously considered taking the case to the United States Supreme Court. But Philip May, her lawyer, advised her that there were many uncertainties in such a proceeding and did not encourage her to continue. Weary after five dragged-out years of expensive legal action, and not a little leery of the whole legal process, she decided against appeal. On August 9, 1948, more than five-and-a-half years after suit was entered, the state supreme court wrote the final sentence, awarding Zelma $1.00 and costs.

149. To Philip May

Crescent Beach
St. Augustine, Florida
March 30, 1948

Dear Phil:

[I am] wondering if we may not stand a better chance than we hoped for, of a favorable ruling by the United States Supreme Court. God, but I hate to take a licking when I'm right—and I know you do, too.

"Where a statute is so vague as to make criminal an innocent act, a conviction under it cannot be sustained."

I must say that the divided decision of 6–3 does not make me too happy. And on the same day, the Supreme Court's refusal to rule in the Florida park case.

I can't remember whether I have seen you or written you since Steve Trumbull stopped off with us. I seem to recall telling you that Steve felt the Miami Herald might well pay part of the bill for trying to take our case to the High Court. I do not know whether this was his own idea, or whether the heads of the paper had expressed such an opinion. He also intimated that Scribner's might well put something in the kitty. I brought this up with Whitney Darrow, and you would have thought I'd dropped an ice-cube down his neck. He said hastily that if we lost, we'd be in much worse shape, and changed the subject. But I cannot believe but that we would be vindicated if the Supreme Court would rule at all.

It is doubtful whether I can afford to put any more money into it. I should know within a week or so whether M.G.M. is definitely going to produce the Lassie story,[1] in which case I get something more. The Yankee house has cost me an absurd amount, I have lived on my cash principal for the most part, for

six years, and unless the movie goes through, I shall probably
have to sell some bonds or securities to get by until I have a
book or something profitable. Of course, I can be supported in
toto by Norton at any time, but Idella and the Creek are my
private luxuries—and the Yankee house, too——.

I know that if we do go on with our case, you would charge a
minimum. There is no reason why you should do it at your
own expense, as you once suggested.

If the Miami Herald would contribute, and if Mr. Edward
Perkins thought we had a good chance, I should be able to talk
Scribner's into putting up a thousand or two.

Let me know how you feel about it.

Norton has been ill with that Virus-X, but has stayed on
the job except for two days. Idella's husband had it, too, and is
now on his third week of absence! But perhaps he had a worse
case. Now Idella and I have a germ, but it is not too severe. Best
to you and Lillian.

Marjorie

[P.S.] I know you will be as enchanted as I with this racy bit.
It was passed on to me by a friend here, Mrs. Parker, whose
daughter Jean is Zora's literary agent. You may want a copy of
this, and then please return it. . . .

"Zora Neale Hurston is due in sometime over the weekend—
ho, and I must quote to you from her last letter: I had mentioned the Baskins to her and in writing Ann she says, 'My best
love to Jean Parker. Please tell her that yes, the Baskins and I
are very close and warm. I consider that a triumph because the
justly celebrated Marjorie K.R. does not usually take to women.
I could have saved all kinds of trouble if she had let me just plain
kill that poor white trash that she took up so much time with,
and who paid her for it by suing her for defamation of character.
Marjorie Baskin does not even know the kinds of words that it
would take to defame that woman. *Everybody* around Cross
Creek says that the creature has a filthy mouth. You have no idea
how good and kind M.K.R. is to everybody. The folks who work
for her are really in soft. She no ways deserves what she got from
that trash. She as a woman is big wood while that strumpet is
not even good brush. If you hear of the tramp getting a heavy

load of rock salt and fat-back in her rump, and I happen to be in
Fla. at the time, you will know who loaded the shell, but you
need not get confidential with the police.' Isn't that wonderful
phraseology—read any or none of it to M. K. R. if you want to; I'm
sure Z. N. H. wouldn't mind."

1. A script MKR had been commissioned to write for a movie.

150. To Carl Van Vechten[1]

Crescent Beach
St. Augustine
July 8, 1948

Dear Cousin Carl:

I have just returned from an emergency trip to Cross
Creek, to find your generously inscribed copy of the "Yale Ga-
zette." Your essay on James Cabell is delightful. I suppose that
during his life-time at least, none of us will dare hazard any
public guesses as to the reasons for his "protective armor"—if
reasons are ever necessary to account for what, after all, is any
man's right to his own personality and character.

I am fascinated, too, by the photograph you made of him. I
have never seen him so tousled! His gray hair lies as smooth
these days as the feathers on the head of a swan. I wonder if the
photograph drove him to what Priscilla insists is his vanity.
She explains his daily walks (taken, I am sure, as an escape
from Priscilla) as being for the sake of his figure. "James is
vain, you know," she says. "He won't allow himself to become
paunchy. He wants to be as trim as a young man."

I was pleased by your mentioning his consideration of young
writers, although he can, and does, devastate them on occasion. In the hub-bub of our meeting, our drinking and eating,
our finding ourselves en rapport, I forgot to tell you the story of
my first meeting with James. I'll try to remember when I see
you again. And his curiosity, as you said, is spectacular. This
spring he followed a perfectly strange girl into a local book-shop
just to find out what she bought.

His letters to me are delicious.

I believe you said you had a volume on the Bogardus line.

My ancestor was William, the oldest son of Anneka Webber Jans
and the Dominie. By his second marriage, to Walburga de
Selle in 1674, he had a daughter named Maria, born in 1681. His
brother Pieter Bogardus also had a daughter named Maria,
born in 1674—seems to have died in 1691. One of these must be
the Maria Bogardus Schuyler (with daughter Catherine) of
my portrait. But the woman in the portrait looks too old to have
been the latter, if my dates are correct. I find a note to check
on a David Pieterse Schuyler at Beverwyck or Bererwyck, with
the date 1660. Of course Pieter was such a common Dutch
name that there is probably no connection there. The date 1660
is too early to tie in with my Maria. But do let me know if
you come across her, so that I may address her properly as
"Cousin" or as "Aunt."

I was so awed at the prospect of meeting you, and it was such
fun to discover that we were old friends and kin-folks to boot.
My husband is in town this morning and is picking up the copy
of my book "Cross Creek" for me to inscribe and send to you.
He can quiet me down at any moment by quoting coldly, "I could
be faithful to you, too." He has the sharpest damned ears.

My emergency trip to my true home, at Cross Creek, was
occasioned by a long distance 'phone call from a son of old
Martha, whom you will meet in the book, saying, "Mama says
come to the Creek right away." I thought my house had burned,
or her husband, Old Will, had died, and I asked what was
wrong. He said, "The refrigerator gone bad and Mama says the
butter'll spoil." I recognized at once the true calamity, which
was that I had been away too long. So under the pretense of
saving the butter, I dashed over, found the refrigerator repaired
and the butter long-since saved, and Martha happy again.

Now I shall write James and tell him all (or almost all)
about my meeting with you, and of my great pleasure in your
study of him.

All good greetings to you and the enchanting Fania.[2]

Cousin Marjorie

1. Carl Van Vechten, American writer (1880–1964). He and MKR were distant
cousins.

2. Mrs. Van Vechten.

151. To Philip May

Hawthorne, Florida
Aug. 10, 1948

Dear Phil:

I know. I have failed you. I should have fought it out to the
bitter end. We might have had a chance of reaching the United
States Supreme Court. Do you know what made me decide to
"end it all"? It was the comment made to Norton by my friend
Edith Pope. If a fellow Florida writer thought I *had* invaded
Zelma's privacy (and I didn't tell you that she also said to Norton, "Marjorie is just enjoying posing as a martyr") it suddenly did not seem worth while to carry on the battle. My own
personal vindication came in the Gainesville court-room, as
you have reminded me.

I wonder if by any chance I have given you the impression
that I felt you had failed in any way. I do not. No one could have
done a more superb job, have kept the whole business on a
higher plane, than you. My only reproaches are for myself, for
not having seen it through, as I swore to do. But I am becoming
almost dangerously frustrated at not getting my book going.
Years more of conflict might make the book impossible to do.
And without my writing, I am nothing.

I *did* want to re-imburse Zelma—if we had won a total victory. This, to show that I was not fighting to protect my money;
and to make a gesture indicating my pity for her, and my understanding. I feel no bitterness for her. . . . But it is salt in a
raw wound to be *compelled* to pay her costs.

My fury is all for the members of the Florida Supreme Court who
took a small-range point of view. I am sure these gentlemen
are among those putting up a noble battle for "States' Rights"—
as against human rights. The failure is not yours, "to make
the judges understand what they were doing." There is a type of
mind that is *incapable* of understanding.

Have you read Lecomte du Nouy's "Human Destiny"? If not,
you *must* do so. It is hard reading in the early chapters, at least
it was for me, but the final rewards are rich indeed. You will
find an application, and a comfort, for our defeat. For in spite of
my dear and eminent friend, Owen D. Young, you and I know

privately that we *were* defeated. But I shall be most miserable if you take any blame to yourself.

With admiration and affection,

Marjorie

152. To the Florida Supreme Court

[August 1948]

To Their Honors
THE FLORIDA SUPREME COURT
Gentlemen:

My health is not of the best, and I am not getting any younger, and it has been in my mind, due largely to an enormous number of requests from readers of my book "Cross Creek," to continue my autobiographical study of my life in the locale of the book.

Unfinished stories have found an end, the war has changed our lives, new and touching relationships have developed since I began the actual writing of the book about eight years ago.

I am wondering if it is pertinent or impertinent for me to ask Your Honors' advice as to whether it is legally permissible to write such a book of personal memoirs. If the Florida law requires that I get permission in advance from each of the individuals concerned in my life story, or to pay, or agree to pay, something to each of them, it will make an almost impossible undertaking. Some of my friends and neighbors have died, but have heirs and descendants. Some have moved far away, with no known addresses.

My attorneys feel unable to advise me in this matter.

Begging the indulgence of your consideration,

[MKR]

153. To Norton S. Baskin

[Van Hornesville, N.Y.]
Sept. 28, 1948

Dear Norton:

After your welcome call last night, I went to bed with a book. Idella planned to retire early, too. Uki[1] had not come in.

Idella called him again and again. I decided he was punishing her, as he had me, for leaving him. So a little before ten, when I was ready to go to sleep, I went down myself. I had on bed-room slippers, a thin silk bed-jacket, and my very best pink satin nightgown, which is as long as an evening dress. I called Uki from the back, then walked around to the front of the house and called again. He answered at once, in his loudest and most anguished voice—and from a great distance. I thought at first he had gotten caught among the boards where the old barn was taken down, and I walked that way calling. He answered every time, and I realized he was farther away than that. I went back to get the flash-light, and Moe, and had to wake up Idella, as I couldn't find the flash. Its light was faint, so we added matches and candles and all got in the car and started down the road that leads up Mt. Tom. I stopped every few feet and called, and as Uki answered, it became clear that he was somewhere up the Mount. I took the flash and set out alone, but Idella insisted on coming with me (she in corduroy house-coat). Moe, the sissy, stayed in the car, wanting none of it, but I made him come, to help track down Uki. Well, there are the remains of barbed wire and an old stone wall between the road and the big field at the foot of Mt. Tom, and I have had to get through cautiously in daylight, and in heavy shoes. The lower part of the field had not been cut, and it was a mass of thistles. We worked our way to the foot of the Mt., until we seemed to be on a line with Uki's voice. Idella stayed in the field with a candle, and I started climbing, Moe following reluctantly.

Let me make excuses for myself right here. Of course, Uki *always* sounds abused, but he was more distressed than ever. I have worried about his running around since I had his claws clipped, as he has little protection against an enemy, cannot do much climbing or get a good purchase. (Damage to the uphol-stery has stopped.) I was afraid a wood-chuck had attacked and hurt him (they fight dogs terrifically, you know) or that he had gotten into something he couldn't get out of.

I am sure I couldn't have climbed that hill in the day-time. It goes up at about a 45-degree angle. From the ice-storm of two years ago, and timber-cutting at the top, it is a mass of fallen boughs and tree-limbs. Under these are rocks of all sizes, some slick with moss, some loose and rolling down the moment I

touched them. Occasional deep wet holes. Very few small trees
to hold to or pull up by. At one point it got so steep that I simply did
not think I could go higher. Then Uki wailed tragically and
sounded a little closer, and I worked on up, on my knees, digging
in with one hand, and holding to the flashlight with the other.
The flash wavered uncertainly, quite dim. Moe began sliding
and slipping back down the Mt. and I had to force him to stay
with it. I got as far as I could, to an over-hang I could not cope
with, Idella's candle the faintest of glimmers far below, and
finally picked out Uki's eyes with the flash. He was up a tree, in
a crotch. I simply could not get closer, and set to work to coax
him down. He was still some distance away, and up. Moe set
to work like a good fellow, and reached the tree. I swung the
light on him, and I think the sight of him assured Uki. I heard a
little crash, which was Uki jumping down, and then he made
his way to me. He was thoroughly frightened, quite unhurt, and
awfully glad to be with me. He stayed right behind me as I
struggled down again. Moe slid down ahead of us. Without much
to hang on to, I simply could not walk or creep down, and did
most of it on my bare rear. The bedroom slippers caught in the
brush, the train of the night-gown got caught in my heels and
the flash got fainter and fainter. It was eleven when we got to
the field, I panting with exertion and Uki with terror.

I really don't know how I did it. I feel good about it, though,
as I have let myself go so soft, and I am glad to know that I
can do a difficult physical thing when necessary. I changed
nightgowns and got into bed quickly, as I didn't want to catch
more cold. I looked at the mountain gown this morning, torn,
muddy and draggled, of course, and it has blood all across the
back, so I imagine my behind must be a pretty sight. Otherwise, no damage, and Uki stayed out this morning only half an
hour, and is back in bed with me. And I thought there was no
trouble here he could get into! Something must have chased
him. He does practically all his prowling around the hop-house,
for the tiny field mice.

Still have not received my research material from Carl Brandt,
and must phone him.

All my love,

Marjorie

1. MKR's Siamese cat.

154. To Philip May

at Cross Creek
Nov. 24, 1948

Dear Phil:

A crew of six and I have spent three days getting the house clean and in order for the Gilkysons. I am lending the place to them for the whole winter and spring. They arrive about Dec. 6. He has had an operation, but is recovering nicely.

All my pettishness has melted away under the old spell, and I am sick at heart at having to leave. I shall never be truly happy until I can live here again. It MUST come about.

The house had been sulking because of my neglect. Now it is cheered up, and while so many things are dreadfully shabby, it has the old cozy appearance once more.

I found myself making notes all summer for new "Cross Creek" chapters. Many of them are sad, as there have been nearly a dozen deaths since the book was written, and several strange tragedies, as well.

I suppose, if I am obliged to write more about the Creek, that I shall have to submit each story to the living participants, in advance. And is "The Trial" now in the public domain, so that I could write of that?

Will soon send or bring you the revised census-taking chapter for legal and personal approval. The character of "Jakey" did not work out at all—did not fit in with Zelma's pungent remarks.

Hope to see you and Lillian soon.

My best,

Marjorie

155. To Horst Heenemann

[Crescent Beach]
Jan. 4, 1949

Dear Horst Heenemann:

Indeed, I remember you well. Your friend was Hans Korth, if I recall the name correctly. But I cannot remember which of you was the son of a Berlin newspaper owner, and which the son of a manufacturer.

I have thought of you often, and wondered what your destinies had been, and Talmadge DuPree[1] has asked if I ever had news of you both.

There have been many changes in the lives of those of us you met in Florida. (It is amazing that your letter reached me, addressed to Orange Grove, Florida, as there is no such place. But since my last two books, the Florida postmasters have been most kind in forwarding mail.) Charles Rawlings and I were divorced in 1933. He has since been married twice. In 1941 I was married to Norton Baskin, whose business is near St. Augustine, Florida. We have a lovely home on the ocean. I still keep the orange grove near Island Grove, where you visited, and go back and forth between the two homes.

Mr. and Mrs. DuPree were divorced, also.

Ed Hopkins, who cooked the guinea hens in the Dutch oven on the shore of Orange Lake, died insane a few years ago. It was hereditary.

I should be so interested in having news of you both. I was sure you must have been involved in the war, and am happy to know that you survived. If you care to talk about it, were you Nazis, by choice or necessity; in what zone of Berlin are you living now; are you married, and with children; and would you like me to send you a food parcel of something in particular?

Surely all of us have learned, or should have learned, that war answers no questions and solves no problems. Ordinary human beings always understand one another, given the least chance. "Nationalism" is a curse, for in the long run there are never nations, or races, but only *people*. Russia is a world menace at the moment, not because of her so-called revolutionary ideas, but because she has reverted to the old Czarist nationalism and has the ancient dreams of empire. It is too late in civilization for any country to work toward any such primitive goal. All over the world, we stand or fall together.

Do let us exchange ideas.

With the very best of wishes to you,

Marjorie K. R. Baskin

---

1. Citrus grower and friend of MKR from Citra, Florida.

St. Augustine
Feb. 4, 1949

Dear Norman:

The pencil note for my book was jotted down perhaps two years ago, as were the others on the same sheet, that have a certain relevance to the theme.

I am glad the notes gave you a feeling of what is in my mind.

It will not be enough for this book to be "a greater work" than "The Yearling," even though "less artistic" as you express it, it *must* be artistic and unified, or it will not be any good at all. The loftiest and most searching ideas are worthless in fiction if they are only ideas. All the thoughts must be spoken through the fictional characters, and those characters must come to life, and seem important, and must resolve themselves into a coherent pattern, and rise to a satisfying climax as to their own destiny and value.

I do have certain alibis for not being further along on the book—the law suit crushed me—the triumphant ending, with all of Cross Creek rallying to my support, did not quite compensate for the anguish—Norton's being over-seas absorbed a great deal of creative impulse, in that I felt I must write him fully, give him of myself, every day, in my letters—five major operations in as many years surely must have sapped a great deal of nervous energy—and I am only now making a reasonable adjustment to a type of daily living that is not in accord with my nature. The death of Max Perkins still seems too much to be borne— —.

All these difficulties could have been over-come by this time if it were not that I am asking so much of myself on this book. The straight-forward narrative of "The Yearling" carried me along with something of ease. The philosophy involved was basic and not at all complicated. Now, in attempting something more, I have the greater problem, as I said, of coordinatiing ideas with characters, of making philosophical concepts a simple, natural part of a story, never obtrusive.

Thank you so much for your understanding.

I do not see how you managed a lime sulphur burn on your

behind————. Was Julie manipulating the spray, and did you literally turn tail?

Best to you both,

Marjorie

Do not ever question yourself as a critic. You are harsh, you demand too much. (Owen D. Young said to me not long ago, "Compromise, when one has standards, is often desirable. Compromise without standards is fatal.") But when a piece of work satisfies you, you should not have the slightest doubt of your critical ability, having as you do, your standards, almost too high. No—never too high.

I had not sealed my letter to you, and Norton phoned, asking if I wanted to go to the movie with him, and I said, No, I was sorting out Maxwell Perkins' letters to me, from 1930 to 1947. Norton said, "I know you're having fun." I said No, my heart was breaking.

As the same moment, I had come to a letter in which Max wrote me: (Sept. of 1940)

"There are very few true writers, and they vary widely, but I have at last discovered that those few share one trait. You would never suspect it, you would think they would be the very ones with supreme confidence. In fact they do have a subconscious confidence, I think. But when they begin a big piece of work they have vastly less confidence than these men who just follow the trade of writing and who always know where they are going and go there like business men, those that we publish to keep the business going because the real ones are so few. I think, in truth, all you lack at this moment in regard to this book is confidence. I wish I could give you that, for I am sure you could make it a lovely book, and one full of the truth of life."[1]

I have 178 letters from Max. I'll keep them here for a time anyway, and you can read them the next time you are here if you would like to.

When Cliff Lyons was at the U. of Florida, he convinced me I should give my manuscripts to the library there. Now that he is at Chapel Hill, he wants me to send them *there*! Meantime, I am practically committed to the library at Fla. The Perkins

letters belong with my manuscript material, in a way, as they
follow along with my books and stories. On the other hand, they
are rich in *general* editorial and critical comment, and are full
of fascinating references to more important writers than I,
Wolfe, Hemingway, etc., and their work-in-progress.

1. *Editor to Author: The Letters of Maxwell E. Perkins* (New York, 1950), p. 179.

157. To Carl Van Vechten

[St. Augustine]
Feb. 10, 1949

Dear Carl Van V.:

I shall have none of this nonsense about age. I was an old,
old woman when you were sporting around. I suppose it is a
part of wisdom to side-step any possibility of heart-break. I was
talking with James Cabell yesterday. He had seen a movie (he
is quite an addict) that was harrowing, but said he had not let it
affect him. I remembered his answering once, when I asked
him (stupidly) why he wrote his particular type of escape literature, "Life is so horrible that one has to escape in one's own
manner." (Quotation not quite accurate, but that was the gist).
So, yesterday, I asked again, "How did you manage not to be
harrowed?" and he tossed it off by saying, "Oh, I realized it
wasn't true."

You may have reached the stage where not being harrowed is
more important than writing creatively. If so, you are quite
right in not having another cat. It is a hell of a nuisance, and a
great injustice, but the writing seems to have to come out of
one's, literally, bloody guts. So if you are not going to do a terrific book of Memoirs, O.K., don't have a cat.

And speaking of animals, Robert Frost was visiting a mutual
friend last week (head of the English Dept. at Chapel Hill),
and my friend reported that Mr. Frost had inquired after me,
had brought along his dog, which my friend Dr. Lyons reported
as being in a class with my own dog, as to manners and intelligence. It seems that Mr. Frost apologized for his dog's not
writing, saying, "It's all a dog can do to talk."

I should be enchanted to have you try to photograph me. I
adored your weird study of Truman Capote. If you could provide

enough extraneous background for my totally unphotogenic
face, we might get somewhere. I am a horrible person, but I
insist that I have a beautiful soul.

Charlie Scribner reported that our Zora [Neale Hurston] had
been in trouble on a "mild sex charge." This is idiotic. Sex is
never mild.

Cousin Marjorie

158. To Norman Berg

[Crescent Beach]
Feb. 16, 1949

Dear Norman:

Yes, I do realize. I have known for some time that I was putting
myself in serious danger. I cannot blame environment, or the
life, anything at all but myself. I may be fooling myself in thinking that the excessive drinking is the effect, and not the cause,
of my mental and emotional disturbance—at any rate, it is
probably the most definite hindrance to some sort of stability.

I am, as you know, unduly sensitive in my need for a certain
type of natural background and type of living. I consider this
a weakness, as my theory is, that the creative person should be
able to work under the most alien of circumstances. Yet to
save myself, I must and shall return to my sort of life. I shall go
to Van Hornesville very early in the spring and stay late into
the autumn, perhaps well into winter. Then I shall go to the
Creek. It should then become a great pleasure to join Norton
here at the cottage for week-ends, or to come for a few days
every few weeks. That was the way I expected our marriage to
be—separate lives and professions—but with a sense of security, of one-ness, from having formally acknowledged our bond.
And with the hope that some day, when Norton has acquired
a financial competence, and I was perhaps written out as to
long books, doing only occasional stories and verses, we would
have a fine quiet time together, traveling to strange places, with
the Creek as headquarters.

I am not ready for that—certainly was not in 1941—and in
the meantime, it hurt Norton so terribly when I felt the need to
be away from him and his sort of life, even though he was as

understanding as a non-creative person could be. I think that he himself will be happier when I remove myself to a large degree. He said the other day that he could not take much more of my desperation. I have been punishing him as much as myself.

As I lay long awake last night, thinking, I may have put my finger on one major difficulty in getting my book going. It suddenly came to me that I should begin the book several years later in my man's life, and should eliminate his mother entirely. Every start I have made has had to do with her, and I believe that she may be not only totally irrelevant to the story, but the worst hurdle, for whenever she appeared, the story became romanticized and unrealistic. (When you get to Maxwell Perkins' long letter about "Golden Apples," you will see how he brings out this matter of dis-harmony of material.)

Please do not worry about me. I go down for the count again and again, but I have a strangely tough core that will never allow me to be "pitifully beaten."

And I must add, that while Bernice Gilkyson identified you as a solipsist, and, the only time it has ever happened; you said, "That's right," when it comes down to bed-rock, in your relations with the few people you care for, you are capable of a very great tenderness and out-going. And I thank you for your out-going to me.

Love to you and Julie.

[MKR]

159. To Norman Berg

[Crescent Beach]
Feb. 19, 1949

Dear Norman:

I realized that I had not been fair to Norton, in the way I reported his reaction to me. When he said that he could not stand much more of my desperation, it was for my sake, not his. He offered to disappear early in the morning and not appear again until I was through working.

I could not let him do this, as there is no place for him to go, to put in the time, and he has spent such a huge sum on enlarging the cottage, giving me the studio, to make me happy, and it is the first and only home he has ever had, and he loves it, and it is truly *home* to him, as Cross Creek is to me. The studio is certainly private enough for me to work here.

I cannot have any blame attached to Norton for my own inadequacies.

I have made still another beginning on my book.

MKR

MKR had an earthy side which included a talent for telling off-color stories and a related taste for practical jokes. One night at a dignified party in St. Augustine she could not resist the sudden impulse to slip a silk stocking into James Branch Cabell's coat pocket so that a generous length of it dangled in plain sight. He discovered it only after everyone else had seen it and did not at the time find it very funny. The following is MKR's letter of apology, sent a day or two later.

160. To James Branch Cabell

Crescent Beach
St. Augustine, Florida
Feb. 26, 1949

Dear James:

From the cold glint in your eye at the theater last night, I got the dreadful conviction that my practical joke with the stocking had back-fired, and that you were anything but amused. I asked Norton if he thought you could possibly be seriously annoyed, and he said you might well be, that he considered my sense of humor quite misplaced and definitely un-funny.

I simply followed a sudden and irresistible impulse. As I told Priscilla [Cabell] at the bridge party, I had the stocking in my coat pocket, to try to match in town, and it struck me that it would be hilarious to embarrass the most pornographic writer in the country, since his personal life was impeccable. Priscilla seemed to be amused, and I told her I should be most disappointed if she didn't tease you thoroughly.

I shall be crushed if I have offended you. My long respect for you as an artist has so combined with my deep affection for you and yours, since I have had the privilege of knowing you, that I shall go in sack-cloth ashes for as long as you wish, if you share Norton's opinion of my conception of a jest.

Although *I* still think it was funny, I am most humbly and devotedly,

Yours,

MKR

161. *To Florida Binney Sanford Baskin*[1]

[Crescent Beach]
March 2, 1949

Dear Mis' Binney:

We are appalled by the week's schedule you described. You certainly must be feeling better, or it would have you laid up.

I've been accepting any and all social invitations for us the last couple of weeks, getting the damned things over with. Even the sociable Norton is crying for mercy. I only hope we finish up before I insult somebody. I can stand just so much *silly* conviviality and then I blow up.

I put in a long hard day in Jacksonville yesterday, but Aunt Ida was fresh as a daisy at the end of it. I had a late morning appointment with my lawyer, to draw up a new will. I made the last one when Norton and I were first married, and thinking he would always be at the Castle Warden, left him my equity in the hotel.[2] Now the owners have been paying off our joint mortgage very fast, so that doesn't make sense. Also, I wanted it fixed so that the cottage would automatically be Norton's without his having to pay any inheritance tax, as he has put so much more into it than my own original investment. Etc.

Phil May took us to lunch to a fascinating "Lobster House," reached by a small boat across the St. Johns river. It was a beautiful day and we enjoyed the water trip. The place has fine sea food. Aunt Ida, at nearly 89, mind you, ate a big bowl of soup with crackers, a huge fillet of flounder, French fried potatoes, peas, salad, rolls, two cups of coffee, and a chocolate sundae. And a glass of Dubonnet wine to start with. I wish you had just *half* her appetite. . . .

My original purpose in going to the big town was to get some spring and summer clothes on order from the Best and Co. traveling exhibit. I wanted some of those cotton cord, I think they call it, things that are cool but still look tailored. They didn't have much, and I settled for two $12.75 sunback dresses with boleros. Norton was cross when he found I hadn't ordered anything else. He would really like me to be a fashion plate, and it just isn't my nature.

Aunt Ida did some shopping while I was looking at the Best exhibit. She had jumped at the chance to go to Jacksonville, as she said she had been looking for a new bathroom curtain in St. Augustine, and couldn't find a thing under $2. When she found they were $5 and up in Jax, she came home most contented.

I know I have told you about her malapropisms, a truly great gift for picking the wrong word, so that the wrong word gives a new, strange and delightful effect. On the way home, she mentioned that Mr. Gibson was in the hospital. She said, "You know, he has been poorly, and Mrs. Gibson thought he had better go to the hospital to *recruit*."

So I said to Norton that I thought I would stay in bed to-day and recruit. He said, "So long as you don't have to do any drafting." . . .

Was amused by something in Ed Durling's column the other morning. (Don't know whether you have him in your paper or not.) He was describing men born under Libra (Norton) and said, "These men demand hotel service in the home. They crave peace and quiet and cannot stand quarrels. They need a wife of strong character, but one with a sense of humor, and who is sympathetic and understanding. They want their wives to keep a school-girl figure, and are upset at any bulges. They want flattery. If they do something fairly well, they want to be told they have done it wonderfully. If they are told they have done something wonderfully, they want to be told it was absolute perfection."

I didn't say anything, but I sent the paper to Norton in the living room, by Moe. Norton called out to ask if I had read Durling. I said I had, with the greatest of interest. I said, "Oh, I've been meaning to tell you, you played bridge last night superbly." He said, "It was better than that." The next morning I took a huge bell into his room and told him to use it to call for any service he wanted. While all this was joking, it turned out that the big bell was just the thing. We have been sleeping in two rooms since he had the flu and I didn't, and found we both enjoyed having a double bed to sprawl out in. I usually have just coffee on a tray at 7:30 A.M., and Norton has been going to the living-room and yelling to Idella to bring his break-fast. So he rang the bell, and ordered breakfast, and it seemed that this suited Idella, too, so he has been having hotel service in his room.

Now all I have to do is get off the bulges, and find out how long a wife of strong character can keep up her strength.

Much love to all.

MKR

1. Norton Baskin's mother.
2. The Baskins had recently sold the Castle Warden Hotel.

162. To Norman Berg

St. Augustine
April 14, 1949

Dear Norman:

I was writing an over-due letter to Sigrid Undset this morn-ing, and I told her that I had let you read some of her letters, and I quoted what you wrote me.

You are terribly right about her and about my beloved Owen D. Young. I have felt that great and cold objectivity in him, yet I wonder——. Perhaps it is only a part of a wise old age. I know that he has suffered, for once, when I spoke of my de-spair, he told me that he had gone too far into the depths, that he had considered suicide. And I said once, brashly, to him, "Have you done what you wanted to do with your life?" He tapped his pipe and looked at me, and said, "no."

We never know the torment that underlies success. We seem to know more of the torment that underlies failure.

Your visit did me good. I do need, terribly, to be loved. To be approved of, aside from my work. But I must say that your loving me for "The Yearling" is cold comfort. (I am joking. Even

after my necessity to be loved for myself, I am nothing except
for my writing.)

Oh God, I can't wait to get to the Yankee house. I think I told
you that I had made one of my usual weird conquests, of the
expensive landscape gardener who has done so much for the
place, much of it without charge. He is ready to start my annual
flowers now, and I have just sent him a long list.

On my visit to Cross Creek this last week-end, I told the
Gilkysons that I should have to be there this winter, and they
were wonderful about it, especially since there was a possibility
that I would lend them the place again. They said I should be
there, that I could really work there, and that nothing must
stop me.

I don't think I agree with you that Bernice [Gilkyson] is cold
and sexless. I think she is very sexy, and that since her husband at 68 probably isn't so good in bed, she has built up a wall
against sexual desire and response. Also, I am sure she annoyed you by pinning you down as a solipsist.

You are a wonderful person, certainly a wonderful friend, but
you do have so many prejudices.

Love,

MKR

163. To Norman Berg

[Van Hornesville, N.Y.]
June 16, 1949

Dear Norman:

I am writing about the matter of an old square piano for
you. The painter who did such a fine job here of re-finishing
things, including the woodwork and my piano, told me last
week, when he came to paint the new screens, that he knew
of an old square piano, a Chickering, which the owner wanted
to get rid of, and had offered to the museum in Cooperstown.
They refused it, as they had several, but said it was definitely a
museum piece. Slim said the woman would undoubtedly be
glad to take $25 for it.

BUT. Since then, a wonderful piano-tuner came out of the
blue, who has tuned and repaired my piano. He is an artist, an

Armenian, he played the most exquisite old Greek and Russian melodies on my piano, he was utterly *true* and charming. Instead of playing up the difficulty of tuning a piano that, he said, had surely not been tuned for twenty years at least, probably longer, he said that the piano here was the finest old one of that sort he had ever worked on, and while it was more troublesome than most, it was a pleasure and a privilege to bring it back into proper tone, even though, as he said when he finished, "Too bad you can't play the darn thing."

I told him of your desire for a similar piano, of the museum-piece Chickering outside of Cooperstown, and he said that it would be madness to buy such a piano, no matter how low the original price, without a check as to whether the works could be repaired. He said that in most cases, the whole works, guts, insides, had to be replaced, at enormous cost. He cannot make that check on the available old square Chickering, as he is moving on for parts unknown in his nomadic, Armenian way. He said that if he should be hereabouts next spring, he will come for another tuning, as my piano should have it for four or five years to make it right for any artist who might be here to play it. And I do have two concert pianist friends whom I should ask here, only to hear them play on this instrument.

I am more deeply grieved than I can say, that I cannot play my now perfect piano, as I am grieved that I cannot play the Kentucky dulcimer James Still[1] had made for me. I began a poem, "To an Unplayed Dulcimer" and it seems to me that both mediums of music are suffering, waiting for the proper and loving hands.

Anyway, I am afraid that it would be not only expensive, but in the end, frustrating, for me to send you what would appear to be a bargain in an old square piano.

I suppose you saw in the papers that my beloved Sigrid Undset had died. I had a letter from her the day after you and Julie were here, and it must have been among her very last letters. She wrote that it was quite all right for me to read her letters to my friends, that I should know when anything she wrote was too intimate for passing on . . . and "I go on chattering when I write to you, being so much alone." She said she longed to make a visit to America again, and I wrote her at once urging her to come to the Creek with me this winter, where she could have her own working quarters, etc. I doubt whether my letter reached her before her death. As usual, her last letter had wonderful comments on the world, especially as it is today. She was planning to do an essay on "Burke's Politics," which impressed her, and wrote: "He just pins down the weakness of all that radicalism which wants to change the world according to ideas generated in brains without respect for the experience of mankind living their everyday life—he has the word for it, the intolerable pedantry of these reformers. And God knows, the thing which is the matter with our governing classes is just this: they are incredibly pedantic about their brain children, immune to the consequences we see everyday— they just kid themselves, by and by their ideas will be made to work all right."

She goes on then into major considerations of another war. Her letter is too long to quote, though it is tempting, and I must go in a moment to water my beautiful garden. I can't resist this from her letter: (anent new war)

"Really to prevent war, I don't know if that will be possible— it is of course a truism to say, the people never want war. But the people usually want a lot of things which their leaders, to remain leaders, will try to bring about, and these things very often lead up to a war. You remember, Prince Metternich, Lord Castlereagh and that gang really did create a system, which would have made war between nations nearly impossible. But the peoples all over Europe did prefer war to the peace of the Holy Alliance. Russian world rule might possibly make war between nations impossible, but the people behind the iron curtain to a great extent are willing to have war rather than the peace they 'enjoy' now. God knows, I hate war, but I think there are worse disasters—that is the worst of the present situation."

More or less along this line of thought, André Gide, in the third volume of his magnificent "Journals," presents a compelling study of his original enthusiasm for Russian Communism, and of his later disillusionment. He gave himself, as what sensitive liberal could not, to the conception, the idea, the ideals of a true communism (with a small "c") which the present Russian regime has betrayed.

I myself feel that it is not so important to fight the bastard, actually Fascist, "Communism" of Soviet Russia at the moment, as to raise our American alleged "Democracy" to valid heights. I deplore the American capitalistic system. I myself would work so happily at my writing on a subsidy, or lacking that, making my living on the land, and writing on the side (as I did at Cross Creek for so long) but I could not endure, as you could not, as Gide wrote that he could not, being subject to any political dictation that violated the individual conscience and artistry.

June 21

Norton arrived here on the 17th, and will leave a week from today. On Saturday night I had my party and square dance for the men who worked on the house, and their families. We were 32 in all. I had wanted the party last year, the 100th anniversary of the house, but could not get the hop house in shape. The party was a huge success, thanks a great deal to Norton's charm and gayety. We had the buffet set up in the dining room, the bar for beer and soft drinks in the wood shed, and we danced on the upper floor of the hop house. Martin Egan, the head carpenter, and his crew, rigged up an overhead light and leveled the floor and hauled off truckloads of rubbish. Idella and I scrubbed and scrubbed, and eventually that floor will be as fine as the house ones.

We had a hired fiddle and a guitar, and a 300-lb. caller. These people are old-fashioned artisans, not workmen, and have a great gentility. The men and their wives feel an even greater pride in the proper restoration of the house and garden than I. The oldest, frailest man proved an exquisite dancer—the square dances were too strenuous for him, but in between we had regular dancing. He said, "You and I could dance together," and for a moment I had a sense of his youth, and it was as though I were dancing with a young man with whom I was sympathetic, and there was a strange sweep, over-lapping in time.

The *next* oldest (about 70) and *humblest* of the men, known as "old Joe Baxter," helps Martin Egan with cleaning up on jobs, light odds and ends of work. His son and daughter-in-law whom I did not know—didn't even know they existed, so had not invited them—brought him, and he had cold feet, and I could hardly persuade him to stay. He was the only one not happy.

MKR's house in Van Hornesville, after restoration.

Toward the end of the dancing, he left his chair by the wall and came over and bowed in front of me. I thought he was saying good-night, when Norton poked me and whispered, "He's asking you to dance." He could not dance, or it was of a vintage too strange for me, and the attempt was painful. But he stuck it out, bowed me back to my seat, and took his departure. If it killed him—and it may have!—he had braced himself to do his social duty by asking his hostess for a dance.

The N.Y. Herald Tribune had a more authoritative story on Sigrid Undset, from Oslo, and she had a stroke June 8 and died on the 10th. Her death strikes in a different way from that of Max Perkins, for I never discussed my work with her. The loss is that of a great friend and a great woman.

The "god-damned" living room looks warmer now that the other bookcase is installed, and the Audubon between. Don't complain about my having *one* dignified room.

I enjoyed seeing you and Julie so much, and wish you could have stayed longer.

Love to both,

MKR

1. James Still, American author (1906–   ).

164. To Norman Berg

Van Hornesville, N.Y.
July 27, 1949

Dear Norman:

I could indeed use you as a critic at the moment. I am toward the end of my third chapter, and I need to know whether I am making sense or not. One great difficulty is that my principal character is almost inarticulate, and almost everything has to go through his *thoughts,* which may be making for inarticulacy on my own part. And I keep getting off-key. I have only one sentence that pleases me.

I may ask you to read what I have written by autumn. Yet I am afraid, not of criticism, but of the questions you would ask— where I am going—what is my theme—and my experience with "Golden Apples" was so disastrous, talking too much about it in advance with Carl Bohnenberger—that I dread a repetition. What I should like, is for you to read the first completed draft, perhaps a year from now. I assume that you would do so as my friend, not as a Macmillan man——.

I had a dream the other night, in which I was showing my three chapters to Charlie Scribner and his son Charles Jr., and Mr. Harcourt-Brace, of all people, a composite little man of the two names, and I was explaining to Mr. H. B. that I belonged to Scribner's, that I had done everything with them except sleep with Charlie, whereupon young Charles remarked, "Too bad."

I remember John Steinbeck's asking me, "Do you find that the job gets more difficult as you go on?"—and it does. So-called "success" is a deterrent, for one thing, and one also becomes more critical of one's own work, so that nothing seems good enough.

Oh Norman, I have been in such anguish. I came closer to killing myself than ever before, except once, last Sunday night. I have always felt that without my writing, I was nothing. And the writing was going so badly. But I made myself wait, and now it is going better.

Sexual failure, lack of happiness, none of it matters if I can say the things I want to say——.

Notes made for the book in the last few days:

It is not death that kills us, but life. We are done to death by life.

Life is strong stuff, some of us can bear more of it than others.

It is not that death comes, but that life leaves.

Death is not a separate entity.

There are two sorts of the living dead. Life has forgotten to inform the dull bodies that it (life) is elsewhere. And there are vital bodies, full of the joy of living, with no minds, and life has forgotten to tell these bodies that it is there, in them.

The timid people, saying, "Life, here I am," but they are by-passed.

Life, a tidal river returning to the sea——.

Marjorie

You understand, I know, that when I write you at Mac-millans, I am writing privately and in trouble.

July 28, 1949

The work going so much better. Spirits higher—I shouldn't have disturbed you. As Norton wrote, "No one has invented a twilight-sleep for book-bearing!"

165. To Norman Berg

Van Hornesville, N.Y.
Sept. 29, 1949

Dear Norman:

I am delighted that the piano arrived in good shape, but I was sure old Martin Egan would pack and crate it well. I know that you have a great musical appreciation, but I must re-mark that if you are making a "key" for temporary tuning, you will find yourself using even "the squeal"——

Julie's use of the burlap bags reminds me of my last week's facetious attempt to gloss over a great embarrassment. I dropped in at the Young's late one afternoon, and said, "Come on home to dinner with me." It just happened to suit them (their most elderly cook had been canning all day) and it just happened that I had already had quite enough to drink (ordinarily Idella

would have fed me immediately on my return) but by the time
she had a gorgeous rib-roast dinner ready, I had been tossing
off the drinks with Mr. Young. The moment we sat down to the
table, I realized I'd never make it. I was seeing two Mr. Young's
and three Louise's. I said, "I'm terribly sorry, you'll have to excuse me, I have to go to bed, I'm drunk." Idella reported the
rest to me later, for I had no memory of it. The silent Young's,
cutting into their beef, heard a great thump on the bedroom
floor above, told Idella to put down the broccoli-Hollandaise
she was passing, and dash up to see to me. She said that she
found me sitting stark naked on the floor, but when she came in,
I gathered my slip across my front, and said, "I'm quite all
right." She said, "Here's your nightgown on the chair, I'll bring
it," and I said haughtily, "Thank you, I can put on my own
nightgown," and so I did. She went down again and informed
the guests with equal dignity that I was "quite all right."

I was too ashamed to approach the Young's later, so when
Norton sent me a message for Louise about their Florida place, I
had Idella deliver a note to her. Inside the envelope, I put a
handful of ashes in one piece of paper and in another piece, a
scrap of burlap from the bags that had been used for moving my
lilac bush. I appended a note, "These are samples of my new
fall costume." Louise of course did not get the idea, made no
reference to it, but the next time I saw Mr. Young, he said,
"Now look here, never mind the sackcloth and ashes, just get on
with that book."

I shall never speak to you if you breathe a word of this to
Norton. *I* think it's funny, Mr. Young thought it was funny, but
Norton would die.

And I *am* getting on with the book. I have written you two
notes, but believe it or not, have torn them up because they
were too cheerful! I wrote you in the full flush of enthusiasm
after a day's work, then thought ruefully the next day, as I re-
read the out-put, "Hell, it isn't going *that* well." But it goes. I
am torn between exaltation when I hit it right for a few paragraphs, and despair over its never being entirely right, and the
dread necessity of doing a more devastating job of re-writing
than ever before.

One day I tell Idella, "I'm so happy, I'm getting somewhere," and the next day I say, "Oh God, my work is horrible" and she rejoices and droops with me in return.

You are most inconsiderate to give such an un-spellable name as, let me look, "Sellanraa," to your place. It also seems to me indecent to have given the name of an ancient Irish heroine and queen, wasn't she, to an Irish setter bitch. If you are so obsessed with the Irish tradition, why in God's name don't you and "Pop" restore your natural name of "Carney"?

Speaking of names of places, friends in St. Augustine have a place on the St. Johns River where two creeks meet, and they call their place "Double Cross Creek."

You ask, "When are you coming home to Cross Creek?" Did you mean to emphasize the *home*? I have almost decided that this is "home." Time will tell.

I plan to leave here the first week in November and after visiting Norton at the cottage, and sending Idella ahead to get the Creek ready, to settle down there for work toward the end of the month. I expect to finish the first draft of the book by Spring, and I do agree that no one should see any of it until I am that far along.

My best to all,

MKR

I am urging Norton to come here soon, as otherwise he will miss again, the gorgeous autumn coloring.

166. To Owen D. Young

Cross Creek
December 14, 1949

Dear Mr. Young:

I promised to tell you the story of Leonard Fiddia (which he pronounces "Fiddy") and the first copy of my first novel, "South Moon Under." Here it is:

Leonard was the prototype for "Lant," the principal character in the book. I first met him about 1929 or 1930 while hunting in the Big Scrub with a mutual friend. He lived then, as now, in the cabin his grandfather had built on a plateau above the Ocklawaha River, about ten miles from the small settlement of Eureka, his only neighbors for perhaps fifteen miles being his

Uncle Enoch and Aunt Eulie and their son, Lester, a couple of miles down the sand road. Leonard was perhaps twenty years old, making an assorted living at hunting, in or out of season, from necessity, farming a little, fishing a little, and when hard-pressed, moonshining. He made a superb corn liquor, which, when well-aged in a charred oak keg, was the equal of the best Kentucky Bourbon. I became his client and then his friend. His widowed mother, "Mis' Piety" (and I could not resist using her true name along with her true character in the book) kept house for him.

My ideas for a novel about such people, strong, self-sufficing, utterly individualistic, part of a passing way of life, began to crystallize, and from 1930 to 1932 I spent a great deal of time, weeks on end, with Leonard and Mis' Piety, at their cabin. I slept on a cot in Mis' Piety's bed-room, under the only mosquito net in the place. I hunted with Leonard, by day and by night. I helped Mis' Piety wash her heavy hand-made quilts. I went

Leonard Fiddia (left), prototype of the character Lant in *South Moon Under*.

with Leonard to the river when he dynamited fish, when fish could not be taken otherwise. I helped him "run" many batches of 'shine.

I told him frankly what I was trying to do, and he was entirely co-operative. He invited friends from across the river, he took me to Uncle Enoch, and to everyone he said, "Marge here, now she's writing a book about the old days and the old ways. Uncle Enoch, tell her about that bear hunt when the bear surprised the dogs."

And because I had been accepted by Leonard, I was accepted by these others, and they told me of "the old days and the old ways." And Leonard taught me more than anyone else, of the Florida flora and fauna, for they were a part of him, and part of his really scientific interest in such things.

So I finished "South Moon Under." And my publishers sent me the usual several first copies, and I took the one on the top of the package and inscribed it for Leonard with gratitude, and went out to his cabin in the Big Scrub to give it to him. He felt only a mild interest, as I had taken the proofs of the book to him, to have him correct any errors in my nature material.

I was anxious to know how his friends and neighbors would react to the book, and a few weeks later I went to see him at the cabin. "South Moon Under" was not in sight.

I said, "Leonard, I don't see the book. Have you loaned it to anybody?"

He said, "Yes, Marge, it's loaned out right now. But I'm mighty keerful where I loaned it. Aunt Eulie, now, she wanted to borry it, but I was feared she'd burn it."

I said, "Why would she want to do that?"

Leonard said, "Marge," (actually, he calls me "Morge") "you know you got right smart of cussin' in the book" (and I had taken the cussin' straight from Leonard) "and you know Aunt Eulie, she's one of them Christian-hearted sons of bitches, and she'd be feared her boy Lester would learn to cuss by the book. Now Lester can out-cuss the book right now, but his Mammy don't know it."

The years passed. Leonard came to see me at Cross Creek, when I had visitors from New York. I told this story in his presence.

I said, "Leonard, are you still lending the book?"

He said, "Yes, Morge, by God, I loaned it out to Uncle Enoch, and he hid it out in the bushes, and there came a little sprinkle of rain, and that book now looks like pure hell."

I said, "I have a new copy of the book, would you like a fresh copy?"

Leonard said, "I shore would, if it won't dis-furnish you none."

I assured him that it would not dis-furnish me, and since in the intervening years I had published "The Yearling" and had been besieged by autograph hunters, I asked with, I am afraid, a certain smugness, "Would you like me to autograph it, to sign it for you?"

"Hell, no, Morge," says Leonard. "That don't benefit nobody."

So that is the end of the story, except that Leonard still has the weather-beaten and suspicious book, the first copy of my first novel. Since he still has, as well, the second copy I gave him years later (and I did sign it for him, regardless) and that takes care of his needs, he was glad to give me the early adventuresome copy for you, and I am sending it along, because of your interest in the circumstances.

I could tell you many more tales of Leonard, which may appear some day in a sequel to "Cross Creek."

With great affection

Marjorie Kinnan Rawlings

(Sorry the rural lights went out, and I finished by candlelight, and this letter now looks like pure hell.)

167. To Norman Berg

Hawthorne, Florida
Dec. 29, 1949

Dear Norman:

I can't ask you to stop being so generous with books, because it's such a great pleasure to receive them. I am saving "Mask of Glory"[1] for the first rainy evening, and the impressive "Literary History of the United States"[2] for the first rainy week. So very many thanks.

Norton was thrilled with his shirt and you will hear from
him.

My brother sent me as a Christmas present the good news
that he had called off the marriage and "severed all relationships." He is just as blunt *after* he's married 'em. I passed on
your suggestion (as my own) that he check on divorce laws in
Alaska to see where citizenship would be least expensive, and
this may have been the bucket of cold water in the face. He is on
such a deliberate wife-hunt, and I tremble for him.

I had begged Norton not to be so extravagant this year, but
if he wanted to know, I did need the biggest alligator purse
available. He passed this on in buying it at the Alligator Farm,
and Charlie Usina said, "Just how extravagant does she think
you can get?" The comic strip character "Penny" said she loves
plain things—plain convertibles, plain diamonds, plain mink.
So I now have a huge "plain mink" alligator bag.

Christmas day itself was a bit dreary in St. Augustine, Norton
couldn't come here Xmas Eve as before, and I took Aunt Ida
to noon dinner at Marine Land in a driving north-east storm.
Norton and I went to a cocktail party and then buffet supper at
Fred Francis' and the worst drunk in town picked on me to
tell me about his misunderstood soul. Even a white orchid and
the pleasing if surprising fact that I could still get into my
best dinner dress didn't cheer me. We made up for it Monday,
when we played bridge with Louise Young and Tressa [Mrs.
H.M.] Johnson, with Mr. Young and H.M.[3] kibitzing, and then
many drinks and a gay dinner by way of helping the Young's
house-warm the new addition to their house, and I must say,
Norton and I are expert house-warmers. At bridge, I made the
mistake of saying casually to Norton anent an odd bid, "Why,
shit-fire, honey,"[4] without telling *first* where the expression came
from. Norton said later that Tressa went pale and was torn
between her own shock and the prayer that H.M.'s hearing aid
was not turned on. It was on——Norton said Mr. Young had
quiet hysterics, his head between his knees.

When Irita Van Doren[5] asked of the three books I had most
enjoyed this year, I was obliged to include "Hunter's Horn" along
with Christopher Morley's[6] "The Man who Made Friends with

Himself," although I was most stirred in a quite different way by the last volume of Gide's Journals, the Kafka Diaries, and the Letters of Proust. To say nothing of Robert Frost's Collected Poems, most of these familiar and already beloved. (When I asked Mr. Frost to sign one of his books for me some years ago, and he suggested his "Selected Poems," I think it was, and I demurred, he said, "Oh, you're being Scotch. You're waiting for the collected poems.")

Now next week I go to work. And stay put here.

Leonard's little girl died a week before Christmas. The funeral services were in the little Fort McCoy cemetery where Leonard's people back to his great-grandfather are buried, and were simple and sweet, if such a thing is possible, with the wind in the pines, and a nearby saw-mill chug-chugging away. Leonard's little boy, aged seven, the dreadful Elmer, wrestled with another little boy at the very edge of the grave——. Leonard insisted that I sit in the front row with the family, and Elmer sat next to me, chewing gum, and fascinated by his new shoes, which he kept rubbing together with a great squeaking, most satisfactory to Elmer.

I promised Leonard and Miss Piety that I'd come to the Scrub this week, and I was sure they would have had some of the east coast rain on their deep sand road, so yesterday afternoon I set out with a turkey and all the fixings in time to cook dinner there. They had not had a drop of rain, the place is 8 miles from anywhere, and I had to dig out twice. But we had as fine an afternoon and evening as possible under the circumstances of their sadness, and the turkey dinner cooked in the old wood-range was delicious, and Mis' Piety put her thin old arms around me and said, "This is like old times." She begged me to spend the night, and I was tempted, for I have always felt such peace of soul over there in the shabby cabin with them, but I was afraid Idella would send the State Police to find me when I did not return. I don't know what inferiority of character is involved, that I am so happy in elemental places and with elemental people. I do know that so-called "Success" is a curse.

Leonard produced the weather-beaten copy of "South Moon Under," and I do hope that Mr. Young can get him a price that will help on the doctor's and hospital bills. Mr. Young made more sense the last time he talked about it, and spoke of $500 as a possible price.

Love to all,

Marjorie

1. A novel by Dan Levin (New York, 1948).

2. Edited by Robert E. Spiller et al. (New York, 1948).

3. H.M. Johnson, secretary to financier Andrew Mellon, former U.S. secretary of the treasury and ambassador to Great Britain.

4. An expression from a novel she had recently read, *Hunter's Horn,* by Harriette L. Simpson.

5. Irita Van Doren, editor of the *New York Herald-Tribune* book review and ex-wife of Carl Van Doren, American editor and writer (1891–1966).

6. Christopher Morley, American writer (1890–1957).

168. To Bernice Gilkyson

Cross Creek
Feb. 4, 1950

Dearest Bernice:

Feb. 12 !!!!

You might say, Look, apparently no hands! I forget what interrupted me when I got as far as the date a week ago.

Idella's husband is practically recovered, and she did not even go to St. Augustine this week-end, but to her home at Reddick. It was a happy day when I met her bus, for old Martha had been particularly exasperating.

Nature finally took care of the matter of Chrissie's calf, if the Mickenses are to be believed. A Hamon bull jumped the fence. The calf is presumably due in April, in which case Chrissie should be getting a rest now, but I am making Martha keep her milked, and while the out-put is not prodigious, there are no signs of drying up. Too many of us cats need the milk.

Goldie lives around Martha's house these days, but one of her female off-spring who looks almost exactly like her lives under mine, along with Tommy, and Uki has not only made friends with them, but bosses them unmercifully. Moe still goes for them (not really meaning it) and they must have gotten wise to him, for Tommy lay purring only a few yards away from him this morning. They are all fat as butter-balls.

Linda sounds enchanting. Uki lost so much of his charm since he became an invalid. Norton says it is only that he has lost his sense of humor.

Oh, Walter, I keep forgetting to give you a message from Chet Crosby. He said to tell you that the "whoopers" are back, at the edge of the Lochloosa marsh, and that there are 26 of them this year, if I remember correctly, at any rate, more than doubled in numbers. As he described them, it seems they must be the sand-hill crane, but he says not, that he knows them, too. I have pored over my large Audubon, and only the sand-hill seems to answer his description. I had thought the "whoopers" were the great American bittern, their cry like a rusty pump, but again Chet says not, and the bittern certainly does not fit the description. Let me know about this. Chet says he will show them to me some day.

At the end of this month and in early March I am to be stuck with several assortments of guests, mostly at the cottage, and while they are beloved, and ordinarily their appearance would delight me, I am simply crushed by the prospect. Every interruption throws me so off stride, and I go a little insane. The book is so difficult and of such poor quality so far, that it is like wanting to get a leper off the premises.

I doubt now whether I can finish the first draft by May first, when I planned to have Scribner's see it, and then go on to Van Hornesville.

I should not be in such anguish if Max were here. He could have told me long ago whether or not I am on the right track, and there is absolutely no one else I could allow to see unfinished work. And even when it's done, there's no one I trust for an honest answer as we trusted Max. I have a list of questions ready to make out, as he might have asked them, and may be obliged to give the answers myself. I have lost all faith in my creative ability, yet there is nothing for it but to go on.

I should not inflict my torments on you and Walter, undergoing your own, except that you know what I'm talking about. Dear Norton claims that he understands, but the last time I was at the cottage I was evidently "out of the world," and he wrote me that he had grieved and been depressed for days after, as he felt I didn't give a damn if I never saw him again. It was only that for the time being, he really didn't exist for me, nor did anyone or anything else, and is that an impossible thing to explain to a nice husband!

Well, good luck to us all around— —.

Much love,

Marjorie

169. To Norman Berg

[Crescent Beach]
March 12, 1950
at the cottage

Dear Norman:

The home address of Pearl Primus,[1] if it has not changed, is 536 Madison Street, Brooklyn 21, N.Y. You may use my name, and if you see her, she pronounces her name Preemus.

I found myself over-working and getting needlessly distraught, so knocked off for the week. I shall not push myself to finish the first draft by May 1, as the quality of the book, already dubious, would suffer too greatly.

You should not have made the too-generous gift of the collected [Edwin Arlington] Robinson, but I appreciate it and am taking a renewed delight in him. I had forgotten how fine a poet he was. When I see you, I shall be interested to know if I drew the analogies you must have had in mind as to "Matthias at the Door"— —.

John Hall Wheelock[2] sent me the Perkins Letters, "Editor to Author," to be published March 27, and of course they meant fresh pleasure and fresh pain. Wheelock has done a fine job of selection, and his editing is discreet and at a minimum, as was proper. I have asked Whitney Darrow if he can wangle another advance copy for me, for me to sign for you, so that you will have it ahead of publication. They used many more of Max's letters to me than I expected, and apparently the only greater numbers were those to Hemingway, Fitzgerald and Wolfe.

The Publisher's Weekly has wired, asking me to review the volume for them, and I am doing so, gladly. I should of course have preferred to do a review for a more strictly literary publication, yet shall be happy to express myself in any case.

I have accepted invitations for all of Friday March 30 at

Gainesville, in connection with the dedication of the new University library, and their announcement of my manuscript gifts, to form part of the Florida Creative Collection, or whatever the name is. I shall speak for no more than ten minutes in the evening. I refused an earlier invitation from Dr. Miller[3] to give a paid "lecture" this spring, as I knew it would wreck my writing. As it is, March seems ruined for writing anyway, what with doing the review this coming week, our Dr. Atchley coming to the cottage for next week-end, and I know I shall suffer almost as much over a ten-minute talk as one of an hour. I pray that at the ceremonies they don't make too much of my gifts and of my value or what-not, for if I get a swelled head, or go too far objectively in this public contact, April will be messed up, too!

The Owen D. Young's are attending the sacred rites, beginning with a small luncheon at Dr. Miller's, and will spend Friday night at the Creek. I have induced Norton to attend all of that day, because I know he would enjoy meeting Douglas Southall Freeman, and being with the Young's and also because, as executor of my estate, which goes finally to the U. of Florida Scholarship Foundation, and all my manuscript material, letters from other writers, books of value, etc., to the Library, I think he should meet some of those people, for if he doesn't do it now, he never will.

The Young's will have my own large front bed-room and bath-room, Norton and I will use the back ones where you and Pop slept, but we'd be glad to have you spend Friday night at the Creek in either of the two remaining bed-rooms back of the living-room, if you wouldn't mind either tip-toeing around to the rear bath-room, or going to the bushes!

The four of us plan to return to the Creek from Gainesville in late afternoon, for a drink, and for Louise Young and me to change into dinner dresses. I MUST stay reasonably sober, if I am to speak even so briefly! But join us then for drinks if you can. When we all get home at night, we are likely to sit up late talking and drinking. I am thinking of making an opportunity for you to talk with Mr. Young about his doing his Memoirs in a personal and creative way.

If you have any suggestions as to a topic for my talk, that

At the home of J. Hillis Miller, president of the University of Florida, before the dedication of a new wing of the university library in 1950. Left to right: Louise Young, Owen D. Young, Jessie Ball Dupont, Douglas Southall Freeman, Nell Miller, Norton Baskin, MKR, Dr. J. Hillis Miller.

would be of especial interest to librarians, I should more than welcome them.

I return to the Creek tomorrow. I came this week-end particularly to have a stenographer come to catch me up on nearly a hundred stupid letters that must be answered. She has worked for me this way for years, does my dictation directly to the typewriter, which saves so much time and trouble, and she is almost entirely accurate. She is due in about an hour, so I must stop.

Love to you and Julie,

Marjorie

1. A young friend of MKR, Pearl Primus was a black professional dancer who was trying her hand at writing.

2. The editor at Scribner's who took over responsibility for MKR's book after Max Perkins' death.

3. J. Hillis Miller, then president of the University of Florida.

170. To Norman Berg

Hawthorne, Fla.

April 13, 1950

Dear Norman:

I think your letter[1] to Mr. Young is very fine indeed. You state your case sensitively, explicitly, and with a perfectly proper challenge. When I was at the cottage the past week-end, I asked Norton to lend Mr. Young his copy of the Perkins letters. I thought that the long letters to such people as E.H. Sothern,[2] Arthur Train,[3] Ray Stannard Baker,[4] and Edward Bok,[5] might be stimulating, perhaps even open something of a door for him as to how to go about such a job. I could see his memoirs, (in a quite different frame-work, of course, and with infinitely more importance, since he made a deep mark on several generations, on the very history of our world) as I see my "Sojourner"—the story of a man's mind.

If he could and would trace his ideas, his philosophy, his standards and ideals, and all their development, from the time he stood as a lonely boy on the snow-bound hill-top of the "home farm"—and when he first became excited over Marconi's experiments, and finally made it possible for David Sarnoff[6] and others to make radio work and become available, his first thought (he told me) was "Now the world can reach the home farm, and all other home farms," through all his years of great financial success, his special moment in history when he toiled over and presented the Young Plan,[7] up to today—when only last Saturday he told Norton and me of his ideas toward resolving the present impasse, in the name of peace, working carefully through two or three other men who have the ear of Truman, hoping that that little man "might see a great light and rise to a great challenge." Oh, it was stirring to hear him.

The practical solipsist Louise Young said matter-of-factly, "Well why don't you go down to Key West and talk to Mr. Truman? I'm sure he'd give you an appointment."

And Mr. Young said, "No, it can't be done that way."

He did not expatiate, but I felt that he meant that such ideas presented directly would receive only the courteous superficial attention given to the Hoover Report on economizing in government, with nothing done about it, that he knew what

he was doing in working as he is. So it is obvious that he
has not settled back in "content of mind." Keep this conversation
confidential.

Now I think I have expressed as clearly as I shall ever be
able to do so, my feeling about the *form* his memoirs should
take. Ida Tarbell gave the "facts," and how stupid they are, as
he is the first to say. "A very bad book," he said to me, "very bad
indeed." No one cares now where he was educated, which
teachers recognized the power of his mind, when he was married
and to whom. Yet if he will do the story of his mind, all the
engaging anecdotes will appear, leading up, (after many light-
ings of the gone-out pipe) to some most pertinent point which
has bearing on world events. Perhaps you would like to save this
part of my letter, to read him or show him, or quote, later, if
he agrees to do this important thing. I could write it to him
myself, or say it, but I sense that if he does go ahead on the
job, he will feel shy, yes, shy, about it, and will not want anyone, perhaps especially me, breathing down his neck, fluttering
around, but will have to do it in utmost privacy, none at all to
know.

I am returning your letter to him for three reasons. I think it
should be mailed from Atlanta, so that he does not know that
I have seen it and that we have corresponded about all this to
such an extent. He respects and loves me more than I deserve,
but after all, he is very male indeed, and it will help your valuable project most now if I keep out of the picture as far as
possible from now on, so that it may become his own compulsion,
never something urged on him even by his favorite female author, and, I do believe, friend. (This is where my half-maleness
comes in. It is almost a curse that I know how men feel, and
react. And then my half-female nature drives me on to protect
that maleness, to want to make any man I care about, feel more
the man. And that partly accounts for some of my own unhappiness, trying never to let a man down.)

Yet if the proper moment comes, I should like you to let
him know of my ideas about the way his memoirs should be
handled.

You did not quote quite accurately, in your letter to him, what
he said—did not say—to me. It was not that "if he had his

life to live over again, that he would have wanted it to be other than it was." I asked him, (I forget the exact words, but this is near enough) "Have you done in life what you wanted to do?" And he looked at me, with his deep, receptive look, tamped his pipe, and only shook his head and said, "No." There is a subtle difference here, and you may re-write the last page or not as you wish.

And a most minor item, but I was coached in England on forms of address, and if I am not mistaken, the envelope you have should not be Mr. Owen D. Young, Esq., but Owen D. Young, Esq. When I was in London, the head of Scribner's there warned me, after my letters to him, before I arrived, that "Mister" or "Mr." was used only for tradesmen, etc., and that one used the name for important people just-so, with "Esq." after the name.

I could not, perhaps, have written you so intensely with my book gnawing at my vitals, except that I am so keyed up this evening over an astonishing death at the Creek. (I think that some day I may be obliged to write something of a sequel to "Cross Creek" which could only be called "Death at the Creek"— and perhaps a more honest book than the first one.)

Yesterday afternoon Tom Glisson went with his oldest son, Carlton, to a beautiful piece of land across the Creek where Tom was planning to build a small, modern home for himself and his wife, having already sold his good fishing camp at the approach to Lake Lochloosa, and he was planning to sell their place next to me. I talked to him a few days ago about his plans, as I have many queries on property here. In the truck, Tom had two jugs that had held Coca-Cola syrup, one containing drinking water, the other a tree-killer poison. Tom took a drink of the poison instead of the water, spit it out, washed his mouth with the water, told his son he was sure he hadn't swallowed any of the tree-killer. The son begged him to take an emetic, and Tom laughed it off and refused.

After hours of unspeakable agony in the hospital in Gainesville, the doctors doing everything possible, blood plasma, glucose injections, Tom died early this morning. It seems that the poisonous ingredient in the tree-killer is lead of arsenate, most concentrated, and that it affects the veins, so that they ooze blood or fluid——. If Tom had downed the contents of the water jug and stuck his finger down his throat, to vomit, he would have survived.

I went to the house the moment I heard the word, and was able to be of some practical help. I drove a daughter-in-law to Gainesville to telephone and wire relatives, and to see Tom's daughter, eighteen miles the other side of Gainesville. . . .

But one thing that frightens me, is that it was Tom Glisson whom I accused of poisoning my pointer-dog Mandy, as I wrote in "Cross Creek"——. Again, as I wrote there, he convinced me that he was innocent, but Tom was always a violent man, and at that time I was hated and distrusted here at the Creek, oh God, so long ago, yet although Tom and I became true friends later, I have never satisfied myself that it was not he who poisoned my dog.

Nemesis? Accident? How lives are tangled together. I must go now again to the Glisson house to see what help I can give.

MKR

1. Norman Berg had written to Owen D. Young on behalf of the Macmillan Company, urging him to write his memoirs for publication. Because of MKR's professional experience as a writer, and because of her close friendship with Mr. Young, he had sent the letter to her for her critical review.

2. Edward Hugh Sothern, American actor (1859–1933).

3. Arthur Train, American lawyer and writer (1875–1945).

4. Ray Stannard Baker, American journalist and author (1870–1946); he sometimes used the pseudonym David Grayson.

5. Edward Bok, author and editor (1863–1930).

6. David Sarnoff, president of RCA (1891–1971).

7. Owen D. Young's plan for the rehabilitation of Germany after World War I. He served as American representative to the Reparations Conference in 1924 and as chairman of that conference in 1929.

171. To Norman Berg

Van Hornesville, [N.Y.]
June 17, 1950

Dear Norman:

You forgot to enclose the carbon of your letter to Owen D. Young as of June 7. He is due here today and I look forward to whatever he may have to say about his memoirs. His children

at last are having a little office built for him, all his own, on the
site of the one-room school house where his mother had gone
to school. He will move his files and vast amount of material
there from New York probably this fall. This should have been
done years ago. I seem to feel the sands running out for him.
Yet such a project may help to keep him going.

I have just had a wonderful visit from and with Robert Frost.
He accepted an honorary degree at Colgate, and Everett Case[1]
insists that I can take some of the credit for his coming. I brought
him back here with me for the rest of the day and the night, and
drove him to Albany the next day to his train for Vermont.
We walked up Mt. Tom that morning and came within an ace of
missing his train——. At the same age, 75, he seems to me
to have more vitality than Mr. Young. He insisted on carrying
his own heavy suit-case, saying, "If I can't carry this, then I
can't farm this summer."

He told fascinating tales of his early days, or the true stories
back of some of his first "colloquies" as he called them, including "The Fear." He said that after his first success in England,
when he returned here and bought a farm in New Hampshire,
he had the same sort of relationship with the village people that
I have at Cross Creek. He felt it his duty to take part in the
Parent-Teachers Association, and began giving readings at the
school house with a small paid admission, to raise money for
the school. Then the wealthy people on nearby estates began
going after him, for lionization etc., and insisted that they could
raise so much more money for the school if they had a big brawl
at the fanciest estate, a reading, a lawn-party, charging a much
higher admission. He protested that the village people
wouldn't go to such an affair and he wouldn't have anything to
do with it. They said all the country folk had already promised to attend. So he accepted.

He said, "They were there, all right. They were there as ser-
vants. They waited on us——."

He waited a moment and then went on, "So I just bought
another farm and moved over into Vermont. Seemed the best
way out of it."

In some ways, he is a greater man than Owen D. Young.

I have been in the longest period of depression I can remember, with no euphoria at all to break it. I am afraid that I am stupid enough to let this be because of Idella's having abandoned me when I needed her comfort-making to get my job done.

I have a rather elderly white woman from Van H. who comes at 7 in the morning, makes breakfast and a hot noon dinner, cleans up and does the laundry, and is perfectly adequate as to work and personality. At first her very mousiness bothered me, but in her three weeks I have become fond of her and have gone back to work.

I have enjoyed writing everyone—and telling Robert Frost— that I knew she had braced herself for any alien and/or writer's oddities, but that she literally staggered when I said Uki, the Siamese cat, always had a scrambled egg, done with cream and butter, on my breakfast tray. I told it that I was sure she was much more prepared for drunkenness and adultery, since these at least were not unknown in Van Hornesville. Robert chuckled and said, "You know, (he says y'know), that cat thing's new to me, too." . . .

Love to you and Julie.

MKR

1. President of Colgate College.

172. To Beatrice H. McNeill

Van Hornesville, N.Y.
August 7, 1950

Darling Bee:

I am sure that my thinking about you drew the letter from you. You did "owe" me, but I was planning to write you anyway.

Let's see now where I left off. I am on the home-stretch of the long-troublesome book, and another month or six weeks should see the end of the first draft. I can't tell yet how much re-writing I'll have to do, but will just have to stay parked here until it is all done. I am pretty well exhausted, but after collapsing a couple of times, have learned to heed the warning signals and stop and take a few days off before I get so low.

Idella left me again, ten days before I was due to drive up here in mid-May with dog and cat and loaded car. Her . . . husband talked her into taking a joint job as a couple in N.Y. city,

which won't work. . . . Up until the moment when I found her
bags all packed, and her living quarters stripped of all her own
belongings, she swore she was coming with me, and even as
she left, said she would get Bernard pacified and join me here.
Not a word more.

Norton drove me up and stayed ten days and did the housework, most capably, to my amazement. He was washing dishes
one noon with the Dutch window open over the sink, and as
he got hotter and hotter, took off his bathrobe and then his
pajama tops, and from the road would of course be apparently
naked. A car full of female "fans," he assumed, drove by and
came to a half-stop and he heard one woman say, "That's her
house," and then they saw him, with his curly hair that happened to need cutting, and he said he is sure the ladies are
satisfied that they saw the author in person, and that her habits
are as odd as is to be expected. (He also needs a brassiere.)

Well, for a while I had a 68-year-old lady from the village
(the younger ones don't want jobs) who came early and brought
up my breakfast, cleaned up downstairs, and did the laundry
(I have a grand new Laundromat, so the washing is nothing)
cooked a sort of hot noon meal, and then I took her home at
one o'clock as I have to go for mail anyway. I would work on a
tray in bed, as I'm doing now (mornings). . . .

Then just as I felt comfortable with Mrs. Hulbert, she announced that she would have to leave me, with regret. She was
not well. I found that after leaving my half-day of easy work,
she went home to her daughter's house where she lives, and did
an enormous amount of work there, big ironings, etc.

Now, the sweet daughter-in-law of the . . . neighbors near-
est, on the short road down to the highway, is coming at 12:30,
fixes a hot bite, cleans and does laundry. She has a 9-month
baby, over 25 lbs., and when she said she'd like to help me, she
expected to leave him behind with Grandma . . . as he has a
long afternoon nap. Lo and behold, she appears with Johnny Jr.,
play-pad, toys, stroller and perambulator, and bottle. The first
day, she came alone, and had everything done in less than two
hours. Now, she is here at least 4½ hours, a good half of it being necessarily devoted to the day nursery. She leaves the perambulator here, for Jr.'s naps. I guess that Grandma, a Polish

bitch, shrieked that she wasn't goin' to take care of no baby while Ruth made money. Visited with Grandma the other day, and she said, "I think I take your job myself. Is easy work, good pay."

Ruth and her young husband Johnny are adorable people, and it is a shame they don't have their own home. I think perhaps Ruth enjoys spending the afternoon here, just to get away. Ruth was a WAC and spent 18 months in France and Germany.

Well, you may tell Sam Wright that he isn't the only one whom Arthur Kinnan neglects. Day before yesterday, I have a letter from Alaska, and Arthur has been married since March 25, and the bride is pregnant, and off-spring due in January! Nice to know, eh? Pictures were enclosed of bride and groom and a letter from the new wife, and I do think Art has the right girl at last. She has both sense and sensibility, and looks most trim and attractive, about 30, I'd guess.

How odd about Dorothy Dwight. She must still have Arthur on her mind, to see you and think of me. She was his best girl through a couple of years at Madison, Mother broke it up——. . . .

Have been having odd things happen to me. A fascinating Armenian piano-tuner appeared last year and took my old square piano apart and tuned it, and said it had obviously not been tuned in twenty years and it would take several tunings to get the tone right again. He appeared again a couple of weeks ago, and I told him to go ahead and when he had finished, he played the most enchanting Balkan music, and then began to sing. His voice was rich and sweet, but in one song that he said was Turkish, it sounded like wolves howling in the distance. He sat down to rest and smoke and I wound up my old Swiss music box, and he arose and bowed from the waist and said, "Madame, shall we dance?" So we waltzed and mazurkaed and polkaed and he danced beautifully and swore that I did, which endeared him further to me, and I cried out, (you know me, always dramatic) "Strange Armenian, I love your soul!" (My mistake.)

I said, "Play one more song for me, and I shall let you go!"

"Let me go, Madame? But must I go? Can you not find it in

your heart to let me stay? You are so alone, Madame."

I have never been propositioned with such grace and courtesy, so I murmured that I was flattered, and he threw his arms wide and said, "You attract me strangely, Madame," and I said "Thank you, but it is impossible," and he said, "Eet eez a matter of preenceepul?" and I could not offend him by saying that it was only his soul and his music that I loved, so I said that it was a matter of principle, and he bowed from the waist and said, "I respect and regret, Madame. Let us congratulate each the other, that we have come through another year in a troubled world. Next year, I shall hope to tune you." ????? !!!!!!

His fee was $7.50, but I snatched out random bills from my purse and pressed them on him, saying the extra money was for his concert and he bowed from the waist and drove away. (The extra money was really thanks for the compliment at my age).

That night I started upstairs to read in bed, an assortment of books under my left arm, a bowl of roses in my right hand. No lights were on. Halfway up the steep little stairs, I missed a step, lost my balance, and toppled backward all the way down. Nothing was broken, not even the vase, but the roses were so strewn down the stairs that as I lay quietly on the hall floor, wondering if I'd knocked my brains out, it seemed that at least a May procession should appear, or the Queen. A most artistic effect, but Norton wrote that from now on I'd better take my roses upstairs one at a time.

August 8

Today is my birthday and how well I remember the elegant party with you so long ago. That visit with you, and our trip, was one of the nicest things that ever happened, and one fine thing was that it gave me the chance to really know your Bill. Oh Bee, I hope the knife-thrusts in your heart are at least not so terribly sharp.[1] But it must be a constant ache——. I think of you so much.

Always with love,

MKR

---

1. Beatrice McNeill's husband, William, had recently died.

173. To Norman Berg

Van Hornesville, N.Y.
Nov. 11, [1950]

Dear Norman:

There was never any question but that Ase Linden[1] would triumph in the end, would justify the failure of his life. You remember, when you read some of the chapters at the Creek, you said, "Of course, but there must be an ultimate triumph."

This aspect, in my re-writing of the last chapters, is working out well. Your feeling about the young Polish boy verifies my own decision to make him the carrier of the torch.

I am determined to stay here to finish the re-writing, for even if foul weather hems me in, my neighbors would bring my mail, my groceries, etc.

It was not quite fair to let Moe [Sikes] report on my auto accident, without giving you details. It was really one hell of a crash. I was turning slowly from my country road, to go left on the main highway toward Van Hornesville, (to deliver my magazines to a friend who reads them and then passes them on to others) when a speeding car came roaring down on me from a blind knoll. In the split second before the other car hit me, I knew it would happen, and there was nothing I could do about it.

To make a long story short, (and the State Troopers who arrived an hour later, listed it as an unavoidable accident) my car was so thoroughly smashed that it is being junked. Both cars were completely insured, and I have just gotten my new Olds, an 88 Rocket, which drives like a dream. The young man in the other car and his friend were not hurt at all, and I was indeed not seriously hurt, but my left leg was amazingly battered, and nearly three weeks later, it is still all colors of the rainbow. My nice country helper drove me to the Cooperstown hospital, where it was found that nothing was broken, cracked or chipped, only a menacing blood clot below the knee, etc., but it has all cleared up.

Thank you for offering to come to help me, but I think I see my way out, and there will be time later for you to read the finished manuscript, and perhaps make suggestions then.

I am sending you a copy of Vogue Magazine, of all things, which has something written by Pearl Primus, page 90-something. This will give you an idea of her style, of her possible ability to do a book. She needs much encouragement at the moment, and if you like this thing, do write her and say so.

Human relationships are so odd and unpredictable, but briefly as I have known her, I feel so close to Pearl, and she feels so to me.

With love and thanks,

Marjorie

I had just finished my letter to you when Gracie brought my mail, which included this disturbing letter from Pearl Primus. Please return it to me. The collapse of her dance plans may be a blessing in disguise, if she can do her book, for she could never have managed much writing with a difficult dance program on hand. I shall write her to this effect. Her husband sounds very much all right.

The grant I tried to get her was from the National Institute of Arts and Letters, which asked its members for recommendations, and I hurried to suggest Pearl, as the $1,000 would have given her some months free from financial worries to get at the book. But Glenway Wescott[2] wrote me back that they cannot give any grants for work in progress, the awards are evidently just *re*wards for something already done. Also, I do know that the top dogs at the Institute all have their own pets, who come first.

I can't finance her myself, without selling a stock or bond, as I am so near out of running cash that Norton insisted on depositing money for me to cover paying for my new car. I'll have about $2,000 in royalties the middle of December, but that will have to last me some time.

I wanted you to see something of Pearl's style of writing. If Macmillan does want to gamble on her book, I suppose they would consider an advance, but I am no believer in advances, unless a writer is absolutely up against it. I consider them a deterrent to writing, rather than a stimulus. And a first-booker is always so disappointed later when the amount is deducted from royalties! The wolf at the door does no great harm when one is young and strong, for even though one doesn't write *for* money, a pressing need is likely to prevent dilly-dallying, a writer's worst curse. Anyway, I shall encourage her on the book, and tell her that she must call on me if she ever hits bed-rock. I could always manage a few hundred to tide her over.

1. Protagonist of her last novel, *The Sojourner.*
2. Glenway Wescott, American author, critic, and editor (1901–   ).

174. To Dr. Blain

Cross Creek
Hawthorne, Florida
March 24, 1951

Dear Dr. Blain:

I should not have attempted to answer your questionnaire, as being far out of my line, except that Dr. Dana Atchley, from Medical Center, our dear friend as well as physician, happened to spend the week-end at the time it arrived, and I showed it to him, with your letter. He told me of the importance of your work, and urged me to do the best I could with answering you.

I presume you know enough of my type of writing to want me to answer for the specific sort of Southern rural community with which I am familiar. Cross Creek itself is a settlement of 50 or 60 people, including children, the largest families, as you would expect, deriving from the more unsuitable parents. Most of the people have always been fishermen on the two adjacent fresh water lakes. A few years ago an outsider established a sizeable fishing camp on the Creek itself, with boats and motors and guides for hire. He now employs many of the men, whose livelihood had been most precarious. Three of us here own orange groves, two large, one small.

Four miles away is the village of Island Grove, of two or three hundred population. The residents there make their living for the most part by working in an orange packing plant and a celery packing plant. The medical problems are the same for both settlements, and for several other small villages within a twenty-mile radius. I give you this background as relative to the problems.

1. The commonest emotional problem in this section is that

of financial insecurity. The new fishing camp and the packing houses have helped somewhat, yet wages are low and seasonal. All of life is geared to the threat of hunger. This is literal. The people are suspicious of "outsiders," most friendly when their confidence is once won. They go much their own ways, but when, for instance, I discovered by accident that one family (this, in our land of plenty, only about a year ago) was actually close to starvation, everyone pitched in, donated what they could, wood for fuel, fish, and in the village store at Island Grove a large box was placed on the counter with a sign, "Something for the Bowens." The box was kept filled until I finally managed, through infinite red tape, to get Welfare Board help for the family. This border-line between eating and not eating has its necessary relationship to other problems.

2. Doctors could help toward solving the problem of the sense of financial insecurity by cooperating in the establishment of free clinics, by urging on the State Legislature such free clinics, by working more closely with the few and not too advanced local hospitals. Illness, operations, are often the last straw with these people, draining off their small savings, plunging them into debt.

3. In my personal estimation, the local doctors have failed to give the necessary help. (Some of these questions seem to overlap. I shall try to follow up on the reasons for their failure.)

4. My answer to No. 3 represents not only my own opinion, but that of the communities I know. The common complaint is that "Dr. So-and-so charged me $150 and didn't do me no good at all."

5. When one doctor failed, these people tried another—and another. Usually, again, with failure. In extreme cases, the patient would be sent to a doctor with a reputation in one of the larger Florida cities, Jacksonville, Tampa or Orlando, or to a good hospital in one of such cities, often with the whole community "chipping in" to pay the bills. When this happened, the results were usually satisfactory.

6. On this question, you have undoubtedly in mind other "emotional problems" in the community than apply to the people of whom I am speaking. Yet I can give one extreme example of a bad handling of an unusual and severe emotional problem.

Again, this relates to another question, the paucity of good doctors, men trained in psychosomatics, in such a community——.

The best doctor serving the several communities of which I speak, is well-trained, over-worked, a true physician. Yet, in the instance I shall mention, he failed lamentably. It is a long story, but I shall try to tell it. . . .

[A local resident] died suddenly, and his only child, a daughter, then about forty years of age, simply went to pieces. She was married, she began sleeping with any chance man, she began drinking, never having done so before, and in the end, began using "dope."

This truly good small-town doctor *understood* her emotional problems—I talked at length with him about her—yet all he did for her was to give her endless prescriptions for dope——. The young woman had become a great nuisance to him, demanding medical attention in a neurotic way, looking for the "lost father," and damn it all, the man took the easy way out——.

7. After all, Dr. Blain, how can I answer "What defects in the medical education of doctors come to your mind?" The defects are perhaps not in the education, but in the soul——. The true physician is part scientist, part Christ——. It is all an extremely individual matter. The writer is a good writer, or is not, the painter is a true artist or he is not, the sculptor brings marble to life, or does not——. Educate your doctors as you will, the spirit must transcend the "education."

8. No suggestion.

9. You are again asking too generalized a question. "The Doctor" is always a *particular* doctor, conditioned by his own personality, patients and problems. Sometimes I think that you psychiatrists live in a more un-real world than the alleged neurotics——. Forgive me——.

10. Again, forgive me, you should have asked "How *should* doctors as a group fit in with the community needs, etc." I think I have answered that earlier in your questionnaire.

One question that does not seem to appear, but which I must answer regardless, is that there are too few good doctors serving their communities.

Marjorie Kinnan Rawlings

175. To Norman Berg

Harkness Pavilion
Medical Center
[New York City]
April 24, 1951

Dear Norman:

The eye people are not quite finished with tests, and I have
another day or so of other tests, but the head man has told my
Dr. Atchley that they are positive that my trouble is *not* glau-
coma, nor anything else serious. They are all sure they can trace
the cause of the pain.

I am so comfortable and relaxed here, and it will make a
good vacation before I get back to hard work.

I have "a room with a view"—I can see the Hudson—I have
"liberty," going in and out as I please, so that twice I have
prowled up and down the streets in the April twilight, watching
the human rats and mice, with now and then a flash of recognition between me and some shabby stranger.

I stopped to buy some end-of-the-day flowers from a Negro
sidewalk vendor. The iris, the snapdragon, the daffodils, were
cheap, and were not meant to last too long. Ahead of me, a little
weasel of a man—and why was he buying flowers in the first
place?—was bullying the Negro into adding another flower to
his bargain bouquet.

I said to the Negro, "Give him another," and he did, and I
stared into the weasel's eyes with contempt and with trying to
make him understand that the Negro was poorer and more
honest than he, and he grabbed his flowers and ran as if the
devil were after him.

I said to the Negro, "He didn't get it, did he?" and the Negro
said, "No, he didn't get it," and we laughed together in the
dusk.

My flowers faded the next day, but all three of us knew they
would fade, for they were florist's left-overs, yet they were
beautiful for a little while, which at the price was all we could
expect of them. And the Negro and I spoke the same language,
and the weasel did not, and did I perhaps do the weasel an
injustice? For he was buying the flower-that-could-not-last for

someone, so that there was sweetness there, and who knows
what treacheries in his life had made him demand a recount of
the frail blossoms, and an additional one, to prevent still another possible betrayal?

MKR

176. To Norman Berg

Van Hornesville, [N.Y.]
May 31, 1951

Dear Norman:

Something of both your reasons for not having written
you — —. I was not in the swivet, almost collapse, of last spring,
but getting here, getting organized, arranging for help, and
finally getting in the mood to work, made letters impossible.
And I was indeed made both angry and puzzled by your pom-
pous preaching about my close communion with the bottle. I
enclose the letter I began to you several days ago — —. I don't
remember now where I meant to go from the end of the second
page.

It may have been to say that the moment I am deep in work
and the drinking *then* interferes, I am perfectly able to stop
short. I must have the satisfaction of absorption in the writing
to make the deprivation worth-while. And I got into the job
this morning — —.

I found the answer to Wallace Meyer's[1] fretfulness over my
never mentioning the Spanish-American War, the matter of
church-going and the Grange, etc., in a sentence I just came
across in the fourth and last volume of Gide's *Journals:*

(Oh damn, I can't find it now. But the translator, Justin O'Brien,
mentions it in his Introduction, anent the amount of space, or
lack of it, that Gide gives to the War II. "In the beginning,
however, he *deliberately* planned to *omit events*—[italics mine]—
noting that thought was most valid when it could not be mod-
ified by circumstances.")

And that is exactly how I planned it for Ase Linden. The more
such mundane detail I drag into his life, the less I validate
his life of the mind and spirit. And I have muffed the last part

of my book, as it stands, in having too much of such detail.
(Among other muffings.)

I thought I could manage alone until Gertrude comes, but
things piled up, after Norton's few days here, and I engaged a
temporary helper from nearby. She is gentle and more than
competent, not as high-priced as Gertrude, and would have
served me well except that she, like Lucille, has a 3-year-old
female child who is noisier, if possible, than little black Chris-
tine. And less disciplined, so that when the mother comes to
speak to me or bring me a tray, the child follows and stands
gaping. All my life I have hated little girls, swore that I wanted
five children if they could be boys, and the more I see of this
she-species, the more they annoy me. This probably goes back to
my memory of myself as a nasty little hypocrite, dressed per-
force in frills, and to my long fight to attain a dispassionate
sexlessness in writing. And I think I can find this from Gide,
which irked me and made me long more than ever to have
known him and quarreled with him—yes, here it is:

"There are always certain regards in which the most intelligent of women, in her reasoning, remains below the least
intelligent of men. A sort of conventional agreement takes place,
involving considerable regard for the sex 'to which we owe
our mother', for many a lame argument that we should not
accept if it came from a man. I am well aware that, neverthe-
less, their counsel may be excellent, but on condition that we
constantly rectify it and expurgate from it that element of passion and emotivity which almost always, in a woman, senti-
mentalizes thought."[2]

Of course, that is a part of Gide's homosexuality. And again, to
be fair, a part of the thinking even of most virile males. One's
thinking is inevitably influenced and tempered by one's sex,
along with one's background and conditioning and a hundred
other elements. Yet I insist that there must be a plane, aesthetic, intellectual and spiritual, where there is no sex, as the
Bible says that there is no marrying in Heaven——.

I refuse to be *only* a biological female. If I had achieved the
normal destiny of a woman, which I indeed wanted, to bear
children, I might have felt differently, but flatter myself that I
doubt it——.

And again perhaps, as you suggested once, I was born half-male, understanding the true male, and resenting the—what shall I say?—well, hypocrisy, *sneakiness,* of the average woman. You are fortunate, my friend, in having an honest woman to wife.

I do hope that you will read all the four volumes of the Gide Journals. A lot of it is not quite up your alley, but I think that again and again some comment would strike you where you live.

So, my love, and I shall not write you again until I report great progress, having begun today.

You may write me, if you care, now and then, but only without sermons. Did I ever tell you of my two dear Quaker friends, the Whittakers? When an unseemly argument arose between them, one or the other would say, "Thee is talking like a husband instead of a friend," or, "Thee is talking like a wife instead of a friend," so, when you preach to me, I say, "Thee is talking like a monitor instead of a friend." I know you *meant* it the other way around.

Marjorie

Oh yes, a fine report on my eyes. Tension and vision registered normal, nearly 8 hours after the morning drops.

1. An editor at Scribner's.
2. André Gide, *Journals,* vol. 4, *1939–1949* (New York, 1947–51).

177. To Bernice Gilkyson

Cross Creek
Feb. 5, 1952

Dearest Bernice:

I don't see how you managed to do anything, losing a young brother in such a tragic and needless way——.

I am glad you are with Walter [Gilkyson] in N.Y. on such a big job.

Yes, the second crate of oranges went off about the time I wrote you. But they do keep well in a cool place. I have a perfect genius for sending perishable things to people who aren't home. I do it to my Dr. Atchley all the time. Once it was a crate of new potatoes from Hastings when they weren't on the N.Y.

market, or something, and he and his wife came home from a vacation to find an incredible affair on their back porch.

I don't remember whether you have a deep freeze. If so, your Betty could squeeze orange juice and freeze it. In small containers, of course, as once unfrozen it does not keep.

Buddy[1] still infuriates me by sleeping on my ear, then scuttling when I move about the house. He is getting a little better.

I started to write a story about the boy-Buddy and may finish it some day. He stayed about ten days, would have stayed forever, but I had such a strange feeling about him. I had been giving him money every day to take to school, enough to treat his two brothers to ice cream and candy etc., and whenever we shopped, he asked me for money to put in the March of Dimes boxes that were everywhere. At the end of the week, he had a pocket simply *full* of money. He said he "forgot" to treat his brothers, and I realized the polio money had never gone into the boxes. He seemed something like a baby cobra.

I have been having enough turkey for once. Think I wrote you I got them from the Guthrie's, 50¢ a lb.

They are picking my oranges, and I felt very cheerful, and thought I could see some checks coming in (most welcome, as I am just about down to my capital, which I don't want to touch) but Chet [Crosby] said gloomily this morning he didn't believe I'd get a thing for them. The price is fair, it's just so darned expensive to get them picked and hauled and shipped.

Chet, of all people, told me a cute political story that Walter might enjoy passing on. Chet apologized in advance for its being "pretty filthy," but he lives a sheltered life.

When Margaret Truman was ready to set out on her recent concert tour through the South, to end up at Key West where the President was headed, he took her aside and said, "Daughter, I trust you, but I wouldn't be doing my duty if I didn't warn you. It's about those Southern men. You've never encountered anything like them. They're slick and they're fast, and if you aren't careful, they'll be in your pants before you know it."

She thanked him and set out, Macon, Atlanta, Memphis, Pensacola, Tallahassee, and finally joined him at Key West. She watched her chance and said she must speak with him very privately, and they went apart.

"Daddy," she said, "you remember what you told me about the Southern men?"

"Indeed, daughter, I do."

"Well, Daddy, I found out something. It's not *my* ass they're after. It's yours."

Much love,

Marjorie

1. The first-mentioned Buddy was a cat, the second a little boy.

178. To Norman Berg

Hawthorne, Fla.

Feb. 13, 1952

Dear Norman:

You asked of me, "Do you exist?"

I think so, but if anyone could make me doubt it, you could.

How much is reality and how much is dream, or a fancy in one's own mind, has of course long absorbed better philosophers than you and I.

You are right, of course, that having a friend absent is quite different from having him *gone*. For myself, somehow, death has lost its power to startle. In all my friendships, I am prepared for the final loss. Often, thinking of a living friend, tears come to my eyes, against the day when, probably shedding no tears at all, I find that I shall never see nor speak with him again. I mourn, as it were, in advance.

I suppose it is possible for there to be the *one* friend, as it is possible for there to be the one love, but a particular value of friendship is that we can have so much of it. We lose one friend and suddenly find another. There is no limit except one's own capacity. And of course when you say that you want to experience deeply the death of every man, as you are struck by that of one close to you, you are asking to be another Christ. We can only approach the universal friendship, the universal love, the universal grief.

And you will have read or heard of the sudden death of Charlie Scribner two mornings ago. Julia wired me.

In my mail today came what must have been one of his last

letters. I had written him last week that I saw the end of my book, with not too much dissatisfaction, and he answered with delight, saying that he was certain it would be good. He was planning to go to London, and thought he would be back in New York just as my manuscript was due. He said that he so looked forward to young Charles' being out of the Navy, as he was a tower of strength, and they worked together so well. I should think that Charles Jr. might well now be released from his Washington job, as his 18-month stint is nearly up in any case.

This loss, while severe, is not that of Max. Charlie was a dear friend. Max had become a part of my thinking. It was perhaps in losing Max that I became more or less inured to death. After too great a wound, there is scar tissue, and one can never feel in that region too acute a pain again.

And with Julia's wire about Charlie, came one of the death of the mother of my dear little Irish housekeeper of the summer. This means that Catherine will be always with me, if I choose. She would have come to Florida with me, except for her mother's illness. She has been writing me as "Dear Mother Baskin." I'll have to see how next summer comes out, when she will be at Van H. with me again.

MKR

179. To Norman Berg

Flagler Hospital
St. Augustine, Fla.
March 2, 1952

Dear Norman:

I was within *two days* of finishing my re-writing—with one more thorough editing to be done when I finished—when I was caught with a severe coronary spasm. I'll hurry to say that there was no residual damage, and will not be if there should ever be other attacks—which may possibly be avoided entirely. I am not to be an invalid in any way—but must never again allow myself to pass a certain limit, in strength or in mental tension. No one can judge that limit but myself. Smoking is forever forbidden. Liquor, later, would be allowed in moderation, but for a year or two it will be easier not to take it at all. I

MKR in 1952, age 56. Photograph by Erich Hartmann.

shan't go into technical details about the type of heart trouble it
is—will try to explain when I see you.

Two weeks ago I thought I would catch my breath before
doing the last bit on my book and drove from the Creek to the
Cottage one Saturday afternoon. I left the cottage about 5 Sunday afternoon, and the thing had already begun. I thought it
was indigestion, which I have never had, so should have suspected something. Norton urged me to stay over-night but I was
anxious to be on the job Monday early.

To make a long story short, the pain was all but unbearable from about 9 P.M. until a doctor came from Gainesville the
following morning about 8:30. I had no way of calling anyone

from the tenant house—they can barely hear me when I stand
at the back door in full health and scream. There was nothing
to do but wait until Adrenna came at 7 A.M., when I sent her
down the road to the Williams to ask them to go to their shop in
Island Grove and phone some, any, doctor in Gainesville—I
knew none.

To shorten the tale again, Norton came over and had a St.
Augustine ambulance come for me. I told the doctor to phone
him and tell him I'd do whatever he said. (The doctor said I
must be in a hospital—of course he gave me a blessed shot that
eased the pain in about 15 minutes). Norton said when he got
that message—that I'd do anything he said, he knew I was
really ill!!!

I will probably be released this Wednesday, and must go to the
Cottage, because of the telephone, and being nearer a doctor,
etc. until I make my adjustment to a more sensible way of life.
As I told Gene Baroff, "How ridiculous to be sensible!" I shall
manage it, however, for the simple reason that it would be too
painful a way to die! A spasm, if one comes again, must never
be allowed to go too long, as it would mean an occlusion.

For all I knew, that awful night two weeks ago, I was dying,
and I have been much relieved to find that I was not at all
afraid. Death seemed cold and dark and lonely, but I seemed to
be looking down a straight road over-arched by trees, and the
road simply went on with no end in sight, and there was no fear
or dread or terror in the thought of going down it. I was interested afterward to remember I had felt this way.

My little Irish Catherine Mulligan lost her mother about
three weeks ago, and she has arrived to take care of me. She
drives the car, you know, and is immensely teachable. Norton
took her to the Creek today to get some of my things, and Moe
and Uki, and my car.

As I was being taken out to the ambulance, I thought to
tell Adrenna to leave one of my rear car doors open, so Moe
could jump in and out. Adrenna wrote me a few days ago, "Moe
take a ride in the car ever day he thinks he be goin. I wish yo
could see him."

Norton just 'phoned from the cottage that the caravan had
arrived. They went the back way to Crescent Beach. He said
Moe and Uki were very happy.

So come to see me at the cottage when you make your trip
South.

I am all right. After I relaxed, I have been more than willing
to be here and do nothing but read. I had every intention of
collapsing when my manuscript was sent off, but seem to have
gotten a little ahead of myself!

I am fortunate in having a room looking out on the Matanzas river. The shrimp boats go out just at sunrise. I love to watch
the tides, and the lights across the river are fine at night.

I am fortunate in many things—this was a *warning,* in
time.

Love to you and Julie,

MKR

180. To John Hall Wheelock

Van Hornesville, [N.Y.]

June 12, 1952

Dear Jack:

I probably sounded quite mad yesterday. The trouble is, that
while I am well physically, I am exhausted mentally, emotionally, spiritually. Trying to do the smallest new bits of creative
writing on the proofs is like (I started to say, getting blood from
a turnip, but Norman Berg jumped on me for "sick as a dog,"
saying, "*You* are not allowed a cliche, not a single one") is like—
is like—oh, damn Norman Berg, is like trying to get blood
from a turnip!!!!!!!!

I had worked for two days doing a few new paragraphs he felt
were called for, and on which I was obliged to agree with him.
After my being in Florida, it seems now as though you are only
around the corner, and I didn't realize until you were on the
'phone that you couldn't put your finger on the special spot in
the proofs I wanted to check. Anyway, I think I have managed
something approximating the needed addition, "Insert Gal. 9 A."
Norm said that I should give a touch to indicate the *effect* the
gypsy love song had on people at the dance where Ase was
courting Nellie, and I decided he was right.

Anyone listening in would have thought we were mortal enemies or lovers, about to slay, one or the other, for we yell so. He shouted, "You don't need much! 'He was a man to plow and sow and reap'! 'Ase Linden had three friends and a flute'! Just some little perfect simple sentence."

I shouted back, "Do you think little perfect simple sentences grow on trees?"

He turned purple and yelled, "I know God damn well little perfect simple sentences don't grow on trees, you have to work for them, well, work for it!!!"

Of course, Max Perkins was even more of a slave-driver (Jack, I love you, but if you want me to adore you, you'll have to be a bit tougher with me) but Max did it in such a beautiful, quiet way, so that you thought it was your own idea and your blood pressure didn't jump. Norman Berg would kill me if he could. Anyway, aside from his feeling that I had "done" it, he said, mused, rather, "I don't know how you do it, the style. I read things I think are good, and then I read something like this of yours, and I know the others aren't good at all, but this is, and it's only an arrangement of words, and I just don't know how you do it."

Don't know myself, and as I told the creature, it's absurd that anything good should come out of me, and I can never believe that it does, because the process is so anguished and *messy*.

Now Jack, I need to have my hand held until I am entirely done with the proofs. It has crushed me to have no letter from you all week long. I live a life, not of Thoreau's quiet desperation, but of overt and blatant desperation, and am ready to— never mind—was about to take a cliche to my bosom.

I enclose notes for our harassed copy editor and the calm printers, who have really done a grand job of type-setting.

"Departments" always startle me. To avoid departmentalization, I send all in your name. Manuscript, corrected proofs. God give me strength to finish the proofs.

It seems really too much to bear, but last night, wakeful, the concept came to me, unwelcome, of the theme for my next book.

I can do it, I can write it, but it is as though I had just given birth, and the sire of my child has obtruded himself.

Marjorie

181. To Norman Berg

Van Hornesville, N.Y.
July 16, 1952

Dear Norman:

Thank you for your good letter.

I am most awfully afraid that it was Jack Wheelock himself who wrote, or at least approved, this blurb. The situation is delicate. He is such a nice guy, and trying so hard to be mother and father, sister and brother, to all of us abandoned by Max and Charlie Scribner Sr.! Yet I have the dreadful feeling that the book *is* getting off to a fatally bad and misleading start. I *must* write Jack—with tact—for which I am not famous.

I am glad that my witch's blood was able to provide some bits of magic for you, when you came so generously to read the galleys.

There have been two more, for the visit of my dear friend Lois Hardy. I took her to the Russian Church, but later in the evening, and we were just in time for late vespers, and the Archbishop himself was there, and presiding. It was a preliminary service for another the following night, the birthday of John the Baptist. After the amazing bearded elders, the unshaven youths, and two plump little acolytes whose bright sports shirts showed under the cherubic vestments, there were half a dozen men, obviously Russians of distinction, one truly noble in appearance, with a Vandyke beard and an elegant but shabby tweed suit. One so wonders about such expatriates, and from how far they had come for these special occasions.

The other bit of magic came last night, and alas, it was not perfect, and it is all my fault——. The very day before my corrected proofs were due to be mailed back, and when I was in constant 'phone touch with Norton about Aunt Ida, the Armenian piano tuner 'phoned me from the village. I was distrait, and brisk and businesslike with him, saying that my piano did indeed need a thorough tuning, as he had not come last year, but that I was finishing a piece of work and could not possibly have him come that day or even evening. He said that he hoped to find enough work in Van Hornesville to keep him two or three days, and he would come the next morning or the one after, and would call me first. I never heard from him again— —. I know that he felt that I was denying him, denying the gifts we had made each to the other— —. I seem all my life to have had a conflict of duties— —.

So. There is a young Austrian, a Viennese, who has just taken his Master's degree from Colgate, and his visa cannot be renewed, and he must return to Vienna to his home, which is in the Russian zone, and where his mother lives, and his father, who is a University professor, and he longs to stay here in America and to have his parents join him, except that he does not see how his father could survive away from the atmosphere of Vienna, in spite of the restrictions and the danger and the past, for the father, being anti-Nazi, emerged from a concentration camp, a tall man, weighing one hundred pounds. Also, getting them out, or returning here again, seems almost impossible.

George set $500 as the amount he needs for returning. He is working here as an assistant to the Young's gardener, actually the town gardener, doing hard manual labor. Halvor the gardener, and another assistant, old Mr. Bronner, sometimes come to me in the evening to work on my garden, as I pay them time and a half. George has come twice, and last night I invited him and Mr. Bronner in for beer when dark overtook them.

He is George Schubert, and he is a great-great-nephew of *the* Franz Schubert. I lit the candles in the tall candelabrum on the old square piano, and George sat down and played and played, with a divine fire. If only the piano had been adequate! He recognized at once that only certain things were remotely possible on it, things suitable for a harpsichord, for the untuned keys have its tinkly sound.

He cried out, "If only my father could be here tonight!" and we embraced.

He is little and ugly, and being, I suppose, in his mid-twenties at the most, suffered from malnutrition durning the war. But he has the soul, and I told him of the Armenian, and of the playing and singing of the wild Armenian mountain songs, the voice like wolves howling, but beautifully and harmoniously, and he was as excited as I had been when it happened. He is starved for reading matter, and I was able to lend him some books, including Bartram's Travels, telling him the story of its influence on Coleridge, to produce "Kubla Khan," and he was thrilled again. He had read "The Yearling" in German, and I gave him an English copy, and "Cross Creek" in French, which he reads proficiently.

Poor devil. But he will be all right, somehow. He is brave.

I was amused at your writing that you expected to spend a night or two with Norton. Unless they were at the Creek, you will have found my brother and his baby at the cottage, and all in chaos.

Love,

Marjorie

With the writing of *The Sojourner* at last completed, the proofs read and returned to Scribner's, MKR was both physically and mentally exhausted, but even now she could not indulge the need for a let-up in her self-imposed pace. Instead, she plunged at once into research for a biography of Ellen Glasgow.

182. To Norman Berg

Van Hornesville, N.Y.
Sept. 19, 1952

Dear Norman:

Without looking up Mr. Webster, don't know the difference between courage and fortitude, except that courage seems aggressive and fortitude passive. Don't know which I'd come under for the last ten years or so, but probably fortitude, with only an occasional flash of courage. The hell with hope. It's only a trap. Let's settle for faith, *work* and charity.

I can tell you exactly why "The Old Man and the Sea" falls just short of being an epic or a complete classic, and I wrote so to Jack Wheelock. The tourists at the next to the end ruin the whole mood. They destroy the *purity* of the magnificent and elemental combination of conflict and harmony. As I wrote Jack, Ernest was taking out a long-time, personal and *inartistic!!!!* gripe against the kind of people who don't know a shark from a marlin. Max would have spotted this at once, and might have been able to show Hem the light, though I'm not sure, he said he didn't edit Ernest ever. But Max would have seen it, and Jack agreed to that, too. I don't think Ernest needed any "contrast," if that's what he thought he was giving, but it wouldn't have been in such dreadful taste (artistically speaking) if he'd even had another jealous fisherman, or perhaps the boy's father, make some deprecating remark about the ruined kill, (by way of pointing up the difference between the sheep and the goats, from a spiritual angle.)

I too could not believe my eyes when I saw Hemingway's full-page endorsement of Ballantine's Ale. He did the same sort of thing a few years ago, that I myself turned down. It was some phonograph record company, and they sent me a statement *they themselves* had written, which I was to sign, for a cool $500. Maybe it was $250. They had first written my passionate acclaim of somebody or other, I forget the name now, then had crossed that out and I was to be passionate and lyric about Jose Iturbi. The statement all written out for me, mind you! I was so enraged that I almost had a stroke then and there, began a furious letter to them, then decided they weren't worth bothering with, and never answered at all.

I forget now, again, who finally signed the Iturbi blurb.

Anyway, Hemingway signed one, and it was published, and once more I longed to write or even cable him, asking what was going on, for it was no more his own style than a rabbit's.

I did a 350-word piece for the Christmas issue of some such magazine as "Woman's Day," [which] is one of those magazines sold in the big chain grocery stores, with an enormous circulation, and I'm giving the check (Carl Brandt is giving his commission, too) to the Foster Parents Plan, and I wrote it because they will announce the "Sojourner" for January and that announcement will answer the questions of I can't begin to tell you how many nice plain women who lived vicariously with me in my book "Cross Creek" and who keep writing "When will your next book be published?"

Thought I had told you about plans for trip to England and Ireland. I wanted to go on a slow cheap boat and Norton tried for a moderately inexpensive one, the new Dutch Maasdam, found it full, got in a panic and took first class passage on

the "United States." I 'phoned him in a rage, offended him, he
snapped, "Very well, we won't go at all," and I said that was
fine, but why didn't he go by himself, and of course the next
morning he called me and explained that he had already paid
for the fares, and there was no rebate, the steamship lines only
promised to "try" to re-sell the space, and I said, all right,
we'd go on the damn boat, but since we are sharing expenses, he
could pay for the trip over, and I'd get us back on a cheaper
and *nicer* small boat.

Anyway, we sail at noon Oct. 3 from N.Y. I'll go to N.Y. a few
days ahead, and Norton will meet me there probably the 2nd,
as he has to be at Marineland *through* Sept. 30 to do his quarterly social security employees chart.

I am certain I wrote you that I agreed definitely to do the
Ellen Glasgow biography. It is too long a story to write now, for I
am swamped with long unanswered correspondence and am
trying to catch up before I leave, well, I just *must* catch up. But
James Cabell is raising hell about it, on the grounds that one
of Ellen's deathbed requests to him, or rather, expressed wish,
was that her own Memoirs be published "as soon as might be"
after her death. Ellen's literary executors are holding them up
because Ellen told *them,* they must not be published as long as
anyone is living who might be hurt. And there is one person
whom I know of, to whom this certainly applies. (Not James). I
don't think he is telling the whole truth—he has some other
reason for making such a fuss. He acted as though I intended to
rush into print over-night with the biography, ahead of the
memoirs, and I couldn't miss the chance to remind him that of
all my friends, he alone kept jabbing at me because I took so
long to write and re-write "The Sojourner."

God deliver me from all Southern gentlemen——.

Will tell or write you the whole story some other time. Meantime, would like you and Julie not to mention the Glasgow
project. It will take me so long that I don't want to have people
asking me questions about it.

Realize I shall have to spend a longer time in Richmond
this late winter and early spring than I planned, and the Gilkysons will probably use the Creek.

Did get some help on correspondence, and may have more,

as Mr. Young set aside some of his work to let his not too good secretary here help me.

Love to both,

Marjorie

183. To Norman Berg

Van Hornesville, [N.Y.]
September 24, 1952

Dear Norman:

There was certainly neither courage nor fortitude when I called you Sunday! You'd better choose the desolate picture after all— —.

Have myself together again, but won't apologize for howling on your shoulder, as I know you realized I just had to let loose, and you would understand that it helps— —.

Well, my admiration for the Oldsmobile increases with every wreck. I seem to be awfully hard on cars! Rather tore up another one yesterday afternoon.

Mr. Young loaned me his secretary for 2 days of dictation and she 'phoned that she had about 30 letters ready for me to sign and I set off down my road at too fast a clip—skidded on the gravel curve toward Redjives, evidently jerked the wheel too far each way trying to straighten out, lost control of the car, ploughed across Redjives' barbed wire and stone fence and knocked down a telephone pole, snapping it right in half.

Stella Redjives and I had coffee and cake while waiting for the bread truck to pass, to call telephone company and garage for me, as all neighborhood 'phones were knocked out. New neighbors passed (they bought the Frederick's place around the other curve) and didn't even slow down. Stella said, "Damn mean people, not stop. Could know you don't jump fence with car for pick mushrooms."

Moe and I not hurt (I have a few bruises) motor O.K., left front of Olds well smashed in.

Of course, these accidents are all impulses to suicides, except that I really don't ever mean to do it that way—it is likely to be both painful and messy— —.

Probably won't ever do it at all—there are other more pleasant alternatives such as running away— —.

Hoped for a letter from you today, but no. Our mail is incredibly slow.

I am really all right—only annoyed with myself.

> Love,
>
> Marjorie

184. To Henry W. Anderson[1]

> Crescent Beach
> St. Augustine, Florida
> December 2, 1952

Dear Col. Anderson:

I have just written a note to Colonel Anderson, the Virginia gentleman. I am now addressing the lawyer, the thinker, the aesthete, and so feel free to use my medium since my university days, the typewriter.

Having been told that you are the most eminent lawyer in the South, and one of the greatest in the country, it occurred to me that you must be weary of evasions, of slyness, of perpetual attempts at traps. I should like to present to you my plans for the Ellen Glasgow biography, with complete frankness, hoping that you will recognize a certain intellectual honesty.

After our first meeting in the home of my dear and long-time friend, James Cabell, I realized that you were filled with a profound (and as I said at your superb luncheon the next day, quite proper) distrust of me and my motives. I stand in admiration before the manner in which you "handled" me. You spoke of Florida fishing, of the fatal "red tide" on our West Coast (and I enclose an item anent that from Sunday's *New York Times,* which you may not have seen, leaving for New York on Monday) and then, using "the surprise element," you asked abruptly, or rather, stated, that you understood that I planned "a book about Miss Glasgow," and that Mr. and Mrs. [Frank and Carrie] Duke[2] "could tell me more about Miss Glasgow than almost anyone else," which of course, if I may begin to be blunt at this point, is nonsense.

You were most wary, Sir, again, quite properly. I should never attempt to out-wit you, knowing that this would be impossible. And actually, I am more honest than you may be willing to admit, so that I have no desire to make of a most serious project

a game of cat and mouse. I shall say my say, and you will do
as you please about working with me on what I hope may be a
definitive biography of Ellen Glasgow.

Irita Van Doren, one of Ellen's literary executors, tells me
that several candidates for literary Ph.D. theses (did I see a Phi
Beta Kappa key on your watch chain? I am a Phi Beta Kappa,
but never took or wore a key, as I know, and you know, that a
superficial facility in passing examinations is no warranty of
scholarship) have written dull and stupid studies of Ellen Glasgow, and that one biography is to appear soon, by someone
named Ross, or Roess, or what-not, which is, to quote her, "mer-
etricious."[3]

Mrs. Van Doren has denied access to these persons of all of
Ellen's intimate material, but will make it available to me. I am
not ready to see it——.

Once again, to repeat what I said while lunching with you,
I have not the slightest intention of *probing, prying,* Ellen's
very few close friends, in order to rush into print with a gaudy
book. My book about her must have dignity, for herself and
for me, otherwise I might better spend my time on working on
the next serious novel that I have already in mind. I have violent ideas about biographies, and next to the dry as dust ones, I
most deplore the over-intimate ones, which are always in the
most appalling bad taste.

I must, in this biography of a woman whom I loved as a person and admired as a writer, know as much as possible about
her private life and emotions, using, as I said to you, only a
fraction of that material in the finished book.

You said to me that "Richmond" had, what was it? accused
you of "everything" and I repeated "Everything?" and you said
"Yes."

Let me deviate for a moment——.

I have been told stories about you and Ellen. In my few
days in Richmond, to which "I shall return," like your Gen.
MacArthur, the most conflicting bits of gossip were given me. To
gossip, to chit-chat, I shall pay no heed.

Since I am committed to this labor of love, perhaps you will
wish to talk freely with me about Ellen. And perhaps not——.

I felt myself oddly *en rapport* with you, and was most dubious about your having a similar reaction. I make no pretensions about "being a lady," preferring to be a woman and, I pray, a creative writer.

As I held your hand in parting after your soignée luncheon— (and of course, you had Carrie Duke as an extra guest, as a barrier against my asking stupid and embarrassing questions, which I had no intention of asking) you said, "I shall be glad to help you in any way that I can."

I need you terribly, to do a proper job on Ellen. She was a complex person, her pseudo-love for animals, for instance, being an example, as a revolt against humans. I am told that she hated her father. I need to know "why."

I need to know whether you and she were ever formally "en-gaged." Whether or not I use the facts (and I shall submit my manuscript to you for your editing and/or approval) I am com-mitted to doing a creative job.

I shall accept from you whatever you wish to give.

[MKR]

1. Henry W. Anderson (1870–1954) was at one time Ellen Glasgow's fiancé. He was rumored to have had an affair with Queen Marie of Rumania during 1918–19, when he was in charge of American Red Cross war relief for the Balkans.

2. Glasgow acquaintances, as were most of the persons mentioned in the letters from and about Richmond.

3. There is no biography by anyone of these names. An edition of the Glasgow letters, edited by Blair Rouse, appeared in 1958, and a general study of Miss Glasgow by the same author, which included a biographical sketch, was published in 1962.

185. To Norman Berg

Crescent Beach
Jan. 2, 1953

Dear Norman:

Although you warned me, and I was somewhat prepared, it is a little hard to take—a little hard to take.

The reviews of "The Sojourner" that I have seen so far——.

I am laughing and crying alternately.

They are:

Saturday Review, done by Louis Bromfield,[1] Jan. 3 issue. (What you have not seen, you can look up). Of this, I can only remark that it seems odd that The Saturday Review would not turn over my book to a critic or a philosopher instead of a farmer!

An advance review, sent by Jack Wheelock without comment, from the Jan. 4 N.Y. Sunday Times, by some obscure writer, Frances Gaither,[2] evidently a minor review on an inside page.

TIME Magazine has just come in the mail and their review there—well, read it. Jan. 5 issue.

MKR in 1952. Photograph by Carl van Vechten.

Strangely, the only other review I have seen is in the January issue of PARK EAST, a "swank" imitation of The New Yorker, where I should have expected a complete brush-off. But the men who did this review "got" the book, except for the major point of the "sojourn," and I am grateful and astonished. Look this up, too.

I am due in New York Jan. 18 to 22, for two radio programs, four interviews, including N.Y. Times and Herald Tribune, and to speak Jan. 20 on Irita Van Doren's Book and Author Luncheon program, agreeing to do this only for love of Irita. At the moment, I am inclined to wire Jack Wheelock that I'll be damned if I'll come, to throw myself to any more wolves, but on the other hand, I'm damned if I'll haul down the flag. I shall brazen it out and fool the boys by talking about the work of other writers!

Actually, Norman, I think the complete lambasting I am taking to date is a good omen. There were "rave" reviews about my lesser books, long ago, books that will die, decently, I hope; and I have held the theory that the best work of most creative people, artists, sculptors, musicians, writers, is not appreciated at the moment of presentation.

I am humble about my work, as you know, and as you know also, I have no mock-modesty. "The Sojourner" is a major novel, for all its faults. I shall stand or fall on that.

I think I may have said, or written, to you, that I expected the book to be much more liked and certainly understood in its foreign editions. And this brings me to Steinbeck. I did not have a chance to read "East of Eden" which you sent me, until our return passage on the Mauretania. It is magnificent, more beautifully and poetically written than almost any other of his books beloved by you and me. And I said to myself, "Steinbeck and I were trying to write almost exactly the same book." (I may gather courage to write him this and to send him my book.)

Yet I felt that I had a slight edge on him because of the co-ordination of my themes, where he dissipated the *immediacy* of his similar ones, by telling his story through two different families, each one fascinating and deserving of a book alone, and by his switching from the third person in two narratives, to the first person. He came as close to getting away with it as any writer could do, yet I deplored what I considered a lack of artistry, a lack, almost, of the Greek unities.

Anyway, the head editor of my British publishers entertained me at the Heinemann (Windmill) Press in Surrey, and they publish Steinbeck and thousands of "East of Eden" were stacked there, and Dwye Evans, in passing them, said, "Your book is infinitely better than Steinbeck's."

I have a lovely house arranged for in Richmond beginning Feb. 3. I shall stay as late into May as necessary for getting material from Ellen Glasgow's old and often frail friends, all of whom have offered complete cooperation. That is the hurry, that the three most important sources are fragile as spun glass.

Also, after I return from New York Jan. 23, I go to Ellen's brother, Arthur Glasgow, in Palm Beach, for two days as his guest, when he will have ready all the material he has been able to gather.

I am tired, Norman, so tired. But the joy of work to which to look forward will keep me going.

And thank you and Julie for the grand books that came as Christmas presents.

When in Ireland, I ordered rose bushes for the gardens of three lovely ladies, and one has just written me in thanks, ending with what she says is an old Irish wish, "May ye be twenty years in Heaven before the divvil knows you're dead."

Love,

MKR

1. Louis Bromfield, American writer (1896–1956).
2. Frances Gaither, American novelist (1899–1955).

During her two-month stay in Richmond in the spring of 1953, MKR wrote a number of letters to Norton Baskin reporting in detail her research activities for the Glasgow biography. She meant these letters to be, as she told him, not only personal communication to him, but also part of the record of information gathered for the new book. Several of her letters to Norman Berg at this time were intended to serve the same double purpose.

186. To Norton S. Baskin

5 Paxton Road
[Richmond, Va.]
Feb. 16, 1953

Dear Norton:

I see where I get no work done on Mondays. George the
yard man vacuums the whole house, singing like mad all the
while, and calling up cheery greetings to me. Mrs. Turner had
paid him for three weeks, but I think I should pay him after
that. I wondered why Mary did so little real cleaning, and it's
because, like Adrenna, she has someone to "do the rough."

Chi-Chi is a little hussy and a hypocrite to boot. She was all
over me at first, simply staking her claim as "the sweet one,"
so she would get first attention. Ditty threw himself down in the
Siamese bid for petting, and when I picked him up and snug-
gled him he purred like mad and has made it plain since that he
is starved for love. He had been so indifferent and phlegmatic,
and it was because he felt he didn't stand a chance around Chi-
Chi. I was cuddling him in bed, and Chi-Chi humped up, growled
at him, and went to biting at my leg, and it really hurt, and she
meant it to! He gives way to her if she wants to eat from his
dish, but when he merely sniffed at a piece of bacon I had given
her, with no intention of swiping it, she slapped him a good
one.

I am enjoying my red tulips so much. They have arranged
themselves most gracefully and will last a long time.

Well, Col. Anderson won't talk. I got blunt and he got blunt. I
had tried to lead him on—fatuous fancy—by wondering why
Ellen never married. He said she gave everything to her work.
He had spoken of her stern principles and a certain Presbyterian viewpoint, and I said that perhaps her restraint had kept
her from marrying. He said, "She was very much in love with a
man in New York in her early days." I said I knew all about
that, but had no intention of using it in my book. He said, "Dr.
Bailey was very much in love with her and wanted to marry
her," and I said, "Yes, Dr. Perce Bailey. She wasn't interested
in him." He glared at me, I said, "One story is that you and
Ellen were engaged when you went abroad." He said, "I have no

intention of talking about anything like that. I learned at my
mother's knee never to talk about a woman." I said, "I thought a
man learned that at his father's knee." He snapped, "My father was very busy."

Norton, I had to change the subject very quickly. He began to
have trouble breathing and turned purple. He tapped his chest and
muttered something about the constriction that hit him. I had
visions of his dropping dead from a heart attack, which would
have been hard for me to explain! I got him soothed, we are to
talk further, he will come here when he feels better, and the
subject is to be Ellen's book "One Man in His Time," on which
he worked with her.

He did give himself away about Ellen in some respects, but I
believe, in view of things Irita knows from the memoirs, that
he told me an out and out lie. I shall write him a letter giving
my reasons for asking him to consider giving me a plain simple
statement about their relationship. I shall also say that if he
does not admit the validity of my reasons, I promise never to
mention the subject again.

After lunch, when I was asking him to describe Ellen's appearance, in her early days, he said he had a photograph of
her that had never been used, that he considered the best and
most typical. He suggested that we go upstairs to his library. I
used the stairs while he went up in a one-man lift. His bedroom
door was open, and the oil painting over the mantel was of a
young girl, probably of his mother, done later from a photograph. It was definitely neither Ellen nor Queen Marie. But over
the mantel in his library, where we finished our visit, was a
large oil painting—of himself—in middle age, rather heavy and
hard-looking—and on either side of it, with a pair of candle-
sticks that could be lighted in honor of him or of her, were two
huge signed photographs of Marie. So that is the truth of *that*
legend. If anyone in Richmond asks me questions, I shall be all
ignorance. (Everyone is dying of curiosity.)

He brought the photograph of Ellen from his bedroom, and
it is most lovely. He said I might borrow it for the book. He had
another picture of her on his desk.

If I could get him mad enough, he'd talk, if only to refute
me, but I am certain it would also kill him. He has my dander

up, and I'd even enjoy being told a provable lie. However, I feel that he will be adamant.

Margaret Cabell[1] calls me two and three times a day. I don't know whether she thinks I am lonesome, or just wants to talk because she is so confined, with James' illness. Her hysteria is really overpowering when it goes on long enough. She has always been more or less that way, but it seems worse now. She had two women in to meet me yesterday afternoon, and one of them, a good friend of Ellen, had some perfectly charming anecdotes. We are to meet again, and I think she will have a great deal of the lively sort of *harmless* personal stuff that gives a certain sparkle to a biography. . . .

Only Anne Virginia and the Colonel are holding me up.

Much love,

MKR

1. James Branch Cabell's second wife.

187. To Norman Berg

5 Paxton Road
Richmond 26, Virginia
Feb. 19, 1953

Dear Norman:

I am most comfortably settled, with a sweet elderly "inherited" maid, and the work goes, I suppose, as well as possible. There have been some set-backs, which are still not hopeless. James Cabell has been quite ill, and I haven't wanted to push his strength by working with him too much. Most of his Glasgow material is in his second floor library, where not even the capable Margaret can hunt it down, and to which he cannot yet climb the stairs. A *most* important old gentleman [Henry Anderson], while giving me his time and confidence, has refused to give me anything at all of the personal story of his relationship with Ellen. He said that he learned at his mother's knee never to talk about a woman, and I rather snapped that I always supposed gentlemen learned that at a father's knee. He is a lawyer, and as a last resort, I have just sent him a letter on which I worked all week, listing the reasons why I think he

should give me a simple statement, clarifying what now stands
as an ambiguous relationship. (I know so much more than he
thinks I know, but after all, I want first-hand information, not
gossip.) And Anne Virginia Bennett, Ellen's long-time companion, secretary, housekeeper, is having another nervous collapse, partly brought on by qualms she developed, after promising me everything, as to whether or no she should talk freely
with me. So much personal material can only be truly verified
by her. But a mutual friend assures me that Anne V. will end by
talking. (The important old gentleman almost had a stroke,
literally, when I asked him a direct personal question, could not
breathe, etc. I can't go around Richmond killing people!)

On the other hand, several people whom I was warned
must be handled with kid gloves, have telephoned and come out,
bearing great gifts of volunteered material. Arthur Glasgow,
Ellen's brother, with whom I spent four days in Palm Beach, has
just sent me three enormous envelopes of correspondence between them, 1905–1939 inclusive, full of treasures. I am beginning to get, in personal talk, delightful anecdotes of Ellen,
true ones told me by the other participants.

A letter from my Aunt Wilmer [Kinnan], the one who never
got to see the leopard, expresses regret that I don't now rest
on my laurels and just have a good time, and expresses astonishment that I care "to write the life of some obscure person"!!!!
My God, if "Richmond" heard of this!

To my surprise, having looked forward to being here, I am not
happy at all. Silly of me, and I don't know why. It is partly
that the loaned material to be copied or photostated and my own
correspondence so accumulated that I have been in a panic. I
think I wrote you that Bert Cooper (who said he spent three
joyous hours on the back steps of his church at Chapel Hill,
talking with you) had been teaching here at the U. of Richmond,
and as a trained librarian, was going to do all the technical
research etc. He was suddenly offered a wonderful job with the
State Department, and is now in Washington, to end up abroad
with his family, so is unavailable, but not without having
pounced on some choice letters at the U. of Va. library, which he
promptly copied for me. Losing him is an irreplaceable loss, but
I have sent for the superb, intelligent secretary in St. Au-

gustine, who finished copying "The Sojourner" when I was ill. She arrives tomorrow to stay as long as necessary.

Did I write you that Uki disappeared just before Christmas, I am sure into the jaws of another rattlesnake. One of the local newspaper stories about my being here mentioned that I was "between Siamese cats," and a woman who had to leave for England to join her husband in the Air Corps there, insisted on bringing out her unrelated pair of 6 mos. Siamese kittens for me "just to meet," as she was most upset that they might not find a proper stepmother. Of course, they came, I saw, I was conquered, and Ditty, (for Bandit) and Chi-Chi (for Banshee) are almost already a part of my life. Chi-Chi is all charm, daintiness and demureness, and is actually a complete bitch. Ditty the male, much larger, apparently phlegmatic, lets her get away with murder, swiping the tid-bits from his dish, biting him and me when she discovers us in the act of making surreptitious love—for I shortly found that Ditty is famished for love, Chi-Chi convincing everyone that *she* is the loving and adorable one.

I know that cats bore you, but Siamese really are different.

Feb. 21

Your letter came yesterday. I am sorry you did not come over from Raleigh. But it still applies, that you had best give me advance notice, much as I shall enjoy seeing you, as surely you know, simply because it is so important that I be at the disposal of the several elderly and frail people.

And if and when I have ever gone as far as possible with them, there are people in Charlottesville, and Ellen Glasgow's sister near Lexington, who have material, presumably, of great value. All this only by way of saying that I can keep a day or an afternoon and evening clear for you, if I know in time.

Normally, I should be a bull in a china shop, in Richmond, but, to mix metaphors, I am, or can be, when necessary, the complete chameleon, and thanks also to two good stories about my project in the morning and evening papers, no one suspects that I am being totally objective.

"Richmond"—who asked me what I meant by "Richmond"?— is a tale in itself. I may end up with a story or novel laid here ——.

I have so much to tell you when I see you.

"The Sojourner" is already a part of my past. Beautiful and understanding letters come in from "plain people," several readers have written me that they have protested to TIME and the Saturday Review etc., the book has crawled into the "best-seller" lists, and it now has nothing at all to do with me. At the moment, I am torn between the Glasgow book and the next novel.

Love to you and Julie. . . .

Marjorie

All this Glasgow talk in confidence, of course.

188. To Norton S. Baskin

5 Paxton Road
Monday morning
[February 23, 1953]

Dear Norton:

I hope there will be word from you today that you are recovered from the dysentery.

I have time for just a note, as Col. Anderson comes to luncheon today, when the fatal question will or will not be answered. Mary and I have planned a nice luncheon, George, the Monday cleaning man, loves to serve and brought his white coat, but I might probably just as well serve cornmeal mush in the kitchen.

I have lost my sense of despair, with [Nike] Grafstrom working steadily and quietly eight hours a day. She is, and will continue to be, exactly the sort of help that I need. She would like to stay no longer than three weeks, and it begins to seem that we can cover the ground in that time. I will still have the personal talks to finish, including the ones at Charlottesville and Lexington. The material continues to pour in.

Carrie Duke is having a cocktail party for me this afternoon.

I spent an hour and a half alone with Douglas Freeman Saturday afternoon. He went at once into the most vicious diatribe against Col. Anderson and poor Anne Virginia [Bennett]. He spoke as if he knew everything in the Memoirs, and I was never so grateful that I had not read them, for he was simply trying to pump me. He is utterly despicable. He has nothing of value for me, and I must keep out of his clutches.

Nike understands, and will not join us today. Margaret Cabell had us both for supper last night. James was in bed, but I talked with him. Nike will go almost nowhere with me. She said she would prefer not to, even if the circumstances were otherwise.

I must bathe and dress and mix the rum cocktails, unless George knows how to do it.

Love—

Feb. 24, 1953

Failure.

Results possibly more interesting than success.

George, luncheon, service, approaching elegance. The Colonel said he had gotten out of bed to come. "I couldn't sleep last night. I got to worrying about things." He had brought copies of his speeches, letters, relating to his political theories which Ellen used in "The Builders." The talk was entirely of this. We had had drinks in the living room, but had demi-tasse in the study, and went over the papers. I knew he would leave at 3. At a quarter of, he said he would have to be going, as he was very tired. I kept my side of the bargain and didn't say a mumblin' word.

At ten of three, he began that alarming breathing again, his chin sank on his chest, and each obviously painful breath ended in something like a groan.

He said, "About that question you asked me. I said I'd rather see you, than write about it. I can't possibly answer you. It would violate the ethical principles of a lifetime."

I said, "You are not willing to make a direct statement as to whether or not you were ever engaged?"

H. A.: "If I told you that, I'd have to tell you why it was broken off."

!!!!!!!!!!!

He realized he had trapped himself and said hastily, "If there ever was—" and just dropped it there.

He was as miserable as an old gentleman could possibly be.

I felt like Lady Macbeth. Who would have thought the old man had so much blood in him?

He said something feebly and unhappily about another of his speeches I had asked for, as though he was sure I was through with him now. I assured him that I wanted it very much, that its date was important, as a probable influence on Ellen for "The Builders," that when I had correlated the speeches with the book, I should like to talk with him further, and he brightened as if reprieved, and I wanted to pat his clean sparse white hair with the sun shining through it.

He stayed until 3:15, and something led to his offering with absolute delight to have his partner's wife alone for luncheon with him and me. Everyone has spoken of Ellen's famous formal dinners, but no one remembers how the table was set, what foods and wines were served. It seems that Mrs. Randolph Williams has a microscopic memory, and he said she would be able to tell even what flowers Ellen had on the table for any specific occasion. He left, a much happier old man, and with, I think, a certain grateful affection for me.

Imagine our mutual astonishment when we met again at Carrie Duke's cocktail party! I had not mentioned the party, and he had said he was going to bed, (which it seems he did, in between) and although I was the guest of honor, I doubt if he knew that beforehand, or that I would be there. Neither of us referred to our joint ordeal———. He took a seat beside me and said that he had found the missing speech, and William would deliver it today. Carrie Duke sat on his other side and he said, "I've had an awful day. An awful day."

I am sure that he was referring to the state of his health, or *thought* he was, but I wanted to say, "I've had an awful day, too, pal. I know what you mean."

He left the party without quite finishing one old-fashioned.

The party was charming. Carrie's lived-in antique shop[1] was bright with open fires and flowers and red damask and Carrie in red and sequins and fabulous special Virginia twisted cheese straws and paper-thin cookies from an old recipe. Martha Byrd Porter took me and brought me home, and I am going to them alone for drinks this afternoon. They live in a large old house near here, you remember. He is the doctor who knows of Ellen's morbid animal activities, and who said, "She had an unhealthy personality." The rest of that story will come out today, I am sure. I shall get the other side from Mrs. Parker Dashiell, whom I shall have here for lunch alone soon. She is the one living in the Episcopal Home, who didn't get her toddy at Miss Roberta Wellford's. Miss Roberta was at the party of course, said she wanted to talk with me alone, wanted me to come to her for luncheon again, but she is coming here Thursday.

Oh, yes, the cocktail table in front of me in Carrie's drawing room caught my eye. It was plainly a very old, well-mended butler's tray, on a new base. I finally asked Carrie's secretary about it. The price was $95, but Carrie said I could have anything she has at cost. I said I would let her give me a discount, but wouldn't hear to cost price, and I am buying the table for Van Hornesville, to go in front of the Liberty-linen-covered couch. I have always wanted a good butler's tray.

Carrie is watching for a convex mirror. She has two or three perfectly stunning low boys and small chests any one of which would be just right to replace the pine desk in the dining room at Van H., but the prices ran from $300 to $700. Carrie said to pay no attention to the prices, they would be adjusted.

I am exhausted today, and shall do nothing more but read Henry Anderson's speeches.

Love,

Marjorie

1. Mrs. Duke was an antique dealer whose home was furnished in antiques, many of which were for sale.

189. To William Kelley

5 Paxton Road
Richmond 26, Va.
February 27, 1953

Dear Mr. Kelley:

Your interesting letter was forwarded to me here, where I am doing some research for my next book.

Yes, it was my father, Arthur F. Kinnan, who owned the farm you mention. It was a mile and a half, or two miles by the country road, from Garrett Park Station. The farm adjoining it

across Rock Creek on the east (if I have my compass direc-
tions correct) was that of Rear Admiral Selfridge. Father was as
you describe him, except that he was 5 feet 10 inches and his
hair was not sandy but almost black.

He was one of the first to co-operate with the U.S. Department
of Agriculture on experiments with the inoculation of seed, ro-
tation of crops, and the planting of alfalfa to be turned under a
certain number of years to enrich the depleted land. One of
Dr. David Fairchild's books mentions an experimental farm at
Garrett Park, and I have always meant to write the old gentleman to ask if by chance this could have been my father's farm.
My father started from scratch with no operating capital to build
up the worn-out land. He went on week-ends and many
nights after his work (he was Principal Examiner in the Patent
Office) by train from our home suburb of Brookland to Garrett
Park, a distance of about ten miles, which in those days seemed
quite a distance, to do much of the work himself. He installed
a hydraulic pump to carry water uphill from an ice-cold spring
to the dairy barn. He began with ordinary grade cattle and as
he could afford it bought registered cows and a registered Holstein bull. I still remember the name of the bull, De Kalb
Second's Paul De Kalb No. 2's Ormsby. I often see the name De
Kalb in Holstein lines today. As he began to have calves eligible
for registration I was allowed to help him draw in the calves'
markings on the diagrams on the registration charts. In the ten
years my father owned the farm he had so built it up along
with the dairy herd that the year of his death, 1913, the place
was self-maintaining and from then on would have been an increasingly paying proposition.

It was his dream to retire when possible and build a home
in those lovely woods toward the B & O. A lovely little brook
ran through these woods and the house was to be above the
brook. We walked there much together, dreaming the same
dream, and it was there and from him that I learned my love
of nature that has so influenced all my writing. My mother
did not care for the farm or for farm life and I have often
thought that if she had died at that time instead of my father
(she died exactly ten years later) I should have lived on the farm
with my father and my writings would have had a Maryland
background.

We used one of the farm horses, Dan, for a driving horse and had a small buggy and a two-seated "surrey with a fringe on top" in which we took Sunday drives, or in which my father and I sometimes drove to Frederick, Maryland, for him to buy mules or cattle, etc. But Father always walked the mile and a half or two to and from the station. In the summers we lived in the locust grove that I mentioned in Cross Creek in a tent colony which appalled my mother but which to me was the essence of delight. There was a very large sleeping tent with a solid wooden floor and partitions, a dining tent, a mosquito netting covered separate arrangements for hot weather, a cooking tent, and the usual country out-house. The camp was enclosed with three strands of barbed wire with a stile and since the dairy herd used the acreage around for night pasture, I heard and loved the sounds at night of the cows chewing their cuds, dropping down heavily to rest, or coming close to the fence and snuffling over it. Sometimes the great bull broke loose from his enclosure at the foot of the hill and went rampaging across the pasture past the camp. The cry went up "De Kalb is loose!" and for years I had nightmares about a white bull!

Father would come walking home from the station on weekends with two enormous market baskets loaded with provisions. He sang or whistled as he came, no matter how tired he was, and when he reached the foot of the hill he began a special bird-like whistle that was a signal to me, and I would run to meet him.

Some of this personal material may not be of interest to you or to your friend but I began remembering——.

I should be very glad to have Mrs. Defandorf incorporate any of this in her typed script for her family.

With all good wishes,

[MKR]

190. To Norton S. Baskin

5 Paxton Road
Richmond, Va.
Mar. 3, 1953

Dear Norton:

Pauvre, pauvre poosy-cats! Chi-Chi the precocious is in heat, and dumb Ditty simply cannot figure out what to do about it. He tried all yesterday until he was exhausted. She was evidently not quite ready, as she did not give him complete cooperation. She sat down with her tail over the adit. Today she is definitely ready, but by now Ditty has decided, "If this is sex, you can have it." She cries despairingly and rolls over and over enchantingly, and Ditty, anxious to go along with her in any reasonable fashion, rolls over and over, too, which of course gets them nowhere. He goes around with a puzzled look and keeps jumping into their pan and tries to wee-wee, then jumps out again with furrowed brow, evidently thinking, "No, that isn't it." Just now she not only rolled and rolled, but inched herself toward him, and Ditty retreated under the dotted Swiss flounces of the tester bed and peered out wildly. You remember Paul Gallico's cat, "When in doubt, wash." Ditty has almost washed his fur off——. I hope to be able to report soon, "The adit's adit."

Last Saturday's luncheon meeting with Maude Williams at Col. Anderson's brought out an interesting supposition. The old gentleman had gotten out of bed against his doctor's orders and was having sharp pains in his right lung area where he had the operations. He sat with us perhaps twenty minutes after lunch then went to bed, telling us to stay and talk as long as we wished. He said to Mrs. Williams, "I want to give Mrs. Rawlings any help I can, but I told her that when it came to talking about my personal relations with Ellen, 'I just ain't going to do it'. I learned at my mother's knee 'Never talk about a woman'."

I said, "And wasn't I very nice about it?" and he said, "You were indeed. You said you appreciated my position and would never mention the subject again, and you haven't said another word."

THEN, as he left for upstairs, he said to Mrs. Williams, "Now you tell Mrs. Rawlings everything you know about Ellen, only she mustn't print it."

I am going on the assumption that since he knows he was to blame for their marriage's not going through, he could not talk about it himself, *but has no objections to it's being told by someone else.*

He had scarcely had time to get up the stairs when "Maude"

stage-whispered, "My dear, Ellen was simply WILD about Henry
Anderson. Do you suppose anybody can hear us?"

I said I was sure that Archer, the butler, could, and that it was
best to talk some time when we were alone somewhere else. It
didn't seem cricket to me to let her gossip under the man's own
roof. In about fifteen minutes Archer came down to say that
the Colonel was comfortably in bed, and if we wanted to ask him
any questions, we could come up to him!!! I said that we must
be leaving.

"Maude" came here avidly in more ways than one, to luncheon yesterday——. She is a large, jolly, rather gross woman
who spilled Mexican pumpkin seeds, served with my Martinis,
down her ample bosom from pudgy, well-diamonded hands.
She wears extremely handsome large hats from Mme. Germaine.
I don't know whether she comes from aristocratic or mixed
stock, but her type of coarseness rather seems that of one whose
position is so secure that she doesn't have to trouble to be
delicate about anything, pumpkin seeds or people.

It was she who brought Ellen and Henry Anderson together.
She says they were definitely engaged, that his romance with
Queen Marie threw the monkey wrench in the works, that he
hurt Ellen dreadfully, that while he was once as much in love
with Ellen as so cold-blooded a man could be, she doesn't really
know whether Ellen's hurt and pride broke the engagement,
or whether by that time he was not only dubious about taking
on an ill, deaf wife but dubious about marriage altogether. After
the post-war and post-Marie breach was healed, they were
platonic friends, and he went to Ellen every Sunday evening for
supper until the very end. Did I write you that Douglas Freeman said he would never forget the sight of Henry Anderson
standing in the doorway at the services for Ellen in her house.
"The ladies" who were running the services and funeral had
not invited him. "He stood there tall and proud, half defiant and
half crushed."

There WAS a portrait of Queen Marie! "Maude" doesn't remember in which room he kept it. It was done by de Laszlo
(sp.?)[1] Not long ago Ileana[2] was in Richmond and spent some
time with the Colonel, and he gave her the portrait of her
mother, as she had none, and he felt that none of his nieces or

nephews would appreciate it as would Ileana. "Maude" is not certain, but thinks the dates are wrong for Henry to have been Ileana's father.

"In any case, my dear, Henry was always too cautious to have *fathered anyone*."

Miss Roberta Wellford, who knew "Maude" was coming, warned me that while Maude would tell all she knew, I myself must be most discreet and not add a single bit to Maude's repertoire, and I was caution itself. I go to Miss Roberta's for luncheon again this Saturday to meet a Mrs. Scrivenor, who knew Ellen well. This afternoon I go to see Mrs. Dashiell, who does not feel well enough to come here. All she will have for me is Ellen's side of the S.P.C.A. story, which will make a nice contrast with Dr. Porter's side. Miss Roberta sent me a box of choice candy after she was here for luncheon, the cute thing.

Carrie Duke 'phoned again to say that this week-end isn't possible for Rebe [Glasgow] Tutwiler³ to have us at Brushwood, but that we will probably go the following week-end.

Anne Virginia is getting the electric shock treatments four times a week. She gets a lift and feels better afterward, then lapses into moroseness. I am terribly concerned, for she is the one person who can sift fact from fiction for me. Carrie Duke keeps telling me just to wait, but I do feel the impulse to write Anne V. now and then, in a general and cheery way, perhaps telling her some of the things that others have told me. I don't know her psychology well enough to know whether this would help or harm the situation. What do you think?

Dr. Porter just 'phoned to say that Dr. Alexander Brown, who was Ellen's personal doctor, will be glad to talk with me as often as I wish. Everything goes well except poor Anne Virginia.

My love,

Marjorie

A DEFENSIVE DITTY FOR A DEFENSELESS DITTY

> I have a cat whose name is Ditty,
> Admittedly uncouth, un-pretty.
> I'VE been called names, so I have pity.
> And ah, we both detest a city.

We have so many things in common.
We share indifference to Mammon.
We play at Scat, but not backgammon.
We both adore a nice fresh salmon.

We watch the birds. (Our reasons vary.)
We're alternately sad and merry.
O'er milk and gin we love to tarry.
We will not fetch nor will we carry.

We recognize our serendipity.
We think each other wise and witty.
What's in a name when one's a kitty?
HE calls ME "Meowm." THAT'S worse than "Ditty"!

1. Possibly Philip Alexius László de Lombos, Hungarian painter (1869–1937).
2. Princess Ileana, Queen Marie's daughter, born in 1909.
3. Ellen Glasgow's sister.

191. To Maxwell Geismar[1]

[Richmond, Va.]
Oct. 23, 1953

Dear Mr. Geismar:

I have just read with great interest your "Rebels and Ancestors."

I am especially fascinated by your chapter on Ellen Glasgow. Several years ago Irita Van Doren, one of Ellen's literary executives, asked me to consider doing a rather definitive biography of Ellen. I answered with a negative vagueness, as I was deep in the writing of a novel published this last January [The Sojourner]. Last summer, when I had finished with proofs, etc., suddenly I wanted very much to attempt this project, and wrote Irita to that effect.

I noticed that you say that there has been no biography of Ellen (a Mr. or Dr. Rouse seems to have about finished a rather academic one) and that you mention among the "studies" of her, one by me. Bless us, I have no recollection of any such "study"! If you do not have to dig too deeply into your files, please refresh my memory on this.

I know that when a book, even a scholarly one, is actually

published, it becomes quite dead to the author, in a way. So forgive me if I bore you.

Your analysis of the Glasgow body of work is magnificent, and I shall eventually ask permission to quote from it. And did you know Ellen personally? And if so, how well?

I knew her, and corresponded with her, and we found ourselves *en rapport*. I loved her as a woman, and admired her books, with some of your own reservations, and others of my own.

I have been fortunate in being accepted by all of Ellen's relatives and friends still living. Last January I spent several days with her brother, Arthur Glasgow, at Palm Beach, at his invitation, when he turned over to me a voluminous correspondence between them. I spent nearly two months in Richmond later, and am here again briefly, gathering personal memories. I have visited twice with Ellen's sister at Lexington, Virginia.

I asked if you had known Ellen, because I am so intrigued by your reading between the lines in her books. If you did not know her, this is even more miraculous. I do not yet know how I shall handle the biography, but at the moment I feel that I want to relate her personal life to her work. I have been given extremely intimate details of her life, lacking only, I think, the final information on what you describe (the middle of page 261) as "a single, brief, fatal love affair in youth and then a lifetime of suffering—."[2]

What I say now *must be strictly entre nous*. Ellen Glasgow was fulfilled at one time, and possibly or probably for a short period at another time. I have all I need to know about those episodes. But Ellen's sister, her friends, her long-time companion and secretary, are still evasive when I insist that from the *context* of the early Glasgow books, there must have been "a single, brief, fatal love affair in youth."

Her truly great love affair ended with the death of the man. The second ended with a strange betrayal of her, but this came long after the early books of bitterness about men, (about 1919).

Yet I have another theory about her early, what shall I call it, sexual bitterness? As you surely know, she became aware that her deafness might be incurable when she was perhaps twenty or twenty-one or thereabouts. Could it be that she decided that she could never be attractive to a man, and so made at that time the gesture of relinquishment, later negated by her actual experience?

Of course, the bitterness continued, as the two men concerned never quite gave her a full devotion, for their varying reasons.

If my project is of interest to you, I should be most happy to hear from you. I am using my permanent address on the envelope.

And let me thank you for a superb book.

Sincerely,

Marjorie Kinnan Rawlings

1. Maxwell Geismar, American critic (1909–   ).
2. *Rebels and Ancestors* (Boston, 1953).

By the time she wrote the letter of inquiry to Maxwell Geismar, MKR had already amassed a considerable body of notes, transcribed letters, and papers for the Glasgow biography. (They can be seen as she left them, in the Rawlings Collection at the University of Florida Library.) And she had begun the task of sifting, evaluating, and absorbing all this material in preparation for writing. As the letter to Geismar indicates, she had also begun to relate her knowledge of the biographical facts to the great mass of the Glasgow writings. Taken together, these were tasks that would have made the most experienced literary scholar blanch, but MKR, in spite of poor health, drove herself so relentlessly to complete them that she never survived to bring to bear that gift of creativity and the hard-won professional writer's experience, which were her most valuable assets, to the writing of the biography itself. A fatal brain hemorrhage intervened.

Nearly two years earlier, after her coronary spasm, she had written Norman Berg from Flagler Memorial Hospital (letter 179, March 2, 1952): "I am fortunate in many things—this was a *warning*—in time." Warning it was, but it was not in her nature to heed it, either well enough, or for long. After brief convalescence, she had returned to the ten-year agony of *The Sojourner,* completing it in late summer. When the book appeared in January 1953, she was already caught up in the first stages of the Glasgow project, and this she pursued with characteristic energy, the urge to carry on stronger than any check of restraining caution. She was struck down by a cerebral hemorrhage on December 18, 1953, swiftly and finally, while she was at the Crescent Beach cottage south of St. Augustine. She was taken for burial to Antioch Cemetery near Island Grove, only a few miles from the weathered farmhouse in the orange grove at Cross Creek, where her spirit had felt so much at home.

index * * * * * * * *

"Letters to" are always listed last in a main entry. Italic numbers in parentheses are letter numbers.